All the
Plagues of
Hell

THE HEIRS OF ALEXANDRIA SERIES

The Shadow of the Lion, by Mercedes Lackey, Eric Flint, and Dave Freer • *A Mankind Witch*, by Dave Freer • *This Rough Magic*, by Mercedes Lackey, Eric Flint, and Dave Freer • *Much Fall of Blood*, by Mercedes Lackey, Eric Flint, and Dave Freer • *Burdens of the Dead*, by Mercedes Lackey, Eric Flint, and Dave Freer • *All the Plagues of Hell*, by Eric Flint and Dave Freer

MORE BAEN BOOKS by ERIC FLINT & DAVE FREER

Rats, Bats & Vats Series: *Rats, Bats & Vats* • *The Rats, The Bats & the Ugly*

The Pyramid Series: *Pyramid Scheme* • *Pyramid Power*

Slow Train to Arcturus

The Karres Series: *The Wizard of Karres*, with Mercedes Lackey • *The Sorceress of Karres*

MORE BAEN BOOKS by DAVE FREER

The Dragon's Ring Series

MORE BAEN SERIES by ERIC FLINT

The Ring Of Fire Series, with David Weber, Andrew Dennis, Virginia DeMarce, Charles E. Gannon, Gorg Huff, Paula Goodlett, David Carrico, Walter Hunt, Griffin Barber

The Assiti Shards Series, with Marilyn Kosmatka, Gorg Huff, Paula Goodlett

The Belisarius Series, with David Drake

The Joe's World Series, with Richard Roach

The Crown Of Slaves Series, with David Weber

The Jao Empire Series, with K.D. Wentworth, David Carrico

The Boundary Series, with Ryk E. Spoor

To purchase all of these titles in e-book format, please go to www.baen.com.

All the Plagues of Hell

Eric Flint
Dave Freer

BAEN

ALL THE PLAGUES OF HELL

This is a work of fiction. All the characters and events portrayed in this book are fictional, and any resemblance to real people or incidents is purely coincidental.

Copyright © 2018 by Eric Flint and Dave Freer

All rights reserved, including the right to reproduce this book or portions thereof in any form.

A Baen Books Original

Baen Publishing Enterprises
P.O. Box 1403
Riverdale, NY 10471
www.baen.com

ISBN: 978-1-4814-8361-2

Cover art by Tom Kidd
Map by Michael Knopp

First printing, December 2018

Distributed by Simon & Schuster
1230 Avenue of the Americas
New York, NY 10020

Library of Congress Cataloging-in-Publication Data

Names: Flint, Eric, author. | Freer, Dave, author.
Title: All the plagues of hell / Eric Flint and Dave Freer.
Description: Riverdale, NY : Baen, [2018] | Series: [Heirs of Alexandria ; 6]
    | "A Baen Books Original."
Identifiers: LCCN 2018041834 | ISBN 9781481483612 (hardback)
Subjects: | BISAC: FICTION / Fantasy / Historical. | FICTION / Fantasy /
    Epic. | FICTION / Fantasy / General. | GSAFD: Fantasy fiction.
Classification: LCC PS3556.L548 A79 2018 | DDC 813/.54—dc23
LC record available at https://lccn.loc.gov/2018041834

10   9   8   7   6   5   4   3   2   1

Pages by Joy Freeman (www.pagesbyjoy.com)
Printed in the United States of America

Dave, who is public-spirited, dedicates this book
to Australia's volunteer ambulance officers.

Eric, who seeks peace and harmony,
dedicates this book to the cat.

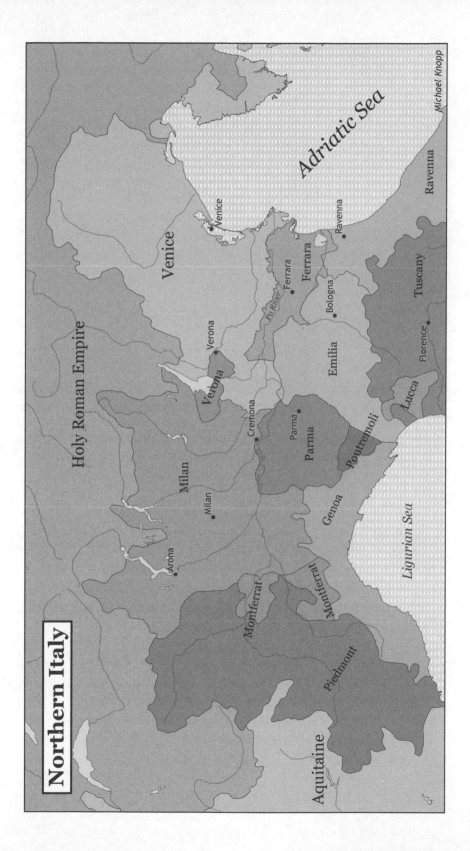

Northern Italy

Holy Roman Empire

Venice

Adriatic Sea

Michael Knopp

Venice

Po River

Ferrara

Ferrara

Ravenna

Ravenna

Bologna

Tuscany

Verona

Verona

Verona

Emilia

Florence

Lucca

Cremona

Parma

Parma

Lucca

Milan

Parma

Pontremoli

Milan

Genoa

Ligurian Sea

Arona

Montferrat

Montferrat

Montferrat

Aquitaine

Piedmont

Prologue

Marco Valdosta greeted the news with a breathless hopefulness. "Are you sure?" He looked around their bedroom as if the sight of the chamber where the child would have been conceived brought some sort of reassurance that the news was accurate.

Katerina Valdosta, the last child of the ancient House of Montescue, nodded at her husband. "I can count, Marco, even without Maria's assurances."

"We're pregnant!" he yelled, jumping into the air with delight.

"I'm late. I may be pregnant. You are just fat." She poked him in the stomach, trying not to endanger her own ears with her smile. "I know Maria says it is definite but it's too early to be absolutely certain, Marco."

He folded her into his arms anyway.

A small, old castle near Arona, in the Duchy of Milan

Staring out the window of her own bedroom, quite some distance northwest of Venice, the expression on the face of Lucia Maria del Maino was not at all like that on the faces of Marco and Kat. It was sour, sullen, disgruntled.

The stirring of life in her womb gave her no pleasure. Firstly, it was too late. And secondly, it was just a tool to get what should have been hers by right. She would have her reward, even if it meant turning the serpent that devoured loose on all of them.

1

She'd already given its blood price—her sister. If the great wyrm wanted more, it would have it.

As a bastard son, and the only child, Lucia might still have ruled Milan.

As a woman, no.

For a while her mind dwelled on revenge. She'd met Carlo Sforza, and he'd paid her no particular mind. She hadn't liked that, even if he was a mere commoner. But then, she too had paid him no particular mind. And it was not as if she'd loved her father. Rather, she had loathed him. But he had been a lever. And now he was dead, by Sforza's hand. Her anger at being thus cheated flamed white-hot.

It took a while before she realized Carlo Sforza would have to take his place.

She steeled herself, knowing it would have to be done. In a way, the serpent had honored the last bargain, given her power to capture Filippo Maria, to snare him away from her mother.

The castello at Arona had been a Visconti holding for time out of mind, perhaps even their original land, her father had said. It had certainly been built on the ruins and with the stones of older buildings. Down beneath the castello were cellars and the dungeon which had been adapted from several limestone caves. And those cellars lay atop of an even lower cellar, the old one, the one with the crude carvings in which the rock itself seemed to have flowed, making them look like a nasty accident. Lucia and her sister had found the key to it nearly eight years ago, now. The room in which it was hidden had once been their father's room, and probably the nursery for every generation of noble children raised in the castello. It had fascinated them: why was it so carefully hidden, in a block that swung out of the wall, when touched just so with something sharp? The indent so painstakingly cut into the rock held the key neatly.

It had taken them nearly a month of dreams of treasure, secret passages and hidey-holes to find the door it fitted at the back of the cellars. Heavy, iron-bound, and with rusty hinges that shrieked. They had always been forbidden to go down into the cellars at all.

What they'd met there had cost her sister her life. Neither Lucia nor the dying, feverish girl had ever admitted where they'd been, or what they'd found there, or what had happened. But what was down there had said that next time she would have to come to it.

And that she would come.

She could have flung that key into the river. But she'd put it back into its hiding place.

In the old cellars, the dark had been hung with trailing cobwebs, touching her face like ghostly fingers trying to hold her back. But they had gone now, along with the light of the candle, so abruptly snuffed as she entered the round black maw in the far corner. She understood: no light came down here. No light ever had. No light was allowed. This was the place of the dark, and of its power.

The tunnel wall was curved and polished to an oily smoothness under her hand. The rock of it was cool on her fingertips as she felt her way, cautious step by cautious step, into that stygian blackness. Lucia needed that wall, for the floor of the tunnel had been cobbled, but the round edges of each hand-sized stone caught at her probing toes. The cobbles too were made of some unpleasant material that almost seemed to give a little underfoot. It wasn't slippery, at least, which as the descent was steep, was just as well. Instead it seemed to cling to her soles. The tunnel wound down, turning left and right, seemingly at random. The silence was such that she could hear her own shallow, nervous breathing, her own careful footsteps, no matter how much she tried to keep quiet. Even her heartbeat was like a fast drumbeat in her ears, relentless, marching her cautious feet onwards, onwards, onwards, downwards, into the pit.

The air was dank and stank of rat urine. They must dare this tunnel, too. Yet her reaching ears could hear no scurry, no chitter nor squeak. Just a silence, heavy and oppressive, as heavy as the hatred and anger that drove her down here. Drove her on, down, down, into the darkness.

Despite the pitch darkness, she somehow felt that the tunnel had opened up. Perhaps there was a breath of air movement, or perhaps...just a feeling. She edged out reaching for the far wall, reluctant fingers leaving the rock that gave her orientation and position. The tunnel had been two arm-stretches wide at the mouth.

"The other side can't be that far," she muttered to herself, as she edged further and further from the security of the wall.

There was a soft, shuddering, susurrating shiver in the very floor of the pit under her.

"Far." The sibilant word came from behind her, and then, as she turned in terror, it echoed back from some vast distance. "Far, far..." The cobbles beneath her shuddered and clattered again, and she fell to her hands and knees, as the vast serpent shook its plate-sized scales, and it moved under her.

She screamed, realizing. The scream, too, echoed. It sounded very thin and small.

"Why do you disturb my rest?" hissed the great wyrm, in a voice cold as its scales.

Milan

Francisco Turner sat at his ease with the ruler of Milan—who occupied that position at the invitation of its people, if not the acclamation of the noble houses of Europe. Carlo Sforza did not insist on protocol unless it served his purposes, and he knew his trusted lieutenant and personal physician well enough not to waste time and energy on show. They'd shared quarters across the bloody campaigns and small wars of the Italian principalities, ranging from palazzos to mud hovels, and Francisco knew appearances worried Carlo Sforza not at all. If he put on airs and graces, they were for other people's benefit. Left to himself, Sforza was rather Spartan in his quarters and his dress. But that was not what was expected of a powerful condottiere, let alone a duke. So now he was dressed accordingly.

"An elegant cotte, m'lord," said Francisco, amused by his chief's irritable pulling at the obviously prickly gold braid at the collar.

"When you have usurped the position, you need to live up to the people's expectations," said Carlo. Much like Marco had done just a short while earlier in Venice, Sforza looked around the luxurious salon in the palace as if to reassure himself that he was, indeed, the new duke of Milan. "But you would think that the wealthy and powerful would put their comfort ahead of fashion."

"Something I have yet to see any evidence of," said Francisco. "Perhaps you could start a new trend, m'lord."

"Perhaps later, when they don't need to be reminded by my

appearance or the sword," said his master. Moved by a restless impulse, Sforza rose from his chair and began pacing about.

"Or cannon. Cannon make very effective fashion statements," said Francisco.

"So, does Venice plan to show us how fashionable they think they are?"

"Not at the moment, m'lord. The leader of their fashion house is not himself yet. And he is disposed to make a grumpy acceptance of your marriage. Not too hastily, of course, as that might cause more problems than it would cure. The gift you sent was well received, and I think they got the message."

"Hopefully one less source of poisoners, for now."

"Oh, I think if he was sure it would weaken Milan, and be to Venice's advantage, there is no doubt Petro Dorma would order you poisoned tomorrow. Marco Valdosta is otherwise. He's too good for this world. If and when he comes to rule Venice, I think she will plunge headlong into war. Too many people will perceive him as weak. I think they may find out that they are wrong."

"Besides, there is Benito," said Benito's father with a wry smile.

"Yes, but having spent time with Marco, there is more to him than meets the eye at first glance, m'lord. Depths most people will not suspect. And there is a magical side."

"A story to frighten children, my rational friend."

"I am not so sure, this time, m'lord. I'm not gullible, but I have spent quite some time with the man. Besides, there was our little experience with the winged horse."

"That was Benito," said Carlo.

Francisco took a pull at his inevitable flagon of beer. "They say that magic runs in families, sometimes. You are undeniably Benito's father. I've been one of your captains for seventeen years now, and seeing him at the Villa Parvitto was a shock to me. It should have been for him too. You looked very like him when I first met you. You have the same turns of expression, the same shape to the mouth and nose. For him, looking at you is a look into the future."

"I hope he is wise enough to learn from that future. Yes, he is very much my son, although the Dell'este strain is there, too. But what does that have to do with it, Francisco?"

"You are as magical as a brick, m'lord," said Francisco with a smile. "Therefore, if it runs in the blood, and if Benito has it, it must come from..."

"Lorendana Dell'este," scowled Carlo Sforza. He went back to his chair and sat down. "And if she used such skills for anything, it was wild idealism and leading my head astray. I would have killed her if I'd gotten my hands on her, Francisco, I was so angry at the time."

"But in the end, you didn't. Anyway, I was about to say the Dell'este line rather than Lorendana."

"Famous for being blacksmiths."

"Famous for being smiths, anyway. Those were reputed to be magic workers back in my father's homeland. Weyland Smith, for example. Magic work... It is one area Milan has little depth in, and Venice, at least a reputation."

"Reputation and fear win wars," said Carlo Sforza. He had used his to great effect. "I hadn't thought about it before, Francisco. I would have thought it right up my predecessor's sneaking alley."

"From what I can gather, the late duke dabbled in magic once, as a young man. The experience, whatever it was, left him deathly afraid of direct contact with it. And he was scared it might be used in the plotting against him. So the Strega and the Jews were persecuted. Or so I heard in Venice, from one of the *stregheria*. They'd have it he was gulled, and it had nothing to do with them."

Carlo rubbed his chin. "He didn't frighten that easily, nor was he entirely a fool. I must admit I want no part in it, personally." He sighed. "We need the reputation, at least."

"I would deny utterly that we have any magic workers, or that we are looking to recruit them."

"That should work in the meanwhile," said Carlo, amused. "So how was Venice, otherwise?"

"Smelly as ever. Better in winter than in summer, though. Less soft than she looks, and I gather Admiral Lemnossa is seeing to her defenses, but you would know that. The Council of Ten are betting on whom you are going to marry."

"Now that I did not know, but should have guessed. And just whom are they betting on?"

"Eleni Faranese, mostly. Although Violetta de' Medici is, I would guess, Petro Dorma's bet."

The self-styled protector of Milan sighed. "They know more than we do. There is the third possibility, of course."

"Lucia Maria del Maino?"

"She has the most legitimate claim," said Carlo with a wry twist of his lips at the legitimate part. "Just not the wealth and influence of the other contenders. So, obviously, she is not high in the betting, but the odds raise day by day."

"So you have heard nothing, m'lord?"

"No. I know from secondhand experience that these decisions are not taken quickly or easily. Or cheaply." He grimaced.

Francisco had over the years been subjected to his commander's opinion on dynastic marriage and the women involved in somewhat pithy terms before. "So the sanctimonious negotiations over the price continues?"

"That's what happens when you have pimps posing as aristocrats," growled Carlo Sforza, who might pose as an aristocrat, but did not have to like them. "But they're being unusually coy about it. One message from Cosimo, and that is it. The fat girl is being contrary, it seems."

"Sometimes the woman is even consulted," said Francisco dryly. "That can add some time, m'lord."

"True with Cosimo, by all accounts, which adds considerably more time and expense to the process. Whores by any name and description price themselves high, so they can afford to come down. It's a waiting game, and they know that time is on their side, since I will need some illusion of right to rule. In the short term, sword and cannon work well enough, but people forget."

"So I assume we will remind them, m'lord?" said Francisco.

The protector of the Duchy of Milan nodded. "You know me too well, my friend. A border action, merely to remind Da Corregio of Parma that a relation by marriage is more pleasant than a wolf on your doorstep. And a reminder to the people of Milan of what the wolf can do. They forget too fast and too easily."

"Nothing like the sound of cannon to remind them."

Carlo Sforza nodded. "And it's a long way from Venice, and they've not been on the best of terms with Ferrara. Now that I have met him in the field, I want to annoy my son even less." He smiled wryly. "It is odd to find myself not wishing to annoy him. But it is not a fight I would choose, for several reasons. And yes, Francisco, I like being in that position."

"It has the charm of novelty, if nothing else," said his personal physician. In all the years they'd campaigned together, he'd yet to see Sforza shy away from a fight. Plan, choose his time and place, yes. But back off, no.

Constantinople

Benito Valdosta simply wanted to go home, to his wife and baby daughter. The once great city of Constantinople, the bridge between East and West, the gateway to the immensely profitable trade in the Black Sea, had no appeal for him at all. Victory, delivering the Ilkhan Mongol ambassador to the lands of the Golden Horde, and retrieving Prince Manfred of Brittany with the remainder of his escort of Knights of the Holy Trinity from the same place were achievements. Lives and great power were affected. What Benito wanted, however, was his daughter's arms around his neck.

Constantinople seemed determined to thwart this. As he peered glumly out over the city from his perch on a balcony, Benito was beginning to wonder how the Republic of Venice, would take to "I wanted to get home" as a reason for burning the place to the ground.

Hungary, a castle once part of the extensive estates of Elizabeth Bartholdy

Count Kazimierz Mindaug, the former castellan of Braclaw and voivode of Zwinogrodek, master mage, and aide-de-camp to various powers, had spent a great deal of his life making sure he was not around when things finally fell apart. In this he excelled, both in his own schemes, and in those of others. Thus he had fled the Grand Duchy of Lithuania, after the failure of his attempt to destroy both Jagiellon and the demon Chernobog—the demon that his then-master Jagiellon had attempted to use and then had been consumed by. He had fled to the protection of the satanically empowered Elizabeth Bartholdy. Through the compact she'd made, she had access to vast magical powers. When, as was inevitable, that had caught up with her, it had been sensible and easy to flee, as he had from Jagiellon's wrath. He'd left before she'd known he had engineered the possibility of her downfall.

Then he'd taken shelter with King Emeric of Hungary. That had been a mistake, as the military power and the vast lands he ruled were no substitute for the king's weakness in magical and spiritual matters. Kazimierz Mindaug admitted he'd been overconfident at the lack of response from Jagiellon or his demon master. He'd thought that he could assume the position of power Elizabeth Bartholdy had occupied, without paying the same terrible price, by using his magical skill.

Now as he lay, groaning, bruised, and drawing desperate, painful shuddering breaths on the stone floor of the abandoned old castle where he'd done his best to hide, he knew that he had been wrong.

Chernobog had neither forgotten nor stopped hunting for him. And now the demon had found Mindaug's magical escape route. The demon had waited for him, entrapped him, and very nearly killed him, when he had fled through the spirit worlds. That had been a battle on Chernobog's home ground, where knowledge and subtlety had counted for little. He'd learned that he'd been stalked and hunted, that every spell he'd used had been visible to his foe like a fire on hilltop in the netherworlds crying "Here I am!" Mindaug had known that magics had their signature, but he had not known how precise it was. He did now, and he wouldn't make that mistake again.

The count still could hardly believe that he was alive. He had only escaped in the end by pretending that he was dead. Yes, he'd managed to hurt the demon, but not enough to win. That was almost certainly beyond his power.

Eventually he sat up. It was probable Chernobog thought him dead. He would do nothing to disabuse the demon of that delusion . . . at least until he had a new protector who could deal with that kind of raw power. And a new way of escape.

Venice

Maria, like Benito, was perched on as balcony and overlooking a city. In her case, the city was Venice, and the balcony was part of the house owned by Marco and Kat. More like a mansion, really, even if it had still not fully recovered from the ill-fortune into which Kat's Montescue family had fallen over the years.

She itched to return to Corfu. It was said that a prophet was not without honor, except in their own country. Venice and her canals were busy proving that held true for the high priestess of the Goddess too. It wasn't that they didn't respect her as Maria Verrier. She'd earned that, working in the canals. Her relationship with Benito was also well known and quite accepted. But the *stregheria* of Venice had no place for foreign goddesses, or their priestesses. They had their own hierarchy and their own internal politics and she was not a part of it.

Chapter 1

Count Mindaug had grown his mustache in the Frankish fashion, suitable for sieving the solid particles out of beer. It did little to improve the magician's face, but it did help to hide his filed teeth. It might possibly have improved the beer, too. The beer was one of the soft Western details he would once, as one of Grand Duke Jagiellon's inner circle, have felt irrelevant. Survival was important, good food or drink, irrelevant. But there was no doubt that having fled Lithuania for the West had softened him too, he thought ironically. Now he was a man with a large library of magical tomes, accustomed to such things, and with no means here in the Kingdom of Hungary of supporting either a liking for good food and drink, his library, or his personal safety. Elizabeth Bartholdy was safely dead, and paying back her debt to the devil. King Emeric of Hungary hung on a gibbet near the Dniester. The result was the lawless breakdown that was happening across Hungary. And in the chaos . . . the Black Brain, the demon Chernobog who ruled his former master Jagiellon, would be seeking him if he showed any sign of still being alive.

He'd used magic to achieve the first part of his flight. Never again! The second journey, to one of Elizabeth's smaller manors in Slovak lands, he had undertaken in disguise, with no trace of spellwork, and there he'd dispensed of the physical witnesses too. The manor had only had half a dozen servants and a majordomo, with a handful of guardsmen and an elderly knight. They were dead after drinking poisoned wine, now. That had required him to load and pack the wagon himself, and pole up the horses. It was not something he was accustomed to, but then, he'd wanted there to be no one left to say when or how he'd left. Somehow, he needed a safe place for himself and his library, and he was unsure where that might be found. It had to be well beyond the reach of Jagiellon, or his sendlings. Right now, he was not sure where that would be, except not in Hungary. Possibly in the Holy Roman Empire—where he doubted they would welcome Count Kazimierz Mindaug.

Filed teeth would be no help against magical pursuit, or even the physical. He did not need them distracting the peasants or the soldiery into trying to kill him as a man-witch or a cannibal either, thus the mustache. It was easier than maintaining an illusion, which he was capable enough of, but would have showed his spellwork.

The mustache was a fine short-term solution. In the long term, he needed far better protection, both in the physical and magical sense. And money to provide beer, servants and good food. Of course he was capable of using magical means to provide those, but right now he cherished the fact that he was officially dead in Mongol lands, and as far as any magical watcher might be informed, dead in the netherworlds. Besides, he had almost a thousand books to look after. That was difficult, without using magic.

Thus he made his way south, doing his best to avoid calling attention to himself. The wagon was very ordinary-looking, with a canvas and wood cover. It was uncomfortable and slow, but the books needed it.

Unfortunately, the party of Magyar cavalry who had been doing a little freelance marauding in the neighborhood decided they also needed it. Count Mindaug had a moment to reflect that perhaps disguising himself as a merchant had been less than clever.

"Here's loot!" shouted their leader.

They surrounded the wagon in a clearing, and the air was full of their savage laughter. The elevation was low enough here that the area was dominated by beech trees, whose height and dark foliage imparted a sense of gloom to an already gloomy situation.

A sword was held to Mindaug's throat; several more menaced. "Where is the money box, you thieving rogue?" They seemed to find nothing odd in engaging in thievery themselves, while saying this. "Janos, Laszlo, Radul, pull the old fool out of the way, search the wagon. We'll make him sing before he dies if we don't find his gold."

The last thing Count Kazimierz Mindaug wanted was to use magic in close proximity to himself. It would be like lighting a beacon in the netherworlds. And even if there was no watcher now, it would leave a trail, which would show his passage, his direction, and worst, the fact that he was still alive.

Unfortunately, these fools might ensure that he was actually not alive, anyway. And, almost as bad, they might damage the books. He raised his hands weakly. "Spare me," he said in a tremulous voice. "Spare old Jusep. I will show you my master's strongbox. It is hidden and has a magic trap on it. If you break it open, you will die. But I will open it for you. You can take all my gold, my life's savings, just spare me and my old books."

The blade had pulled back, but two of the men had dismounted and grabbed him by the elbows. "Give it to us, you old fool."

"He'll have more hidden somewhere," said one of the men, as they pushed him into the covered wagon's darkness, into the narrow gap between the carefully packed and corded oilcloth-covered boxes.

Giving them illusionary gold would not work, then, thought the count, quite coolly. To someone who had survived in the court of Grand Duke Jagiellon and then with Elizabeth Bartholdy, these were merely dangerous puppies.

"What's in the boxes, old man?" demanded one of soldiers, poking the oilcloth with his sword, and nearly getting himself killed.

Mindaug controlled himself. "Books. I am a bookseller."

"Go on! There aren't enough books in all Hungary to fill that box."

Mindaug thought, *yes, and there lies your country's weakness,* but he said nothing of it, just: "There is my strongbox," pointing to a small iron box next to the bedding.

They let go of him to haul it out. He could have stabbed both of them. They would not have lasted a week in Lithuania. Instead he took the time to uncork a metal flask which was dangling from the crossbar.

The box was heavy enough to fill them with greed and stop them noticing what he did. Mindaug was almost tempted to let them have the contents. Their fellows would kill them for stealing a box largely full of lead, and something less appealing. He'd seen fit to wrap that particular book in sheet lead. It had been a precaution, but he was fairly certain that the book itself was more than just a book. The lock was to keep it in, not to keep the thieves out.

They hauled it out into the daylight, which was a good thing. What was in the box was best viewed in daylight. Not that he had any intention of letting that particular book out, but still. He climbed down from the wagon after them. "Weighs a fair bit," said one of the carriers. "I think our luck just turned."

"Open it, you old fool," said the Magyar lieutenant who had turned his small contingent loose on the countryside. "Let's see what we've got."

They'd put the box down. Men jockeyed their horses around to get a closer view. The two who had dismounted and gone into the wagon stood peering. A third man was holding their horses. Mindaug made sure he was close to the horse holder, before he started his performance. He bent down behind the box and tapped on the lid. They stared. He began drawing a suitable complex pattern with his finger across the lid. Their attention was all on the box, and on him now.

From the wagon, the creature he had let loose began to emerge. The horses noticed first, of course. First with an uneasy tossing of the heads, a whicker...and then full-blown panic. Mindaug had been ready. The horse holder did not even see the knife before it pushed up into his heart. The lieutenant saw it, but his horse was rearing wildly and even a great horseman had other things to do besides avenge the killing.

Mindaug clung to the reins he'd seized from the horse holder. He had the advantage of being on the ground, ready for the shrieking thing that came gibbering out of his wagon, and besides, he was protected against it. It had been one of Elizabeth's creations, one of her little experiments in breeding with trapped magical creatures. With any luck, those who might suspect Mindaug was not dead would blame this on looters. It would stink of her magic and bear no trace of his workings.

They'd know that she was dead.

Some of the fleeing Magyar would be, too. The ones on foot had fled along with their companions. Someone had managed to loose off a wheel-lock pistol in the distance. And again. That would just make it angry. Now, to take the box and follow the wagon. With luck the horses would stay on the road, even without a driver.

He used the dead man's waist sash to tie the box to the nervous horse's saddle. Then, he mounted himself on the second horse. He was, after all, a nobleman and a reasonably good rider, and having organized a lead rein from the tack of the third horse, rode off to find his wagon. He was both luckier and less lucky than he'd hoped to be. It was barely a mile away, but the wagon had suffered a broken pole and the horse was tangled in the traces. The count soon got the horse untangled and calmed, but for the crosspole...he would be obliged to try and effect some kind of repair, and although he was a great master of magical knowledge, practical woodwork had not come his way much. He might have been stuck there, or forced to use some of the magic he had avoided with such effort, if it hadn't been for two frightened young peasants scurrying along the road like nervous rabbits.

Mindaug saw the opportunity, and realized that in practical terms, he needed them, as much, perhaps, as the obvious runaways needed him. The girl was limping, the husky-looking boy doing his best to support her. He kept looking back warily but plainly did not regard a merchant as a danger—which, Count Mindaug thought to himself, merely showed how wrong ignorant people could be. Not that he was an immediate danger, of course. Still, the presence of three Magyar warhorses—the third having followed the other two—would have alarmed most intelligent observers. But perhaps it was simply that these two youngsters did not recognize them as warhorses. They would have had little experience with such.

The peasant boy bobbed. "Uh. Kind sir. You would not have a drink for my...my sister? She is very tired, and we still have far to go."

Count Mindaug nodded. "I do. I can hide her too, and you, if you help me to fix this wagon. Is it your master or her father chasing you?"

The look of terror on their faces would have been amusing if the count had been anything like Elizabeth Bartholdy in nature. He was not. He had, in the course of acquiring the knowledge he now held, committed some terrible deeds. He would kill without qualm or query if need be. But Mindaug was a man who had really no interest in doing so for pleasure. It was just work, as a peasant might regard butchering a hog as work which had to be done sometimes.

So did calming fears. "I said I could hide you," he repeated, his voice even. "There is really no need to be quite so afraid."

"If our lord catches us, he'll beat us to death," said the girl tremulously. They were both, on closer examination, slightly better dressed than most peasants. That was a thing of small degree. King Emeric had made sure that he got every groat out of the peasantry.

"He won't," said Count Mindaug. "Get in the wagon, young

woman. Do not fiddle with anything. There are a few blankets piled in the back. Hide under them. You, boy. Let us change your hair color and clothing. A moment." He reached in and took out the bag he had packed for the emergencies of magic while traveling. It was not something he had sufficient experience of, he had to admit. There were a number of compounds in the bag which had multiple uses, including a bottle of plant killer taken from the green husks of Vinland walnuts. It was stronger than that made from local walnuts, for some reason. A basin was very useful for thaumaturgy and also for filling with water, and a bit of plant killer, which had other properties.

"What is it?" asked the boy.

"Hair and skin dye. Dunk your head and hands in. Be quick now. I've a spare cotte here, too. How far behind you are they?"

"My lord will be looking for her before nightfall. He may be looking already. I..." he looked fearfully around.

"Get on with it," said the count. "I've a hand-cannon that will see no man gets into my wagon."

He gave the trusting peasant a spare cotte which he'd used for some experiments, and was thus not too clean or particularly nice-smelling, and inspected his handiwork. The blond head and white cheeks were considerably darker. "Again." He said. "We'll have you too dark for a local."

The boy stared at his hands "I will look like a gypsy."

"And not like a runaway serf."

"I'm a miller."

That accounted for the slightly better clothes, but didn't stop Mindaug pointing at the bowl again.

A little later, they were busy working on lashing the crossbar together when the sound of horses disturbed them. As he had promised, Count Mindaug returned to the wagon and took up the hand-cannon. "Keep working. Say nothing."

The hand-cannon had been added to his store of things to take with him on a whim. It would probably have gotten him shot by the Magyars, but the minor noble and his handful of retainers who came briskly trotting down the road saw it and were wary.

"You. Have you seen two peasants pass? A young woman and a man," demanded the lordling—addressing the frightened looking boy at the horses' heads, pointing with the whip in his hand.

"He is dumb," said Count Mindaug. "And the answer is yes.

Running over that field beyond those horses." He jerked a thumb at the three Magyar horses, now grazing a few dozen yards away, still with their tack on.

The lordling took the sight in, plainly recognized them as the warhorses they were, and type of tack, gawped at them, and then asked weakly, "Where are they from?"

"Back up the way we'd come from. They stopped here, I suppose, because horses look for other horses. Nothing to do with me. As soon as we've fixed our wagon, we'll be on our way. I'd like to find a town by nightfall."

"Creki, one of my villages, is not more than four miles off," said the lordling. He indicated the direction with a pointing finger.

"We'll likely seek safety there," said Mindaug. "There's something back there unhorsing soldiers. I want no part of it."

By the looks of the minor noble's face, he didn't either. "Which way did they run exactly, merchant?"

"I wasn't paying much attention. I yelled at them to come help me, but they took off toward those woods."

"Our thanks."

"You'd best take the horses with you."

The lordling shook his head. "We'll go and come back with the dogs. I thought to find them on the road, trying to run to Perca-town. Come on, men. We'll just go and check that copse over there."

A few minutes later the count and his wagon were ready to leave, and the lordling and his entourage were already out of sight. "Thank you, master," said the boy humbly. "We owe you our lives."

"Where will you go now?" asked the count, knowing the answer full well.

"Away. We don't really know..."

What peasant, even a miller, who was a step up on most, would know of other options? Their masters kept it like that, and fed them on horror stories, for good reason. "I have an offer for you," said the count. "I have a need for some servants, and no need for young girls." Barring certain rituals, that was true enough. "I'll see you clear of this place, if you will work for me."

The boy nodded eagerly. "We did not know where to go."

And thus it was that Count Mindaug acquired two servants. He was later to wonder why he had done so. But at the time, they were both exceptionally useful.

Chapter 2

A villa in the Tuscan countryside

Violetta looked around the salon where she was sitting a few feet away from Tuscany's ruler. Because it was hers—well, her mother's—and not the duke's, the salon was small and not lavishly furnished. Still, she thought the paintings on the walls were quite nice. Her mother had always been willing to splurge a bit on the artists they employed, while they scrimped elsewhere.

Stop avoiding this, she told herself sternly. It required some exertion of will, but she forced herself to give her uncle a level and—she hoped—reasonably calm gaze.

Well, in truth he was a second cousin, but he had always been Uncle Cosimo to her. She should be quaking, but she had decided long ago that she did not approve of such behavior. Her mother would have been: she ascribed more power to Cosimo than to the devil himself, and with only slightly less malice. It was not a side of himself he had showed Violetta, up until now. But she would try to use as much tact as possible.

It would be difficult, though. She was, by nature, far too inclined to say exactly what she thought.

"No," she said. "I will not marry him, Uncle Cosimo."

His eyebrows raised, but only the outer edge, making him look rather like the devil her mother said he could be. "Is there perhaps some reason, Violetta?"

"You and mother did not provide me with an appropriate instructor of poisons, Uncle. So I would be obliged to use something unsubtle. Just think of the terrible embarrassment that

18

would cause the family. And he is probably—as an experienced condottiere—not easy to slip a knife into. So it would be unsubtle and probably messy. Not at all the image the de' Medici seek to cultivate."

Cosimo's face betrayed little that he did not want to show, but she thought he was amused. That was a good start. "I am surprised, little one. I would have thought martial vigor would have helped his case."

"It does. Just not enough to cover a multitude of other sins."

Little one! Indeed! Well, it was more flattering than "Butterball," but not at all accurate. Not for some years now.

"Suitors without sins are few on the ground, Violetta."

She sat up straighter in the chair, trying to look as self-assured as possible. "I am not in a hurry to marry, and even less so to marry a man who would marry a midden if it gave him a legitimate claim to the Duchy of Milan," she said, forgetting her resolve to be tactful.

He raised his eyebrows at her forthright speech, but replied calmly: "It would also give you a great deal, my dear. I doubt, beside the formalities, he would have any interest in you. However, you would become a duchess, and be able to buy a great many more books."

"You're a better temptress than my mother. She talked about jewelry and fine dresses. And feasts."

"Which you would enjoy, too."

"Which I like, of course. Too much. It's why they call me 'Butterball' behind my back."

"The raw garlic you have been eating would probably get you a less flattering name, Violetta. Dragon breath, perhaps. But there is a political aspect to this, and as head of the House, I ask you to reconsider," said Cosimo. "There is potential advantage not only for the de' Medici, but also for Florence and Tuscany. Sometimes we do not what we wish, but do what is needed of us."

She'd been afraid it would come to this. It was a lot harder than jewels and dresses. Harder too than books or even food... which she did love more than the jewels or dresses. "I do not believe," she said slowly, "that it is of that great a value. In fact I think it would bring us into conflict with Venice, with the Holy Roman Empire, and also possibly Rome. Don't think I don't understand, Uncle. Or that I set myself as more valuable than the family. That is part of the reason I refused. That and the dislike of being little more than a stamp of legitimacy for a man who is a usurper. He who would take that step would value the de' Medici not at all. He would use us and betray us."

Cosimo sighed. "Your mother wrote that you were merely being mulish. I had my doubts about that. She does not think women can comprehend politics. How she reconciled that with having met my mother and sister is beyond me. You know, and I know, that we do not marry to please ourselves. I have had similar thoughts about his actions, Violetta. But, to be honest with you, I can see no real difference in Carlo Sforza's behavior with, or without, his marriage to you. And I can see some possible advantage for you. You are twenty-four years of age, long past the typical age of marriage, have, to be honest, little in the way of inheritance, and besides the Visconti relationship, little in the way of value as a dynastic marriage. You are a second cousin, and there are de' Medici that would seem of more value to the outsider. They do not know, or care, how fond I am of you. It would be a position of wealth and power, and thus good for you."

He gave one of his infamous twisted smiles. "Especially if he dies, which, even if you are not a skilled poisoner, military men do."

"How cheerful," said Violetta, giving him her own twisted rictus of a smile in return. "You say: 'Marry him, Violetta. You may soon be a widow.' Uncle Cosimo...I can only see war coming for Milan. He has not a friend to turn to, and his enemies will not chance him being able to devour them one by one. They won't rest until the Duchy of Milan is torn into gobbets, and the winner of the city will take his widow, especially if she has a claim to the Visconti bloodline. And wouldn't it be nice if it were Count Andrea Malatesta, as seems not unlikely," said Violetta grimly.

Cosimo was silent for a while, pacing. Finally he said: "You do manage to paint the most unattractive pictures in my mind, Violetta."

"Yes, and you can be sure Malatesta would use the lever you gave him, and be even more sure to keep me out of striking distance of his exquisite person."

"That does suppose they can unite against Sforza. I may tell you I have had approaches. Not from Malatesta, of course. Parma and others, but it was obvious to me he would be in the alliance—and better within than without. But I have heard rumors that Venice is being neutral. That could change the entire picture. It is a very fluid game, and Sforza is, if nothing else, a master of applied force."

"Venice will not sit out when the others threaten to devour their northern borders. And there is no love lost there. The people of Venice would be demanding war, too."

Cosimo nodded in agreement. "You know, Violetta, you are wasted as a woman. You would have made a great condottiere."

She snorted. "Most condottieri would have made poor women. They have far more resources, and they still lose. Usually with great expense and noise."

"With the general exception of Carlo Sforza. In a way, I am glad the two of you do not make a marriage. It another way, though, it is a pity. I rather liked him, the time that I met him. A blunt, powerful man."

"Not precisely a nobleman," she said, with an instinctive lift of the chin.

"No. But then neither were we, not many generations ago, although we pretend otherwise. Andrea Malatesta is, though."

"You also paint the most unattractive pictures in my mind, Uncle Cosimo. What do we do now? Sforza will take offense, and make that an excuse, I think."

Uncle Cosimo was a great deal better at business than he was at warfare, reflected Violetta. It was a good thing he tried to avoid it. She had studied Sforza's history, as much of it as was known, long before his unattractive proposal came. She enjoyed the reading of military tactics, which was just as well, because there was more of it than any other form of writing, besides the ecclesiastic, which had less appeal to her. It also irritated her mother, which, Violetta had to admit, was something of a reward.

He shrugged. The gesture did not exactly project indifference, but something fairly close. While Tuscany's ruler was not going to treat Sforza in a cavalier manner, he was certainly not terrified of him, either. Cosimo de' Medici didn't have the military skills—and certainly not the fearsome reputation—of the Wolf of the North. What he did possess, however, was lots and lots of money, with which he could and had hired very capable mercenaries and even more capable designers and builders of fortresses. Tuscany was the proverbial tough nut to crack.

"I will play for time, of course," he said. "Then, with luck, he will attack someone else, probably Parma, which will spur the forming of an alliance against him. I want no part in yet another expensive war, but I think we will have no choice."

Her mother was not going to be pleased. Mother had dreamed, somehow, of that romantic marriage, despite what it had brought to her. She was a widow of almost no means, thanks to her father's disastrous military venture and her own decision to marry against the family wishes. If it had not been for Cosimo, they would not have had the moderate comfort of a country villa and the small estate that went with it. If Cosimo had insisted, Violetta would have had to accede to his wishes.

She was grateful he had not. Grateful, and yet sad, somehow. She would like to see more of the world than just the view across the vineyards and, on all too infrequent occasions, the city of Florence. It was just too far for a comfortable day's travel, there and back. That made economic sense, but did leave them a little lonely and isolated—a little too noble for most of the local land-owners, and a great deal too poor for life in a great house in the city. The food was good, and plentiful, and Uncle Cosimo saw to her getting quite a large number of books. He took perverse pleasure in that, it seemed. If his wife Catherine could read, she never did. She had no interest in what she termed with a sneer "men's boring doings," but devoted herself to fashion, music, and grand entertainments, to which they were sometimes invited. Violetta's mother bemoaned the expense, and reveled in the experience. Violetta found them dull, as did her uncle, judging from the mechanical civility he displayed at the events. She had seen him animated only in philosophical discussion, and in talking of books or politics.

He had married, as a dutiful son should, for the family.

Chapter 3

Venice

Marco had wondered why he would get a request from Patriarch Michael to visit him at his palace. The Church was...just a little wary about the connection between the Lion of Etruria and the House of Valdosta. Still, while it was politely worded, and merely an invitation, the Church was powerful in the Holy Roman Empire and Venice.

"It's not, politically speaking, an invitation you can refuse," said Lodovico, handing the message back to Marco, "even if you wanted to. And he's not a bad old fellow, Michael. Quite moderate, really."

Marco shook his head. "I know. It's just that, well, the *stregheria* are very suspicious about the Church, and I've been hoping for medical help from them. There are some plants..."

"Marco, if they can't live with you visiting the patriarch, especially after his defense of Benito, then they're crazy," said Kat firmly. To emphasize her point, she planted her hands on her hips and leaned forward a bit.

"Yes, but they have been persecuted, at times."

"Not by him. And anyway, he's near ninety and was looking quite frail the last time I saw him. It's probably about medical help."

That was a very persuasive argument as far as Marco was concerned. So he went, not that he had that much choice. He was escorted in to a small withdrawing room—a place in some contrast with the wealth displayed in the rest of the building. It was Spartan and simple, with plain wooden settles and an open fire, and a wooden cross on the wall. The patriarch himself was seated there, not on anything like the inlaid golden throne he sat on in the cathedral but on one of the settles. He rose, not fast, but still quite spryly for someone of his age, when Marco was ushered into the room. "Welcome to my sanctum," said the old man.

"Thank you, Your Holiness," said Marco bowing. He'd met the patriarch before, at functions at the Doge's palace, and seen him at the Basilica of St. Mark, of course.

"It tends to surprise people," said the patriarch, plainly understanding the expression. "I let them make a fire in here now, as a gesture toward my aging bones. But I was a Haitian monk for some years, before the Grand Metropolitan of Rome called me to serve here. Venice and her great families love and expect the display of wealth and power. Simplicity does not impress them. I am uncomfortable with such display. Much of the wealth and artwork was, however, gifted to the Church to use, and cannot merely be disposed of." He sighed. "Powerful families like to show the value of their piety. They know full well what their ancestors gave, and expect to see it displayed."

"Oh. I had heard Lodovico...my grandfather-in-law Lodovico Montescue, mention the Montescue candlesticks."

"Given your upbringing, young Valdosta, you are probably unaware of the fact that the cloth of gold used for Martinmas was a gift from Alberto Valdosta. There is quite a list of other items too."

"Well...those could be sold without offending me and I don't see Benito caring a fig either, Your Holiness." Was this why he'd been asked to come?

"Thank you. Of course people are used to seeing some of them, and this is Venice, so one does not wish to start nasty rumors. They breed quite well enough without help. Shall we sit?" He gestured toward the settles. Marco sat in one of them and the patriarch sat in another.

"Ulrico has gone to fetch the gentleman that I asked for you to come to see me," continued the patriarch, "so that you could meet. He has been sent from Rome, by the Grand Metropolitan."

"I, er, do think matters of state should be dealt with by the Doge. I am only his ward."

"I believe this to be a matter above the state," said the patriarch, with a mischievous smile more fitting for a boy of four than for a man of almost ninety. "Marco Valdosta, I have invited you here as the rising physician of Venice, not as the ward of the

Doge. I have had a fairly substantial number of reports from the poorer parishes about your work. That's more important to me, but we won't tell Petro Dorma that."

Marco's surprise and embarrassment was interrupted by the entry of a tall man in clerical clothes with a rather long bony nose. "Ah," said the patriarch. "Father Thomas. Father Thomas Lüber of Baden, this is the young gentleman I wished you to meet. Marco Valdosta, the ward of our Doge, and also a man of some repute of medicine and healing."

The newcomer bowed. "I have heard a great deal about you, Signor Valdosta. Eneko Lopez wrote to me of you." His Frankish had a decidedly Mainz accent, and he plainly suffered from some shortness of breath. He breathed audibly at each sentence.

Marco rose, bowed and made haste to shake the hand of man. "I also know a great deal about you, Father. And about your work with Professoro Ghini. I have an interest in the plants described in *De Materia Medica* myself. I've been trying to combine them with the system of quantifying dosage for treatment suggested by Dacetto, and Von Hohenheim's *Lexicon of Toxicology*. He took the approach that it was dosage that made some substances toxic, and noted that bigger persons took larger doses to kill, and I was reasoning that the dose had to be proportional to the weight of the patient."

The priest looked thoughtful. "Yes. A different approach. And one which has merit! I have been following up on an idea I had, oddly based on apples. I grew two plants, from seed from the same fruit. One at the new botanical garden Signor Cosimo has ordered cultivated in Pisa, and the other in Montfalcone, where my brotherin-law has a small estate. The fruit look alike, but the taste is quite different. Those from Montfalcone, barely three leagues away from the Botanica, are tart, delightful apples, but those in the Botanica are watery and of poor flavor, and much larger. I had wondered if it was perhaps a virtue of the earth of a particular place. That would go a long way to explaining why the curative properties of some of the plants Pedanius Dioscorides recorded, those that we have found and cultivated, are in some cases not effective."

"Well, I have been told that the same grapes produce different wine from different places," said Marco. "Those growing on the clay in the valley floor are quite different to those on the granite slope facing north, and different again on those that face south. But—please have a seat."

Marco sat back down on his settle and motioned for Father Thomas to join him. Once he'd done so, they resumed their conversation.

"Precisely!" said Father Thomas. "And that is an easier example for most to grasp than my apples. Not all of the same plants produce food alike, thus why would they produce medicines of equal value?"

"I can see I have brought together two kindred spirits," said the patriarch. "But before the two of you become entirely absorbed in the academia that interests you, let me remind you of the matter of business that you are here about, Father Thomas."

The priest's face fell. "Yes. It is a grim business, Signor Valdosta. You know that the Patriarchy in Rome keeps a group of clerics whose work it is to magically scry the future, to try to divine where evil will strike next and so help to prepare our defenses. Eneko Lopez was senior among those practicing this form of sacred magic, and that was one of the reasons that the Grand Metropolitan was so reluctant to grant him leave to form his new monastic order. I am not a man of any knowledge of magic, myself, but I believe he was among the most skilled at this field of magic, and is sorely missed. But I digress, a bad habit of mine. They have identified a new threat."

"Not to Venice again?" Marco could not see how this could not be a matter of state.

"No, or at least not immediately. But the symbol which has been repeatedly oracularly derived is one that should be familiar to Venice, and has endangered her in the past: the crowned devouring serpent." He moved his forefinger through the air, as if drawing the image of the serpent.

"Milan. I still don't see why the Doge..."

"He will be informed. But what they have foreseen is not a war. Or not just a war. It is the reason I have been sent here, and the reason that Patriarch Michael sent for you first, not Doge Petro Dorma. Disease is what is foreseen. And not just any disease, but a disease that has not affected Europe for centuries, but devastated the cities and countryside like no war could."

"Plague." The word itself carried terrible fear.

"Yes. If we are correct in our foretelling, somehow this is the Justinian Plague reborn. Visions of rats, too, have been described by the seers; rats, a strange monstrous face, dead cities, and the countryside laid waste. And famine and war following in its wake. Millions dead, men, women and children. That is why I have been sent here, to Venice. That is why trusted messengers have been sent north to the Holy Roman Emperor in Mainz. That is why men are being prepared for action, and called to readiness. It will need hard, effective and fast action."

"What can be done? There is no certain cure for the plague. Some live, many die. Most die, if the plague is virulent enough."

"We will be working on whatever treatment we can, Signor Valdosta." He ran fingers through his closely cropped hair. In that moment, he looked both tired and ridden with anxiety. "I will confer with you, and others at the academia. We need to prevent panic as much as anything else. But the disease must be contained. And the problem, as we foresee it, will begin in the Duchy of Milan, with whom the patriarch of Rome has poor relationships. These have not been bettered by the train of events with Carlo Sforza taking control of the duchy and its territories. And we know, from what remains of the historical record, that isolation and quarantine were all that was sure as a treatment."

He paused. "It is known that you had a friendship with Caviliero Francisco Turner, who is the personal physician to Carlo Sforza."

"Yes, I did—and, hopefully, still do. Francisco is the very man I would pick to head a fight against the plague."

"Unfortunately, politics would get in the way of that idea. The states of Parma, Rimini and Ferrara are vehemently opposed to any form of cooperation with Carlo Sforza. I wish we could rise above that for such a dire situation. But it is not so. I had hoped, through a neutral, or at least not so violently opposed party, and personal contacts to, well, make them aware. To get them to make such preparations as they can, to contain and quarantine." He grimaced. "Military force will be needed. And people fleeing in panic will spread the disease. Fear and war will merely make it worse and spread it wider."

"I see. So, what you are asking is that I send warning to Francisco, and through him to Carlo Sforza."

The priest nodded. "Yes. We would thus set up a route of communication that would not be open to us otherwise."

Marco sighed. "I don't know what my word means to Francisco. He is a clever man, and, I think, an honorable one. But he is not an easy man to read, and he is intensely loyal to Carlo Sforza. That said, I am willing to try at least."

"Thank you," said Father Thomas.

Chapter 4

The Border Marches

Count Mindaug had discovered in his few days of rough traveling that having been born with many servants to wait on your needs, even a master magician could struggle. Simple tasks like hitching horses to the wagon—an unobtrusive choice for travel, perhaps, but very slow—were more difficult than he'd realized. The runaways Tamas and Emma had been a spur-of-the-moment decision, and might still have to die, but they had eased his passage somewhat. His two servants had, as he guessed, been lovers: she was a pretty peasant girl who had caught the eye of the local lord, and he, amusingly enough, was a bastard child of the same lord, a fact to which he'd owed his elevation to the important—in a minor village—position of miller. It meant he had some skill with things rudely mechanical, which could indeed prove useful.

The problem, of course, was a passage to where? He had thought about various possibilities—Vinland, Alexandria, one of the remote Iberian states. The issue was that physical distances were not the same in the netherworlds, where Chernobog held such power.

The more he thought about it, the more Count Mindaug realized he would have to go either to the Holy Roman Empire or to one of its vassal states. The problem with that, of course, was that their rulers would kill him as surely as Grand Duke Jagiellon, for his role in working with the grand duke and for his aiding of both King Emeric and Elizabeth Bartholdy. He would have to keep his true identity secret. That would be easy enough in a physical sense, but difficult in a magical one. He could protect himself reasonably well, both magically and in combat (as a noble, little as he'd enjoyed it, he had had some training with the sword, main gauche and lance). But against armies and forces of magic such as the Empire or, indeed, the grand duke could muster, he could not stand. At least, not against both at once. He wanted a secure position, where he would be protected, physically, and he could prepare for a quiet departure again, if need be. It was a situation he had realized he would have to live with, or he would not remain living for long.

He would avoid Pressburg and head northwest, and cross the black water of the March River, he decided. The far bank was the territory controlled by the Knights of the Holy Trinity, but it was formally part of the Holy Roman Empire. And then he would be going south, to Italy and the sun, and also various small states and principalities. A place where he could possibly find protectors, and return to his art.

In this, he found his awed new servants invaluable. For the first time in his life, the count had servants who did not fear him, but instead felt they owed him their lives, and it seemed were very conscious of that debt. They were both awkwardly eager to please. It was something of a revelation to him: their desire to repay him made them more industrious and more ingenious than fear or money had made his previous lackeys. There had been some wary jealousy on the boy's part that Mindaug might try to exercise *droit du seigneur*. Mindaug had very little interest in women, or men, for that matter. He had had his pick and fill as a young and powerful noble. He had, in the course of his researches, encountered more and varied sexual practices than most people. He'd realized what a lever they could be, and had taken certain steps to prevent himself being thus entrapped.

He hadn't realized that it would also make him totally uninterested.

To his servants, however, with their small knowledge of sex and power, that indifference obviously made him seem even more benign. They traveled steadily, with not more than minor brushes with authority, which he was easily able to dismiss with a touch of arrogance, and a little money. Ahead lay the March River, and the border of the Kingdom of Hungary. It looked a very similar country on the other side of that river: meandering streams and lush vegetation. The count, however, knew appearances could be deceptive, and for him, the other side of the border was much safer from his old master.

Now he just had to cross that border. That sounded simple enough, and would be if he used his magical skill. Only that would most likely call unwanted attention to himself. It really was very inconvenient.

The trouble was, the eastern Marches were patroled by the Knights of the Holy Trinity. Long ago, Emperor Magnus had given them lands there, as a simple way of protecting his border with minimal expense. It had not been a dangerous border for many years, but the abbeys built back then were old and large. They served as a place of rest, recovery and recuperation for Knights back from more dangerous fronts. That meant that there would be magic workers and doughty warriors here, who would not be in these relatively peaceful parts otherwise.

The answer, of course, was money. Not as bribes, which he gathered might just be counterproductive—a most odd and unhealthy situation as far as he was concerned—but as a distraction. Most people seemed to find it so. Elizabeth Bartholdy had had an ample and generous supply of money, a side effect of the bargain she'd made. The devil provided generously, but did extract interest. From his researching, Count Mindaug had decided that adding interest to the bill... was probably foolish. But then, he'd never rated her intelligence that highly. She'd thought herself too clever, too powerful, and ended up wrong.

They had stopped and camped some distance from the peat-stained water of the river, near enough to see the spire of the church and the tip of the watchtower's roof at Marchegg, but not close enough to be observed. His researches had indicated that the narrow bridge that had been built there had helped the town to grow a little. But it was still little more than an outlying fortress for the Knights, who permitted, but watched, the trade that was allowed across it. It went no further than the walled town, and the gates out of that required a permit chit. Well, once in... he could get out.

Perhaps some vague strand of that long-forgotten thing, guilt, had plucked at Kazimierz Mindaug's mind. He had bought good fat Kenyersalonna bacon and a string of small onions in the last town, and Emma had had Tamas carefully trim hazel twigs into skewers, and she'd cut squares off the bacon side, and slashed it carefully, and then stabbed the bacon onto the skewers, and then half an onion. They carefully toasted the rough rye bread and grilled the bacon, holding the skewers down at an angle so that the fat dribbled into the onion, and then carefully brought their master a wooden platter with the best pieces, and the toasted bread, and strong ewe's cheese.

It smelled better than most of the feasts he'd had in Lithuania, or in Elizabeth's castles and palaces, or in the retinue of King Emeric. Tasted better, too.

Here." He handed them a pottery jar and a bottle he'd also bought in the village. "We leave the Kingdom of Hungary tomorrow, and it may be a while before you taste anything from your homeland again. Enjoy them."

The peasant girl looked at the two gifts warily. He'd gathered that even bacon was a rare treat. Meat had been a sparse thing in her life, cooked with grain and pulses, and cabbage to make it stretch, and the bacon and bread a princely meal. "What are they, master?"

"Honey wine and some cherries in brandy."

She curtseyed, peasant fashion. "Oh, thank you, master. I have never had those. Have you, Tamas?"

Tamas had come from the fire, so he opened the bottle and smelled it. "Here, Emma. Smell the spices! I was given some of the honey wine, once."

The count realized that the spices he took as a normal part of fare, townsfolk took as special treats, and to the peasants, depending on their poverty, they would be far more rare. Brandy, too, was beyond their means. They were as excited as small children—something else the count had had little to do with—tasting it cautiously, sampling one cherry between the two of them, and conscientiously offering him some of their treasure. That had surprised him so much that he had almost laughed, not something he had done for a long time.

"No. Enjoy. It is not from my homeland or unusual for me." How easy it would be to poison them had the need to do so arisen.

"May we keep them in the wagon, master?" she asked, carefully closing the bottle and clay jar.

"But they are for you to enjoy. To eat. To drink."

"Oh, but they are too good to have all at once!" she answered, shocked.

And not all his reassurance could persuade her otherwise. Well, if these were treasures, then tomorrow's plan would work well.

A goose woman, with a flock of six geese coming along the track as they broke their fast, provided the portal.

"Hola, old woman. Where are you going with those?" asked the count, slightly warily, because as a young boy he had discovered that geese are no respecters of rank.

"Ah, master, I'm off to sell them to the foreigners. Across the river. They'll give me a better price than I can get here."

For a brief moment, the count considered killing her and taking the geese. But . . . money would be easier.

"How much for your fine geese?" he asked.

"These geese! Why, your lordship, they're worth a silver penny each, but to save me driving them, I'd sell the six for four copper pence each."

"Why you cheating old hag!" screeched Emma, taking a menacing couple of steps toward the old woman who, for her part, flinched back the same distance. "They're not worth two copper pennies. Look at them. Scrawny, they are!"

Battle was about to be joined when Mindaug intervened. "Here," he said drawing out this pouch. "It is your lucky morning, old woman."

"But, master," protested Emma. "They're not worth that much!"

He looked at her quellingly. "It is my day for doing good deeds. And this lady looks tired. We will eat one goose and sell the rest. I have spoken."

She was instantly contrite, at least with him, but the look she cast at the smirking old besom was less so. Still, ownership of the geese was handed over, along with the strings attached to the creatures, who did not seem to like Mindaug any more than he liked them. He hastily handed their leashes to Tamas, and watched the goose woman walk off the way she had come. The vegetation on both sides of the track was thick; within a few seconds, she had completely vanished from sight.

"What do we do with these, master?" asked Tamas, pointing to the geese.

"You will be taking them to sell across the river, making

a way for me to cross with less notice. We need to cross into Frankish lands, and they will not just let us do so."

"Ah! I wondered why you were paying so much! They aren't worth half that. They will let us across with the geese?"

"They will let you and Emma across with the geese. You will create a distraction. I will follow."

They both nodded. "Yes, master. What do we need to do?" asked Tamas.

"Go across the bridge, go into the market and set loose these geese. With any luck people will chase them. Then run up the street and strew around the money that I will give you. People will be so busy chasing the money, they will not be watching the gate."

Mindaug knew the idea was entirely ridiculous, but hoped that they would hold out under torture for a little while. He found, oddly, that he hoped that their deaths would be quick. They would create a distraction, of course, but more in the sense of being taken to the garrison, and probably immediately, under escort to the nearest chapter house. Guards being guards, the senior and most skilled would go running off with them, eager to claim the credit for catching them. And the last thing they'd expect would be a second infiltrator, so close behind those inept two.

They would not realize that their guilt would betray them. What knowledge did they have of borders or guards? He took out the two bags of coin he'd prepared last night. There was a good weight to them, more money than either of them—or quite possibly their overlord—had ever seen. Human greed would do the rest.

"This side of the border, you're peasants. Across the river, with this, you would be rich," he said, to prevent them running away here and now, and too early. "All you have to do is lie to the border guard and say you have come to sell the geese, and then go scatter the money, and I'll follow in the chaos."

Big-eyed and solemn, they nodded. A little later they got underway, driving the geese with him following behind.

The count soon found that his plans were not as complete as they should have been. The geese were not fast movers, and the track they were on led to join a larger track, down which several other people were heading for market, driving a few beasts, carrying baskets and bundles. Mindaug had not envisaged such a crowd. He stopped the horses for a brief moment while fiddling with the tack, and allowed a few of the other traders to get between him and the geese, and the bait.

The bridge had been built for rapid demolition. Three sets of pilings in the river, each linked with logs planked with riven oak—barely wide enough for his wagon, and enough to make his horses balk. The last piling had a gatehouse on it, and entrants queued up for the guard to examine them.

Count Mindaug had expected a commotion ahead. Instead, he and the wagon were causing it. The horses just didn't like the bridge, the river, or the other traders.

But by then he was already on the bridge, completely unable to get off it. The scene that followed was completely contrary to the plan. The guard, several stout farmers and, to his dismay, even Tamas, came back to help him move. Urgently, he waved the boy on.

It took half an hour, and great patience and determination from a large cowherd, two guards, a shrill and irritable woman with baskets of eggs, and a great deal of swearing to get the wagon into Marchegg. No examination or paperwork had taken place. One guard went back to his post. The other, still shaking his head at the stupidity of bringing horses across that bridge, said: "You're lucky not to end up in the river, you old fool. What brings you to Marchegg?"

Obviously, his plan of chaos on the bridge with the arrest of the two peasants had not come to fruition. Or if it had, he hadn't noticed. If all else failed, Mindaug could use magic, but that would undo his attempts at secrecy and probably bring him into a dangerous conflict with the Knights of the Holy Trinity.

"Sir," he said humbly, "I have a number of books in the wagon. The castle of my old overlord, Count Gastell, when King Emeric executed him, had a library, and I was able to buy it cheaply. Well, the truth be told, the new lord was going to burn them as rubbish. I am a scribe and love books and I had heard that the Franks love books. There are a few tomes I had hoped to sell to the great Knights of the Holy Trinity, as they appear to be on the subject of magic."

The guard shook his head. "Only a scribe would do something quite as stupid as to try to bring that wagon over the bridge. They're good horses and a solid wagon, Scribe. How did you come by them?"

"My mother was...um, a favorite of the count," said Mindaug, making up the tale on the fly, preparing himself for action. "I was destined for the cloister, but he took me to be his scribe. I and my mother had a little put by for the wagon. The horses were his gift to her. She's dead now, God rest her soul."

"Fair payment, I suppose. And the reason the new count didn't want you around."

"Or me to remain in the area."

The guard nodded, set his spear aside and said: "Well, show me some of these books."

So Count Mindaug opened a carefully wrapped box—one of the front ones which contained little that would make a churchman unhappy, not some of the hidden tomes.

"They look of value. Not that you're likely to sell them in Marchegg. I'll give you a chitty so you can go on to the chapter house at Eikendal. And don't come back this way, for heaven's sake, Scribe. There are better, wider bridges at Pressburg."

Mindaug, all his cunning plans it seemed in vain and unneeded, had a little time to wonder where he was going to find some new servants and just how far he could be from here by nightfall, while the guard walked back to the gatehouse and returned with a scrap of parchment.

"Here you go. Avoid narrow bridges!"

"I shall," said the count gratefully. He moved on, passing the market where several people seemed occupied in chasing geese, and out of the far gate, into the Frankish Marches.

He hadn't gotten very far—just to the first copse—when Tamas and Emma came running to join him, their faces beaming, eagerly holding out his pouches of money. "We didn't have to use very much, master. You gave us far too much. Emma went to the wine merchant and changed twenty silver pennies into small coppers, and we bought five bags, tied them around the necks of the geese, cut small holes in them and set them loose in the market."

Count Kazimierz Mindaug, who had kept his calm and not been at a loss for words with the murderous and demon-possessed Grand Duke Jagiellon, had coolly answered the satanic Elizabeth Bartholdy, and had urbanely dealt with the foaming spittle of King Emeric, was now at a loss for words. He just looked at them and shook his head.

Emma looked at him worriedly. "I am sorry, master. Did I spend too much? You can count the money..."

For the second time, his new servants surprised the count so much that he wanted to laugh, and this time he actually did. That was something he had not done for so long he had almost forgotten how. It was obviously such an odd noise that it worried the two of them. "Are you choking, master?" asked Tamas, plainly perturbed, stepping forward.

"No, I am laughing. I have had no cause to laugh for a long time, and I have lost the skill of it," he said, shaking his head, feeling a bubble of it still within himself. He looked at the second, larger bag Tamas was holding out. "And what is in that bag? The city guard?"

"Oh, just the goose, master. You did say you wanted to eat one, so I brought it along. I kept the fattest one. I did kill it. I hope that is all right?"

And this time Count Mindaug managed to laugh with somewhat more skill. "I am going to have to get used to this. And now, I think we should remove ourselves from being too close to the goose-infested town of Marchegg."

So they proceeded on their way, Emma calmly plucking the goose and Tamas driving, while the count found himself as comfortable a place in the wagon bed as the rough road would permit. He attempted to read, and to readjust his ideas around the idea of people who served out of loyalty and, when given a small fortune—brought it back to him.

That had possibilities and possible advantages, even. He was able to grasp that, and to realize that it was a conditional thing, worth keeping alive, at least until he understood it. The joy of it was that Jagiellon, and the demon that owned him, never would or could understand it. Mindaug was not sure he could himself, but at least he knew of its existence now.

Chapter 5

Venice

Marco Valdosta had labored long over the letter he had composed to his friend the Caviliero Francisco Turner. It was dangerous and difficult ground. He knew he was spied on, as indeed were most of the *Casa* Longi to some extent. In his case, he knew that the watch was fairly intense, because he was the Doge's ward and well-connected in other areas, as well as having some associations with the *stregheria*. And there were others that spies and the political overlords of Venice and elsewhere feared—the creatures who were not of this world and beyond their machinations, like the Lion of St. Mark and the tritons of the lagoon. There were spies from Rome, other states, and naturally, Venice herself. Normally, this didn't worry Marco much. After all, he lived a fairly blameless life. He was sure they found him boring, which was his best defense. And he had an ally they could not reach in the Winged Lion of St. Mark.

But in writing in secret to Francisco he risked two things. The first, obviously, was that Francisco was the trusted confidante of a man the Venetian Republic considered at best a threat, and at worst, one of their most dangerous enemies. Writing to him in secret, well, that made Marco guilty of conspiracy. Marco had done his best, telling Doge Petro that he would be writing privately to Francisco about medical matters. The Doge had raised his eyebrows. "Not my health. Not unless you are telling him it has returned to robust strength and I can at last increase my consumption of the pate made from the livers of fat geese. I am sure as they're made of livers they must support mine. And best not about the condition of your wife. Those are matters of state, Marco."

"No. I wish to talk to him about the prevention of the spread of infectious complaints. We get a lot of that every spring and autumn." That was the truth, but not what this letter would be about. The Doge would have spies listening, night and day.

And that was the second reason Marco was so afraid of the contents of this letter. People, even spies, remained terrified of the plague. It had been centuries since the last exceptionally infectious strain had swept across Europe. The fear still remained. Marco knew that those infected with it, but not yet dying, had also tried to flee, and had carried it with them, spreading the disease. There had been outbreaks of what could be the same disease since, but oddly, they had been contained by their own virulence. The victims had died too fast to pass it on beyond their community, become too sick too rapidly to travel.

It was a terrible thing to hope for, and yet it would spare many lives.

The letter itself was carefully phrased making reference to several of the books that Marco knew his friend and mentor in the Arabic medical tomes would recognize.

My friend in Medicine.
Using the medical methods much criticized by Alpharabius, but that we nonetheless have found completely reliable, we predict that the coming season, particularly in the low-lying areas near the rivers—that is for both Venice and Milan—will spread the swelling condition of which Avicenna refers to in the first book we studied together.

That had been a tome on anatomy, which had described the glands in the groin which typically swelled with the infection from the plague. They'd talked about it at some length and, in Francisco's dry manner, some humor. "A pity the swelling is in the wrong place," he'd said, "or I'd have customers prepared to get the plague, aye, and pass it on, just for the swelling."

I must advise you that we are taking such steps as we can to prevent the spread, and hope you will do the same.

Seemingly an innocuous letter, which would probably still attract suspicion and considerable reading of medical tomes and ones saying that prediction and divination by astrological means were nonsense.

And now to send it... But how best to do so? With the sanction of Petro, who would want to know what it meant? With a private messenger? There would be a good chance of him being intercepted with that message... intercepted, robbed and killed, most likely. Marco wished his grandfather Enrico Dell'este was back in Ferrara. The Old Fox had his reliable networks and methods not available to other men.

"So do you," said the voice of the Lion within him. "They will rob men, but they'll be hard pressed to take the message from an undine or one of those they do traffic with."

"Oh. I hadn't thought of that. I suppose I could be a little more direct then. But I better write it on something waterproof," said Marco to the inner voice of that magical being he shared his mind with. He got up from his writing desk and went to the room he had converted into a store for his medical paraphernalia, drugs, and instruments. Finding something waterproof was not hard. Finding something he could write on that was also waterproof, and where the writing would not suffer from immersion, was a lot more challenging. Finally he hit on the happy and simple answer of merely using a bottle that he could seal properly.

He went back to his desk to find that someone had bumped over the precariously balanced quill and little ink bottle. It gave him something to clean up and to think about. The letter he'd worked on was ruined, so it was just as well he was writing it again, in more direct terms.

He really didn't like spies here. Especially if they were going to be that clumsy! He would have to find out who they were and do something about it, because he did not want them accidentally ruining a medical preparation. He didn't wait, but took the new letter as soon as the ink was dry, folded it and put it in his pouch, and took the bottle in his bag of medical implements and medicines, and headed for the Chapel of St. Raphaella. There he spoke with Brother Mascoli and then went below, through the water door, to call for one the undines.

He had treated several of the merfolk over the last while, and as the Lion he could command anything that lived in the lagoon or marshes of ancient Etruria. But he would rather ask. He had one of Francisco's books with him, one of those he'd retrieved from the Signori di Notte after Francisco had abruptly left Venice in the wake of Alessia's disappearance. He'd offered them back to the caviliero when he had returned as Carlo Sforza's emissary.

Most of them, Francisco had taken with gratitude, but this one he had presented to Marco. "I have another copy, and they're not easy to come by. This is a later copying and there are a few errors. But it was my original copy, and I did put corrections in when I got an older version."

One of the undines, Chloe, came to his call. *"Healer. Lion,"* she said respectfully, as they always did. She was one he had treated before—in the last year he'd treated infections, had sewn up injuries on a fair number of the magical non-humans. Just because they were not human did not mean they could not be hurt, or that they could not become infected, or as he had discovered, that they could not have stomach ailments. That had been difficult. He had no idea what or how often they ate, or what their normal body temperatures were, or how to treat what was plainly a fever for the merfolk. He'd started developing treatments and learning about their physiology, which he had been painstakingly recording and drawing. He wondered, suddenly, what the spies made of that! He would hate it used against the merpeople. He would have to devise a way to keep it away from them.

"A long silence, Healer. What do you seek?"

"There is a sickness coming among the humans, and I need to send a message to another healer, one who lives in the city of Milan, to warn him. I cannot send the message through the normal human ways, and thus I thought I would ask here. My need is great."

The undine was amused. *"You do know you can command, as the Lion."*

"But I would rather ask, as a friend and your healer," said Marco.

"And as such we can hardly refuse. Some of our kind do swim north, and they have built canals from the Adda and Ticino rivers. At night we pass through the locks... But reaching humans in their city fastness, and even finding them, if they do not come to water is hard."

"He talked of going running along the canal path. I have drawn a picture, and this book was once his property."

"Wait. I go to call my sister Melisande," said Chloe. *"She is from the river-lands. Her nyx-kind like the fresh water."*

So Marco waited.

A little later the undine Chloe returned with two others. They were both smaller than the lagoon undines, but also had that greenish pallor and bare breasts, which they seemed to enjoy showing. He wondered if they did suckle their young, and why he had never seen any.

Once introductions had been done, Melisande and the dark-eyed Rhene said they came from upriver. "We come to feel the salt on our skins," they explained, without explaining why. Marco had discovered to his surprise that a lot of humans didn't even think about why. Perhaps the merfolk were similar.

"We came from the Ticino River," said Rhene, *"and often venture down the big ditch they call the Naviglio Grande, to go and watch the humans."* She sniggered. *"Especially the young men, swimming. Chloe says you seek to send a message to a one who runs, not just when he needs to flee or to chase. Does he look like this?"* And with a long, sharp fingernail she traced the outline of a face with a little water on the slate paving around the edge of the water-chapel. She had an ability Marco's artist friend Raphael could not rival for capturing the essence of a face shape in a few lines.

"Yes. This is my picture of him," said Marco, taking out his attempt, feeling a little inadequate about his artistic skills.

"Ah. Yes, he runs nearly every day, along the path at the water's edge. We like to watch him. In summer he will swim, and always he stops to wash. He is much cleaner than most of you humans." She sniffed.

Marco was faintly affronted. Why, he bathed his hands often, and always between patients now, since his conversations with Francisco, and his whole body far more frequently than most. Sometimes even twice or three times in one month. There were many who only did so once a year.

But the nyx continued: *"And then he will stop at the taverna that is called the Grosso Luccio, next to the water, near the Basilica of Sant' Eustorgio. In fine weather he comes and dangles his feet in the water and drinks beer."* Rhene gave a wicked little laugh. *"We talked of pulling him in."*

That seemed to confirm it to Marco. Francisco's fondness for beer and running were notable. "I wouldn't. I suspect he can be quite dangerous. But that is the man I need to send my message to. He is a healer, but a soldier, too. This is his book." He held out the battered copy of Alkindus's *De Gradibus*. "I don't know if you also trace people like the tritons do?"

"*Oh, yes. We know the taste and flavor of you humans,*" said the nyx, taking it. Marco suppressed his immediate instinct to tell her to dry her hands first. This was more important, although it was hard to accept that. Books needed to be treated as the valuable things they were! She held it between her fingertips, sharp face intent, and then held it up to her little retroussé nose and sniffed, looking, despite the bare breasts, like a disapproving countess being asked for a charitable donation. Then she stuck out a long slim tongue and licked it.

"*Yes. It is difficult to separate your flavor from that of the runner. But I think that is him. I would know the owner of the book if I tasted his essence.*" She handed it back.

Marco hastily dried the book on his cotte. "So could you take this message to him? I have put it in a bottle so it will stay dry. Please?"

She shrugged. "*For the Lion, and the licence he gives us to come into his waters, yes. We go north tomorrow, to the sweet water again. I will give it to the runner. I like watching human faces as we come up and show them our breasts.*"

Some instinct made Marco say: "And then?"

"*Then we drown them. We can't leave them alive. They would hunt us down.*" She paused, perhaps reading something in Marco's expression. "*Or sometimes we seduce them, draw them into the water for loving, and then drown them. Would that be better?*"

"Er. Not really. I am sending him a message," explained Marco, thinking that the nyx was proof that beauty and brain did not have to go together, and being lusciously curved didn't mean that you couldn't be a cold-blooded killer either. "What would be the use of my doing that, if you killed him before he could read it and act on it? Besides, he is my friend. I don't want him drowned."

"*Oh. That's difficult. We don't show ourselves to humans otherwise. It's not like here.*"

"*We have to be careful here, too, sister,*" said Chloe. "*Still, it is quite useful to have traffic with them sometimes.*"

Rhene giggled and nudged Melisande. *"Oh, yes. Remember that last fisherman, Meli."*

"They can be very virile," said Melisande.

"Well, there are other uses," said Chloe, gesturing at Marco. *"This one is a healer and the Lion's human."*

"So is Francisco," said Marco. "A healer, anyway. And he will not betray or hunt you. And"—his voice burred to the deep-throated edge of a roar of the ancient and magical Lion within him—"you will not kill him. If you do, I will banish you and your kind from my water. Understood?"

The undine and nyxes, wide-eyed and silenced, nodded.

Sometimes it really is easier not just to ask nicely, thought Marco, on his way home.

Chapter 6

Politics, places various
Rimini

Count Andrea Malatesta, Lord of Rimini, Forli, Cesena, Pesaro, Marquis of Ravenna, and Protector of Romagna was a nobleman's nobleman. He traced his lineage back to Roman times and, as he said with pride, even his distant patrician ancestors had shown their breeding. They had, as he did, derived their wealth from rents or conquest. Venice and its new-baked "Longi" chaffered in trade like the commoners they really were, and as for the likes of Florence's de' Medici...banking. Ha. *Usury.* By rights, it should be restricted to Jews who could be executed if they got too insistent about repayment.

The problem for Count Malatesta was that the peasantry simply did not work hard enough. Rents were down again this year, land lying fallow. And war had become expensive. The last major territorial gains had been by his father, who had taken Faenza and the surrounds from the de' Medici. They had failed, rather spectacularly, in their venture to recapture that, but while Andrea had enjoyed the victory, it had brought no territorial benefits, and little in the way of ransom. He had been a bit too hasty in making an example there. Urbino still held against him, and expansion to the south would be difficult, and not that rewarding. The Po Valley was where the money lay, but it had thrown him back.

This time, however, things would be different. He had a powerful ally in the fear that Carlo Sforza had spread among the nobility of the northern Italian states. He was entertaining some of them, right now. And they were eager, willing, greedy... and afraid.

Duke Umberto Da Corregio of Parma and Viscount Lippi Pagano of Imola listened as Malatesta read to them from a letter that gave him great pleasure. Pleasure great enough that he paced back and forth as he read it, gesturing all the while, as if he was an actor on a stage.

"We do not currently"—here he waved a hand in a dramatic circling gesture—"see any immediate possibility of such nuptials, and would suggest a longer term approach, and considerable caution..."

"Bah. What kind of man is Cosimo de' Medici?" said Umberto, swilling back his wine. "A coward and a fool. To advise 'caution'—with *Sforza*?"

"Nonetheless, it does tell us that the Butterball is not to marry Sforza," said Lippi Pagano, who had a cool head and had drunk relatively little. That was all that Andrea Malatesta could find as redeeming qualities in the viscount. He had, de facto, allied himself with Ferrara, and Andrea Malatesta fully intended, at the appropriate time, to shorten the tall dour man of his head for that. A skirmish with Enrico Dell'este had not ended well for the protector of Romagna. But they would need Ferrara and Venice, to at least stay neutral in the war, and preferably to attack Sforza. That was why the count had invited Lippi: so that he could act as a messenger to Dell'este. One thing in Count Andrea's favor, though: He might have fought a skirmish with Enrico Dell'este, but the man's hatred of Sforza was legendary.

Venice... Venice would reach her own decisions, play things for her own unpredictable ends. If anything, Andrea disliked and distrusted La Serenissima even more than Ferrara. In his grandfather's time, they had raided Rimini on the thin pretext that her vessels had been engaged in piracy against vessels of the Venetian Republic. But they too had little reason to love or trust Milan, or indeed, Carlo Sforza.

"We have torn up his letter, and sent it back to him with a suitable gift," said Umberto. "The hand of his messenger and a piece of excrement, to show the depth of our disdain."

"I wonder what Cosimo will make of your actions," said Viscount Lippi Pagano dryly.

"What does it matter? Cosimo is an old woman, more interested in money and art than war," said Umberto. "He who hesitates will be left out. We have money and backing from at least half the states in Italy now."

"I do gather Florence is mobilizing her reserves," said Lippi.

"Cosimo does that without doing anything at least twice a year. It impresses no one anymore," his host informed him. Indeed, getting rid of Viscount Pagano of Imola had risen in importance. Did the fool know no better than to cast doubts in Umberto's path? There were certain protocols to be observed in assassination, and he had his value . . . for the moment.

Now, it was a waiting game, waiting for Sforza to make a move—any move—against the allies, and then they'd have due cause for a war. They did not really need due cause since war was their plan anyway, but it would bring in the laggard and the reluctant.

Arona, Duchy of Milan

It was said that the first steps to hell were the easiest. They were wrong, reflected Lucia, walking down to the cellars, the heavy key hung on a ribbon around her neck and resting like a cold snake between her breasts. Asking the serpent, back the first time when they had not even seen it, to make her father love her . . . that had been terrifying, especially when she understood what the serpent and her father understood of "love."

Now she was going down to the lowest cellar and the pit, again, with the tokens that would bring death to two women. And she felt nothing.

The great serpent had said to her: "You understand that it is far easier for me to destroy a city full of people than just one person. That is my power. That is what I can give you."

"Nonetheless, for now I need two people to die. And they must die as if by natural causes."

There had been a shaking of the scales. "All death is natural. Humans die, all that lives dies, and their dying and fear is my food. I hunger for the great feasting again."

"I mean no daggers or obvious poisons."

"I do not use daggers, and my poisons are subtle. You have

paid my price, and will pay my price again, so I will do as you command. But you will need to provide a way I can find and identify those who must die."

"Eleni Faranese, and Violetta de' Medici. They are my rivals. There are lesser claims, but I do not need to kill them yet."

"Names are important to mortals, but they mean nothing to me. For me to know them, I need their essences. I can derive that from hair, skin, nail clippings, sweat, blood or their body's waste. Give me that and it will allow my minions to find them and work your will. Otherwise, you would have to point them out to me."

That had given Lucia temporary pause. They were in Tuscany and thus far from her. But she had some wealth, and most things could be bought. It took a little bribery, and some intimidation. Some hair from the heads of those she'd sent out.

Her sendlings believed her to be a witch, one of the dark *stregheria*. She could get killed for that, despite the foolish Hypatians' cries for tolerance. Her room was pointedly empty of the paraphernalia of magic. And if they found the key, and followed her path to the cellars . . . they'd never come back.

The two men she'd sent to do her work would be dead soon anyway. She would not leave them alive, just in case they brought trouble. That level of poisoning she could deal with herself. Assassination, like seduction, was an important skill for the line and the house, and she had worked hard to learn as much as possible about both. Fortunately, her father had agreed with her about the need for her to learn both. An old courtesan and a half-blind alchemist had been his gifts. She had liked neither, but learned as much as she could from both. The problem with poisons, of course, was that they could be traced, and showed signs.

Since her father's death at the hand of Carlo Sforza, her mother had retreated further into herself, withdrawn into her chambers, and often did not leave them at all. That had started when her sister died, and Lucia had encouraged it, because she had more space and more power as a result. She'd become the de facto chatelaine of this place. No one would question her decision to go anywhere, not even the lower cellars. She still took great care to do it only late at night, and make sure she was not observed.

The cold rage at Carlo Sforza when she might still have done something foolish was long since burned out. Now all that was left was a bitter ash that would go on etching her mind and actions forever. She would have what was hers. What she had paid so much for. And in achieving it, take as few risks as possible.

In the darkness she put down the two oilcloth bags. "I have hair from Eleni Faranese, and a cloth marked with the sweat of Violetta de' Medici. How soon will they die?"

There was a long silence. And then the serpent spoke in that cold sibilant voice that made her scalp prickle: "What is time to me? How long does it take a rat to scurry through the night, or the viper to slither thence? That is how long it will take, no longer and no less."

And not all her questioning could get a more precise answer. It was only later that night, when she washed again to try and get rid of the rat stench that seemed to cling to her after she'd been to its lair, that it occurred to her that it might possibly have spoken the literal truth. She had assumed the death would be magically inflicted. But perhaps a snakebite...

That was quite a natural death, really. Hard to call assassination. She expected Milan and Carlo Sforza to be engaged in war, but at the time and place of Milan's choosing, and once she was ensconced, not while she was still living in the borderlands.

The smell just didn't seem to wash out. She used more perfume.

Mainz, the Holy Roman Empire

Moving slowly, as men do who are afflicted with arthritis, the old man eased himself into his chair. The piece of furniture was expensive and well upholstered, although not as large as the throne in the main audience hall. But it was considerably more comfortable than the throne and the small chamber could be kept quite warm.

"Nothing," he said peevishly, "is ever simple, is it?" Which might have seemed like a grumpy complaint from almost any man of advanced years, but this particular old man had the lives of millions balanced on his decisions and actions. And he took that very seriously, not delegating the responsibility as much as he could have—and should have, in the opinion of most of his advisors. He spent much of each day reading reports, hearing from his emissaries and ambassadors, and writing personal instructions himself, despite an army of scribes, in a crabby handwriting that had no doubt caused chaos and quite possibly war by being both illegible and enormously important.

"Don't answer that, Hans," he said, waving a large hand which was still sinewy despite its little tremor. "I am glad to see you back, even if you doubtless bring me more complications.'

"My efforts in Aquitaine have not been crowned with great success. The more I tried to change anything, the more irrelevancies they put in my way, my liege," admitted Hans Trolliger.

"Perhaps for the best," said Emperor Charles Fredrik tiredly. "The more we try to fix, the more new things break. Anyway, I called for your return because I need men I can trust. Things look... awkward. There are too many thunderheads piling up."

Baron Trolliger blinked. He had heard a certain amount of news if, obviously, not as much as the Emperor. It had seemed good to him. "I had thought the last communiques from Manfred had been full of good news. Or so I had been led to believe."

"Oh, they were. We have protected access by sea from Jagiellon's armies to the underbelly of Europe, secured the goodwill of the Ilkhan and the Golden Horde, and acquired a powerful new ally in Prince Vlad of Transylvania. Unfortunately, that has left a power vacuum and chaos where two less-than-competent leaders have been deposed. Emeric of Hungary and the Emperor Alexius were foes or, at best, untrustworthy allies. But they kept control over their territory. The breakdown of power in Hungary and its territories, and to a lesser extent Greece, opens the potential doorway to an invasion into Slovakia by the forces of the Grand Duke of Lithuania, or the new proxies and allies for our foes—right on our border. Hungary under Emeric was at least a buffer state, as much an enemy to Jagiellon as to us, meaning we only faced the monster of the East directly in Polish lands. Now... we stand on the edge of a possible precipice. Of course, there are upstarts and pretenders to the thrones of various nations that Emeric had overthrown. Some we will support, some are as bad or maybe worse. It all depends what happens to the crown of Hungary."

"Emeric of Hungary did not leave any heirs, I know. But who stands in the succession? Is there someone we should favor?" asked Trolliger.

"As with everything Emeric touched, it is a mess. He, or that aunt of his, had gone out of their way to kill off any obvious claimants or rivals. There was no heir named, and not even a living bastard child, although he fathered a few. At the moment, my informants say the principal rival claimants are John of Simony and Christopher of Somolyo."

"Ah." Trolliger knew something of both men, as was inevitable in diplomacy and the small pool of noble houses. Neither were of such a reputation that he could be enthusiastic. That was probably why they had been allowed to survive.

"And then there is Lazlo de Hunyad."

Baron Trolliger sucked his teeth. "I thought he was living in Moravia."

"He made his return within days of the news of Emeric's death. He obviously had it planned. He is not in the direct descent, but he's a good general and popular with the minor nobility and commons."

"And a very strong-willed man," said the baron, who had once had the misfortune of having to deliver a message from Charles Fredrik to him. Of course, the former Ban of the Puszta was no longer young.

"True. But at least a man of strong principles. It is my feeling that we should back him in this race."

"With troops? It would be difficult to find a commander he's not going to drive to drink, Your Majesty. Or vice versa."

The Emperor shook his head. "No." he paused, and then continued. "Hans, I say this only because I trust you, but I have news out of Rome that makes it unlikely the Holy Roman Empire is going to commit troops or engage in anything but defense for the next while. They have been employing magical means, and their predictions have a good record of accuracy. This must go no further, but they predict a major outbreak of the plague in northern Italy. If that happens, it will spread, and our foes will take advantage of us while we are weakened. It destroyed the Eastern Roman Empire. It could destroy us, far more surely than an invasion from the East could. We will prepare as well as possible, but..."

Now Baron Hans Trolliger knew just why the Emperor looked so weighed with care. The last great plague still lived in the memory of men—as did the worst of them all, Justinian's Plague of a millennium earlier. And it was not just the disease that killed. Crops had rotted in the fields without men to harvest them. People had starved, although the seasons had been, reportedly, benign. The wheels of commerce ground to a halt. Trade stopped as people feared the spread of disease that came with the traders and, of course, war came down on the decimated people.

And walls and armies, magic and prayer...all had proved ineffectual.

There had been many outbreaks of some infectious diseases since then, destroying people and settlements. But the last great sweep by the plague had been nearly five centuries before. There were more living people now. More roads, more vessels. More likelihood of more contact with noisome places, from whence the disease was reputed to spring. Just, all in all, more possibility to spread the plague. This time it could quite easily be worse. The horror was almost too much to contemplate.

"I see," said Hans Trolliger. "Well, you know that you can trust me, my liege. What do you want of me? I am wholly at your service. This calls for all good men to stand against it, no matter what other differences we have."

"You'd think so, Hans. But there will always be a few who'll try to play it to their advantage. I'm afraid my task for you is a difficult one—or, rather, to be dealing with a difficult man."

"De Hunyad."

"Yes. We cannot offer him the backing of men, which I suspect is what he'll ask for. Money, and even weapons, yes. But we'll need some form of agreement. He'll hold to that, if we don't give him weasel space." The Emperor sighed. "We have a somewhat more dangerous—to us, and indeed to Hungary—claimant on hand to introduce if he fails."

"Who would that be, Your Majesty?"

"The castellan of Braclaw and the voivode of Zwinogrodek. Count Kazimierz Mindaug."

"A Lithuanian!"

"He is of that origin, yes. Somewhat out of favor with the grand duke, to put it mildly. His castle at Zwinogrodek was razed to the ground and the count had fled to his cousin, Elizabeth Bartholdy. And following her, and King Emeric's demise, he has fled again. He crossed the March River some days ago, and is traveling southwest. He is a very competent magic worker, a schemer and a scholar of note. Unfortunately for him, he is not aware of all of the methods of the Knights of the Holy Trinity.

He is in disguise, traveling with no escort, masquerading as a traveling bookseller. He is being watched carefully, both magically and physically. He still, by blood, has as good or better claim to the throne of Hungary and, indeed, the Grand Duchy of Lithuania, as any other rival."

"I'd put him in custody, until you need him. Perhaps put him to the question, too," said Trolliger.

"The spymasters want him to reveal his associates first. Someone like that does not move without a plan."

"Sometimes I think we are all too devious for our own good, Your Majesty."

"It would be nice if life was all simple and straightforward. I also think the spymasters see devious plots in people drawing breath. In the case of Count Mindaug, however, they may well be correct. Now if we can discuss what I can permit you to offer De Hunyad..."

The discussion moved on to what the baron would be authorized to offer, what compromises he could accept, and what was nonnegotiable. But Baron Trolliger had to wonder just what the Lithuanian Count Mindaug was doing sneaking about the Holy Roman Empire. It was a little worrying. All very well to say he was being watched and was needed, but such men were dangerous and had skills that were beyond that of most watchers. And worse, they were unpredictable. If there was one thing Hans hated in his ordered life, it was unpredictability.

Even dealing with a hot-tempered elderly Hungarian like De Hunyad was at least something where he could guess, with reasonable accuracy, what the man would do.

Chapter 7

Venice

Maria had longed to return to her daughter and to Benito. To leave the cool halls of Aidoneus, the Lord of the Dead. The longing to see Venice again, too, had been like a dull ache within her.

And now that she was here in Venice, had held Alessia in her arms... she found that longing seldom lived up to reality. She had gone to the marshes, and set out to reestablish the old religions among the *stregheria*. That had gone so well, for a while. She had told Aidoneus in no uncertain terms that their marriage of four months a year was over. She had found a potential new bride for him and she could not wait to tell Benito that she had solved that problem.

And that was where the matter stuck. She found herself, perforce, for Alessia's sake continuing under her brother and sister-in-law's roof. She could have rented a lodging for herself, but as the Church would not recognize her relationship with Benito, his money was not available to her. As Umberto Verrier's widow, she had a small pension paid by the Arsenal. The Arsenal's guildsmen did not forget their own, and he was, she found, accepted and remembered as one of the heroes of Corfu. Her old boat was still here, waiting for her. She could have gone back to poling the canals. Between those two she could have afforded a room somewhere and have bought food, even it if was a long, long, long step down from the comfort and safety of the *Casa* Montescue.

But she knew that would reflect badly on Marco and Katerina, and they would be very hurt by it, Marco in particular. They certainly had done nothing to deserve being hurt—the opposite was true. Katerina, with generations of *Casa* Longi blood, treated her like a friend, a sister, even an equal. Marco...

Maria had looked after him and Benito, and Marco had been a romantic fool. Back then, she'd always felt ten years older than him. Benito might be Marco's younger brother, but somehow he'd always been the one who had been less the innocent child, more able to cope. Now, that too was different. Marco had moved on, moved up into a world she really didn't grasp, a world of intrigue and politics, and also of academic study. He was still Marco, still as soft, as gentle, as kindly. But being married to his love, and part of a still-functioning ancient and noble *Casa*—and especially being part of the Lion—had changed him. She knew they had looked after, fought for, and nurtured Alessia, as if she was their own beloved child. She couldn't be that ungrateful.

And secondly, there was no way it would have been as good or as safe for Alessia. For that, Maria would put up with being part of a great house, full of servants, where she was but a guest.

That wasn't easy when she was used to running and commanding her own household. So she had turned to worlds she knew... or, rather, thought she knew. She was a priestess of the Great Mother. She was a woman of the canals of the *popula minuti*.

She would do the work of the Goddess here, in Venice's lagoons. Among the swampers, and among the *stregheria*.

Very rapidly she discovered two things. Time was like a river. It moved on, and she could not go back. She still had relations, and even people who were friendly, if not what she would have called friends, among the canalers. But... she was Benito Valdosta's woman. And she was Marco's sister-in-law, and half of the poor of Venice regarded him as the greatest physician ever to breathe. They regarded the *Casa* Montescue as part of the Longi, a core part of the Longi. And that was where Maria lodged. As far as they were concerned, that was where she belonged and who she was now.

Oh, they were proud of her. They thought she'd gotten somewhere. But she wasn't one of them anymore.

And in truth, she knew she wasn't. Not that she didn't understand them and love them, or at least, some of them. But their world, especially for the women—some of the men had been on Venetian ships to Flanders or Outre Mer or Trebizond on the Black

Sea—was the canals of Venice. Few of the women had been more than a league from where they had been born. Once she had been like that too. But, since then, she had lived in Istria, and Corfu, and then Aidoneus's shadowy halls. And because of Benito, she had mixed with men from far further afield: men—and in the case of Francesca, a woman—of very different orders of society, from princes and dukes, to thieves and powerful merchants. It had changed the way she saw things, given her a bigger picture.

Or made her too big for her boots, according to the canal women. And by the time she realized that they were saying this, it was far too late. They might like her. They might possibly listen to her, sometimes, but in general they listened to her the same way they'd listen to the Schioppettieri. Which was when she was watching or when it suited them.

When it came to the worship of the Great Mother, among the *stregheria* ... it wasn't that they didn't give her respect as the priestess of a powerful, old goddess. It was just that, away from Corfu, she was not their priestess. They had those of their own that they called on. There were secret shrines, secret rites, secret places of worship. She hadn't even realized it when she went trampling in, full of missionary zeal.

And now she found that she was not welcome among them. Really, seriously we-will-kill-you not welcome. The *stregheria* varied and were divided. But on this they seemed at one. The Great Mother was the first and oldest of the fertility goddesses ... but the lagoon gave primacy to the Lion of Etruria.

On Corfu, her role as the Bride and as priestess meant she was the most powerful woman, certainly among the women, and as a result, with many of the local men. That had taken a lot of getting used to, and then it took a lot of getting used to its absence.

Chapter 8

The Duchy of Milan

Francisco Turner had just come back to Milan with Carlo Sforza. They'd been readying several regiments, and a fair number of cannon, for the move to the West. Sforza always liked to prepare well first, and then strike hard and fast. And he liked to oversee a part of the preparation personally. "They believe you know everything then, Francisco," he said dryly.

"Or they're scared you might," said his physician. They'd reached the entrance to the ducal palace that Sforza preferred to use for all but formal occasions. "Well, if you have no further need of me, m'lord, I'll go and take a run."

"When they finally catch up with us, my friend, your running won't get you away from the cavalry," said Sforza, amused.

"Very true. But I just have to run faster than the rest of my troop," he said lightly. "It keeps me fit and makes me feel better, and gives me the excuse for a mug of beer down at the water's edge."

"Don't drink too many and fall in," said his commander. "I shall venture on some of my paperwork in the scriptorium with my overanxious secretary and the scribes. I'd rather be at war." He turned away and passed into the palace.

Francisco thought about the situation they found themselves in as he kept to a steady pace along the canal path. The canal would make something of a defensive perimeter, but it was too shallow and too long, and not well overlooked with a clear field of fire. Taking Milan had seemed a masterstroke when Carlo Sforza executed it. No one outside a small clique of sycophants had liked the last duke much. Certainly not the peasantry, nor the minor nobles, nor even the heads of great houses and lands.

The problem with the latter was that they liked Carlo Sforza even less, if for different reasons. They feared his military prowess; he was not one of them and not a known quantity. And if one lowborn condottiere could seize power and make himself an overlord in their place, what was to stop others from doing likewise?

Francisco had to admit... fairly little. All that stood between many of the Italian city-state rulers and their mercenaries was a certain lack of competence among the condottieri, and the possibility of the citizens and minor nobles successfully resisting. He did understand why they should be worried about Carlo, but the sensible arrangement would be to strengthen their own armies and make themselves somewhat more popular with their peasantry and minor nobility, and the craftsmen in the towns and cities. They preferred to get rid of an upstart who was upsetting their normal way of doing things.

It wasn't going to work, but there might be a fair amount of bleeding and dying done before that was established. Ferrara clove to its lord, Enrico Dell'este—his habit of winning, and working iron like a tradesman, and not employing mercenaries, made him safe if unpopular with his peers. It was a shame that he hated Sforza since they were more alike than either of them realized. That was something that Francisco was never going to point out to either man, but the reason Duke Enrico Dell'este's daughter Lorendana had been attracted to Carlo Sforza was probably that very similarity.

Venice had a fair degree of loyalty to its nobility—they went to sea together with the commoners, and lived in crowded cantonments with them. And, as a second string, the *popolo minuto* adored the two Valdosta brothers as part of themselves, and the Valdosta brothers were loyal to the Doge. Cosimo de' Medici's contributions to grandeur and the quality of life in Florentine territories meant he was more popular than most. He was a shrewd man, who knew when to display the common touch. Admiral—now Duke—Doria in Genoa had a support base at least among the sailors and ex-sailors. However, the bulk of the people in the rest of Italy's states cared very little who their next overlord might be.

Francisco had reached the end point of his run, so he gave a brief last sprint and stopped at the water's edge to scoop up a handful of water to wash down his face and hands. The water flowed into here from the Ticino River so it was not of the order of filth that the canals of Venice were, but he still had a roof-top collection system for his and—to the best of his ability—his commander's water. You might get bird droppings in that, but not human ones. Several times in the course of his soldiering, Francisco had seen flux that could only have come from the well water, and had no faith in that either. It was better with a bit of alcohol in it. That seemed to kill or least weaken whatever it was that carried the diseases. On that thought, he decided to go and have a beer.

He must have bumped a reed or something in the water, because a bottle bobbed up, just short of his fingers. He resisted his natural instinct to grab hold of it, and stood up and walked across to the taverna, Grosso Luccio, and bought himself a mug of beer. It was dark and frowsty in there, and not unpleasant outside, so he took himself back out into the late afternoon spring sunshine. He sat down on a stump that had been dug in there as a hitching post, and looked at the water. It was, for a place on the edge of the city, quiet at this time of day. The tradesmen were still at work, but most shoppers had gone home, markets had packed up and the farmers or their wives headed home.

But it really was still too cold to enjoy sitting outdoors for long. He might as well go back inside and finish this mug. His man would be here with his horse soon, and they would ride back to his apartments in the Palazzo Ducale. To run anywhere near his quarters would be to run through the streets, and this was more pleasant than having to constantly explain to worthy citizens that they didn't have to hold you for your pursuers, or to let them hide you from the same. Or have to explain to stall-holders that throwing fruit which was past its best could cause the runner to stop and do some surgery on their tripes.

With this thought, he started to stand up...only to find a slim, delicate hand around his ankle, with a grip that was more to be expected from a steel manacle.

He looked down at the face of the slight woman in the water.

A foxy little triangular face, alive with mischief and a little malice. There was a greenish pallor to her skin, and there was a lot of that to be seen.

"*Scream and I'll pull you under,*" she said in a tone that suggested that she could, quite easily. "*I'm not to drown you, but I know how to take you to the very edge of it. And I can do it any number of times.*"

Francisco prepared himself to reach for the main gauche at his belt. He had a second knife in his sleeve, too. He was an old soldier. He wasn't going to show either unless it was to the fish-girl's guts, if he had to use them. No sense in forewarning the enemy, unless one hoped to frighten them out of something, and it was too late for that.

She held up a bottle—the same one, by the looks of it, that had bobbed up when he was washing his hands. "*A message for you. The healer who is also the Winged Lion of Venice wanted it delivered privately.*"

It took Francisco a second to grasp just who that had to be. It was going to take him a little more time to get his head around the evidence of the truth of that rumor. "Next time, tell Marco to send two bottles. The one with the message and the other with some grappa to help me get over the shock of meeting his messenger!"

"*You don't like the way I look?*" she said, pouting, thrusting her nubile bare breasts above the waterline.

Francisco thought that if anything showed her to be non-human, beside the slight greenish tinge to her soft-looking skin, it was, firstly, the perfection of those breasts, and, secondly, the fact that she wasn't a mass of shivering goosebumps. He did not think her nipples were pert from cold either, but rather, for other reasons.

He also knew just what was reputed to happen to young men who found the charms of that flesh irresistible, and had the feeling that she might not take well to being resisted. "You are, of course, beautiful. You quite take my breath away."

He'd bet that she would, too. Permanently. "Alas, if it wasn't the stern duty of seeing what this important message was about, I'd have stayed to drink the grappa with you."

"*I don't like grappa. You can bring me some of that sweet pelaverga wine next time.*"

"Only if you decide not to drown me."

She wrinkled her nose at that. *"I suppose since I have made an exception for you once, I could do it again."* She let go of his ankle and held up the bottle again, which he took. *"I will tell Marco about the grappa for next time."*

Francisco retreated from the water, bottle in hand, half tankard of beer forgotten, but his wits not lost. "Thank you," he said politely.

His mind was in more of a ferment than the beer had been, anyway. This type of messenger was something he had to tell Carlo, and then get Carlo to believe it. That would be difficult. The Wolf of the North did not like tales of magic and superstition. He wouldn't like the fact that Venice had agents who could come and go freely in these waters, either.

Francisco was a rational man, and didn't much believe in what passed for magic. But he also knew he hadn't imagined the delivery of the bottle, either. He saw his man had arrived with his horse and was waiting by the tavern door. There was always a saddlebag on the horse containing a cloak in case the weather had turned unpleasant and a brace of wheel-lock pistols in case anything else turned unpleasant on the ride back.

Francisco pushed the bottle down below the cloak, and drew one of the pistols out and put it in his waistband. "Let's go, Balco," he said to the old sergeant, who had watched this and reached his own conclusions. "I want to get back in a hurry."

They mounted and rode off at a brisk trot. Francisco noted the sergeant was carefully riding point, and had loosened his own rapier and hastily checked his big horse pistol, but the ride was uneventful. It wasn't always. The people of Milan were wary about their new overlord, but there was still the occasional jeer or brat throwing a stone. They had been grateful to Sforza for reining in his mercenary army, but human gratitude was a fairly shallow cup. They'd need something else soon, Carlo had been saying on the ride back, either another lesson or a show of grandeur. Francisco hoped it would be a suitable wedding.

Back in his chambers, Francisco pondered briefly how to get the letter out of the bottle and settled for the easy way—giving the bottle a smart tap with the heavy pommel of his knife. Being a physician and a surgeon, and well aware of just how nasty a weapon glass could be, he did so over a large basin, with caution, but no one got injured. The letter, when he unsealed it, however, could do that well enough on its own.

> *Dear Francisco,*
> *I am sending this letter to you to warn you of a situation of which I have been made aware, but have been asked to keep secret, thus I beg you to do the same. My informant requested that I find the means to communicate this with you, and I am using contacts which are unlikely to be intercepted or available to others. The Church has, in its attempt to foresee and manage threats, used a team of scryers. While I know you do not have much faith in this, I can vouch to some degree for its accuracy and success at prediction. They believe there will be a recurrence of the Plague of Justinian, and the Church is quietly preparing for the possibility of an outbreak. This is predicted to happen within Milanese territory, and thus I urge you to quietly ready yourself, your master, and the forces at your disposal to respond to the disease with quarantine, and to stockpile such treatments as you think may help. I would like your advice on what these may be, and what, if any, preventative steps we can take.*
> *Yours in Medicine*
> *Marco V.*

Francisco stood and reread it carefully. His first reaction was to burn the letter forthwith. But he would need to show it to Carlo first. Marco Valdosta remained an innocent, doing his best to heal and help, even if he was caught up in the tides of Venetian politics—and had the power to make murderous water nyxes run his errands for him.

He folded the letter carefully and set out to find Carlo Sforza. He was, as he had said he would be, in the scriptorium. Sforza might not like the tasks of governance but he did them scrupulously, if just as brutally as he would run a military campaign. *That might take the civilian administration some time to get used to, by the look on the secretary's face,* thought Francisco, entering the room.

"My lord." He bowed. "I have some urgent business that must be discussed privately. Can I disturb you?"

"Everyone's business is always urgent and private," growled

Carlo irritably. "I'm not sure if you're the fourth or fifth this morning, and none of them were at all. This paperwork also needs my attention."

But he set down his pen and swiveled in his chair to face Turner more directly. "Spit it out, Francisco. You need a new drain under your running track?"

"No, my lord." Francisco stared at his commander, trying to convey with his eyes alone that they really needed to talk, without other ears listening in. Venice wanted those ears to hear, and so did Rome. He did not plan to oblige them.

Something about that stare must have gotten to Sforza. "This woman of yours is really giving you trouble, Francisco," he said, getting up and clapping an arm around him. "Well, I can spare you a few minutes. It may stop me killing someone." He looked hard at the scribe in the corner who bowed his head and industriously scratched away with his quill.

"The drains are best discussed from where we can see them, my lord," said Francisco. "The tower will do nicely."

Sforza raised his bar of an eyebrow, but walked with him to the stairs which led up to one of the small corbelled turrets ornamenting the palazzo.

He closed the door, checked the small room for people, and then led his master up the spiral stair to the arrow-slitted small room above. "You are never insolent, so I assume that look wasn't that this time either, Francisco. Or have you made me puff up all these stairs for nothing?"

Francisco did not say that he thought his extremely strong master was out of condition and beginning to put on some middle-aged weight, if such a flight of stairs made him puff. This was not the time for that.

"No, my lord. I have received a message which was sent to me with the intent to be intercepted, to cause panic. I want you to know what they're trying to do before I destroy it. I also wanted to tell you just how effectively Venice can penetrate our defenses to send messages. This is something we need to add to our calculations."

"They have spies and messengers, just like us. Or are they training rats or birds to the work?"

"They may for all I know. But this was a naked woman."

"That's an old one."

"Not when she swims up the Naviglio Grande underwater, and has greenish skin and drowns men, m'lord. I have explained it badly. This messenger may look like a woman, but it's not. I didn't believe in such things, but I have now changed my mind. And it appears Marco Valdosta can make these creatures carry messages for him. He sent me this in a bottle carried by this nyx."

He handed the letter to Sforza, who held it out at arm's length and read it.

Carlo Sforza seldom let his expression betray his emotions, and did not this time either. But he said at the end of it: "I think I understand why you wanted to speak to me in secret. But if this is what they choose to do, they will start the rumor anyway. Not everyone will be so careful and not everyone has that kind of messenger. I'd tell you to stop drinking that stuff, but for the winged horse incident."

"They plainly intend to sow panic. But in all seriousness, I doubt if Marco Valdosta was more than their cat's paw, my lord. The choice of method of sending this was his, and thus he foiled their plan. I don't think he bears you that much ill will. Also, Byzantine plotting is more the style of Venice's Council of Ten than his."

"I'd agree. I remember the boy when Lorendana was my mistress. He was a serious little fellow, and too good for this world. I can't say I paid him a lot of attention back then, and now I wish I had. Still, he is being used."

"And except for the 'little' part, he has not changed that much," admitted Francisco. "I had gathered, peripherally, that he does not hate you, especially once it was revealed who had actually killed Lorendana. Of course it was not a subject I encouraged him to speak to me about. I didn't want to betray myself."

"I would have killed Lorendana if I had gotten my hands on her, after her last tricks. But my orders were always to bring her back to face me, and not to hurt the children. I doubt if he'd believe that, but it is the truth. Never leave anything but a dead enemy behind you, Francisco. Otherwise, make peace with them. Hmm. In this case, send back a message saying we have had similar rumors or tales or foretellings, but that the source predicted it was Venice, and that we have taken precautions..."

"Magical ones, as he'll know there are no non-magical ones."

"Perfect. And suggest that, for her safety, I would like my

granddaughter out of that pesthole that is Venice. My spies tell me her mother is back in Venice from wherever she'd got to, and I think they'd be safer in Corfu."

"That's true enough," agreed Francisco.

There was a thunderous knocking on the lower door of the turret. "My Lord Sforza! You commanded us to call you if any messengers came from Parma or Florence."

"Some people have no notion of the privacy of their master," said Carlo, with a sigh. "Come, Francisco. Let me see what new farrago of nonsense they have sent me. I had a three-page waffling non-letter from Cosimo de' Medici only yesterday, saying discussions were ongoing, but the lady was reticent."

The footman who had interrupted them stood waiting at the foot of the stair. "My lord. I put the messenger in the Giotti salon, so he could repose." He took a deep breath. "My lord, he needs a physician. He has been grievously wounded."

"Better come with me, Francisco," said Sforza, quickening his pace.

So Francisco went with him. The messenger had not taken advantage of the gold damask chaise longue which had plainly been drawn up for him, but his face was nearly as sallow as its cover. He was standing awkwardly instead, with a posture that Francisco recognized after seeing many combat injuries. He was upright by force of will, nothing more.

"My lord," he said, and bowed. The bow was not a very deep one, not for lack of respect but to enable him to remain standing. He didn't manage that for long, as Carlo took him by the shoulder and sat him down on the chaise longue. "What's happened to you, man?" he demanded.

For an answer, the man held out the stump of his right arm. "This was done by the order of the Duke of Parma for daring to bear your message about his cousin, my lord."

"Hell's teeth!" Carlo Sforza did not bother to restrain his fury now. "I'll have the stupid *testa di cazzo's* head shoved up his own hind end and his body displayed on his gates for this. You were a messenger, damn him."

"He sent you his reply," said the man, through gritted teeth. "My severed hand holding a *pizza de merde* from a mongrel dog."

"I'll give him mine in the shape of cannon. Francisco, see what you can do for this man."

To the injured messenger he said, as Francisco began to examine the stump and its rusty dressing: "This happened in my service. I can't give you back your right hand, but you will be cared for. I'll give you your pick of the Duke of Parma's estates when I am done with him."

But the man had quietly keeled over onto the chaise longue. Francisco felt his pulse in the throat. "Alive," he answered the unspoken question in his master's eyes. "Pulse is weak and tumultuous, but he's alive. He's lost a lot of blood, and got himself back here by sheer willpower and anger. I'll have to take him to my chambers and clean the wound, check it and cauterize it while he's unconscious."

"Do that. Keep him alive if you can. I want him alive to see the Duke of Parma suitably chastised." Sforza was still plainly boiling with anger, at his most dangerous. In this mood, other men were rash, but Francisco had been with his commander long enough to know that it would make him cold and brutally efficient instead. "You," said Sforza to the footmen. "Carry him on this daybed."

So Francisco left with his patient. There was considerable work to be done—bones were shattered and there was septic tissue to be dealt with. Still, the man was tough. He would probably survive to see vengeance done.

Francisco was summoned again, late that evening. "You'd better get your message off to your Venetian friend tonight," said Sforza. "I'm trying to make sure I have only one foe to face, Francisco. Cosimo de' Medici has his faults, but he's not going to harm a messenger, and I think you can be my most honest and insightful set of eyes. Go to Florence and get me a straight answer. I'd rather have Cosimo as an ally and a banker than the fig leaf of legitimacy I'd get from marrying that cousin of his. I'd get that from marrying Lucia del Maino. But Cosimo as an ally... for that I'd rather have his cousin, but I do not read this as very likely. Go, and get the best diplomatic compromise out of it you can. I doubt if Cosimo wants war, and I'd guess he'd rather not be dragged into one. He knows of you, and knows where you stand with me. That will give you some advantage. In the meantime, I'm going to invite Lucia del Maino to the court here, in preparation for the inevitable. Try and be back in three weeks. I'll be moving in force majeure against Parma in four. This is not just about a few border villages anymore."

After he had gone back and checked on the health of the

messenger again, Francisco returned to his quarters. He poured himself a mug of beer, and calmly and methodically burned Marco's letter. Then he wrote a reply, couching it in careful terms.

> *My dear friend in medicine, my thanks for the letter. We had been told of a similar problem, but Venice had been identified as the area from which it would spread. Precautions of a magical, as well as a practical nature, are being undertaken, and we believe ourselves reasonably safe as a result. My friend and mentor has suggested that his granddaughter be removed to a safe spot, to keep her safe from contagion.*
>
> *Yours*
> *Francisco*

On the spur of the moment, he collected a bottle from his store of herbs and medications, put the letter inside, and then corked and sealed it with a mixture of beeswax and Venice turpentine. He would go for an early run in the morning, along the canal path, and see if he could send a reply back the way the message had come. It could be useful. He was due to leave with a small troop escort, at the Terce bell, with a letter to Cosimo de' Medici that Sforza would have written by then.

He packed his gear, finished his beer, washed, and went to bed. The next morning he was up well before the dawn, rousted out his yawning orderly from next to his peculiar, and took himself to the stables, and then down to the canal path. He ended up sitting on the same stump, looking out at the mist drifting above the water. The sun was not yet up.

"Nyx. Water woman. The pretty one . . ." he said, feeling mildly foolish.

She stuck her head up near a couple of water-lily pads. *"Why don't you keep normal hours like other men?"*

"I suppose because, like you, I am not just like other men."

"True. You bathe more often and like to run. But like other men you are enchanted by my body." She flaunted it.

"Also true, beautiful nyx," Francisco lied, guessing by her conduct that saying otherwise would not be welcome. "I have a boon to ask, for my friend Marco. The one you called the Winged Lion."

"My name," said the nyx, *"is Rhene. You are a healer, too?"*

"Of sorts. My skills are more those of a chirurgeon. Marco is better with other ailments," answered Francisco, used to the preamble that people wanting treatment gave. "My abilities are more what is needed in times of war."

"Then I will do what you ask. Chloe says having a healer has been of value. And I may not drown you. Therefore it is better to befriend you and have you in my debt."

"Almost exactly as my master, Carlo, put it last night...on a different matter." He handed her the bottle. "Now I am in your debt."

"Oh, good. So come into the water. I need a virile young man."

Francisco thought to himself, *I walked into that one.* "Alas, beautiful Rhene. My man will be here at any moment. And also, you want me in your debt, and if I repaid you thus, I would not be."

She wrinkled her forehead. "I have not allowed any men to see me without drowning them, except you. I'll have to think about these debts."

She slipped under the water silently, without a ripple, and left Francisco looking at the twisting trails of mist wreathed above the water, wondering if it had all been his imagination. But the bottle—which would have floated—was also gone, somewhere beneath that limpid water. Behind him, Francisco heard a horse stamp and his orderly cursing and understood that perhaps it wasn't just his eloquence that had saved him from, at the least, a thorough, cold wetting.

But in the meantime he had breakfast to eat, and his gear to finish readying before a long ride. He might also find time for another wash. Those were always tricky in foreign towns, let alone in roadside camps or in village inns. He might even be longing for the cold wetting by the time he got back.

He was rather looking forward to meeting Cosimo de' Medici. The man was exceptionally well-read, by all accounts. He just wished the meeting could be on a less bootless and awkward mission.

Chapter 9

The Duchy of Milan

Lucia looked at the letter from Carlo Sforza, inviting her mother to bring her to the Palazzo Ducale for an extended stay of a month or two, so that he could become properly acquainted with her, as one of the late duke's kin. She understood precisely what the letter meant, and fierce delight and triumph leapt in her breast. *Milan!* To go to her own. That was, after all, what she'd waited for, worked for, tried relentlessly to achieve. And now it was barely a step away from her.

Then, standing there, looking at the letter again, she realized that being just that close to her goal was going to be more difficult than being far off and striving for success—because she would be so close that the smallest misstep would take her down completely. Lucia also knew she was going to be much further from that which gave her power, that which lurked in the darkness below the Castello di Arona.

She took the key from its hiding place and made her way down to the cellars. Familiarity had not bred contempt, but at least she felt less in the way of sheer terror as she walked down the stairs in the darkness now.

"And now?" asked the sibilant voice in the darkness. There was a kind of terrible languor about the way it spoke, something that would make the listener abandon all hope and give over to the serpent.

"I go to Milan. Your killers have worked well."

There was a long silence. Then it said: "They are not dead yet."

"Oh?" Had she gone through all that expense and difficulty for nothing? "Well, I go to Milan. But I may need you there. Is there any way I can reach you while I am in the city?"

There was a long drawn-out hiss. "I will go there. But I need more time before I can move out of the pit. It is still too cold. Summer, stinking summer is when my little ones thrive. But I can send one of my serpent lackeys with you, if you will carry it between your breasts and keep it warm and safe."

"A snake? You want me to carry a snake? Carry it there! Are you mad?"

Again the scales shifted under her. "A serpent. Not a mere snake, but a part of me. He can bite and poison for you, give you that which you desire, and send word to me. But yessss, you will have to carry him. Feed him. He likes his mice trapped and helpless. But he does not require many."

Lucia paused at the thought of having a snake nestled up against her. She wanted to scream just at the idea. But ... but she had come so far. And she knew she would need to go further still, before it was all done.

"Very well." And then she screamed and clawed at her leg. Hauled at her skirts.

"It is your little helper. Do not hurt him or he may bite you," said the great serpent as the snake wound its way up her leg and thrust under her girdle, cold scales slithering against her skin. Almost rigid with fear, Lucia stood and panted ... but controlled her hands as the snake slid up between her breasts and stopped, resting there like a vast weight on her heart.

"I can't breathe," she panted, resisting the urge to tear at the fabric. Firstly, she knew she must not, and secondly, it might bite her.

"You will grow used it. You will even assume it is normal, soon," said the serpent, unconcerned. "Others have told me so, the last time, and the time before."

"I can't."

"But you must. Or you will die."

Eventually, she got to her feet and began the long walk up to the cellars. With every step she could feel the scales move against her flesh. It must be a very small snake, really. That didn't stop her flesh wishing to crawl away from it.

She went to inform her mother about the letter. Her mother

had once been something of a beauty, in a slim, childlike way, but all that was gone now. All that was left was a shrunken, sad-eyed woman. A woman who had given up. Even with a snake in her bosom, Lucia felt anger and scorn seeing her like that. She'd let herself come so close to power and then let it get away from her.

"Milan. I don't think I can, again," her mother said weakly. "The expense. Yes, I know we would be fed, but court clothes will cost. And the noise. No, Lucia, I don't think so. No, it would be better if we stayed here, where we are safe and it is quiet. Why would you have anything to do with some lowborn soldier anyway?"

"Don't be stupid, Mother. Our living here is at his whim. Yes, the court clothes will cost us, but stay here? What is there here for me? A bare half-dozen servants and a rotting old stone pile. We have no power and no influence. The local great families pretend we do not exist. At least in Milan they will bow. And afterwards, the families here will grovel before us."

"Lucia, it is not as simple as that. You don't know the court. I do. I was raised there. I can't do it."

As Lucia drew angry breath to harangue the stupid woman, a woman who had known full well what her father had done, when a little voice from her breast, or possibly within her head, said: *I will deal with this.*

Lucia knew the woman reposing on the daybed was as good as dead. That did not worry her. But she would need a chaperone, and the letter had invited her mother to come back to the court to present her there. Even without her, with someone compliant in her place, a funeral would take time to organize, and then there would be the mourning period to further waste time she did not have.

"Not dead," she said hastily.

"What?" said her mother, and then she gasped, her eyes going round with fear, as the serpent slithered out of Lucia's bodice and, as Lucia watched in the wall mirror, balanced itself upright, swaying slowly, and staring cold-eyed at her mother.

The snake did not lunge or strike. Just swayed slowly and steadily. *Tell her what to do,* said a quieter version of the voice of the great serpent below. *She will obey now.*

So Lucia gave her mother instructions. In two days the household would be packed up and the castello closed, with just old

Aleta left behind as a caretaker, and they would go to Milan. To the Palazzo Ducale, where she would present her daughter.

Her mother had not answered back, but had nodded obediently, all the while looking at the swaying snake's eyes, not at her daughter.

Later, back in her chamber, Lucia asked the serpent in her bosom. "Who are you and just what can you do?"

I am the asp. I serve those who are in a pact with the great wyrm. I have served others. I have served queens. I have bitten ones, too, at her command. Octavian would have had her killed.

"You are not to bite me, I command you."

I am yours to command.

But it would lie, part of her mind said. Had she been in the same position she would have lied. She would plan to kill it... in time. For now. "What can you do...and what can't you do for me?"

I can kill, slowly or fast. I can induce paralysis, either in the whole or in any part. I can cause great pain. I can hypnotize, as I have done to your mother. I am but a small part of the great wyrm. I cannot deal with more than one foe at a time. There are some who can resist my hypnosis, but they are few. I can help heighten your own charms. That magic, too, is in your grasp.

The great wyrm was correct. She did get used to having the asp in between her breasts, although she had been afraid to sleep the first night.

Two days later they left for Milan. For her goal.

Chapter 10

Francisco had been—as was his habit—observant and taking mental notes during his journey to Florence. The first observation was that this principality had become rich pickings under the de' Medici. The second observation was that even for Sforza, it quite possibly wouldn't be worth the cost of taking it. Someone had put a fair amount of thought into the fortifications and defenses. And there were many soldiers drilling. These had the look of levies about them, but when it came to massed harquebus fire, a well-drilled squad of levies could still do a lot of damage. Less than the same number of well-drilled professionals, but still, a great deal, especially if they could choose their own ground and time. The fortifications had also been built recently, and for cannon. They weren't the showy tall stone towers of many castles. Instead they were low, broad-walled structures, built in a star shape with triangular ravelins on the star points. Francisco wished he had the liberty to walk and measure them, but no doubt Carlo would have had his spies do so.

Two days later he arrived in Florence, presented his credentials, and requested an interview with Cosimo de' Medici. He knew it was perfectly possible that he would be refused, or be left to cool his heels for weeks on end. That could happen, but there were worse places to have to do so than Florence. The beer wasn't bad and there was, of all things, a library which was open to the public, where a man could sit and read. The city was cleaner than Milan and smelled far less than Venice. Its citizens seemed reasonably fat and happy.

Francisco repaired to the library, to see what books the benevolent master of the city had seen fit to let the people read. The stock of some two thousand books and a great number of manuscripts was enough to make Francisco green with envy. Books were expensive to produce, and even the twenty-eight books Francisco owned added up to a year's wage for a manservant. The use of woodcut presses had brought the price down a great deal though, from when the books were handwritten. Now a press could do two thousand pages a day!

The downside of the place was that they would not let him drink beer in the reading room, or eat there, for that matter. Still, there were benches, with the backs to serve as reading desks, and the smell of books. Two librarians kept an eye on the place, and kept it quiet, and there must have been a good forty people inside.

He was engrossed in Plutarch when someone coughed, delicately, in front of him. Looking up, Francisco saw a man in a large loose cap, and what was probably a false beard, looking at him and smiling. He had not lived as a soldier for all these years not to realize that the two men on the flanks, also in very ordinary clothes, were almost certainly bodyguards—and good at their work, for all they were pretending just to be there.

"I am glad to see you enjoying a book, Caviliero Turner," said the one in the middle. "You do realize I cannot meet with you, so perhaps you would walk to the back of the stacks on your left and take the small door on your right. I will join you shortly." He walked past and pulled down a book from the shelf.

Francisco calmly returned the Plutarch to its place and went down the stacks to the small door. It led into a room which had considerably more books in it than the library, but most of them were piled against the wall, except for those on the large table obviously in the process of being repaired. "His Grace said that he would be here presently, so find yourself a book that isn't too badly damaged," said the librarian, who was painstakingly stitching the pages back into a book.

"A lot of them get damaged, do they?" asked Francisco.

"Sadly, yes. We also buy and repair damaged ones for the library. Some books are very popular."

As a way of increasing the popularity of a ruler with his subjects, too, Francisco had to approve. He would suggest it to Carlo, if they could brush through the next few years.

Cosimo came in with his bodyguards before Francisco had comfortably settled into a damaged copy of Boccaccio's *De Mulieribus Claris.*

"Your reputation, Caviliero, appears to be accurately derived," said the duke. "How worrying!" But it was said with a disarming smile.

Francisco rose and bowed. "Yes. If we are to start believing all these reputations...I am very impressed by your library, Your Grace. Florence is a great city, but nothing I have seen here could delight me more than this."

"It needs a bigger building. And more books," said Cosimo disparagingly. "My wife says we should rather spend the money on a great public camerata for the musical arts, or a theater for drama to rival Rome."

"I'm sure that would be popular, but for me, this is the finest gift to the people. But then, I like to read."

"And to drink beer," said Cosimo.

"The simple joys of life, Your Grace. I blame it on my English ancestry, if I have to excuse my tastes. But then, I am a soldier and it is not expected that I be refined in every direction or, indeed, any."

"I envy that freedom at times. I myself am not musically inclined, but it is expected of me. Anyway, Caviliero, we could discuss books for hours, but I am expected to give an audience shortly. So let us come to the point. I know why you are here, and you know that I will not be meeting with you...officially. You must also know that I have no real desire for conflict with your master."

"Carlo Sforza feels likewise, Your Grace. He does not excel at the niceties of diplomacy, but he holds you in some considerable esteem." That was true enough. "Which is the reason he sought an alliance by marriage with your house."

"Nothing to do with seeking to bestow legitimacy on his usurpation?" asked Cosimo urbanely.

Francisco decided to play it the same way. "There are other candidates for that."

Cosimo sighed. "I am very fond of my cousin Violetta. Her father was one of my closest friends, before he embarked on that reckless venture of his. Aside from political considerations which, let us be honest, do not place her in a good position, Violetta is, shall we say, a determined woman. She has made up her mind.

I cannot see a great advantage in the short term for Florence, so I will not bring pressure to bear on her, even if I could. I admit, I actually do consider the match favorably, but she does not. Nonetheless, Caviliero, I shall take you to meet her, and you can put the matter to her personally. I am, I will be honest, trying to keep Florence out of war. Now, I am committed until Thursday of next week. You will fail to see me, for obvious reasons. I suggest you petition every day, and spend your days kicking your heels, possibly here in the library."

"That will be a great hardship," said Francisco with a smile.

"Indeed, I hope it will be as hard for you as it would be for me. And then you will leave on the Friday morning in high dudgeon at being ignored. Do not move too fast, and choose the north road. We'll overtake you, as I ride out to see Violetta and her mother."

Francisco blinked. "That...is very generous of you, Your Grace."

"I merely hope to make you understand why this would not work, and that it is not an insult to Carlo Sforza. Violetta is no pawn. I shall see you on Friday."

Francisco bowed. "I will enjoy your library and petition to see you with increasingly visible anger."

"Excellent. I look forward to talking of books with you. I shall leave now. If you don't mind, wait for a few minutes before you leave my man to get on with his repair work."

He left Francisco Turner with considerable food for thought, and access to a large number of books. Francisco had been around enough Italian courts to know that Cosimo de' Medici was generally held in some disdain, but that he usually ended up getting what he wanted. Francisco knew Carlo Sforza did not share that disdain, an opinion he now shared himself. Cosimo might try to please everyone. Florence was not worth attacking, because her money was very important. Everyone borrowed from Venice, or Florence, or both. A failed attack might end up in future loans not being forthcoming.

He did not hold out great hopes of persuading Violetta de' Medici into a marriage with Carlo Sforza. But at least he could tell Carlo, firsthand, that Cosimo was doing his level best to avoid an armed conflict with Milan. He would probably succeed, barring something exceptional happening, Francisco judged. Of course, exceptional was less rare than you'd think it could be.

Still, he went through with the charade of being ignored by Cosimo so that the spies of various other states could gleefully report that Sforza's emissary was being given the cold shoulder. On Friday, he regretfully bade the library farewell and rode out in a suitable display of high dudgeon.

Nearly two hours later he was joined on the road, relatively close to Croci di Calenzano, by Duke Cosimo de' Medici. His escort and Francisco's far smaller one gave them space so they could ride and talk without being overheard. By the way that the duke's troops needed no instruction for this, Francisco guessed they'd done it before. They were relatively well-drilled cavalry: good, if not of the caliber of Sforza's men, or Dell'este's forces for that matter. Those troops had a degree of skill whose final polish came only from being blooded. Often. That, Cosimo's pacific nature had avoided.

"I should have specified a time for you to leave," said Cosimo. "I am more accustomed to midday departures, than ones at first light, Caviliero. You keep military hours, and my wife had a soiree which did not end until after midnight last night. We had to make our usual leisurely departure and then ride like hell."

"My apologies, Your Grace. I've had a lovely ride admiring the countryside. It is verdant and so well-protected," said Francisco, gesturing at a windbreak grove of chestnuts.

Cosimo laughed. "The trees or the fortification on the hill?"

"I had noticed those, yes. They have an interesting design."

"Oddly enough, they owe their design to Violetta's late father. In defensive terms, he was a very good engineer. A genius, you might say. That led him to believe he'd be a great conqueror. Alas, the two did not actually go together. I learned something from his unfortunate demise. I hold my base well. I do not risk all in expensive and dangerous ventures. However, I wouldn't mention that to the Signoretta Violetta. She can be quite touchy, and she's well-read on military subjects."

"She is? That's ... unusual."

"Oh, my little cousin is very unusual. She's also let herself get sadly fat since her father's death. I think she ate for comfort, and it became a habit."

Further confidences were ended by a rider—not a very good one—who came racing over the brow of the hill towards them. Both Cosimo's and Francisco's men took defensive measures, but unnecessary ones, as they could soon see. The rider was waving furiously whenever he could take a hand off the saddle horse. He was, by his dress, plainly a servant.

"Ah. One of the Lady Calimet de' Medici's footmen," said Cosimo. "She only has two, at my insistence. I wonder what is wrong?"

The servant pulled his steaming horse to a halt. "My lord! Come quickly!" he panted. "The mistress... and the young mistress... bitten... by... snake."

They spurred their horses to a gallop.

The neat little manor house was in chaos. Screaming women—not the injured ones—and there were people running around frantically.

"Be quiet!" commanded Cosimo, with an icy and effective authority that Francisco had not seen him employ before. In the sudden silence, he said, "Now. You," he pointed to one of the older dames. "Take us to the ladies. Caviliero, I believe you are a physician, so could you accompany me? The rest of you remain here. Be quiet and wait on my commands."

Francisco drew his traveling kit from his saddlebag as he dismounted. "The snake. Did it get away and, if so, did anyone see it? I need to know what kind it was," he explained to Cosimo.

"The signorina. She cut it in half," said one elderly servant, by the looks of him a gardener.

"Bring it to us. And be careful, they can still bite and poison, even when dead."

He followed Cosimo, led by an elderly servitor, into a salon where the two women lay, on a settle and a daybed, surrounded by the entertainments of ladies of the gentry—tambour frames, a basket of delicate whitework, and a number of books. Francisco wasted no time, checked for a pulse on the older woman, found it weak but racing and erratic. She moaned feebly and panted. Then to the plump girl—and that was worse. At first, taking the limp, cold, clammy hand, he thought she was dead, but there was a pulse at her throat—he could find nothing on the wrist—faint, slow and weak.

"Is she dead?" asked Cosimo.

"Not yet, Your Grace," said Francisco, loosening the neckband of her dress by the simple expedient of cutting it.

The gardener came in with a still-twitching snake—both halves speared onto a garden fork and held as far from himself as possible.

"What is it?" asked Cosimo.

Francisco had seen a fair number of snakes in Africa and Arabia as a slave, and a few in Italy. This one was the color of a savage bruising: purple heading toward black with a dirty yellow underside. It also had a vee pattern in brighter yellow on its head scales. The head had been cut in half, so that was less easy to see. It was very distinctive, and yet new to him. "I've not seen the like of it, I'm afraid."

"What is to be done?" asked Cosimo. He was maintaining an icy calm but Francisco could see that the man was as taut as a bowstring, and despite the façade, deeply upset.

"I will find the bites and apply a tincture to them. I don't know if it will help, Your Grace. And then it will be a matter of managing the symptoms and time."

"It bit Lady Calimet on the hand," said the gardener, "and when she screamed and the signorina ran to her—she had been cutting some herbs with me—it lunged and bit her on the leg. She cut it with the shears in her hand."

"How long ago did this happen?" asked Francisco.

"Oh, not long, master. Just before the None bell."

Like most rustics, he probably could not read or tell the time, but nonetheless, that could not have been an hour ago.

Cosimo must have seen his expression. "That's bad, is it?"

Francisco nodded. "It is very soon for this extreme a reaction. Your Grace, I will be honest with you," he said, as he located the two puncture wounds on the feebly panting older woman's hand. "I'd send for a priest. And get me a couple of men to move the bed and settle closer together. I'll want a stool so I can sit between them. And I'll want someone who can understand what I tell them to do and will obey orders."

"That will be me," said Cosimo de' Medici calmly. "Unless you have one among your men who will have more experience?"

"No, Your Grace. But it is likely to be grim," said Francisco, cleaning the wound, noting the swelling and mottled bruising developing up her arm. The hand was clammy and her brow was beaded with sweat.

"I can cope," said Cosimo. "I will go and give the orders."

He came back to find Francisco cutting the fabric away from the younger woman's thigh. Francisco stopped briefly to allow them to move the settle. "Should I have them fetch a bed?" asked Cosimo.

Francisco shook his head. "Later. Your Grace, it appears she only got one fang—I can only find one puncture wound. But her heart rate is decreasing and very weak. I am going to administer a tincture of belladonna. It's a poison, but it does increase the heart rate. But it may kill her if she gets too much."

"She's dying anyway," said Cosimo, his voice harsh. "Do it. I've heard you are one of the best physicians in Italy."

"An exaggeration," said Francisco as he carefully measured out the dose. "I do know someone who will be, though."

As he said that, his other patient began to twitch and moan, and that took their attention. "One with barely a heartbeat, the other with a weak racing erratic heart. An odd poison," said Francisco, "although different toxins affect the body differently."

The priest came at this point. Francisco left him to his business and paid attention to the younger woman again. The heartbeat was faster and at least discernable now.

But then things went from there to worse with the older woman. Francisco tried various stopgaps, even a low dose of the belladonna. It was not particularly effective and he tried several of his other drugs, with no better result. Eventually, her heart fluttered its last and stopped. Fortunately, the younger woman had gradually started breathing slightly better during this time, but then she, too, had a relapse, and Francisco was too busy dealing with her to concern himself with the dead. Violetta, however, did respond to a second dose of belladonna tincture. The trouble was the response was just so slow, administered like that.

He was in for a long afternoon and then night. But by just after dawn the next day, he began to feel he would not lose the second patient. She was still comatose, and still had clammy extremities, but her breathing and pulse had stabilized. Cosimo came in, looking gray and exhausted himself, bringing with his own hands a goblet of wine for Francisco.

They had long since passed from "Your Grace" and "Caviliero" to first name terms. "I have sent two of my men back to Florence, to fetch the best of her physicians, Francisco. I should have thought of it last night. At least they could give you some rest."

Francisco took a deep gulp of the wine. He felt he'd earned it. "Well, the good news is I think that they will not be needed. She's certainly gotten no worse and has possibly improved slightly."

"You, sir, are a miracle worker," said Cosimo. "I curse myself that I thought this would be a suitable place for them. It was the only one of my cousin's estates that he had not sold to fund his military adventure. And that, purely because there was a lawsuit pending on it at the time. Lady Calimet resented my charity, and I am afraid my wife disliked her very much. But Violetta... she was always my favorite among the cousins. I pray she lives."

"It might well have been a miracle," said Francisco tiredly, "or the prayers of the priest. Look, she was young, strong and had only one fang of venom, and was the second person bitten. Whatever that snake was, it was very deadly. I'm sorry I couldn't save her mother, but Cosimo, you must realize that it is not over yet. Her heart or her liver—they could be damaged. So could her nerves. She may never recover consciousness, and may never recover movement. We just don't know."

There was a long silence. Finally Cosimo said: "Earlier, much earlier, you said you knew the best physician in Italy."

"What? Oh. I know the young man who will become that. Marco Valdosta. I assisted him in the treatment of the Doge when the Doge was poisoned. Privately, I will tell you I was sure Petro Dorma would never recover. But Marco seems to have, and I mean this literally, a healing touch."

There was another long silence. Then Cosimo nodded. "I will write immediately to beg him to come to see her. May I mention your name?"

"Certainly. But, to be realistic, we should wait a day or two, and see if she makes any progress or...relapses. I'll stay on hand to stop these doctors of yours from undoing my good work." He smiled, which turned into a yawn.

"Do you think he would come?" asked Cosimo, patting the girl's hand.

"Marco? It would be difficult. The Doge seems determined to keep him close, I gather. But...well, you could arrange to send Violetta to see him. I don't think travel will make a great deal of difference to her. It is not as if she has any broken bones. It is some distance, but a part of the journey may be accomplished by river and by sea. I will be going some of the way myself and could watch over her. But we need to check that she is stable, first."

"I will immediately send a messenger to the Doge to beg this favor, at least to have Signor Valdosta examine her."

"Oh, Marco Valdosta's problem is that he would help anyone," said Francisco tiredly.

"I will still send messengers, and have my men organize transportation and a suitable escort. But I would be further in your debt, Francisco Turner, if you could at least see her safe to the river, and bestowed on a fast, comfortable vessel for Venice. And...if you ever look for another employer, look no further than Florence. Land and titles are yours for asking."

"I'm flattered, but I merely did what I could. And the girl is far from safe or healed."

"I saw your effort, read the stresses on your face, Francisco Turner. If you could have dragged them through by sheer force of will, you would have. You are a physician born, not a soldier, I am afraid." It was said with a smile and a hand on his shoulder.

"Funnily enough, that's also what Marco said. You're both wrong, projecting yourselves onto my nature. I'd rather be a man who drinks beer and reads books, and avoids sick or injured people."

"I don't particularly believe you, but I shall send you a suitable gift of books," said Cosimo. "Which brings me to another subject. One I wished to broach in some security that I could not be overheard. The Church is apparently preparing itself—and giving warning to a few trusted individuals—that there may be another outbreak of the Plague of Justinian, in the Duchy of Milan. Church warnings are not always to be trusted, but I would still like to send word on to Carlo Sforza. And as his personal physician, I should imagine you would be consulted."

"We have had this rumor already sent on to us," said Francisco. "I'm not sure that it is anything but an attempt to destabilize the Duchy of Milan, Cosimo. The disease is always recorded as originating in the East, and has always spread from the ports into the interior."

"Ah. I did not know that. Still, I suppose someone could sail up the Po River with it. I doubt that the rumor is being set about as a tactic against Carlo Sforza. I could be wrong but, well, Monsignor di Marino is a man of some honor. He's a great humanist."

"I hope I'm right, simply because we have never successfully stopped the plague. It just burns itself out, when it runs out of people."

"That is even more terrifying coming from you, Francisco. Well, I hope it is a mere vicious rumor then. How odd to hope for that."

Francisco was too tired, just then, to analyze what Cosimo had said. He was just grateful that the girl survived his short sleep, and he was able to somewhat forcefully dissuade the physician from Florence from cupping her. Violetta de' Medici showed no signs of recovering consciousness, although the circulation to her limbs had improved somewhat. Francisco took that as a good sign: less blood was being directed to her vital organs and some could be spared to warm her hands and feet. Of course, there was no telling what damage had been done to those organs already.

Cosimo had arranged a horse-borne litter for his cousin, a letter to Marco Valdosta, another to Doge Petro Dorma, and a majordomo to bear the letters and to see to the transportation and any other matters. The man had suitable funds and the right to draw on more from a certain banker on the Rialto Bridge. They would have an escort of fifteen guards.

"Enough to make it not worth an attack by petty bandits and unlikely to attract the attention of the large ones," said Cosimo. "Sometimes indistinguishable from the local nobility. A sick woman, though, is not likely to be considered a valuable hostage, or worth their trouble."

"And I will have my eight rascals to add to that, as far as the Po River, where we will put her aboard a vessel. She'll be safe enough, and travel fast enough."

By now, Francisco was quietly certain of what he had begun to suspect the afternoon before: Cosimo de' Medici was in love with his "little" fat cousin. Probably not as a lover in the physical sense, but as an affair of the heart. There was a gap of many years between them and Cosimo was married, but Francisco had seen that often enough. He'd probably have accepted her marriage to someone suitable, because that was the nature of the man. But he would cherish a soft spot for her and woe betide the fellow if he hurt Violetta. Cosimo de' Medici might seem a mild and sensible man, but Francisco had seen enough of him during the period they'd fought for the women's lives, to realize he could be brutally efficient, and was very well able to outthink most Italian nobles. Cosimo was also fabulously wealthy. He had the money and the intellect to crush them, even if not the martial prowess.

So, besides for other reasons, that made Francisco hope the girl lived and recovered fully. He was Carlo Sforza's man, and Sforza needed allies, especially ones like Cosimo de' Medici.

Chapter 11

Venice

Marco had received a message from Brother Mascoli that some of the water-people wished to see him. By now, even Venice's spies accepted that he spent time in the poor Hypatian chapel, and had also accepted that they could not follow him in there. There wasn't much, besides spend their time pretending to pray, that the most ardent spy could do in the chapel. They'd tried watching the place, and found it was empty of other people waiting for Marco, and that no one came when he went there. It was not a rendezvous that they could see. They'd even searched it and found the little water-chapel below. But that—while odd— definitely could not be accessed unless one were a fish, except through the church above. So a man might as well have a mug of wine, in the tavern across from the door, and wait...and see which other agents were doing the same.

Those who came to see Marco in the water-chapel had no problem swimming there, of course. But people preferred to deny the existence of tritons and undines and nyxes and others of that kind, unless they were in trouble, and then they'd believe anything.

"Your friend Francisco did not want to be my lover," said Rhene, pouting a little. "But he did give me this message for you."

Marco took it eagerly, cracked the sealing wax, drew the cork with his teeth, and then fished in the bottle with the tweezers from his bag of medical supplies to extract the folded letter. He read it hopefully. He'd been doing considerable research into the subject, and so far, found little to comfort him. But Francisco's knowledge was years ahead of his! And indeed, he hadn't disappointed him—although the idea of it starting in Venice horrified Marco. He had a pregnant wife here, apart from anything else. The very idea of his precious Katerina being at that sort of risk was enough to make him shudder.

"Oh, this is wonderful! I need another message taken back to him. I didn't know Francisco knew anything about magic in the area of healing. I thought he was very skeptical about it."

"He is in my debt. I will be going to see him again. But I think that he has left Milan."

Marco bit his knuckle. The need to prepare for the onset of the disease was obviously urgent, but another secure way of sending secret messages was not apparent to him. "I will give you a message for him anyway. Please, give it to him when you next see him."

He dug a piece of paper from his bag, blessing the fact that he had a quill and several small bottles of ink in different colors that he used in various medical situations. It was amusing in a way that it was Francisco who had showed him how to do this, to mark the progress of inflammation. "They'll believe that it is magical, of course. They always do, for anything they don't understand. Sometimes it seems that very belief helps."

Marco trimmed the quill and wrote:

"My dear Friend in Medicine,

I thank you so much for your reply, which has brought me much relief. The good Father Thomas Lüber of Baden, who informed me of the problem, had told me that no cure or effective treatment has so far been known. Please, I beg of you, share this knowledge with us.

I shall see what can be done to persuade Maria to return to Corfu. We will miss my niece terribly, but her health is a priority with us, too.

I have as yet been unable to identify the snake which bit the patient you consigned to my care. Her progress is very slight, and I do not know that she will ever recover.

Later, after he had given the resealed bottle to Rhene, he left the chapel and went to the Doge's palace. He had less trouble in securing an interview with Petro Dorma than most people, but he still had some time to kick his heels before he was ushered in. Petro was thinner than he'd been before the poisoning, and was still prone to get tired quickly and to grumble almost incessantly about the dull diet. On the other hand, his old energy with work and his sharpness of focus did seem to be returning. That was good for Venice, and good for his young physician's happiness, if not because it turned more of the rich and powerful and terrified of poison to Marco for protection. He'd always seen himself as tending the sick because they needed help, not because they were wealthy or poor.

"You've come to tell me that I am cured at last and can eat what I like?" said the Doge, mock hopefully. "That fat goose-liver pâté studded with truffles is good for me?"

"No such luck," said Marco. "I heard you felt quite queasy after buttered scallops yesterday."

"I suspect the quality of the scallops," said Petro. "Anyway, you were not quite called. I started feeling better soon after."

"Which did not affect any other person present at the meal. No, Petro, I'm afraid we have to consider that the damage may be long-lasting." Marco did not say "permanent." He didn't think Petro was ready for that! "Anyway, I have come to talk to you about a message from the physician who assisted me with treating you, when you were poisoned."

"You really need to be less cryptic in your letters. The Council of Ten got quite worried about what it might mean."

"It wasn't them I was trying to confuse. Seriously, it is time medicine was above such spying. Disease knows no borders and does not care if the victim is rich or poor, a friend or a foe."

"A nice idea, Marco. But that would simply be viewed as a window to all the spies."

When Petro used that tone, there was no point in debating the matter. Marco had heard him use the same finality in dealing with his sister. The subject was closed. "Anyway, he had also heard that the coming season would be bad, and says they have taken various measures to prevent it, including magic. I've asked for help in getting that protection for Venice."

Petro pursed his lips. "I don't think we wish to be beholden to Milan, or to be seen to be. There have been developments, not encouraging ones. I will say no more now, but we'll be glad to see your brother back soon with the fleet."

"I was wondering whether Maria could go back to Corfu and meet him there. I think, by a few things she's said, that she is not too happy here in Venice. And it's a healthier place than Venice in high summer."

"I want no reason for Benito Valdosta to linger on Corfu, or to think he's not wanted in Venice," said Petro, also in tones of finality. "The sooner he and Enrico Dell'este get back, the happier I will be and the safer Venice will be."

Marco attempted to direct the discussion towards taking some preventative measures against the bad air which was reputed to carry disease. But that, too, was not a subject—as it involved cleaning up Venice's canals—that he got very far with, either.

He had to hope Francisco would come up with some form of magical charm against the disease.

Chapter 12

Rimini

Duke Umberto Da Corregio of Parma had not yet managed to outstay his welcome with Count Andrea Malatesta. He was trying, though. It was, however, a case of him being too drunk by midday to make much of an impact besides passing out and spewing his host's red wine. The planning of the campaign against the usurper Sforza had not gotten very far as a result.

Viscount Lippi Pagano of Imola had returned to his city, and not a day too soon, reflected Malatesta. He'd rather put up with puking drunks who had all the decent women of his court locking themselves in, than the smart-mouthed Lippi. Still, he had committed troops to the coming war.

Money was, of course, still a problem. They really needed Florence. And for that he needed allies, because for all that Cosimo de' Medici was scrupulously polite, Count Andrea was very certain he still held a grudge about his cousin's death at Faenza.

Count Andrea had been fairly certain that today would bring more of the same as yesterday. However, the morning brought instead a messenger who had ridden in haste from Parma, and demanded to see Duke Umberto as soon as possible. When that failed, as the duke was still abed, and the count's majordomo was under no delusions that waking him would be a good thing, the messenger begged for an audience with Count Andrea. That, too, would have failed, but as it happened, the count had been on his way back from the stables just then and overheard the request. As he had seen the man's exhausted horse being led away in the stables, Andrea knew the messenger had plainly ridden far and fast. That was worth finding out about, even if Umberto would be hung over and unpleasant when he woke naturally, let alone at this time of day.

"Spit it out, man," he instructed.

"My lord, I beg that you would have the duke woken. It's rather grave news about his niece."

Count Andrea was in some doubt that Duke Umberto would care if a messenger brought him news even of his mother's demise at this time of morning, let alone grave news about a niece. Then something occurred to him. "Which niece?"

"Lady Eleni, my lord—she's dead," the messenger blurted hastily. "Poisoned!"

"Go and wake Duke Umberto," said Count Andrea to his majordomo, rather pleased at the news. That put a whole new complexion on the day.

Umberto shambled forth from his chambers some half an hour later, his cotte askew. His cameriere must have had a great deal of difficulty dressing him. He had a large flagon of wine in one hand. "One of your footmen woke me," he said blearily. "Said there was an important message."

Count Andrea was already dictating letters to his scribe for the various allies, paused at the interruption, and stood up. "I will take you to him," he said, as if he normally conducted his guests in person. "I told my men to put him in one of the salons off the great reception hall."

He went along to see the reaction. It was as furious as he had expected. "That dog Sforza! Next he will try to poison me! This means war! War!"

"Absolutely despicable," said Count Andrea. "Is there no end to the depth of his depravity? A woman refuses his unwelcome advances and he has her killed. Tell us exactly what happened?"

The messenger looked to the duke, who nodded. "We're not sure how the poison was administered, Count. Her tirewoman heard the lady calling out, and went to her. She was in great distress in her bedchamber, panting and sweating and thrashing about on the bed, although the weather was cool. She was delirious, and a physician was called to cup her. During the process, she had some kind of spasm and died. She was fine and healthy when she retired to her chamber. The physicians all declared it had to be poison, my lord."

"What else could it be?" said the duke, gulping his unmixed wine so hastily it slopped down his chin.

"And who will be next? We had better warn Cosimo."

"The Butterball would eat poison and call for seconds," sneered the duke. "But by all means, let us tell him. It may frighten Cosimo into hiding under his bed. I need to return to Parma, Andrea, to ready my men for action."

"Quite understood, Duke Umberto. Quite understood." Count Andrea was quite happy to have the duke gone. Firstly, the troops of Parma were intended to blunt and occupy Sforza's mercenary troops. They had no hope of beating them, but they would make them bleed. Andrea used enough mercenaries himself to know how little they liked that, even if Sforza's men were, reputedly, more reliable than most. Secondly, Duke Umberto had two con-dottierie of a reasonable level of competence to lead his men, so he could safely get drunk in the afternoon without losing a war.

It could be that Sforza had ordered the bitch killed for the slight. It was more likely that the duke's niece's penchant for experimentation had gotten the better of her. She had had something of a reputation. It did not matter, for it was all the pretext they had needed. If he'd thought of it, Andrea Malatesta would have ordered her poisoned himself.

It was only three days later, when the news via one of his spies in Tuscany reached him, that Cosimo's cousin had been bitten by a snake at roughly the same time, that he began to wonder. He did, like all of Italian nobility, take some precautions against poison and assassins. He decided it would be wise to increase these, especially as he was related to the Visconti himself. Quite closely, but he had not pointed that out. The time would come when the duchy was to be carved up.

Chapter 13

Milan

Lucia came to Milan without fanfare and, arriving just after noon, spent a great deal of money on suitable court dresses and all the other items of fashion that a woman might need, especially perfume, before they would proceed to the palazzo. She and her mother would remain, quietly, in a house hired for the purpose until the dresses were ready. It was a wonderful sign that the asp had her mother under perfect control, in that there was not a whisper of protest at the expenditure which might have kept them in reasonable style back at the Castello di Arona for several years.

The truth was, she was somewhat nervous. She had met Carlo Sforza at her father's court, as a young woman of fourteen, when many of her peers had already been getting married off. That had been a time when favor from the duke's bastard daughter could have possibly been valuable. Yet Sforza had made not the smallest effort to acknowledge her, let alone charm her or even show respect. Of course she had done likewise, but that was to be expected. He was a mere condottiere. Rich yes, successful yes, but still not what she had wanted then—and still, she admitted, not what she wanted now—which was a nobleman who desired her because she was who she was by birth.

Had he ignored her then because he was beneath her touch? She doubted it, since he had had Lady Lorendana Valdosta, a duke's daughter, as a lover. He had exchanged the polite flirtations of court with several well-born ladies. He'd been, to Lucia's ear, heavy, awkward and unskilled at these, but the comments and flattery had been well received because he was a man of power and wealth, if not noble birth.

This time, of course, she had considerable value to him, even if she intended to see him dead for it. The heir to the ducal throne was already in her belly. She would rule as the regent until the child reached majority. And then... she'd see.

One thing did gall her, though: Milan had forgotten her. She had been shown respect as a customer... up to a point. But the tradespeople had demanded money before the shears cut crisply through the silk. She knew they had not done that when she'd gone to the dressmakers and silk merchants when she had still been known as Duke Visconti's illegitimate daughter. She and her mother had never dared spend too freely then, but that was because Filippo Maria had not been generous with the allowance he had given their mother, and would have been angry if they'd outspent it. He had been strange that way. Strange in other ways, too, she supposed. Mother had been very talented when it came to making a good showing on a small stipend, buying frugally and seeking bargains. She made no attempt now, and Lucia had not bothered. Now it would be all or nothing. If this failed...

And in the street... no one knew who she was, or gave her any deference.

That would have to change.

It will, said the asp in the quiet, terrible voice that seemed to be inside her head. She hoped so, and it seemed that was true. The first time it had spoken when other people had been present, she'd been afraid.

Now she knew that they should be afraid. That she quite enjoyed.

There were various tasks to be undertaken before they officially arrived in the city—hiring several new servants, as well as awaiting the work of the dressmakers of her new wardrobe of court clothes; and, of course, measuring the response of the citizens to the usurper, while she was still anonymous. It was a shock to discover that Milan did not yearn for her father. About Sforza... feelings ranged from outright fear to a sort of perverse pride in his brutally effective conquest.

That was not what Lucia had expected at all. In a way, she had expected to be welcomed as the returning rightful Visconti ruler to the duchy. She'd never had a great deal of time for the commons but discovering their lack of due respect to her blood lowered their value even further. She did, however, find out that Sforza was away from the city and would only be back later in the week. That suited her fine.

Three days later, when the first of the court wardrobe was ready, with her hair suitably dressed, chopines trimmed with gilt on her feet, her eyes widened with belladonna, and jewels at her throat, she was different from the young woman who had come in from the country a few days earlier. An elegant carriage had been hired to transport them, and they made their entrance in a suitably grand style.

Of course, Sforza himself did not come to greet them, the great peasant. The courtier—one she knew from when they had come to the court more frequently—was suitably apologetic and made all the excuses she'd heard him make for her father. Still, they were settled comfortably in a pleasant suite of rooms on the third floor, and were presented to Carlo Sforza that evening. He hadn't changed a great deal. The gray at his temples had increased, and he was somewhat more tired-looking. He was still too broad to wear the current mode, which favored tall slim men. He looked like a big mongrel walking through a pack of carefully bred greyhounds, with the same slight stiff-legged gait. *Watching the courtiers,* Lucia thought. But she favored him with her best smile, nonetheless.

His response showed that at least he had learned to conduct himself as a pretense of a courtier. He bowed, kissed her hand. "My dear Lucia," he said, "it seems to have been such a long time since I last saw you here. May I bid you a heartfelt welcome back to Milan? And this is your charming mother. I remember you well, madam, when you were not a great deal older than your lovely daughter."

That was a lie, of course. At that time, the usurper had been a minor condottiere in the service of Lucca. But her mother favored him with a mechanical smile, as if she had no reason to hate him either.

Lucia's estimation of his potential rose slightly. Not a great deal, not enough to let him live overlong, but somewhat. He was, after all, behaving as a good Italian noble should.

Sforza did not dance, but he did circulate among the guests. The principal topic of small talk—the new style of lace out of

Mantua—was one where he did little more than smile and nod. He did venture the opinion that the current high price of spices was largely due to the Venetians and Genovese having trouble in Outre Mer, which he predicted would resolve itself.

"Or we'll resolve it for them, eh, Protector?" said one courtier, making a shooting gesture.

"Not at the moment," said Sforza coolly. "I have other . . . less spicy fish to fry."

That caused laughter, although Lucia could not see why. But perhaps laughter was the safe option, and thus the courtiers used it a great deal. If it was real information, it would be worth a fair number of florins. But it could be that he was misleading them.

When Francisco arrived, tired and somewhat muddy, he made that an excuse not to join the proceedings in the great hall. He had no particular taste for that type of affair and was glad to make the need to get out of his mud and traveling clothes an excuse. He needed to talk to Carlo as a matter of some urgency, but that was not going to happen privately at a grand reception. And he'd prefer it if they weren't overheard. He got one of his men to carry the message that he was back to one of Carlo's bodyguards. He did not, despite the temptation, go to bed. He knew Carlo Sforza too well for that.

Sometime after midnight his commander arrived. "Clear the place out," he said to his bodyguard, "and watch the door. Outside. If I need to watch my back with Turner, I'm several years too late about it."

"I might have changed my mind," said Francisco, smiling.

"And you might have stopped running and drinking beer, too. So, to test that, you'd better pour me a tankard and yourself one. It'll help to wash the taste of that load of two-faced crawlers out of my mouth. Have I told you how much I hate courtiers?"

"Not more than five or six hundred times," said Francisco, giving his commander a mug of beer and drawing himself one. "You could purge them and get a better mix, you know. These are mostly still Filippo Maria's cronies and yes-men. Not of much worth."

"Give me time. When I have a little more stability, it'll happen." Sforza took a pull of the beer, sitting down on the table and straightening each leg in turn. "Dress boots. Worthless for campaigning and hell on the feet for standing. So what happened in Florence?"

"Well, Cosimo refused to see me officially, although he was very much more forthcoming in private. But, in short, you should forget marrying Violetta de' Medici. The girl may well be dying, and she's in no state to marry anyone, even if she were willing."

"What has happened to her? She was reported to be in robust health by several of my courtiers, who had seen her at some Soirée in Florence." He paused. "Cosimo is playing both ends against the middle again, is he?"

"I'd say he is genuinely reluctant to go to war."

"That's Cosimo. He'd rather impoverish his enemies. Or appease them."

"Florence is well defended, though. It's wealthy, as I'm sure you saw when you passed through it on your way back from the pilgrimage."

"They were working on some new fortifications back then. I've bought the plans. Some people would sell their own mothers. They're intended to withstand cannon, and might even do it. I've no desire to prove how effective they are, in case the idea spreads."

Carlo Sforza's use of heavy cannon was well known. What was not well known—Sforza and, indeed, Francisco Turner hoped—was that the artillery was successful because it was substantially better than that owned by other states or condottieri. Success was not just because Sforza applied more force and larger numbers than others. Carlo went to some lengths not to make the difference in the quality of his guns or bombardiers obvious.

"So he is reluctant to go to war with us, and we, with him."

"And we will continue, if possible, to let him think he is the one who doesn't want to fight," said Carlo with a wry smile. "So tell me what has happened to Violetta de' Medici. I'd heard she was a fat termagant."

"She's certainly not thin. I can't say much about the termagant part. I don't know if she'll recover. But she's brave enough to take on a snake with a pair of garden shears. Cosimo thinks very highly of her. He values her a great deal."

"She was his mistress?"

"I doubt it. There was genuine affection, Carlo, but I didn't get the feeling of anything more. Not from the responses of the servants or . . . well, anything else. He took me there in person, to see if I could persuade her to change her mind about your proposal. That's not the act of a lover."

"Yes. I will grant you that. I didn't know he'd go that far for my sake."

"A complex man, Cosimo. I think that if he did decide to pursue a war, he would be devious and relentless. And far tougher than most guess. I saw a different side of him that night." Francisco went on to tell his commander as much as possible. "He's also had this plague rumor fed him, by the way. The Church is mixing quite heavily in politics as far as you are concerned."

"Oh, they do, while they pretend not to. I think the Hypatians have decided I'm a bad man, despite spending time and money in their hostels on my way to the Holy Land. And they're in the ascendant at the moment." Sforza sighed. "It would be all very well if the Paulines had not also decided that I was a bad man."

"So: It's not them being right that is a problem, but them both being right at the same time?" said Francisco, pouring more beer.

"Precisely. Now all we need are problems from Venice. Ferrara I have against me just by breathing. Next thing I know, we'll have the Holy Roman Emperor sending troops over the Brenner Pass to kick out the usurper. And given that Eleni Faranese will not be my bride, and Violetta de' Medici is comatose and on death's door, even if she was willing, it'll have to be the bastard daughter. She arrived today."

"Ah. And is she willing?"

"Well, she hasn't treated me like something you'd scrape off the bottom of your boot, this time around. She was wearing enough scent to make my eyes water. I suppose it was always a case of something I would have to put up with, a marriage in name, but I was hoping for something else. Not that the choices sounded much better."

Francisco grinned. "If it leaks out, my friend, that you are a starry-eyed romantic, you'll have even more of the states going to war against you."

"Romance? No, thank you. I once made a fool of myself with a woman, and once is enough for a lifetime. But I'd hoped for someone who would at least be able to make conversation that did not bore me to tears, and make sensible decisions when I was away campaigning. Condescension has never sat too well with me. I've known a few nobles I'd respect: Dell'este, for all that he hates my guts, and some fine soldiers born on the wrong side of the blanket. I'll not hold it against a man, but Lucia's 'I-am-the-duke's-daughter-and-don't-you-forget-it' used to get up my nose and itch. Filippo Maria publically acknowledged that she was his get, but never made any effort to legitimize her, so he didn't think much of her nobility."

"Well, Carlo, it's what choice you have."

"I know. I'll start to take steps tomorrow. And speaking of tomorrow, I must ask you to go to Arsizio. The troops there are afflicted with a flux that makes them near useless for combat, and it keeps coming back. I'll need those men. I'll need them fighting fit, and soon."

That, by the way the thunderheads were piling up, was true. But Francisco had great faith in his commander. As long as Sforza headed them, his mercenary soldiers were worth considerably more than the soldiery of most of the states that opposed them, in skill, experience and loyalty, and his artillery even more so. The reputation of the Wolf of the North had been dented by the Venetians and Ferrara in that attack down the Po, but he had rebuilt it with his men, and, to the limit that he had been allowed, with Milan's enemies.

They might discover that with the Wolf in charge, and not the mercurially moody Filippo Maria Visconti, things were quite different, Francisco thought, with some grim satisfaction, preparing himself to rise early and ride out.

Three days later, having shot a thieving cook and had a new well dug, Francisco got a visit from Carlo Sforza and his personal bodyguard troop. "I thought I'd check on your progress. And tell you the news in person."

They met inside the tent that Turner had set up as his headquarters. He'd had the tent erected in the city's center, in the square that fronted the shrine of Santa Maria di Piazza, as something in the way of a none-too-subtle political statement. Normally, Francisco—like any sensible commander inside a city rather than in the field—would have used a large tavern with good sleeping accommodations for the purpose. But he'd suspected corruption from the beginning and had used the tent to reinforce his image as an untainted outsider.

"I found out that a cook and several of his apprentices were using the old salt meat, and selling the new. I shot him, and hung his apprentices." He gestured with his hand to the open flap of the tent, beyond which could be seen part of the square and one of the arched windows of the shrine. "If you'd gotten here yesterday, you'd have still seen their corpses out there, displayed for the education of the troops."

Sforza nodded approvingly. The Wolf of the North wasn't given to pointless acts of cruelty, but he was no stranger to savage disciplinary methods when he felt they were warranted.

Francisco wrinkled his nose in disgust. "And you should have smelled the well! You couldn't tell it from a sewer, it had gotten so bad. So I had a new one dug some distance from the privies. I think we'll see an improvement in the number of melted entrails."

"Should have forced him to eat his own melted entrails," growled Sforza. "On another subject—I won't be able to give Eleni Faranese to the men for a communal slut, after all."

"Why? Did you find out how much she'd have liked that?"

"Pure rumor, Francisco. No, she's dead, and I am blamed for poisoning her even though I do not and have never resorted to poison. But Umberto sees it as a reason to go to war, and to urge his camp followers to do the same. Oh, and I have become affianced to Lucia del Maino. She deigned to accept my offer, on the condition that her child will be heir to the ducal throne."

"I suppose congratulations are in order," said Francisco.

Sforza snorted. "Yes, it should be a nice little war."

Chapter 14

Venice

Maria had had enough of Venice. She had loved it, once. It had been all she'd known. She could have imagined no greater, better place. And now she was longing for the sight of Pantocrator, the mountain on the north end of Corfu, almost as much as she longed for Benito. The canals stank and La Serenissima left her feeling anything but serene.

She had gone down to the dock to see if there was any news of the Venetian fleet—sometimes coasters would make better time than a laden fleet, especially if they had stopped for repairs. Well, that was the story she told herself. It did happen. And it gave her an excuse to go down to the docks along the Ponto Lungo. She had dressed appropriately, so that they would know she was not a woman going down to the docks, without her own boat, for the reasons they usually did. She'd gone in one of the Montescue gondolas, rowed by a family retainer.

She'd been the very model of decorum and had not taken the oar out of the incompetent fool's hands.

There had been no news in from the fleet, but there had been a vessel loading for Corfu. A good, well-found vessel with a Corfiote captain, who knew who she was. He knew her, she knew him, and she knew his wife and their new babe.

A berth to Corfu was easily arranged. She would get back to the island, back to the Mother's temple, and be there when Benito arrived. She would see him far sooner than waiting for him to come to Venice.

Feeling very pleased for the first time since she had come back from Aidoneus's shadowy kingdom—well, very pleased since the first time she had hugged her daughter after her return—she had to stop herself singing on the way back to *Casa* Montescue. Now she just had to tell Marco and Katerina. They'd fuss, of course, but she and 'Lessi would soon be away.

"Well," she said on her return, finding Marco and Katerina together. "Good news. You will soon be rid of me."

"The fleet has been sighted?" said Marco, with palpable relief. "But you and Benito will be here with us a while yet, with things as unsettled as they are. The Doge will not send Benito away from Venice until...I have said too much, but you may be here for the summer. And we love having you and 'Lessi!"

And it was plainly true that Alessia loved having Marco and Kat. She toddled to them as fast as her fat little legs could carry her, and was now using Marco's elegant slashed breeches to wipe her nose on. "Um, no. I found a captain about to set sail for Corfu. I can meet the fleet there. I...I long to see Benito again." She did, so badly it hurt. "I am sorry, but I—we—must go. My role on Corfu, as I have explained to you a little...is important, too."

"I don't think you can go," said Marco slowly. "Not that I would try to stop you, Maria. But, well, I suggested it to the Doge. Suggested it would be safer for Alessia. He said no."

"I don't see what it has to do with the Doge," said Kat.

"Or how he'd know." Maria felt her anger rising. "It has nothing to do with anyone else. I am my own mistress. I do not take orders."

Marco shook his head. "I would guess the Council of Ten's agents have already reported it, Maria. And please, dear God, you would not be stupid enough to disobey that sort of order. Not from Petro Dorma."

For a moment, she was tempted to tell him there was only one stupid person here, and that was Marco Valdosta. But Marco was not stupid. Blind sometimes to the obvious, but never stupid.

He interrupted her. "A poor choice of words, I am sorry. Not stupid but crazy. And we have enough craziness just with Benito, surely?" he said plaintively. He then hugged Alessia, who snuggled into him, which took the wind right out of her sails.

She shook her head at him. "Marco, you obviously thought it would be good for me to go."

"Yes, not because we don't love you and Alessia, but because I thought it would be safer for her, and make you happier. But when I suggested it, the Doge simply vetoed it out of hand."

"But you won't tell him I am going, will you?" she asked.

Marco sighed. "You do know how to make things difficult, don't you? I am not looking forward to explaining this to him."

"I'll say my farewells here, and leave most of our things with you. We will just need clothing for a couple of weeks' voyage, and you can claim that you knew nothing of it."

"I'm a poor liar," said Marco ruefully, looking at his wife. "And I wouldn't try to lie to Petro Dorma. I've used up my ration of trying to deceive him. But I will not betray you."

Maria did feel faintly guilty, but she thought Marco was taking it all too seriously. After all, Venice would barely notice she wasn't here. She said her farewells and found them tearful, nonetheless. Then she got into a hire boat that she hailed from the water door, refusing Marco's offer of an escort, or sending her with a boatman from the *casa*.

"The less you are seen to have to do with it, the better," she said firmly, playing on his ridiculous fears. The truth was she relished being independent again, even if it cost her money.

"Ponto Lungo, the south end," she said, while making sure Alessia was securely seated. She didn't recognize the boatman, which, she thought, just showed how long she'd been away.

He nodded. "Right, Signora Verrier." Well, he obviously knew who she was. He rowed out skillfully onto the Grand Canal. However, he did not take the San Troverso. Just kept going.

"You've missed the Rio di San Troverso. Where do you think you're going?" asked Maria irritably.

It was broad daylight, there were dozens of other watercraft within fifty cubits and even a bunch of Schioppettieri going the same way in a caorlina about ten yards off. Maria was more irritated than worried. She knew that one did not mess with a boatman on his own vessel by choice, but she'd spent too many years staying on her feet to be any kind of pushover.

"Doge's palace," said the boatman. "Orders from the Signori di Notte."

Maria felt the blood drain from her face. "I get the message. You can just take me back to the *Casa* Montescue."

The boatman shook his head. "I have my orders, Signora."

For a brief, mad moment, Maria considered tipping the *testa di cazzo* into the canal. Or yelling to the Schioppies that she was being molested, and leaving while this bastard explained who he was and why and what he was doing. But then she realized that the Schioppettieri weren't just accidentally going the same way. And neither was the boat on the other flank. They weren't in uniform, but they were just too well fed a set of bullyboys to be anything but enforcers of some kind.

That feeling was confirmed when they escorted her and Alessia, and the boatman, in through a water door into the Doge's palace. No one said anything, not even Alessia, who plainly realized that something was wrong and clung to her. Alessia had gotten rather upset at leaving Uncle Marco and Aunt Kat and all her other friends in the *Casa* Montescue—and everyone, it seemed, was her friend. Except, of course, when they wanted her to do what she didn't, when matters were loudly proclaimed to be otherwise.

Maria was escorted up several flights of stairs, and then into a small empty salon. And there they waited, Maria getting steadily more nervous. It was the silence that made it so alarming.

Of course, Alessia soon got bored and squirmed free and engaged in exploring the high ceilinged room. Maria let her. She traced patterns on the tapestry. And then there was a startled, but very adult curse. Maria stood up hastily, to find her daughter poking a plump little finger through a hole so much part of the pattern that it was very difficult to see. Maria had to smile at the idea that some spy had got a finger in their ear or eye. It served them right.

A few minutes later a footman came in. He bowed perfunctorily and said: "The Doge will see you now."

Maria had little choice but to pick up Alessia and follow him down the passage, past several more footmen, and into another salon which plainly served as a study. She had met the Doge, and knew most people considered that a great privilege, at the great celebration of Katerina's and Marco's wedding. But a private meeting? She knew it had happened to Benito, and Marco—as the Doge's trusted physician—saw him often. But for an ordinary citizen of the Venetian Republic? It was almost unheard of. And she had been doing something he had explicitly forbidden. Yes, she had lived with an ancient god as his bride, met with and found remarkably human Prince Manfred of Brittany and various grandees who had come to Corfu. But...this was Venice, and she was Venetian. The worst part was, she realized, that it had to hurt Marco, because no one would believe he hadn't known.

Petro Dorma was sitting, looking out past San Giorgio Maggiore towards the sea. Calenti coughed. "The Signora Maria Verrier, Your Grace."

The Doge turned slightly to look at her. He did not show any sign of pleasure at seeing her, or utter a word of greeting. Maria curtseyed, bowing her head deeply, wishing she was somewhere else.

The Doge pointed out to sea, at a coaster galley. "That could be your vessel. Her captain claims the ship is going to Istria. She is actually heading for Ancona. Her purpose was to make sure the goods that had been ordered were delivered to the right person."

"What?"

"The goods in question were you and your daughter," said Doge Petro, steepling his fingers. "Did it not occur to you that you would make a very valuable hostage? There has been one attempt already to take the little girl. Did you think that meant that there would never be another? That Corfiote captain showed up just by chance, eager and willing to take you...anywhere you could have asked for? But as you have spoken of going back to Corfu, that would obviously be what was offered. Did not even the fact that he asked for no money up front and less than the normal passage fare strike you as odd?"

Maria blushed to the roots of hair. "I...uh, thought it was out of respect. I don't believe..."

"The Council of Ten's agents are very thorough, Signora. And since that first incident, our watch has trebled. We have intercepted the messages. And we're not your only watchers. Agents of Carlo Sforza saw to it that that vessel would not sail today."

The Doge sighed. "Benito Valdosta is one of our greatest assets, Signora. He has, repeatedly, shown his loyalty and faith in the republic. He has risked his life and well-being for us and, I believe, for you. He trusts us to do our best for his family. He does not fail us, and I will not fail him. If that means putting you in a nunnery or putting you in one of my cells—and I have some well-appointed ones—until Benito gets here, I will do so."

Maria wondered in a moment of anger just how he would

respond to her calling on the power that was hers, through the Mother Goddess, and the Lord of the Dead... and then she realized that she had given that up, when she'd walked away from being the bride of Aidoneus for those four months. And besides, from what she now knew, Venice was the realm of another ancient power, the Lion of Etruria.

"You are a bad man," said Alessia in the silence.

The Doge's mouth twitched, the first sign of any softness Maria on his face. "Yes. I am."

"Tell Marco on you," announced Alessia, looking sternly at him.

"I will be sorry," said the Doge, while Maria tried to hush her. "But this has to be done. Now, I suggest you both go. My officers will see to your safe transportation back to the *Casa* Montescue. Tell Marco and Katerina Valdosta and Lodovico Montescue that I await the pleasure of seeing them this morning."

"They knew nothing of this."

He peered at her from under heavy brows. "Try not to undo the good your daughter has just done you. I understand family loyalty, but stupidity is intolerable. My Lord Calenti, see them out."

He turned back to the window.

Maria was escorted out of the salon, still seething, afraid, and wishing desperately she had not brought trouble to her brother and sister-in-law, the best friends she had in Venice. It was a long and silent trip back to *Casa* Montescue. Well, it would have been, except Alessia was now in the mood for playing; the fact that her mother had much to reflect on was her mother's problem.

She was rather dreading her return to the house, especially having to deliver the Doge's message. She was fairly surprised to find that her return and the summons to the palace were not unexpected. Kat hugged her. "Stop looking so upset. There's not a lot the Doge can do to the Lion's vessel," she said cryptically.

"I've learned enough now, to be very afraid of what he knows and what he can do," said Maria, as her daughter prattled away to Marco. "I'm sorry I even thought of it."

She was left alone with her thoughts and her daughter, as they went off to the palazzo.

Even out on the water in their *felse*, with their own gondolier rowing them along, Marco, Kat and Lodovico kept their conversation casual. Katerina was a little more worried than she let on.

Petro Dorma might not be able to do much about the man who wore the mantle of the Lion—her beloved husband—but he was still a powerful figure in the commerce of the city. The *Casa* Montescue had made some recovery, and looked to make more. But expenses were high, and just a blighting word from Petro Dorma could hurt.

Kat really, really did not want to go back to running secret cargos around Venice at night. True, she sometimes missed the excitement . . . very slightly, on evenings when Marco worked late into the night, or when they had to attend something particularly tedious. But she really did not miss the insecurity and the fear that had always gone with her.

She loved Maria dearly, who'd been a friend when friends were few. Maria had given her a great deal of good advice about Marco—whom she'd known forever—and about children. But she was plainly unhappy in the *casa*. It just wasn't her place, Kat guessed.

They arrived and were conducted in to see the Doge. Marco politely enquired after his health.

"I have been reliably informed that I am a bad man, and that you were going to be informed of the fact," said Petro. "So I imagine my health, or at least my diet, is about to get worse. But otherwise I have no need to see my physician."

"Except to alarm my sister-in-law," said Marco.

"Well, yes. But I did it for good reason, Marco. She very nearly ended up as the 'guest' of Count Andrea Malatesta, which would have annoyed me, your brother, Enrico Dell'este, and quite possibly Carlo Sforza. And they would have been angry with me for failing them. If you could, by those channels you are so carefully not telling me about, tell Sforza that I do not appreciate his spies taking direct action in my territory. Informing my men is all very well, but they overstepped the mark."

"What did they do?"

"Drilled several holes below the waterline of the galley. That part of the port will now be out of action for several days until we get the boat lifted." The Doge did not sound particularly displeased. "I'm tempted to have them ornament my interrogation chambers. The Council of Ten are mostly in favor of having them found floating facedown in the back canals, along with the captain of the galley, except that they mostly seem to be here to watch your niece."

"I suspect that didn't help the captain of that galley," said Lodovico dryly.

"Your years of experience have not misled you," said Petro Dorma. "Now, I wish you all to understand that Maria and the little girl are not to leave Venice. Not without going as part of the whole fleet, not without my consent. I expect to be informed of any attempt at such folly. I expect you to tell me if it is contemplated. Family considerations aside, there are things afoot that make her and the little one valuable hostages. You will tell her this is what you are constrained to. I do not think she will ask it of you again, but you are watched. I would like your word on this."

They all gave it. What else could they do?

Petro smiled. "As I said, we are watching. After last time... anyway, actually Marco, I asked you to come to see me because I have a request from... a very powerful person for your medical skill. You were recommended by the man you called in to help me when I was poisoned. Francisco Turner thinks if anyone in all Italy can do anything for the young woman it will be you."

"Oh. Of course, if I can help, I will. Although Francisco flatters me. He knows so much more..."

"He seems to think it goes beyond mere knowledge. He says you have a healing touch that he does not."

"Just what I have always said," said Lodovico, with satisfaction. "I liked that man, for all that he was a bit rough and ready, plainly spoken, and liked beer."

The Doge nodded. "A testimony of some worth that, Lodovico Montescue. But I would be very obliged if you would give this woman your especial care, Marco. Usually one ends up owing Cosimo de' Medici. It would be good for Venice if the boot was on the other foot."

"Who is the patient, where are they, and what is wrong with them?"

"It is the Lady Violetta de' Medici, Cosimo's second cousin. My men have carried her into chambers on the northern side of the building, as she arrived by boat this morning. I believe she was bitten by a serpent, but her majordomo will tell you more and provide you with a letter from Francisco Turner. I would like to know just what he achieved in Florence, as I was under the impression he'd failed to meet with Cosimo, and had left in a high dudgeon, information which it would seem was...misleading. The young woman in question is, as you may know, one of the closer female legitimate blood relations to the late and unlamented Filippo Maria Visconti. There are only two others closer, and the one is somewhat disqualified by being an illegitimate daughter, and the other is, according to my messengers last night, dead."

"Someone is doing all they can to deprive Carlo Sforza of the fig leaf of legitimate rule. I would be guarding that bastard daughter very closely."

"I sent a message, indicating that I thought that would be wise," murmured Petro Dorma, as if talking about the weather. "I should imagine that it hasn't passed him by, though. On the other hand, Sforza had been refused—rather pointedly—by the woman who died. He is being blamed for poisoning her. And I gather the duke of Parma and his allies—who just happen to include the person who ordered Maria and her daughter kidnapped—now go to war over this matter."

"If you don't mind, I think I had better go and see the patient," said Marco. "The sooner the better."

"Of course," said the Doge. He tingled a bell. "Barossa will take you down to her immediately."

Katerina had to smile to herself. The Doge might rule Venice, but when it came to the sick, it would seem nothing could stand in Marco's way, and it would seem even the Doge knew it. Marco was meek and mild most of the time, but every now and then the Lion in him was very visible.

"Interesting times," said Lodovico, with the relish of a Venetian for intrigue and politics.

Kat could swear she'd felt her baby move in her belly. She had no appetite for interesting intrigue at all, as Marco took his leave of them.

Petro looked at her. "Now, while I do my best not to be overlooked or overheard, I will speak somewhat cryptically here. Some of your old connections from harder times have been engaged in trafficking information. Word of Maria's unhappiness and her desire to return to a...religious sphere of influence she holds on Corfu had leaked that way, I believe, from what my informant in Andrea Malatesta's court tells me. I don't actually know the precise source. I would hate to ruin Venice's reputation for tolerance. Perhaps you should go shopping, my dear, and leave old

Lodovico and me to talk. Lord Calenti will provide you with an escort. I suggest you use your family gondola, I will have the others conveyed home in my vessels."

Kat knew what she was being asked to do, and where she would go on the Campo Ghetto, after a number of other stops, and with a few more after that. Also, she knew her grandfather well, better than Marco. As the interview was going on, she'd realized that of the three of them, he was the one with the most reason to be nervous but had not been. It was probable that the Council of Ten's spies had ferreted out a great deal of this plan. It was likely that Sforza's men had sunk the boat. And extremely likely that her grandfather had sent one of his old friends on the Council of Ten word of Maria's intention. He had made no promise not to tell, and had apparently not been privy to all of it, or was not paying that much attention. Ha, when he was obviously not attending, *then* you had to be wary.

Lord Calenti, that sinister devoted servant of the state, had an unobtrusive footman for her and, thoughtfully, a bag of coins. "It's unlikely that you would have brought much with you. One does not always wish to leave traces of debts behind."

Kat wondered just how much he knew of her past dark-night delivery of gray goods to the *stregheria* and other magic workers of the city, who did not like to advertise their purchases or leave traces of them either. "I suppose if I am doing Venice's business, I may as well spend her coin."

"Precisely," said the spymaster, giving one of his reputedly rarer-than-diamond smiles. "A little pleasure will make it look like it is not just a cover."

And will, no doubt, get various businesses, silver- and gold-smiths and a few cloth merchants onto a list they'd rather not be on. *Even if their noses are clean*, thought Kat, making a mental list of a few that had, in prior years, given *Casa* Montescue no reason to love them. It was an odd wheel, but it turned.

She spent quite a lot of silver and some gold, and made the footman work, carrying parcels and boxes, before arriving at the goldsmith in the Campo Ghetto. She'd already made it clear to Calenti's man, in their visits to several other establishments, that his job was to stand near the door, out of easy earshot, and make sure that Katerina was not overheard. She had several other people to visit but the old Jew had been a friend and a major contact in her trafficking days, and had passed information to the Doge via Marco before. He was, she was aware, a Cabbalist, and had some magical skills with precious metals.

The goldsmith's shop was just as tiny as Kat remembered; and, as she always had in previous visits, she wondered how the old man could get any work done in such tight quarters—or, for that matter, where he had sufficient space to hold his tools and supplies. Granted, gold and the other metals he worked with were not bulky.

His appearance hadn't changed much either, if at all. He was wearing a wool black-and-white tallit katan, a fringed garment designed rather like an Incan-style poncho. The distinctive knotted fringes called tzitzit were attached to the garment's four corners. It was a style of dress favored by particularly devout Jews—or, Kat suspected, by Jews trying to avoid the attention of Venice's sometimes-overbearing rabbinate.

She was pretty sure this goldsmith fell into the latter category. At least, the cheery twinkle he usually had in his eyes didn't seem to fit very well with a man pondering the miseries of the world.

There wasn't a twinkle in his eye today, though. In fact, he seemed quite worried. Before she could even start, he said: "I've been wanting to pass word to the Council of Ten from the *stregheria*. Some of the *stregheria* I know ... they dabble in foretelling. Some even get things right. And three of them have gone mad in the last few weeks. I got to talk to Donatzio before he slipped away. He said something about seas of dead bodies. And the Serpent ... and that was all. But the talk is going around. A few people are leaving, quietly."

"Well, I have something for you to pass on to them, from the Council of Ten, and unless they want to leave Venice fast, something needs to be done." She explained how news of Maria's desire to get back to Corfu and to the shrine of the Mother Goddess had been reported to Count Andrea Malatesta, and what had nearly happened as a result. "The Doge said he would hate to ruin Venice's reputation for tolerance. Read that as a warning to find the informant and deal with them, Itzaak."

The old man nodded. "I like it here. I want to stay, to call this home. And"—he gave a little smile—"I would think the *stregheria* want Benito Valdosta hunting them even less than the Council of Ten."

"If Maria or, heaven help anyone, Alessia got hurt, I would think you might have Marco after you, too. And that could just be worse, Itzaak."

"We know that," said the old man. "Trust me, we know that. For those of us who work with things not of this world, we'd far rather take on Benito and the Council of Ten's agents than the Lion."

Two days later, Marco, on his way into the palace to see his new patient, was met in one of the passages by Lord Calenti. "Please tell your wife that her little shopping spree was successful. The Schioppettieri fished a body out of the canal this morning, with a message pinned on it. It said: *this one will not be sending messages to Ancona again.* The woman was a fertility charm seller. Perhaps she had a grudge against Maria Verrier for that reason."

"Oh. Kat did say something about it. I'm sorry, I have been so deep in research. This snake bite..."

"How does your patient do?" Lord Calenti inquired politely.

"She isn't dying," said Marco, grimacing. "Her swallowing reflex seems to work. But if the poison of the snake does not kill her, the poison from the hemorrhages it has caused may. She was fortunate it happened to bite her on the thigh, where she has plenty of flesh. If it had been a hand, the swelling might have been too much for the circulation. She's fighting for her life. I've had to open and drain several of the pustules. She has messy, pussy sepsis."

He saw the spymaster was looking faintly green, and stopped there. It was strange that a man who had without doubt ordered deaths and torture, and quite possibly done and overseen them, should be affected thus. So he said no more and went on to the room when the man and woman chosen from among the Doge's staff were busy changing her sheets again. It was a job they'd done a number of times already and doubtless would many times again. He checked Violetta's pulse, temperature, the circulation in her limbs, and the state of the necrosis around the bite. That had, at least, not become any worse, although it was still weeping and the dressing would need changing soon. The circulation in her right leg—the bitten one—was poor, so he set about gently massaging it while trying to decide if anything else should be done.

The problem was that he was on unknown ground. Francisco

had carefully described the purple-black snake, and even sketched it in the letter he had sent. He hadn't recognized it though, and neither had anyone else that Marco had shown it to. Something about it made his flesh crawl, and the part of him that was the Lion even felt the drawing as of something evil. He wondered, not for the first time, if it was actually just a snake, or something magical. But that was a more difficult question still, and he had no one really to ask. He'd searched the Doge's library, and at the Academia. He'd finally asked Professor Balti to find him two dedicated but poor students that he could pay to go on searching, as he really did not like to leave his patient for too long. He knew liquids had to keep going into her or she would die, but these had to be carefully administered, a sop at a time, or they would end up in her lungs.

If she lived, it would be a good thing she'd been a fat girl, he reflected, because broth was the most they'd been able to give her.

The little majordomo who had accompanied her came to him while he was busy dealing with the wound, which had grown into a necrotic hole. If she recovered, she would have bad scarring on that leg. He just hoped it would not affect the bone.

The majordomo did not interrupt Marco, but watched patiently. Eventually Marco paused and asked what he wanted. He bowed. "My lord. Is there any news I can send to my master? I have just received another message from him asking how she goes on."

"Not right now. Let me finish here and I will see what I can say. I'll have you called," said Marco tiredly, also thinking that it might take a little consultation with Petro Dorma on how best to phrase what wasn't a particularly happy state of affairs.

The man nodded. "I will write at least what I have seen your lordship doing, the hours you work and the goodness of your helpers."

Well, that was a start. And fair.

Chapter 15

The Holy Roman Empire

Count Mindaug was enjoying the mild spring in the Marches as they made their way west into forest country, avoiding Vienna, and then onward into an area of extensive apple orchards, all in blossom. Many of the blossoms were still pink, but most were starting to shade into white. In places, the trees were so plentiful that the entire landscape seemed to consist of huge pink and white mounds.

There were many vineyards, especially on the hillsides. On several occasions they also passed by patches where asparagus was being grown. Mindaug had a great liking for the vegetables and was sorely tempted to have Emma and Tamas pluck some for him. But there was always the risk of arousing the ire of a local farmer with that sort of petty thievery. Mindaug wasn't afraid of farmers, of course, but a confrontation that escalated too far or too badly might draw the attention of those he did need to be wary of. So, with some regret, he resigned himself to an asparagus-free diet, at least until such time as he might be able to purchase some in a market.

For the count, it was … an odd time. For the first time in his adult life, he was not in service or hastening to be in service to a master of magical and state power. He'd begun that journey as a boy of eleven. He was now fifty-six. He felt as he imagined an old war-horse put out to pasture might.

In a while, he might yearn for the use of power and long for the intrigues which had been a normal part of his life. In a while, he might want a suitable palace, or at least a noble residence. He might yearn for the company of other nobles...perhaps.

But right now, he desired none of that, and they had no idea that he was even still alive. He was free to enjoy things he had never dreamed of even wanting to enjoy. To look at the sights and to eat well. Yes, home was merely a traveling wagon and his bed a straw pallet. But the weight that had lifted from his shoulders made it all seem good. And, by comparison, the country was safe, fat and prosperous. His new servants fussed over him as if he were a precious chick. He found that very strange and not a little amusing. They, it seemed, were terrified by the idea of being masterless. They'd fled not to be freemen but because Emma was afraid of being made the concubine of their overlord, and her lover was jealous.

They'd had no idea that life could be better and would have been terrified to go and look for that small degree of greater comfort, more food, or more rest. But having a master, who, by the standards they were used to, was almost ridiculously generous and soft, was their ideal. Somehow they'd hooked onto the idea that they had to show him they appreciated his kindness—which was purely accidental on his part. For the count, the instruction of servants had been for those who oversaw servants. It appeared those people were somewhat harsher than he was. He had never done any personal disciplining of lazy or recalcitrant servants himself. That had fallen to his underlings.

Only there were none, now.

It worked well, at least for the moment. Tamas and Emma could not imagine braving this big world without a master to protect them, and yet they thought of him as in need of protection from it. The count had long gotten used to the idea of letting Emma chaffer for their food. She loved doing this, considered it a vast privilege and actually had some idea of what they needed, once he had persuaded her that they could eat as if every day was what to her was a once-a-year feast day.

They were neither of them stupid, just ignorant. They were painfully honest and deeply religious. The two of them spoke in their own Hungarian bastardized with a fair bit of Frankish that had crept across the borders, and had proved very adept at rapidly picking up enough words to communicate with others of their own order. It still kept them from becoming too familiar with the locals. Mindaug himself, of course, spoke fluent Court

Frankish. What he hadn't been prepared for was that local dialects could be almost incomprehensible, especially coming from the peasantry. Sometimes Emma and Tama understood the ditchdiggers and wood carriers better than he did.

They crossed the Danube at the toll station at Muthusen. It was the first substantial town they'd stopped in, having skirted all the others—there were always tracks and long ways around everywhere, if you had strong horses and some patience. And the count wasn't going anywhere, so he was happy to be patient. By now, the count felt he'd avoided the suspicious scrutiny given to strangers close to the borderland and, this deep into the empire, could go into the market town with some impunity.

It was a market town and it was a market day, to the vast excitement of Tamas and Emma. Mindaug had to admit he found it quite entertaining himself. There was music, some dancing. A traveling troupe of actors with a stage-wagon were doing a series of religious tableaux. And, of course, there was drinking, bawds and bullies, as well as stalls offering food and various goods, medicines, charms, saints' relics...all being hawked at the top of the stall-holder's voices.

"Best put your money safely, master. Or keep it in your hand," said Tamas, big-eyed at the scale of it all. "I've heard such places are full of cutpurses."

To the count, it was a small country-town market, but to them, something vast. And it probably did have at least three cutpurses, reflected Mindaug. No one had ever dared to try to rob him. There was a place in the wagon intended for safe-keeping and the bulk of the remainder of his gold was there, in a small kist that would kill anyone unwary enough to open it. Both had their protections, but he had some coin in his pouch. He took out a piece of silver. At such a fair they probably could not care what face there was stamped on it.

He handed it to Tamas. "Get provisions. I'd like another ham, Emma. And get yourselves some more clothes." He realized he had no real idea of the cost of those and took out a second silver coin. "For the clothes. Hold on to them tightly," he said with some amusement. "I will take a walk around."

They looked at the coins, no longer in shock at being entrusted with what to them was a lot of money, but still plainly delighted. And then Tamas shook his head. "Emma and I will watch the wagon, master. I know places like this are not safe for a woman alone. And if we leave the wagon untended, it will be robbed."

That would have fatal consequences. Count Mindaug did not mind the deaths, but he could do without the fuss and notice that it might cause. He did notice that other wagons had some kind of watcher, so this probably wasn't mere peasant foolishness. But he wasn't interested in chaffering for ham, beer, bread or clothes for his servants, who looked a little too much like runaway serfs—and very poor ones, by the Empire's standards. The peasantry were plainly wealthier here than in Hungary or Lithuania.

"You go and buy. I will remain here." He was not being generous, just not wishing to shop for the sort of wares a country fair might offer, and not that interested. As usual, Emma and Tamas concluded he was the kindest of masters and probably due for sainthood, which seemed vastly unlikely to Kazimierz Mindaug.

"Oh, we couldn't go first, master. You go, we will watch the wagon, water the horses and give them some oats." They did, it was true, consider giving the horses oats a treat, only for the steeds of the nobility, and thus terribly exciting to do for horses that would draw the wagon, but it was a frequent pleasure, unlike the fair.

Mindaug went, even though taking it in turns was not what he had meant. Perhaps they would sleep in an inn tonight. He roamed the fair, which was set on the town green, amused by the quaint charms being sold—the misspelling and ignorance on the cantrip scrolls were truly startling. There were a handful of books for sale. A juggler was performing some tricks which the audience suspected of being magic, and Mindaug knew were not. He decided to get himself a mug of hot spiced wine, and returned to the wagon . . . only to find that his pouch had been slit.

His first reaction was a dangerous fury that they dared do something like this. He'd turn those coins to scorpions . . . and melt their entrails for daring to take his money. He could put a tracing spell . . .

He shook his head. Folly. Not worth it for a few coins. He was still angry, but on further thought it did tell him something good and valuable: he had successfully posed as what he was supposed to be. No thief would have dared touch a magician's pouch, let alone the pouch of a noble of high degree who was also a master magician who could inflict a torturous death on them. Theft was something the lesser orders were prey to. They could, he thought irritably to himself, now that his own funds were somewhat more limited, less afford it.

So he went back to the wagon and sent the other two off, with no more than a warning to hold tight to their money and to stay together. He was still somewhat annoyed. While camouflage was all very well, some respect and the protection that gave were going to be necessary. And he would, in a few months, need to find a protector, or at least a source of income.

His thoughts were interrupted by a loud belch from the man who had just walked up to his cart, which occupied the space next to the count's wagon. The fellow had his charm cantrips over his arm, and a mug of beer in his hand. He flicked a small copper coin to the urchin who had been sitting on one of the poles of his cart, drained his beer, and set the charms in his cart, before turning to go and unhitch his scrawny horse tied to a post some yards off. Mindaug noted his pouch bulged. The fellow gave the count a wave, and out of professional interest, Mindaug walked across to help him harness up the horse. Not that he knew much about harnessing horses, but possibly more than the fellow knew about writing spells. That would not be hard.

"I won't help you kill your wife. Or your mother-in-law. And I'm all out of love philtres," said the fellow cheerfully.

"I have no real need of those," said Mindaug. He hoped the scorn didn't show. "So this is regular business of yours? Do people often ask you to kill someone?"

"Oh, all the time. Don't go there. The Church will get onto you before you can say 'Emperor Charles Fredrik.' Where are you from, fellow?"

"I am from Bohemia. My mother was Hungarian."

"Ah. And you have come down in the world, have you?"

He was fishing. Mindaug's barriers rose...and were dispelled. "I can tell your fortune for you. My magical arts can show what the future holds," said the mountebank. "The past and future are an open book to me. I know you were born to wealth."

My accent betrays me, thought Count Mindaug, knowing he'd have to do something about that. He chose to ignore the offer, and instead passed the strap to the man. "Your accent is not from here, either," he said calmly.

"I come from sunny Italy, my friend. Where I will be again before the bitter winter bites here. Now that Duke Visconti is dead, I'm for Milan. They say that the new Protector is not hiring magicians."

"This is different?" asked the count.

"Visconti was too busy hanging or burning any he found to be not hiring." The fellow, realizing he did not have a customer, got into the cart and took the reins. "Farewell. I want to make the real city by nightfall. Linz calls. There's profit in these small towns but the city is the place for me."

Count Mindaug let him go and went back to the wagon with some food for thought. It seemed that he might find employment in Milan. If a mountebank and charlatan could fill his purse, well...he could be a far more effective mountebank. He could, without resorting to real magic, fool a more intelligent audience than this. And so...the Church did watch but tolerated these frauds? There were obviously lines not to cross and he would have to establish where those were. Spying magically on the Empire, and reading about it—those did not add up to the same thing as being here.

Emma and Tamas returned, loaded with purchases and small change they punctiliously returned—which they expected him to inspect and assumed he would know how well they had done. They were excited by the shows and the music, disgusted by the prices, and amazed at the variety. Well, they'd see a bigger city in Salzburg before they traveled on to Linz and then Italy.

The naturally frugal Emma had, of course, not wasted money on made clothes. The idea seemed to shock her when her master mentioned it. "Oh, no! They were far too expensive, master. And not well made." She could, like any peasant, sew, and better than most, it appeared. She had bought cloth and sewed for herself and Tamas, and shyly presented him with a fresh shirt of finer linen than the wool she had bought for their clothing, about which she had obviously labored with especial care. He'd have to actually make sure tailored clothes were included in her next purchase, as he planned to move up the social scale in his disguise, and thus his servants would have to do likewise.

She was furious with the town of Muthusen, its inhabitants, and the Franks in general when he asked her to repair his slit pouch. It was a good thing she had no magical skills, or they'd be suffering with everything from scales to boils.

❄   ❄   ❄

Archimandrite Klaus von Stebbens knew just what a high responsibility the Knights of the Holy Trinity, and indeed the Emperor, had laid like a cross upon his shoulders, to follow such a one as Count Mindaug. The man was a monster and an associate of monsters. A killer. Someone who should be destroyed without compunction and with all the haste possible. At all costs, his evil designs had to be thwarted.

They watched Mindaug both magically and physically. Von Stebbens had a number of men with his troop who had been poachers, and one who had missed his ship home to Vinland. He was a man of one of the forest tribes there and could track a ghost, or sneak up on a rabbit and cut its throat.

And, so far, the count had given them a very pleasant holiday and had engaged in precisely no magical activity, nor committed any of the habitual brutality he was expected to. It could be that he was trying to hide. It could also be, as Abbot Goldenbuss had theorized, that he had no idea that his cargo of books made him very easy to track magically, even if he was lost in their distant view. Mindaug might well have become so accustomed to the evil aura of some of those tomes that he didn't realize that, for some magicians, they were like so many beacons in the night.

They thought they'd found out what he was up to at last, when he had headed for the round pyramid deep in the forest between Zwettl and Gross-Gerungs. But he had driven straight past the track to the witch place as if he hadn't even known it was there.

They had tried to investigate his two assistants. So far, either they were innocent dupes or mere servants—which seemed unlikely on the face of it. Klaus had nearly fallen over backward, though, when he was told the young man and woman had gone into a small church in the hamlet of Waldenberg and asked the priest if he could marry them. The priest had wanted them to wait until he could announce their names before mass to ask if there was any impediment to their marriage. The girl had burst into tears and said their master could not be kept waiting.

The priest had heard their confessions, though. And was being obstinate about the sanctity of that confession. The archimandrite had to respect that, but surely... he had sent a letter to the bishop, asking for his help. He hoped it would be forthcoming.

But the very fact that someone as evil as Mindaug could have associates who would willingly enter a church and confess...was simply hard to grasp.

Von Stebbens's troop followed and watched at Muthusen. As a matter of course, they'd taken into custody a charm-seller from Italy, who had had words with Mindaug. The charm-seller's pouch had revealed more money than was remotely plausible and some of it Hungarian gold thalers. Count Mindaug had spent a little time in the man's stall, looking at the wares. It had not been obvious how they had known the other would be there, or what had happened or been passed, but Klaus intended to find out. The reputation of the Knights of the Holy Trinity helped to open reluctant mouths. The charm-seller nearly melted with terror when the archimandrite, in the full spiky armor of the order, walked into the cell where he was being held, followed by two other burly knights in the same garb.

"I didn't know! How was I to know? I would never steal from the Knot...uh, the great Knights of the Holy Trinity," the fellow burst out before Klaus could say anything.

"You stole from us?" *What?* wondered Von Stebbens. Some precious relic that Mindaug had come to fetch? There were traps ready to try and prevent him escaping magically.

"Yes, but I didn't know. He just looked like a rich merchant or a noble's by-blow. How was I to know? You've got it all back." The man was almost blubbering now.

"What did you steal? Tell me everything," said Von Stebbens relentlessly. The answer had to be here.

The man was either the best actor in the world or genuinely dumbfounded by the question. "His money. He was so green that he looked at the sackbut when Malky played the blast. I gave him one thaler."

The certainty with which the archimandrite had approached the prisoner was now in tatters. Malky, it turned out, was a sackbut player with whom the charm-seller had a regular arrangement, when they were at fairs together. When the charm-seller had a fat mark, he would signal the sackbut player, who would let loose a mighty noise, and in the distraction, the charm-seller would slit the pouch and later give a small cut to the musician.

It seemed too much of a story just have been made up on the spur of a terrified moment. But the archimandrite was a thorough man. He sent two knights to find the local magistrate and track down a sackbut player called Malky. And then he asked what exactly had passed between Count Mindaug and the charm-seller.

The charm-seller told him. "I didn't have a chance, straight off to see what I got, just pushed it in my pouch...as soon as I looked...I went to get a beer to celebrate, and only then I saw the gold. I knew I had to get out of there. It was too much money! He had to be a wealthy powerful man. I gave Malky a coin, and grabbed my wares and got out of there. And there was the mark sitting on a wagon bar, next to my cart, not guessing a thing. He even helped me get my horse. I told him I was going to Linz and then back to Italy. I even offered to tell him his fortune, since I wanted to find out where he was going. He said his mother was Hungarian but that he came from Bohemia."

"So you are asking me to believe you stole from one of the most powerful and deadly magicians in Europe. And that he did not take revenge?" asked the archimandrite, with a disbelieving snort. "Steubel. Just on the off chance that he isn't lying to me, you had better have that money placed in a suitably consecrated and protected spot, and have all those who have touched it bound in rites of protection. Heaven alone knows what sort of magic he'll use, but it's bound to be nasty."

The prisoner, already pale, turned sheet-white and started weeping.

It did not take long to find the sackbut player who was nearly blind drunk on his sudden windfall. He rapidly confessed his role in the thefts when he realized what trouble he was in. It also transpired that the charm-seller had been up before the local magistrate before for theft, and had managed to not be convicted...but he was still suspected.

The archimandrite went back to the charm-seller. "Never before has a man been so lucky to end up just imprisoned for theft," he informed him. Personally he found the so-called charms, all scrawled with badly penned useless doggerel just as much of an affront. There were signs there that the fellow had tried to dabble in more knowledge, some of it of questionable virtue, and even failed at that. And yet the gullible had bought his wares, and probably derived comfort from them.

They were no closer to finding out just what Kazimierz Mindaug was up to, or who his associates in the Empire were. The situation did not improve when, with the local bishop—a stout

Pauline cleric—they reinterrogated the priest from the church Mindaug's servants had entered.

The priest was an elderly man of military bearing, which the Knights who had questioned him earlier had not told Klaus von Stebbens. One look told the archimandrite that he and the bishop were wasting their time. He did a little polite asking and was not surprised to find that he was correct. This was a man who had served in a mercenary company, found God, and had used the money he'd accumulated to study and enter the priesthood. Eventually, he'd ended up in a quiet country parish.

Klaus told him of the manner of man they were following, of the fact that he was a foe who would send his little congregation screaming to their deaths...and got exactly what he expected. A shake of the head.

"That may be, but the two servants spoke only kindness of their master. And their sins were sins of little people, my lord. I know those, I know how to read the truth, and the omissions of parts of the story. I have dealt with peasants like them for many years now. They made full confession, and I had no difficulty in granting them God's forgiveness. I only wish I had defied my bishop," he inclined his head to that man, "and married them, then and there. I will not betray their small sins to you, or what they said to me. That is between them and God now. You can ask them or God, but you will get no answer from me. You or I might easily have done the same, or worse. I see no need, or gain, in breaking my vows to tell you."

The bishop tried, but failed. Klaus von Stebbens did not. One did not batter oneself to death against a rock. And he had learned a little more. Mindaug, who was one step from Satan, had possibly outsmarted them by employing young innocents who were not of his kind. No matter. They would see, or be shown, the evil of his ways. Or fall into the pit with him.

When Mindaug turned south at Salzburg, the archimandrite sent hasty messages to his archbishop and also to Mainz. Surely the man would not be allowed to leave the empire for Italy? Tracking him would be much harder in foreign territories.

Somewhat reluctantly, Von Stebbens decided he had no choice but to employ the services of the monk which had been offered to him by the man's order. Reluctant, because the order in question was the Aemilines, who had no official ties to either of the great factions of the Church, but clearly leaned more toward the Peterines than the Paulines to whom the Knights of the Holy Trinity adhered.

Healers, for the most part, as had been the martyred saint from whom they took their name. But some of them also practiced a sort of quiet magic, with which they communed with the spirits of wild animals. Small and timid animals, as a rule, since they favored such.

Still, by all accounts the archimandrite had heard, such an Aemiline sage could perhaps track Mindaug where the Knights themselves could not.

It was worth a try. "Send for that monk," he ordered one of his subordinates. "The hesychast the Aemilines offered us. I've forgotten his name."

"Brother Dimitrios."

"Yes, him. We need him as soon as possible."

Chapter 16

The Duchy of Milan

Carlo Sforza rose in the predawn, as was his custom and, with his usual troop, exercised his horses. It was as much a habit with him as Francisco's running was. He knew that patterns got one killed and to that end he at least varied what he rode, where he rode and the precise time he was out for, or would start. The troop varied somewhat, from day to day. But they were all veterans, all men who felt a personal loyalty to him.

The ride was his thinking time. One did not talk to the commander when he was taking his ride. Carlo was glad of the silence, because he had a fair bit on his mind. He had taken the step to depose Filippo Maria Visconti for one simple, clear-cut reason: he had held a small child in his arms briefly. She had trusted him, knowing, heaven knew how or why, that she could. Generally, Sforza did not regard himself as an emotional man. He did not let his heart rule his head. When he'd been younger, he'd made that mistake once with Lorendana, Duke Enrico Dell'este's daughter and another man's wife. And when he'd found out eventually that she'd wanted him not for himself but for her damned Montagnard cause, he'd been nearly as angry as when he'd found out that the duke of Milan had dared to have his granddaughter, that child that had held onto him and trusted him, kidnapped.

I must be getting old, he thought irritably. Benito . . . he'd established, could look after himself. He was oddly proud of the boy. He had kept an eye and ear on his career. Sforza had accepted that the boy might come to kill him one day, and that that would be a bitter fight. But Visconti had dared to step on ground that was not to be touched. And, worse, he had tried to make Carlo Sforza appear to be the perpetrator.

For that threat, there was only one possible response from Carlo Sforza. Killing Filippo Maria without resorting to mere open warfare, when the worm could have slipped away, had meant taking over the Duchy of Milan.

The problem was that having ridden the beast, now that he was in the saddle, there was no safe way off. Not for him or his officers anyway and, quite possibly, for many of his men. They were loyal to him, and he was loyal to them. A marriage to one of the female heirs seemed to be the answer.

Then last night, he had received a letter from none other than Doge Petro Dorma. Venice was one of the few states to send an ambassador to the court of the new Protector of Milan, a gesture of appreciation for giving the Venetian Republic the man who had nearly succeeded in killing the Doge. It was a step of unusual generosity, as Sforza had been the condottiere in several wars which had eaten Venetian territory, and had been en route to destroy her, at his master's bequest, when Dell'este had stopped his barges on the Po, and neatly ambushed and entrapped him.

The letter had informed Carlo that Venice had been asked to join an alliance against him and offered as its share of the possible spoils a great deal of territory to the east of the Po. It pointed out—as only a Venetian could—that someone had plainly set out to see that his plan to legitimize his rule by marrying a Visconti heir was being sabotaged by killing the possible contenders, and begged him to take extra care with Lucia del Maino's welfare, lest she become the next victim.

That just hadn't occurred to Sforza. He detested poison and poisoners. Francisco had seen the dead snake and believed that it had bitten them. He'd sent a message to Cosimo to that effect. Viewed that way, the killings were entirely logical, and indeed, he'd immediately put Lucia under a far heavier spy watch and guard. And the marriage would have to be rushed along. That would give the states who were less willing and eager to engage in battle with him more reason not to. Without Venice and Florence, and with Dell'este away, he could deal with the rest, probably.

But then there had been the message from his two men

engaged to keep an eye on his granddaughter. They'd be well rewarded for their actions, but it was true that his being Protector of Milan had not made them leave her alone. Well, it was likely Venice's Council of Ten, who liked assassination, would have delivered "messages" to those involved. But he must see if the Venetians would also tell him who had been behind it. His messages tended to be louder, with cannon fire for percussion.

Sforza. Bah. I really do despise him more with every moment that I have to deal with him, thought Lucia. His proposal—if you could call it that—had been as brutish as his nature. Only the fact that it handed her, finally, the key to her inheritance, that which was hers by right, had stopped her schooling him appropriately.

And then suddenly his soldiers were on guard at her door, his bodyguards were checking her food, and even her apartments. As if he owned her!

There will be those who will try to kill you. They always do, whispered the asp. *I can keep you safe from poisons, but not from the knife.*

"I've no objection to suitable guards but some of these have not shaved. And they have no idea of the deference I am due." She knew she was being petulant. But that, too, was her right.

They will learn. Later, said the asp in a whisper as old and dry as the legendary tombs in Egypt, from whence, it said, it had been drawn.

"He wishes to send messages to the noble houses, which could take months, and then there will be the ceremony with pomp and display. And much as I would like them to see me finally take my place"—there had been all the small slights over the years at court, especially as her father simply had not provided enough for them to dress as if they were really equals—"I am more than three months pregnant. Can you delay that, too?"

A little, said the asp. *The unborn will take the milk of the serpent from your blood. That will slow its development.*

"The milk of the serpent from my blood?"

As is suckled from the breast of adders. Hist. Sforza comes.

He entered her chambers with, to her disapproval, two of his men. He bowed. "My affianced wife. How do you do this day?"

"Very well." Actually, she was feeling nauseous, but that was not for him to know.

"I have had a disturbing communication from Petro Dorma, in Venice, which was why I set extra guards on your door last night, and had my personal taster attend you breaking your fast." He grimaced. "Spies and poisons. What I like least about the noble houses of Italy."

He would doubtless prefer force. He lacked finesse of any sort. But all she said, while idly waving her fan to hide her mouth, lest the expression show was: "And what did the Doge say to cause this alarm?"

"Ah." He paused as if struck suddenly by something, then shrugged. "This is a little awkward, but I must be direct. After all, you will have to deal with my bluntness in our marriage. As you may know, there were three female relations of Filippo Maria Visconti, all with some claim to the Visconti lands."

She lifted her chin slightly. "I am aware," she said coolly. He could have allowed a tissue of illusion. By blood, hers was by far the strongest claim.

"What you don't know, and I was unaware of until Dorma pointed it out, is that someone or some persons, seeking to prosecute war against me and to dismember and spoil the Duchy of Milan, has killed one of those women, Eleni Faranese. The duke of Parma has blamed me and foolishly seeks to engage in war as a result. One of my captains, Francisco Turner, was able to intervene in the incident in which both Violetta de' Medici and her mother were apparently bitten by a snake. The dead snake was even provided, but I suspect that a poisoned stiletto was really used."

Lucia wanted to know just exactly what this Turner had been doing there, to foil the great serpent. But then...the killing had not actually been necessary. He had asked her, after all. "Did neither woman see the attacker?"

"Neither were conscious when Francisco got there. He was too occupied in trying to save them to follow it up properly, for which I don't blame him. The mother died, and the girl, well, Francisco holds her chances of recovery as not very high."

She will die, whispered the asp in her bosom. *Nothing lives through the poison of the great serpent, unless the serpent wills it...and even then, they live but for a while.*

"I see," said Lucia.

"As Francisco, and Cosimo de' Medici did, I blamed it on an accident, a snake in the garden, which could possibly happen.

It took our Venetian friends—whose Council of Ten are all too prone to use poisons in their assassinations—to point this out to me. And to point out that I should keep an extra guard on you, my dear."

"Ah. Are you sure that Venice is our friend?"

"Who knows? Venetian politics are as murky as their canals and filled with even more dead bodies. But I think it a fair warning, and it brings me to a subject—awkward though it may be—that I wish to broach to you."

"Speak your mind...my lord," she said, getting her tongue around the words with difficulty.

"Once you are married, there is nothing to be gained by killing you. One of their pretexts for war disappears and some of the weaker camp followers may decide the Duchy of Milan has a rightful ruler. If even one leaves, their alliance will disintegrate, and those who remain can be dealt with easily. I hate to press the idea of a rapid marriage on you—I know all women long for the pomp and ceremony and show—but I think, for your safety and that of Milan, the sooner we are wed, the better."

To think she had worried about how to press this forward. She put on her best show of coyness and reluctance. "Not for myself, but for the sake of my father's duchy," she said.

"Good. Hopefully our union will be blessed with a child and they can put all this behind them," said Sforza, blissfully ignorant.

There is something to be said for a marriage of convenience to a fool who has no nobility, thought Lucia. "Let it be soon, my lord."

"I will have the banns read out in the cathedral this Sunday, and letters will be dispatched to all the noble houses. Let them wonder about the haste, and whether I have to marry for other reasons." He laughed at his own coarse jest.

She did not, but then he did not seem to expect her to. He took his leave.

"Mother and daughter?" she said to the asp. "I gave orders that it was not to be obvious. Not that it has not worked out precisely for the best, but I do not like being disobeyed."

I will send a message to the great serpent. It will know. I will be told.

"In the meanwhile, I have nine days to get suitable bride clothes," said Lucia.

Before the hour was out, her orders had gone far and wide

across Milan. She did not go to dressmakers and silk merchants anymore. They came to her and, if they knew what was good for them, came quickly. Sforza's coarse mercenaries were useful for that purpose, at least.

The letters Carlo Sforza's scribes neatly wrote out and various messengers took to their varying destinations did not include Parma, but did include Venice, Florence, and—though it would have been impossible for a response, let alone attendance—even Rome and Naples. The letter provoked varying reactions, but most of them had a common theme.

It was not going to be a very well-attended wedding.

Carlo Sforza expected that. But he had more important matters on his mind, a war to prosecute in the Northwest that, unless he judged incorrectly, would soon spread to several more fronts. He knew all too well how expensive war could be, but this was the first time he had, so to speak, been drawing on his own coffers to pay for it. That was proving a shock! The only thing, he thought sourly, that seemed to have more ability to spend money than a regiment of cavalry was his bride-to-be.

Venice

For the first time that Marco could recall, Petro Dorma—living as he did in close proximity to Milan, at least when compared to Rome or Naples—was quite pleased that he had been poisoned.

He had called Marco up to the public chamber from his latest visit to his patient. "And how is she?"

It was a public audience, and Marco knew enough to be aware that anything he was asked here was for a greater audience. He knew... and still doubted Petro's theory that this had been assassination... but just in case he was wrong and Petro was right... he shrugged. "No real progress, Your Grace."

That wasn't strictly true. The flesh had stopped dying around the wound. The honey treatment seemed to be working, even if it was a mess to apply. The circulation in her foot was definitely better than it had been. Her pulse was slightly slower and slightly easier to find, but she was still comatose and showed no signs of recovering consciousness.

"How very sad. Poisons can be so terribly debilitating, and it is about that that I called for your advice: I have been invited to attend the wedding of the Protector of Milan to the lady Lucia Maria del Maino, the former Duke Visconti's natural daughter. An occasion of some pomp and ceremony, which is taking place in a week's time. As my chief personal physician, would I be fit for such a journey? It would have to be done in a great hurry, as...well, you know my work schedule here in keeping our great city running."

Marco understood that, too. Petro probably would suffer no ill effects that a bit of rest would not cure, provided he didn't overdo things or eat unwisely. But...this was politics.

"I am not the Doge, Your Grace. I am merely your medical advisor. If I were the Doge, I would absolutely forbid Petro Dorma from undertaking any such exercise yet. It could have fatal consequences, as you know. In easy stages, undertaken over a few weeks with traveling by galley, it would be risky. At speed, suicidal. I hope the Council of Ten will concur with my opinion and advise you not to go, purely on the grounds of your health."

"That is most awkward, because I would very much like to attend," said Petro. "I will have to send a delegation in my place to wish them well, as well as my personal message of congratulations."

"I am sorry I cannot advise otherwise," said Marco. Which was also true, but for a different reason. What he'd heard from Benito had begun to make him put his own youthful memories of Sforza in context. Marco had been his mother's darling, and had been largely ignored by the bluff mercenary commander. Then had been the time when Mother had broken from Sforza, and the memory of those furious fights, and her belief—which he'd shared and passed to Benito—that Sforza wanted them all dead and had hired assassins to kill them.

He'd been his mother's partisan then, loyal to the last drop of his blood. Now, as an older person, knowing more of her cause and more of the people who had supported it, like the slave-trading Dandelos and the black Lotos smugglers...

He'd begun teasing out the truths from her ardent beliefs, particularly since Alessia's kidnapping and Carlo Sforza's part in rescuing her. The condottiere had never taken any real interest in Marco as a child, or even in Benito, who was his own son.

Marco had resented that, at the time. On the other hand, they'd always been well fed and well housed, and had never been abused by him. Well, he had gotten a most unfair box on the ear for something that Benito had actually done once. But he realized, now that he was working in the city often with sick and injured children, and he'd seen for himself what could happen to step-children, they'd been lucky.

Also, he could forgive much of a man who had Francisco Turner's loyalty and had sent his own physician to watch over his granddaughter.

Peace between Venice and a Milan ruled by Filippo Maria Visconti was never going to be anything but an excuse for Milan to regroup. But perhaps there could be a real chance with Sforza.

Marco would always choose peace over war. "But if they come to take my marshes and lagoon," said the Lion of Etruria within him, "they will have war."

And that, too, was true, and Marco knew his name would be right up there, first on the lists of volunteers in Piazza San Marco. He had fought for his city before, and would do so again, if need be.

Chapter 17

Milan had a week of frantic preparation. The reason given for the hasty marriage was the war with Parma. So far that had amounted to very little, and in truth, no one believed that to be the drive behind such a hasty marriage. But none but the most sanctimonious would suggest that marriage as soon as possible was not a great idea. They put either Lucia del Maino or Carlo Sforza down as fast workers, depending on where they stood politically. Some felt tradition and Visconti blood was a good thing. More had a good gossip that a conqueror like Carlo Sforza was all too adept at lifting skirts and not taking no for an answer. But at least he would marry her, not that that would stop him! The well-informed said it showed in the behavior of Benito Valdosta, known to be his son and also known for his drunken sexual exploits with wanton dancers on bridge arches. The fact that Benito appeared to be reformed was not something they let weigh with them.

Oddly, it did Sforza's popularity no harm, as Francisco Turner found, returning to Milan the night before the wedding. He and a few of his men had stopped to play off their dust, and among the carters and grooms in the taverna, Francisco was surprised to hear the rapid marriage treated as a matter to brag about in there. Human nature was sometimes peculiar, an observation that Francisco had made many times before.

Well, it mattered not. It might help to keep some combatants out of the war that was coming, and if Carlo wanted a duchy to retire to, this one could be very wealthy if it had better management. Francisco didn't like Milan itself, especially in summer, but there were plenty of pleasant places on the slopes of the Alps not that far away. And the beer in the North, with the Lombard influence and the Swiss that close, was better than in the rest of Italy.

He didn't care much for his commander's wife-to-be, but on the other hand, neither his opinion nor, in fact, her desires and opinions, would make a lot of difference to Carlo Sforza. Francisco was here as one of his commander's officers, not because he thought it an event of celebration which he wanted to support. It was a political event, and as such, nobles from the various parts of the duchy had been asked—or told—to take their roles as supporting the groom or the bride, rather than as old friends. Francisco had been rather touched that his commander had apologized for this. As a result, he and the other officers had to be there, but had not a great deal to do except eat and drink. Still, it was no time for a run.

Carlo Sforza had had a week of arrangements and organizing, and some preparation for a little war. He would rather have been doing that. Still, there had been some essentials, matters he had never considered, particularly in setting up a suitable dowry for Lucia. She did have some possessions of her own, or at least her mother did, but by noble marriage status she was a pauper. And as she pointed out with surprising honesty and bluntness, in wars and with him being older than her, she could end up widowed and very insecure.

The nobles of Italy would never accept her as the legitimate ruler—she'd plainly been bitter about that, and Sforza had felt some sympathy, so she had to have a contract that settled a part of his wealth on her child. The contract specified that he should remain the protector and the regent—or in his stead, she should act for the child born of their marriage until the child reached its eighteenth year. There had been some dickering about that. She'd actually wanted it longer, to his surprise. But nineteen years hence, at the earliest, seemed a long time away, and the nobles of Italy would hear of it. A longer period would seem as if he was trying to remain in power forever. Sixteen would have been not unusual.

She seemed rather fixated on protecting her children. But that too was only natural. She had to know of Benito and his granddaughter, and given her own uncertain inheritance, she was making sure.

Carlo found himself in some sympathy with her, if not with the bills she was running up. But that could wait until after the wedding to be reined in a bit.

A few replies to the hastily written letters of invitation came in. Many had not.

None of the invited guests from outside the state of Milan would be there. Several—Venice, Florence, Imola—had offered some sop of representation. Venice, oddly the most, sending several of the *Casa* Longi and a rather handsome gift. His spies did confirm that Dorma was advised not to travel, but that too could have been arranged. Still, the Venetians were plainly feeling generous towards him. Carlo had sent them the person who had tried to poison the Doge, and had almost succeeded. And they plainly would rather not seek war at the moment, with so many of their men still away with the fleet that had gone to Constantinople and places to the east.

As for the rest: well, he had grounds to rule now. More so, if Lucia managed to get herself pregnant.

Lucia had reveled in the untrammeled spending on bride clothes. She'd also taken great delight in the fact that the great oaf seemed blind to what he was signing. He failed to realize that after he was dead, she would rule until the child in her belly was eighteen. And if it died, too, then she could continue to rule. She might almost have thought he did not care about the power and the great glory of ruling the Duchy of Milan. But such an idea was entirely ridiculous, and it had to be a charade.

She had suitable noble maids of honor chosen, had they but known it, to repay old scores. He had given her a free hand in the selection of the groomsmen, too, and she had promoted a few old favorites there.

Her mother continued dazed and cooperative. She would have to stay like that, or die.

Actually, perhaps she would keep Sforza hypnotized, too, at least for a while.

The asp answered her. *Some cannot be hypnotized easily, or at all. You will have to let me kill him.*

"How do you know what I am thinking?" she asked, suddenly suspicious.

You speak your thoughts to yourself, so softly that others cannot hear, but I can. I have an answer from the great serpent as to what happened to the women of de' Medici. The scent marked both.

It was possible that the handkerchief had been used to blot two brows... not that she cared or that it mattered.

With both hands, she leaned on the sill of the open window in her chamber in the palace, and spent a moment gazing up at the huge cathedral across the Piazza del Duomo. She was quite unmoved by the architectural splendor of the Duomo; she just felt a mild resentment that it was so much larger and more imposing than the palace itself.

"Will she still die?" she asked the asp.

Oh, yes. The venom alone will kill, and if it does not, the flesh will rot, and the sweet scent of that kills. There is magical part to it all; that will kill, too. She is dead and triply dead. But she lies and dies within the demesne of the Winged Lion of Etruria. The serpent will not challenge that great creature until his full strength is raised.

"And when will that be?"

When it has fed enough on dying.

She turned away from the window. At the moment, she had no vast quarrel with Venice, so she gave no further thought to the Lion. Lucia was not given to thinking in the long term, and what really galled her at the moment was the absence of the grandees of the Italian states at the wedding. She had spoken to her bridegroom-to-be about it, but he had just shrugged the matter off. "Give them time to admit that their greed will get them devoured, Lucia."

She was not sure that she should make him free of her first name, but that too was a small price, which would wait until after the wedding. "And then?"

"And then we will see. You'll have a wedding night, and then, early the next day, I will go to join my men in countering what Duke Umberto considers a lightning thrust to give you a gift: my dead body in exchange for his."

She blinked. "What do you mean?"

"If I am killed, several of these gallant gentlemen," he said sarcastically, "will follow their conquest of Milan with either your death or your remarriage to one of them. So: there is some reason for you to hope I don't lose. I have met some of them."

"You will not be defeated," she informed him. And he would not. She had come too far to lose Milan now.

The voice within her bosom informed her that she had but to say the word, and the great serpent could kill all. Nothing could stop the dying, once she turned it loose.

"He can try first," she murmured. She suspected, more by what it had not said than what it had said, that once it started killing it would be hard to stop.

Her wedding day came with its triumph. It was very sweet indeed to finally sit upon the seat next to the ducal throne which would be fully hers too, in time.

The wedding night was all that she had imagined. Hopefully, she would not have to put up with that very often.

He left well before the dawn.

The officers who had attended the wedding rode out in a body with their commander, with an escort of cavalry and with scouts out. Someone made a bawdy comment to Carlo. He quelled it with a raised eyebrow. There was a little silence before the talk turned to the forthcoming campaign. A little later, Carlo Sforza signaled that he wanted to talk to Francisco alone, and the two of them were given space.

"You're not yourself, Carlo," said Francisco, once he was sure the others were out of earshot. "Are you not well?"

"Fine. Well, that is not true, but I'm not close enough to death's door to need your treatments, my friend. Except for the fact that I wonder what I have gotten myself into."

"It's a bit late now," Francisco said wryly, mildly puzzled. Carlo Sforza wasn't a man given to introspection. He tied knots and went on. "And it may be she will find it's what she's gotten herself into."

"Yes . . . but I wasn't expecting that in my bed. She wasn't a virgin," said Carlo. "She uses perfume by the bucket and still has an unwashed rats-nest stench about her. Clammy bitch. It's not a bed I'll be rushing back to."

Francisco did not quite know what to say to that.

Chapter 18

The Sea of Marmara

"Finally," said Benito Valdosta, looking over the stern rail, taking enormous pleasure in the sight of the great city at the gate between East and West. He had a superb view of the great wall of the Hippodrome from his current position in the Sea of Marmara.

All the more superb in that he was looking back at it as he sailed away—which was, in his considered and now well-informed opinion, the very best way to see Constantinople. And definitely the best way to deal with the petty bickering still going on there.

"Yes," said his grandfather, sounding amused. "But I daresay we'll be back in a twelvemonth with Alexius back on the throne, or something worse."

"I should think that the people of Constantinople would welcome him back. He was depraved, murderous, treacherous, but at least he is not Admiral Borana."

"They're certainly alienating the Greeks and will, in the fullness of time, lose the city," said Duke Enrico Dell'este, speaking of the triumvirate of rulers left to govern the conquered city. "With any luck, your man will retain the Venetian quarter, if the fellow is wise and keeps out of the machinations of the eunuchs, as ordered. He seemed fairly level-headed."

"If the Golden Horn's survivors will let him," said Benito. The foreign traders in Constantinople, many of whom had been there for generations and had taken local wives, had been made the emperor's scapegoats, and had been enslaved and suffered murder and rape as well as having their assets looted. When the tables turned...

Benito thought the only answer now was for them to leave the city forever. They had been far more vicious in their revenge, and restrictive in the demands they placed on the Greeks than the conquerors. It had to go badly, as they were outnumbered by five to one, and the countryside that surrounded and fed the city was entirely Greek. Benito understood the bitterness, but he also understood the need for a degree of pragmatism that didn't really exist on either side.

"Well, never mind. I dare say that there will be some fresh wars and skullduggery going on in Italy. I just want to get back to Corfu and my wife and my baby daughter, and rot there peacefully, sorting out fights between people who drink terrible wine and grow good olives. I understand entirely how Guiliano Lozza feels now."

"Somehow I suspect that will not happen for long," said Enrico. "Besides, that island of yours is too far from Ferrara, young man. We need to talk about your long-term future there, too. I intend to name you as my heir, you know. I'm not getting any younger."

Benito stared at him. Enrico Dell'este, the Old Fox of Ferrara, was nearly as much of a fixture in Benito's life as his brother and Maria. Rather like the iron he would go and hammer, working as a swordsmith and binding himself to his people and his city by doing so. He had always seemed indestructible.

Yes, Benito had known that he must die one day. But surely that was long and a far way off? His ironlike nature had meant that Benito had never considered what the duke's line of succession was. There had been uncles...his mother's brothers. But they, too, had died without heirs.

He bit his lip, shook his head. "Marco is your heir, Grandfather. Not me, um, I'm..."

"Carlo Sforza's bastard son. And the finest grandson a grandfather could ever desire, and what the city of Ferrara needs. I will talk to Marco, Petro Dorma, and of course my own nobles, and the leaders of my people. But Marco is bound to Venice. And while we're on good terms with that city, Ferrara stands on its own. I am fond of your older brother and proud of him, but he belongs to La Serenissima, and will probably end up as its doge, in the fullness of time. Ferrara...it's an iron worker's city, a place where we make swords and use them to hold our own. We are not serene, we have no lagoon to guard us, and no magical guardian. We only have our swords, our courage and our heads. We need you, Grandson."

"I don't . . . know quite what to say."

"Nothing is best in that case," said his grandfather cheerfully. "But you and Maria and your daughter must come to my city, and soon."

"Maria . . . that's going to be interesting." He meant because the Church refused to marry them. And because Maria was a Venetian canaler at heart. But then she'd taken well to Corfu.

"The city has been there a long time. It'll probably survive the experience," said his grandfather. "Ah. Good day, Prince Manfred."

Prince Manfred of Brittany, Baron Eberhard of Brunswick and some ten of the other surviving Knights of the Holy Trinity were aboard the Venetian flagship. Almost half of rest of the Knights who had been on the diplomatic mission to the lands of the Golden Horde, bordering the Black Sea, were scattered through the fleet. The other half were with Erik Hakkonsen.

It had been an interesting argument . . . to be on the sidelines of. Hakkonsen was coming back across the Balkans, along the old Via Egnata, with the remaining Knights, his bride the Princess Bortai—who was sister to Kildai, the Great Khan—and about fifty or so of her personal retainers. And her dowry. Some of it, anyway—the part that could not easily be transported by ship. Horse transports were few and far between, and Princess Bortai came with a lot of horses. Some of the finest bloodstock Manfred had ever seen, certainly for horses ideal for light cavalry. They had sufficient sheep, too, but merely as food.

They would travel under the shelter of Iskander Beg's hand—not that that group needed very much shelter. By the looks of those Mongols, any horse thief might as well commit suicide. They would meet again in Corfu, where Manfred and the other Knights would join them to be transported to Venice. By then, between his ample purse and imperial augustness—he was, after all, second in line to the throne of the Holy Roman Empire, preceded only by his brother Conrad—Manfred should be able to assemble the vessels they'd need for the voyage.

Then, from Venice, by any one of several possible routes, they'd go north to Mainz. That would be the end of Erik's and Manfred's service as confrere Knights of the Holy Trinity, and the end of Erik Hakkonsen's period of service to the Hauhenstaffen.

Benito wondered if Europe was any more ready for Erik and a small tribe of elite Mongol warriors, and a large number of horses, than Manfred was for his loyal bodyguard and close friend's departure. Hakkonsen was headed for Vinland, across the Atlantic, to where Erik and his new bride planned to settle.

"I'm very disappointed in the fittings on this ship, Benito Valdosta," said Manfred, slapping him on the back with a huge, meaty hand. "I thought you'd improve matters while we were in Constantinople, but there are no bridges, and still a serious lack of exotic dancers on board. I know, I have just searched it from stern to stem. The wine is of mediocre quality, too. It can barely compete with qumis."

"If only I had known how much you liked qumis, I would have gotten a couple of mares for you to milk, and the barrels to ferment it in," said Benito, thinking his shoulder might recover one day.

Manfred shuddered. "Erik must be deeply in love. He says he is getting used to it. The qumis, I mean, not the being in love with the pretty bear-wrestler."

"He is, you know. And I am glad for him."

Manfred nodded. "But rather him than me."

"Well, she's quite a girl, but I do understand that the qumis could put one off," said Benito, reading a great deal into the light-hearted banter. Manfred was not wearing the loss of his friend and bodyguard easily, and was determined to make light of it. Benito thought he was probably still missing Francesca, as well.

"Barbaric stuff. I should think they'll be very happy on the plains of Vinland. It's a fairly barbaric place."

"If Kari was anything to judge by, yes. And I should think it'll stay barbaric for about a week after Erik, Bortai and the Mongols get there."

"That long?" said Manfred. "I may have to go and check this out for myself. After all, Vinland is part of the League of Armagh, and so is Brittany. Anyway, it's cold out here, and I came to tell you Falkenberg is preparing some hot mulled wine in our cabin."

Venice

Maria Verrier, in the comfortable quarters of the *Casa* Montescue, found herself with both the time and need to reflect on the latest happenings and the situation she found herself in. There were sufficient servants that she never needed to lift a finger in the *casa*, and it upset them very much when she did. Alessia, of course, took a fair amount of time and energy, and there was no way on Earth or below it, that she would let that child out of her ambit again.

Alessia did play by herself and slept for hours longer than Maria did, and of course she spent time with Marco, and Kat if she got half a chance. Children seemed to know Marco was a good toy just by looking at him. Kat—Maria had to laugh. Kat could take on the darkness, smuggling, and shoot someone calmly with a wheel-lock hand-cannon if there was need. She'd fought for family and her *casa* with cool courage. But she was still wary and a little nervous around small children. She'd get used to them with one of her own, Maria reflected.

But she had too much time for that reflection. Venice's *stregheria* had made clear they did not want her, and then had betrayed her. Venice's canalers were fond of her, but they—and she—had moved apart. Corfu, and the Mother Goddess, and the service of the women there were not something she could really do any longer.

Effectively trapped in the *casa*, she turned to something the *casa* had quite a lot of, by *Casa* Longi standards, and a vast amount of by anyone else's standards. Books. She started reading. Reading and writing she had learned later in life than most, and hadn't enjoyed very much, either.

But now, as she practiced more, that changed, too.

Chapter 19

Tyrol

The trip through the Alps was extremely chilly, muddy and relatively unpleasant, except where the ground was still frozen. Count Mindaug, having been beguiled by the early spring mildness, began finding the nomadic life less charming. The same wagon that had so often in the weeks gone by seemed cozy and comfortable, now sometimes reminded Mindaug of an engine of torture. His back ached, his behind ached even more, and both of his shoulders were bruised from being flung about by unexpected slips and slides and twists of the wheels.

There was still considerable snow around, too. Despite the spring, it was necessary for Count Mindaug and his two servants to spend some nights in various hostelries along the way. People did seem curious as to where they were going and why, so the count set out to provide them with what they wanted. The books were going to Baron Otto von Wisselbacher, outside Villach. The name was chosen from memory. The man was a minor magician and bibliophile with whom Count Mindaug had had brief dealings many years ago.

That justified their direction, their cargo, and it seemed an acceptable reason. But, he decided, he would need a profession in Italy as well. If the Duchy of Milan was absolutely not hiring magicians, it was probable the rest of them would also not be—in the same sense. That could push up the price for his services nicely. And, it seemed, these Imperials, and probably the Italians, were terribly trusting. He could be a magician. Not

Count Kazimierz Mindaug, the castellan of Braclaw and voivode of Zwinogrodek, but a charlatan—good enough to fool most people, but as unmagical as a brick and thus attracting no unwelcome attention from the great powers. Not, at least, until he had a secure bolt-hole and more security and defenses.

There was something very appealing about the idea. Mindaug knew a great deal about many chemical and physical processes, which could pass for magic to the untutored, and he could write very convincing cantrips. He even had quite a few of the chemicals that such deceit would involve. True, he had them for arcane purposes, but who would know?

He began thinking his way through his large collection of lore for suitable tricks. He had a number of books on alchemy, and had a very helpful translation of a book from China, which included recipes for making various pyrotechnics, and the colors that burning them could produce. With this in mind, he bought some beeswax and made a few experimental candles, to the fascination of his two servants. Part of the fascination was the careful notes he made of the ingredients and the weights he used.

"Is it magic, master?" asked Tamas, watching him write.

"No, no more so than your making a loaf of bread or pot of stew. You use the same quantities of flour every time you make a loaf, do you not?"

"I've got a little rhyme my mother taught me," said Emma doubtfully. "But the writing is magic. Just like all books."

Mindaug, who had gone to some lengths to not even hint that he trafficked in magic, discovered that both Tamas and Emma had assumed he was a magician because he read books. Writing definitely confirmed this assessment. Far from being terrified of it, they were rather proud of him. Still, he did his best. "This will not be magic. It is just knowledge of what will burn in what color, and what will make smoke. I plan to pretend to do magic. It is a trick."

He went on to discover they were quite aware of tricks, but could still regard that as magic, just magic that could be learned. He lit the candle some few yards away from the wagon one evening. He put it a little distance off, because in his experience, such things smelled, and he didn't want the smell getting into the books. As he had intended, the candle burned for a while and then began to produce smoke. Emma squeaked and both she and Tamas hid themselves behind him.

This proved very wise, as the candle spat several great, slow-burning sparks with a shriek, instead of producing a nice bright yellow glow, and then exploded.

It showered him with wax fragments, frightening the horses and Mindaug, and terrifying Tamas and Emma thoroughly.

Kazimierz Mindaug resolved that any future experiments would be performed at a greater distance from himself and his camp, with smaller quantities. Still, in itself, it was fascinating. He could magically produce remarkably similar effects. Perhaps this could enhance or substitute for it.

The second of Archimandrite von Stebbens's poacher-trackers did stop in the village over the ridge, barely five miles from Mindaug, where the thirty Knights waited. It was difficult to move and house so many, and yet stay close to the quarry.

The first man, who had been on watch with him, disappeared so effectively that he might as well have been murdered by Mindaug in some vile ritual, for all they knew.

Unfortunately, he'd found the poacher who did stop merely clung to the feet of a Ritter. The poacher gibbered insensibly for some time, until Ritter Hartz poured water on his head.

Von Stebbens gave the man a mug of wine instead. It clattered against his teeth. "What happened man?" he demanded, getting ready to shake the fool.

"M'lord, defend me. I need magical protection. You should not have sent us out against the wizard without it."

"We will defend you. What happened?"

Wild-eyed, the man looked around. "I'll tell you . . . in the church. We'll be safe in the church, won't we?"

They took him to the little village church. "Demons don't come into the church, do they?" he asked fearfully, kneeling.

It was some time before they could get any sense out of him. "I want the priest. I want to confess my sins first." And not even a good shaking could move him from that. So they had to wait. "Check on the thaumaturgic watch, Hartz," the archimandrite instructed, while he waited.

The Ritter came back at a jog. "They report there is no sign of movement or magic, my lord."

The poacher came back from the altar with the local priest. "I have granted him absolution," said the country priest, "but he is a troubled man, sir. Tell the archimandrite your story."

The little poacher nodded. "Hans and I, we were hidden about thirty cubits away from each other, Hans in some bushes and me in the ditch on the edge of the road in the dead grass, watching the fiendish sorcerer. And next thing... the magician walks toward me, lights a magic candle and then there's a huge cloud of magic smoke. Then this screaming yellow demon flies out, all sparks and terrible baleful light, and it pounces down on poor Hans. It knew exactly where he was hiding. He screamed. I knew it was going to drag him off to hell, so I crawled away... but they still shot me. I felt the curse-bullet hit. But there is no blood. No blood," he said hysterically. "Look!"

He showed Von Stebbens his cheek, which had a red mark on it. It did not look magical or accursed to the archimandrite, but it would leave a bruise.

"It could have been a stone or ricochet."

"It was a shot!" insisted the poacher-scout, his voice rising hysterically. "In the dark. Magic, black magic. You can't shoot someone in the dark otherwise. They could never have seen me."

And there was no way he was going back to his task.

Too late, Von Stebbens began to see the folly of telling the peasant trackers what an evil magician Mindaug was. There was no inducement that could make this one ever dare follow him again.

But more worrying was the fact that he and his fellow Knights, prepared to attack and magically neutralize the count, watching for any magical sign, protective wards at the ready... had seen nothing at all. The archimandrite had been waiting on orders by messenger. Waiting for the instruction to pounce on Mindaug. There would be magical safeguards and escape mechanisms, and he would have preferred the go-ahead to kill Mindaug first, before he had a chance to use either. They had a line on whom he been heading toward and Baron Otto von Wisselbacher had been under observation for some time. He was not in the same league as Mindaug, although very rich. They could strike and question with a great deal more safety, there.

It would be necessary to take chances if Mindaug had found some way of circumventing their magical watch. He might well be aware of their observers. He could be playing a cat-and-mouse game. He certainly had a reputation for deviousness. The Knights placed the ward candles, and set about the prayers of summoning, and then made magical contact with Bishop Pelmann in Mainz.

Such contacts were always difficult, and the sending of precise messages hard. And then, the bishop had to go and consult with Emperor Charles Fredrik himself, before they did it all over again. The Emperor wanted him alive, and so, it seemed, did the Knights. But they would take up position before dawn and strike at first light. With someone like Count Mindaug, combat at night was to be avoided.

Only, during the night, the snow began to fall. By morning it was apparent that they weren't going anywhere.

Of course, the comfort was that surely the villainous count was not either.

Except... he was.

"Weather magic?" asked Ritter Hartz, looking at the blizzard outside. Visibility was down to a few feet, and the snow already piled soft and high.

Archimandrite von Stebbens shook his head. "Even small weather magic is hard and loud in the thaumaturgic sphere. This would be no small magic. For Mindaug to use something that powerful that precise, and yet have no trace of it leading to himself? That is hard to believe, even for such a one as he. If it were true, then he could have destroyed us like a man brushing off a fly. And if so, why bother to travel slowly and in such discomfort? He's been very afraid of something—and I doubt very much if it's we Knights."

"He has the luck of the devil."

"He may quite possibly be in league with Satan," said the archimandrite, with a sigh. "Let us see what the Aemiline hesychast can do."

Von Stebbens was appalled by the methods Brother Dimitrios used to guard himself. Instead of the usual wards used by all Christian magicians of the archimandrite's acquaintance, the Aemiline hesychast seemed to be satisfied with mere candles at the four points—and, more bizarre still, four mice held in small cages stationed next to the candles.

"They are my watchmen," explained Dimitrios, with a little

smile. "Well...watchrodents, I suppose I should say, since three of them are female."

"But..." Ritter Hartz shook his head. "How do you expect them to protect you?"

"Protection is for mighty mages, young man. My magics are far too modest for such martial methods. Like my little mice, I will run and hide the moment any sign of danger appears."

He lay down on the thin mat positioned at the center of his peculiar "wards." Then, he crossed his hands on his chest and closed his eyes.

"You needn't worry, Ritter," the hesychast murmured. "I shall be quite safe, I assure you—because this fearsome Count Mindaug fellow will never notice me at all."

Since this was his first contact with Mindaug, it took Brother Dimitrios's wandering mind a fair amount of time to find the wagon. But, eventually, he sensed the contented feelings of a mouse, basking in a degree of warmth that was unusual for the season.

Thereafter, it took Dimitrios very little time to track down those sentiments, and before long he was peering at the world through the eyes of a mouse hidden on a small wooden ledge in the interior of a lurching wagon. At the front of the wagon, somewhat hunched over, sat a small man holding the reins. Dimitrios couldn't see his face from the mouse's vantage point, but he was almost sure this was Count Mindaug.

Less than a minute later, his supposition was confirmed. The mouse's gaze shifted, and now Dimitrios could see the stacks of crates that filled most of the wagon. Those had to be the Lithuanian sorcerer's notorious books.

Brother Dimitrios had many virtues, but perhaps the greatest he possessed was patience. So, he spent the next many hours simply observing...

Not much of anything.

Chapter 20

Northern Italy

On the other side of the Felsen Ridge, the count and his servants were making haste for the pass. It had taken Mindaug a little time and the acceptance of his absolute authority—and some brandy—to get Tamas and Emma calmed down. And then, Tamas had started sniffing as if he smelled something bad. "It's going to snow, master. Soon."

Perhaps it was the brandy. Or perhaps it was wisdom, or perhaps it was just the idea of being stuck here in the snow without as much as a village alehouse for shelter, that made Kazimierz Mindaug say: "Well, we'd better pole up the horses then and move."

The moon had risen now, and although there were scudding clouds, it was possible to see the track. A little further on they came to a fork, and chose the more traveled route, which took them slightly downhill and was definitely in better condition than the rutted steep track that was the alternative.

They walked on, Tamas leading the horses, into the increasing dark.

The downhill and the quality of the track had both been temporary situations. Indeed, the count might have been inclined to think them illusions. They were, by the occasional glimpses in the moonlight, out on the mountain, with no sign of habitation and no easy place to turn the wagon. Indeed, they'd had difficulty negotiating some of the turns. The only comfort was that it was plainly a well-traveled track, with deep wheel ruts into which the wagon's steel-banded wheels fitted. That was just as well, too, because a flake of snow settled on the count's nose, as he sat on the box.

They stopped. "What is it?" called the count to his man.

"Pole across the track, master."

Mindaug and Emma got down to have a look. It was plainly a deliberate barrier, and on kindling a lamp, there was a stone-built cross between a hut and a fortress there—unoccupied. "It must be a toll post. Protection from bandits around here, I shouldn't wonder."

The hut was a two-story affair, with a stable beneath. It had a stack of wood at the back. As it was snowing steadily by then, Mindaug made the decision to stop. The horses were stabled, rubbed down with hay and an old sack, and given oats. Mindaug himself took a hand because, by the looks of Tamas, he might just fall over before the horses were cared for, and they were too valuable to risk here.

In the meantime, Emma had a fire kindled and had shaved dried meat into a pot, along with crushed wheat to make a broth of sorts. It was warming, and they were out of the snow, and were probably three hours travel on their way. It did not look as if the single-room hut was normally lived in, but rather used as some kind of billet. There was a rough table, a couple of straw pallets, a fireplace, and not much else. Still, it was warm, out of the wind, and out of the snow. They slept peacefully enough.

Morning brought a leaden sky and occasional flurries of snow, although it looked a lot worse to the north. And they were in daylight, at the top of the pass, with the trail winding through snow and then into clear fields. Far below, there was a village with smoke rising from its chimneys.

It was somewhat amusing, thought the count, that he'd spent the night in the place he'd been concerned about getting past— the border post between the Holy Roman Empire and the Italian states. By the looks of it, the weather-wise locals had abandoned their post and gone home. The question now was whether they could do likewise. Well, at least to abandon the post. Go home? The count thought of the draughty castle at Braclaw that stayed chilly even in summer, despite its huge log fires. He had lived out his early years there, and then been taken to be introduced to his first steps in magic. As a younger son, it should not have been his inheritance, but the others . . . died. Jagiellon had burned the castle, by way of revenge, when the trap on Corfu had failed and Mindaug had had to flee to Hungary.

Home was a concept which obviously meant something to other people, just not to him. He called Tamas, and they went to look at the trail. The snow lay fetlock deep and powdery. "Can we get the wagon down it?" the count asked.

They'd been along steep mountain trails for weeks now, and while those on the worst places had been fitted with windlasses, they'd replaced the brake blocks on the wagon once already. This slope looked steeper, and in worse condition. Mindaug had learned to trust his servant's judgment on such matters more than he did his own. The ex-miller had a great deal of practical common sense, more than most men of education.

Tamas kicked the snow. "It could help, if we put something to drag behind us. If there's ice, that could be treacherous. There are some eight- to ten-cubit logs beside the shed, waiting to cut for the fire. We could chain one to the tail, to make a broad anchor to drag in the snow behind us."

"Let us do that then."

Emma had come out to join them. "But is it right to take their log of wood, master?"

The count almost laughed, but she wasn't joking. And ... he needed their respect and goodwill, as he'd come to realize.

"Of course, we'll pay for it. Do you think a silver penny fair for the lodging?" Mindaug had no idea what a reasonable price would be for such a thing.

"Oh, that's far too much, master. We only used twelve of their fire logs, and I have given the place a good cleanup." She sniffed disapprovingly. "I'd say two coppers for lodging and one for their log. And, if it please you, there's porridge and honey ready for you to break your fast. I've baked some pot bread for the road, too."

One day, thought Mindaug, he'd get used to their way of thinking. But he doubted if he'd ever be able to share it. In many respects, he was still a nobleman of Lithuania, and always would be.

Using the log as a snow anchor, they crept their slow way down the pass. It took care, ropes, patience, and Tamas's inventive and practical skill to get them down, but they managed. Count Mindaug was glad of it, because there was an inn at the foot of the pass as well as a border watchman, who was happy to have his palm silvered. The little mountain village was not much of a place, but it was warmer. The air seemed warmer here, too. They had lost a lot of altitude. The border guard seemed mostly interested in collecting money and was not concerned with invasion, even if he was mildly incredulous that anyone could have been crazy enough to bring a wagon over the pass in the snow. At least, that was what Mindaug thought he was saying. His Frankish was so accented that it was hard to tell.

Still, it was without let or hindrance that they proceeded lower, and to the west. The count was beginning to think of finding a good place to stop traveling now, somewhere on the borders of the Lion of Etruria's territory. That would hopefully make it possible to flee there if there was an attack, but not so close to Venice as to call attention to himself.

Sooner or later he would have to wield power, build himself a demesne, or find himself a protector. And, of course, build a bolt-hole. In that regard, Northern Italy had several possibilities: Padua with its university and library sounded attractive; Milan had a ruler who was recruiting magicians; and Verona was, from what he had read, a beautiful and cultured city—although one always had to be wary of the city's ruling family. The Scaligeri who ruled Verona were prone to lawlessness, even by the standards of Italian nobility.

He had to sneer at himself, a little, in an amused way. Going west had made him soft. The Holy Roman Empire worked on their roads and bridges, policed their little towns, hunted down bandits, and had nothing worse than toll posts for a traveler to deal with. In Lithuania, he could not have undertaken such a journey without a troop of horsemen.

As they rounded the spur, it was brought home to him that this was no longer part of the Empire, but was one of the Italian principalities—and Scaligeri territory, known for brigandage.

It had been a steep upgrade, and the horses weren't moving very fast, when the horses shied and one man jumped out of the thick bushes at the roadside and grabbed their bridles. His companions bundled out of the brush on either side of them, armed with what peasants-turned-thieves had—cudgels and knives. From the way the first one thrust at the count, it was apparent that this wasn't a holdup and robbery. This was intended to be the murder of a few travelers—they'd rape Emma in the bargain before they killed her as well—followed by dumping their bodies in a ditch after stealing what they had.

Mindaug leaned away and hit the forearm of his attacker, before slipping his own knife up under the man's ribs. To someone trained to survive murder in Lithuania, it was ludicrously easy. His two servants did not have his advantages, though. Tamas was down but not out of the fight, wrestling with two men next to the wagon. There was a knife being wielded. Emma, seized by a man who hadn't killed her because a woman was a prize, was screeching like a wildcat and clawing and fighting—fiercely, but not very effectively.

Mindaug picked up the dropped whip and sent the lash around the throat of the man who had pushed aside his dying companion and was yelling for help with the count. A hard jerk and the scream stopped, suddenly. The pommel of the whip then cracked the one wrestling with Emma over the head.

Mindaug muttered a quick spell that slowed the three fighters—Tamas included—as if they were trapped in thick mud. There was no time right now to avoid magic, much as he would have preferred to. He stepped up to the trapped men and dealt with both of the attackers with his blade, and then pulled Tamas free and to the seat where Emma hauled him up. The lad was bleeding profusely.

Now there was just the varlet holding the horses—and half a dozen more men straggling out of the bush. The whip dealt with the horse holder, and the surging panicked horses did the rest. Mindaug gave them their heads, merely trying to keep the wagon on the road while they put some distance between themselves and the attackers. A keening Emma tried to deal with the injured Tamas, attempting to staunch the blood. Mindaug hoped he didn't bleed on the books. Leaving aside the mess, it would not be wise with some of those books to let them taste human blood.

A mile or so further, the horses tiring anyway, he pulled them to a halt. There were open fields on either side of them and little chance for another ambush. "Look to see if there is anyone following," he said to Emma. "I will deal with Tamas's wounds as best I can."

He was irritated with himself, and somewhat shaken as well. To let such a little incident break his cover! Those who watched this world and others for traces of magic might now be aware that Count Mindaug was not dead. Such a minor working would be hard to pinpoint, true, but he'd preferred them to think him dead, his corpse lying among the bodies on the steppe where Emeric's forces had failed.

It would have been wiser to just let the bandits kill the boy. But...that would have left him short a loyal servant, which this journey had made him value. And, truth be told, Mindaug simply hadn't thought of consequences at the time. He set about look-ing at the injured Tamas. He knew a thousand good ways to kill people, but had little knowledge and no experience at healing or even at dealing with the injured. He did have several books on medicine, simply because he collected books.

Tamas, it appeared, was at least not dying this instant. He was trying to sit up, and kept rubbing his eyes, which was not helping the cut on his forehead at all. He was plainly confused and ready to try and fight the count, too, by the way he milled his hands around. "Lie down and keep still," Mindaug said sternly.

The wrinkling of his eyes did not help the bleeding; he was plainly trying to focus, and failing. But the familiar voice had an effect. "Yes, master," said Tamas, in a slurred but plainly relieved tone. "Emma, is she...?"

"She's fine. She's safe. Lie still, I told you."

Mindaug ripped aside the man's rough shirt to expose consider-able blood and a long wound—from midchest and onto the belly. It was bleeding...but he'd seen enough sacrifices to know that this was not the pumping out of major arteries. Emma was back at his shoulder, so he told her to fetch him water and cloths. A quick wash-down of the wound had Emma at his shoulder whispering prayers, wide-eyed because imbedded in the blood and torn flesh was a small, cheap copper icon—a head of St. Arsenius, now with a slit in it. The overhand stab had been forceful enough to go through the leather jer-kin, and hit the little saint's medal and gone partly through it—which had undoubtedly saved Tamas from being opened up like a split carp.

Personally, Count Mindaug doubted divine intervention, but nothing short of a chorus of angels would ever convince Emma that the saint had not personally put his hand out to save her man. The rest of his wounds amounted to a nasty cut on the head, basi-cally a split from the crack he'd got from the cudgel, and two other minor cuts on his arm and shoulder. The bandaging that Mindaug and Emma managed was rough, as the patient was not cooperative. Eventually, Mindaug fed the fellow a little poppy juice, and he did subside into uneasy rest, as they made their way to Vicenza later that afternoon.

They found an inn there. Mindaug decided he'd be wise to leave Emma with Tamas and search out some help. The young woman, distraught, was not good at making sense of the local bastard Frankish. It was hard enough for the count.

He found an apothecary, but two minutes' talk convinced him the man was nothing but an ignorant fraud and that what he sold was close to worthless if not dangerous.

In the process, the count found himself wondering why he was taking so much trouble over a servant. He supposed the truth was that he'd probably spent more time in the company of this pair of servants than he had of anyone, since being a small boy. A few further questions of a merchant put him on the trail of a physician who was, by dint of coin up front, persuaded to come look at Tamas.

"He's suffering from an impairment to his wits from the blow on the head," said the physician.

"I needed to give you gold to tell me that?" muttered the count. "What can we do for it?"

"I would say bleed him to remove the excess phlegm," said the physician.

"I should say he has bled enough," said the count irritably.

"Oh," the physician was plainly a little alarmed by the tone. "Well, he should recover with sufficient rest, unless the demons have taken hold of him. He may suffer terrible headaches. I can provide you with a preparation of my own for that."

The count did not kick him down the stairs, but it was tempting. Demons! Ha. He knew more about demons than ten such idiots. Instead of buying his quackery, he went and dug out the books he had on medicine. It took a while, although each box had been labeled and the count had allowed a narrow passage down the center of the wagon. When he returned to the bed where they'd put Tamas, he found the man had thrown up and was, by his own account, feeling better if weak, and keen to see to the horses.

"The hostler has seen to them. You will rest," commanded Mindaug.

Emma asked permission, timidly, to go and give thanks to God and the blessed St. Arsenius, and to pray for his healing. By the looks of her, she had been weeping, and Mindaug had nothing else that needed doing. So, he sat and read while Tamas slipped into a shallow sleep, and the count moved between Galen and Rhazes.

Emma came back with food for him. "They say there will be war soon!" she said fearfully. She could not tell him much, as she struggled with the language. But people were buying supplies against the possibility of siege. So, although it was early evening, the count went out again. He found what he was looking for quickly enough—a gunsmith. Next time the horses shied from a roadside bush, the count planned to be ready.

Not only could the gunsmith sell him two wheel-lock hand-cannons and tell him that, yes, the Scaligeri, long-time allies of Milan, would go to war against the usurper Carlo Sforza. That hadn't yet been officially declared, but everyone knew it.

The gunsmith was quietly packing up. "They talk of rights—but this is Sforza they fight. I'm going to my cousins in the mountains until it is over, sir. So I'd be glad to let you have these at a good price."

He and the count disagreed about the good price part, but Mindaug had been in cities under siege before. He, too, had heard of the reputation of Carlo Sforza, the Wolf of the North, the con-dottiere who had only ever been bested by Duke Enrico Dell'este and the Venetians together. And then only with magic added into the mixture. Sforza was perhaps not the master of grand strategy that Dell'este was, but his tactical strength was legendary. And he destroyed the cities and towns that resisted him.

So, it was time to move on again. Despite Tamas complaining of a terrible headache, and protesting about not being allowed to pole up the horses and do the other tasks he normally did for the count, they left early the next day, going west.

Mindaug waited until they were well clear of the town and in a clearing surrounded by trees that blocked sight and would muffle sound before getting Emma to practice with the hand-cannon. The count tried it out first. It kicked, and left the firer in a cloud of blue smoke.

Emma eyed it fearfully. "But... am I allowed to use such a thing, master?"

Mindaug knew King Emeric had strongly disapproved of an armed peasantry. Yes, they had knives and pitchforks, axes and billhooks and here and there an old spear, and many had bows, but weapons that could threaten a knight? No. Not to be tolerated.

"This is not Hungary," he said.

She looked puzzled. "Yes, I know that. This place is not as good, of course, but it was... nice, in some ways. Until we were attacked. It is not safe here."

Mindaug had to think his way around the "not as good" part. It had never occurred to him that his servants might yearn for the fields and the mill, things they knew. But that was peasantry for you, where "safe" was life and death in poverty at your lord's whim. At least it was certain, thought the count, like life in Jagiellon's court had been certain. If you showed too much competence you'd be killed. Too little and you'd be killed. Sooner or later, you would step over one or the other boundary.

Neither Elizabeth Bartholdy nor King Emeric had been that different. Not quite as murderous as Jagiellon, but then, who was? Mindaug was beginning to like the idea of dying of old age, as unlikely as that possibility had ever seemed to him in the past.

"No one here cares, Emma. If you had had such a thing at the ready, you could have shot the man who attacked you."

She plainly thought about this, nodding. Mindaug wondered suddenly if it was the idea of killing that worried her. He'd come across that notion in some books before. A curious concept.

But her reply showed that this was not the case.

"Yes, I could," she said, quite thoughtfully. "I could have shot him and the man who attacked my Tamas—and you, master! I could have shot them dead. Show me."

So he had, once he was sure there was no one to see what they were about. This time, in another clearing, Mindaug set up a target for her to shoot at. It was nothing fancy, just a dead branch propped against a tree stump. She was delighted when she blew the branch apart on her second shot—and her first shot had not missed by much.

Tamas had wanted to try, too, but the count had settled for showing him the mechanism and telling him to lie down again. Then he had Emma shoot a few more rounds against other targets he set up in the clearing. Despite the recoil, Emma was quite successful at hitting them. She had strong hands and wrists, and seemed to have a genuine knack for the handcannon.

There was a point, thought the count, in keeping these weapons from the commons or from the women. Women of rank had always used guile, poison or magic to win fights. These weapons— particularly if they got smaller and better—could change that.

Mentally, he shrugged. Mindaug was only worried about his own future, and even if his earthly foes were armed with handcannon, sword or spell, he could deal with most things. Let those who could not cope, deal with it in their own way.

On the other side of the pass, in Imperial lands, Von Stebbens and his men were still coping with the snow. Sleds and horses were moving about again, the trail was being cleared—but they were advised not to follow the pass that Count Mindaug had taken for some days yet. The magical watch on the count continued. And, at last, they saw some sign of him using his powers.

"Deaths," said Ritter Hartz, who had been the one gazing on the thaumaturgic sphere. "It was a small working, though."

"But with Mindaug, there would be deaths, no matter how small his use of magic was," said Von Stebbens grimly. "We push though the pass tomorrow, snow or no snow, Ritters. Or we will go further east and take a lower pass."

So they did. The guard had gotten to the border watchtower fort barely an hour before the Knights did. Yes, someone had slept and stabled their horses there—and they had left some coins for payment. The guard produced the coppers to prove his claim. "Not everyone is so honest," he said.

The Plocken Pass took the Knights most of the day to lead their horses down. Von Stebbens knew there was something of a delicate balance to their behavior here. They were no longer in the Holy Roman Empire and were mere travelers like anyone else. Not that most people or even the local nobility would interfere in their business. But it could cause complications, especially after the Knights had been used to unwittingly transport Chernobog's demon into Venice. The Knights had redeemed themselves since, but they had a good reason not to start any diplomatic incidents.

They rode hard to catch up with Count Mindaug. Orders or no orders, the archimandrite was determined to take the man into custody now. The information about Baron von Wisselbacher had plainly been a false lead. Whatever associate Mindaug was heading for must be in Italy somewhere.

Only, as it proved, those few days' lead that Count Mindaug had gained, had been crucial ones.

The city-state of Verona was at war with its neighbor, and military patrols were now guarding and setting up barricades on the roads. And the count and his wagon were on the far side of those barricades and patrols.

"Milan. He must be heading for Milan. We had better send word to Mainz."

So once again magical communication was made.

❁   ❁   ❁

A discordant note, however, was introduced by Brother Dimitrios. When told of Von Stebbens's plans, the Aemiline hesychast shook his head.

"I think you may be acting precipitously, Archimandrite," he said. "I have been able to watch Mindaug at very close range, using my little friends. So far I have seen no sign at all that he is engaged in any sort of dark magic, and it seems very odd that he would have two such servants if his intentions were really those you fear."

Von Stebbens was skeptical. "And who, exactly, are these 'little friends' of yours who make such reliable spies?"

"Mice, mostly. Squirrels, sometimes. Once in a while I'm forced to use a bird, although I try to avoid that for this work." His expression was rueful. "I'm afraid there is a reason for the expression 'bird-brained.' It's hard to keep a bird focused on anything for very long."

"I should think hawks or owls would be able to concentrate."

The hesychast's rueful expression was replaced by one of distaste. "I do not like to spend time in the minds of raptors," said Dimitrios. "Their thoughts—and they generally have only one: *kill and eat*—are not pleasant."

The archimandrite was still not satisfied. "Are you saying you can get these 'little friends' of yours close enough to Mindaug to really be able to spy on him?"

"Oh, they can get very close—within a few feet, usually. The count pays little attention to mice in his wagon, so long as they stay away from his crates of books. Even squirrels, he generally ignores. He's odd, that way."

Dimitrios smiled. "Of course, my little friends have little brains as well. So while they can hear what he and his servants say, they are just meaningless sounds to them."

"You can't translate?"

"Oh, no. I hear only what they do. But there's nothing wrong with their eyesight, and I see everything that transpires quite well. I tell you, Archimandrite, whatever the count from Lithuania's plans are, there has been no indication at all that he is seeking confederates beyond his two servants. And he's refrained from using magic except once when he and his servants were attacked by robbers on the road—and that was a minor spell."

Von Stebbens frowned. "But he fended them off? How?"

Dimitrios made a little grimace. "Even without magic—even as small as he is, and at his age—Mindaug turns out to be quite deadly. If you should happen to engage him in personal combat at some point, I strongly recommend you stay at sword's length from him. Up close..."

The hesychast shook his head. "He is very adept with a dagger. A whip, too."

"What one could expect from such an evil man," said Heinrich von Tarnitz, nodding his head sagely.

Dimitrios gave the Knight a none-too-admiring look. "You think so? Let me ask you, Ritter—do you think a hawk is evil?"

"No, of course not. A hawk is just a wild animal, doing what its nature calls for."

"Indeed so. I don't like to spend time in a raptor's mind, as I told you once. No more would I care to spend time in the mind of Count Mindaug. But did you ever once consider"—he glanced at Von Stebbens—"either one of you, what it would be like to be born and raised a very high-ranked nobleman in the Grand Duchy of Lithuania? Mindaug's even in the line of succession."

He paused, waiting for a response—but all he got were blank stares.

"I thought not. How much time have either of you ever spent in Lithuania?"

Von Tarnitz shook his head. "None at all."

"I visited Vilnius once," said Von Stebbens. "Thankfully, only for three days."

"Yes, well—I have spent a great deal of time in Vilnius and other cities in the Grand Duchy, as well as in those vast, ancient forests. My little friends make excellent monitors of Jagiellon's doings. It is a wicked country—more so than ever since Jagiellon was possessed by Chernobog. The only man who could have survived Count Mindaug's upbringing, no matter how inclined he might have been toward kindness, would have soon learned to think like a hawk himself."

Dimitrios shook his head. "Do not be so certain, Ritters, that you understand the workings of such a man's mind. I make no such arrogant claim myself. I simply pass on to you what I have observed for weeks now—that there has been no indication from Mindaug's actual deeds that he intends any of the things you suspect him of."

He paused briefly. "Have you heard that miners use canaries to warn them of the presence of dangerous fumes?"

Both Knights nodded.

"Well, you might do well to consider those two young and quite innocent servants of Mindaug's as your canaries. If you wish to know what evil the count plans, watch them. If they die—if they faint, or grow ill—then you have your warning. Until then . . . be cautious in your conclusions."

Mainz

Emperor Charles Fredrik sat in one of the smaller rooms in the palace to discuss the matter with Abbot Goldenbuss and two of his other advisors. "Milan. Carlo Sforza. We had assumed that the worst of the rot in Milan had died with Filippo Maria, but we were wrong. It continues, apparently."

"He's a very capable general, but outnumbered—vastly so, if we intervene," said Baron Saasveld.

"Which may well be why he has brought Count Mindaug into the equation," said Count de Bressy, who was a rising strategist in Imperial circles. The Emperor liked him. The man was cautious when it came to military affairs, but thoughtful and never lost sight of practical matters like how to keep an army supplied in the field.

"But when we add the possibility of an outbreak of Justinian's Plague, we cannot take military intervention lightly," De Bressy continued. "We could just wind up making the situation worse than it is already."

The abbot looked grave. He leaned forward in his seat, planting his hands on his knees. "Our largest concern is that the three things tie together; that, somehow, Mindaug has found how to magically control the plague, and Sforza plans to use it for military expansionism. There are hints of something similar in a few documents in the Church's possession."

There was a silence.

Then the Emperor said heavily: "If I had known this earlier, I would have ordered Mindaug's immediate capture and, after questioning, his execution."

"We did not know . . . or, rather, we never guessed," said

Goldenbuss. "One of the scholars searching for treatments for the plague came to me only two days ago. He found reference to such a possibility in a very old text, somewhat distorted by recopying. It took us a while to work out that when it referred to the purple bites of the summoned destroying serpent, it was not merely using poetic language to describe Satan. Parts of it are literally indecipherable but we think it refers to a pagan rite of the sacrifice of a virgin to a dragon."

"It's a common story," said Baron Saasveld, chuckling a bit sarcastically. "Invariably, a knight saves her."

"But what if it had a real origin?" said the abbot, sitting back up straight. "Stories often do, after all. Monks and nuns of our orders are researching it urgently, going through manuscripts and record from that time." He looked directly at the Emperor: "You do realize, Your Majesty, that Count Mindaug has one of the premier collections of old books and writings, particularly of magic? That was how we first spotted him approaching our borders—the books contain so much lore, much of it very dark in nature, that they emitted a faint aura. He has that very dangerous library with him, and he is, apparently, an indefatigable researcher."

"It all does seem to tie together, does it not?" mused De Bressy. "Your Majesty, what about the Venetians? They seem, by all reports, to be on relatively good terms with Carlo Sforza. Surprisingly so, all things considered. Could they be asked to intervene?"

The Emperor nodded. "They can be asked, certainly; hard to know what their response would be. Abbot Goldenbuss, send some of your men to Venice. I will send a message to my ambassador there, as fast as possible. Firstly, Petro Dorma must be apprised of these developments, and secondly, perhaps they can arrange for the Knights to travel to Milan and exchange this man for some concessions."

"Venice being Venice, and the Council of Ten being what they are, they can always just have him killed," said Saasveld, with the brutal practicality for which he was famed as a general.

That thought had gone through the Emperor's head, too. But all he asked was: "And what news from Hungary?"

Chapter 21

The Duchy of Milan

Actually, Count Mindaug and his two servants were at that very moment having their first encounter with the mercenary troops of Carlo Sforza. The soldiers were guarding a bridge over the Adda River, and had positioned themselves in such a way as to direct flanking fire from their harquebuses to support the half-dozen lancers on the bridge. They weren't in loot-and-destroy mode yet, thankfully, because Count Mindaug would have had little choice but to use magical means to survive such. Two hand-cannons weren't going to go far in changing the balance of power.

Unfortunately, no one had explained that to Emma. She kept the weapon pointed unwaveringly at the lead horseman.

"Put that down," snapped the sergeant in charge of the patrol. She obliged him by turning her aim on him. Holding the hand-cannon two-handed and rock-steady, she provided, Mindaug thought, a good distraction, and would stop them watching him too closely. He would see how he could play this.

The count raised a hand pacifyingly. "She doesn't speak Frank-ish, Your Honor. We were attacked and her man badly injured by men dressed as soldiers outside Verona. So she is very scared. I don't want her to panic and kill you. Then your men would kill us. We mean no harm, but please don't alarm her. She's, um, upset by her experiences. Not quite rational yet. I am hoping to take her to a convent for help."

The sergeant didn't like the weapon pointed at him, but it was obvious her fixed expressionless stare must have convinced him that there was some truth at least to the *don't cause her to panic* part. So he concentrated his attention on the small older man with the huge mustache. "What is your business in the Duchy of Milan?"

Before he could answer, another horseman came clattering across the bridge from behind the guard. This was an obviously, by the more ornate uniform, a senior officer. The sergeant saluted him.

"And what have we got here, Sergeant?" he said, looking at the wagon. "The Scaliger invasion force?" He took in the hand-cannon and the woman holding it. "Armed to the teeth, too."

Mindaug was a good enough judge of character to say: "I will try to tell her it is all right, Your Honor. She is just scared." He repeated his story, and then told Emma in her native Magyar that she could rest the gun on her lap.

"Hungarian?" said the officer.

"My servants are, yes." He repeated his tale about being a bastard who had inherited his old lord's books, but gave his origins as Moravia.

"And so what is your business here?"

"Please, Your Honor, I am a scholar and bookseller."

"Well, Francisco Turner will be glad to see you, even if no one else will. Don't you know there is a war on?"

"No, we were just trying to get away from Verona. Actually, I hoped to go to Florence. I have heard books are much valued by Duke Cosimo."

"I've been there. He even has a public library, so you'd lose your market."

Mindaug shrugged. "Reading causes more reading, Your Honor. Please do not send us back into that lawless country behind us."

"If you're spies, you're cleverer than most. We'll need to check your wagon."

"Certainly. I can show you my books," said Mindaug, eagerly.

The officer snorted. "I think I'll save that privilege for the sergeant. Go and have a look, Sergeant."

So, accompanied by Mindaug, he did. They opened several bales and boxes at random. Fortunately, luck served the sergeant well—as it did Mindaug himself. Of course, it was unlikely a man as untutored as the sergeant would have realized the dangerous nature of some of the volumes. In any event, the presence of the bandaged and bloody Tamas inside the wagon bore out their story. They were allowed to proceed, which they did, towards the city of Milan.

It was not an unappealing city, thought the count. But that could also be because he was tired of traveling. He hired a small house near the lazaretto, and began the process of making himself comfortable. Count Mindaug knew something of spies and would have cheerfully bet that a man with a large collection of books arriving in the city would be known and noted quite fast. They would approach him in their own time and manner. The house had a cellar, which was good, because Mindaug wanted to perform some more experiments of the pyrotechnic nature. If you counted the fact that most of the rooms could have his books arrayed in them so he could find them easily, and a central, windowless one had a solid door and good lock, it was adequate. The weather, creeping toward summer, showed that it might be rather too warm for comfort here, later in the year. But Tamas, besides complaining of headaches, had largely recovered.

Milan might be in a state of war with its neighbors, but it was not yet showing any signs of it. Goods were still freely for sale, and farmers came in from the surrounding countryside to sell their produce every day. Emma apparently found the food acceptable, even if some things were far too expensive in her opinion. Mindaug found it slightly amusing how conservative she was of his money. The food was plentiful, not rationed in any way, and neither was the wine, which was better than he'd tasted before. No one appeared to anticipate a siege. Well, the count knew that that did not mean anything, and so long as he kept looters away from his books, why would he care? He could, if need be, take magical steps to see that happened. He had, gradually, carefully, without using any of his power, set up certain traps and wards that he could activate quickly.

Still, it had all cost rather a large proportion of his gold. He would need some more soon. If that had not been the case, he could have considered himself very comfortably situated, safe, hidden, and working on a bolt-hole.

Chapter 22

The disadvantage, Benito Valdosta found, of having had the tritons advising the fleet on winter weather on their outbound trip, was that he had become accustomed to it. There had been no warning of the storm coming down the Adriatic that had struck them a day out of Cerigo, driving them southwest. There was little they could do but to ship oars and run before it, and hope it blew itself out before it left them shipwrecked on the coast of Africa.

"According to Grandfather's maps, the good thing about this is there isn't a lot of land to hit," said Benito. "The bad thing about it is there isn't anything to shelter behind, either." Benito was standing on the heaving deck with Manfred. Neither of them suffered from seasickness, and the smell belowdecks was enough to make anyone think about being sick, even, as Manfred said, without drinking any wine.

Manfred shrugged. "It might get warmer if we reach Africa. There's a smell of snow on this wind, as well as the bite of it. It is spring, but I shouldn't wonder if Erik is stuck in a felt tent somewhere in the Balkans. Not that he'll be complaining with the company he has, but it'll hold him up as much as it does us."

"I want to get home. Home to a quiet life with my wife and baby," Benito complained.

Manfred laughed. "Now, you are doomed. There'll be at least another war by the time you get home, if not two."

❀ ❀ ❀

Marco Valdosta had largely despaired of finding out what sort of snake it had been. He'd had some success in getting a swallowing reaction from the young woman, but that still meant she was being fed, painstakingly slowly, a small spoonful of broth at a time. It was a good thing she'd been well-covered and healthy or she'd have starved by now.

He had also largely despaired of hearing from Francisco Turner. The nyx Rhene had not returned to the salty waters of the lagoon. He had no messages, but the Doge's agents had brought word that war had begun, with soldiers from Parma and Lombardy ravaging the northern Milanese countryside. And now, it seemed, the Scaligeri were also about to attack Milan in the east. Probably his friend was away on military duties—but that did not make Marco worry less, or prevent him from wondering why he had not heard anything. He decided that the chief role of being a father-to-be was to increase the amount of worrying he did, a hundredfold.

A summons to see the Doge privately did not ease matters. Petro Dorma received Marco in one of the small chambers in the Doge's palace that he used for small meetings he wished to keep very private. He was already seated when Marco entered and he gestured at a chair nearby.

"Please, have a seat." Once Marco had done so, Dorma continued: "I have had a troubling message from Mainz, sent by their fastest courier. And as you have . . . um, magical connections with La Serenissima, I think you need to know. A very powerful and very unpleasant magician has now arrived in our back yard—a man who was Jagiellon's confidante and worked for a time with Elizabeth Bartholdy. He was also, the Imperials inform me, Emeric of Hungary's mage when he invaded the territory of the Golden Horde. He is thought to be in Milan, suspected of being in alliance with Carlo Sforza. They are attempting to locate him there."

"Do they know what he's planning?" asked Marco.

The Doge shook his head. "Not that they informed me of. He's a nasty piece of work, though. I suspect Sforza may end up being used and devoured by the fellow. They've asked for our help in neutralizing him or, at least, locating him. They ask for my support in dealing with Carlo Sforza. They have a team of Knights of the Holy Trinity monitoring his magical works. It appears serious, whatever it is. Sforza does have a problem with the sheer number of enemies he has, but I cannot feel that adding the Holy Roman Empire to them is going to be worth having this fellow. My spies will be advised, and I will let you know, just as soon as I know any more."

And with that, Marco had to be content. It was not information he could share—but it was shared with him, by back channels, by old Itzaak the goldsmith in the Campo Ghetto.

"There's an evil and powerful new magician arrived in Milan, M'lord Marco," he whispered in a very harsh croak, after Marco arrived at his shop. "Out of Lithuania. And anything from there means bad, bad, bad."

"But... didn't some of your family come from there?" asked Marco.

"Yes. That's why we left. Because of his kind."

He would not say how he'd heard about it. But something he did let slip was that the news was not from Milan, but from a source in Venice. "Filippo Maria purged almost all the *stregheria* in his duchy. We don't hear much from there. There is no one in Milan, um, right now."

Chapter 23

The borders of the Duchy of Milan

Duke Umberto's finest men marched toward the town of Fidenza, which had so recently been taken from the Parman forces. His pennants fluttered bravely on their lances, as the troops advanced as if on a grand parade. Those cowardly mercenaries of Sforza's kept trying to draw them out with little darts forward on the flanks of his tercios. They would caracole, fire their horse pistols and then retreat. Ha. Sooner or later they would be unable to run. He had them pinned down, and they would have to engage like men eventually. Just as they talked of Dell'este, soon the name of Umberto Da Corregio would be hailed as one of the great commanders.

He stopped for a stoup of wine from his steward. And then, just because things were going so well, he had a second drink.

It saved his life.

Carlo Sforza watched the duke of Parma's tercios moving forward, from the shelter of the coppiced oaks on their northern flank. It was almost as if the fool was unaware of having flanks, or had not wondered why Sforza's cuirassiers were merely firing and retreating, with no real casualties on either side. That was to keep the Parman tercios tight, and prevent the scouts from riding out. It kept them where they were supposed to be—advancing along the easy ground toward Fidenza. From his viewpoint Carlo could see the southern flank, where on the slight rise of ground in the shelter of some elms his artillery waited, men swinging their slow matches.

166

He turned to the trumpeter. "Sound the call."

That startled Duke Umberto, several drinks into his day, and he fell off his horse, just as a cannon fusillade began its dreadful mayhem. The fourteen-pounders were loaded with grapeshot, ranged on the tercios.

Tercios of pikemen were effective against horse, and could hold their own against other pikes. But they were chaff before the cannon's flail. And then into the chaotic melee Sforza took his own cavalry, down onto a flank that had no pikes to defend it.

There was, of course, still opportunity for things to go wrong. But Carlo Sforza left little to chance. There were troops waiting in the wings. Umberto's soldiery might outnumber those of Milan, but they were scattered in several different thrusts, uncoordinated and out of touch with each other. When they met here, Umberto was not only ambushed, outflanked, and outgunned, but also outnumbered.

At grand strategy, Sforza might have a few superiors, but at battlefield tactics, none. His troops, with several dozen valuable prisoners, were not following the rout, bar the handful of light cavalry assigned to keep the enemy running for as long as possible, harassing the rear and providing the illusion of hot pursuit by Sforza's army. Sforza's scattered allies would rush there to their rescue, instead of here, where the rest of the cavalry were providing a screen for the artillery to retreat, and the infantry units were already moving out.

By the time Umberto's rescue got back here, there would be no one to fight. The bastard culverins and falconets were being moved, the wheeled gun carriages hitched to teams of horses. That was the drawback of using artillery in the field—moving the cannons fast, because if you failed to do so, they could be lost. Carlo Sforza had settled for largely employing lighter cannon and was thinking of moving to still lighter ones for field artillery. The drilling that his artillerymen had in rates of fire, in aiming, and in moving the guns gave them an advantage. Some of the Italian city-states did not even have trunnions on their cannons. They used the big guns largely for siegework, and if they moved them at all, did so by hauling them about with oxen, and used wagons rather than gun carriages. Horses were more expensive and lacked the sheer slow-speed power of oxen, but they made up for it, as far as Carlo was concerned, with speed.

Speed and communication won wars. Other factors might

win battles, but wars were won by he who could know what was happening, and react the fastest.

Sforza had refined that. He had a properly organized system of scouts and messengers, and worked on making his troops as mobile as possible. He had lost the battle of the Polestine Forts because, partially, he had trusted Filippo Maria's assurance that the forts themselves would be neutralized. He didn't place reliance on allies—or employers—any more. If it could not be scouted, it was to be avoided if possible.

Somehow, someday, he must get to talking to his son about these matters. The boy was learning strategy from the grandmaster Dell'este of Ferrara. But Sforza's skill was different.

Two messengers rode up. "The cannon are hitched and moving out, milord, save one, where they're trying to change a broken wheel."

"Which piece is it?"

"One of the old demiculverins, m'lord," said the messenger.

"Tell them to spike it and get the horses out of there." One of the newer falconets might have been worth trying to salvage, but the demiculverins were only there because he hadn't yet had the spare funds to replace them.

The next pair of messengers came in, with the report from the cavalry. It appeared Duke Umberto had gotten away in the confusion, although they had his condottieri and a selection of his nobles.

It was time to move on. The entire conflict had lasted less than thirty minutes; the retreat and regroup would be over in an hour. Carlo yawned. He wasn't bored, just tired. That was unusual enough for him to notice. He'd better not tell Francisco or he'd probably make his commander swallow muck and do exercises. Carlo Sforza was very fond of his physician, but the laconic Turner was far too fussy about a few extra pounds on the waistline of a fighting man. It could keep you alive in a siege or even a case of the flux.

The fighting would slow down now, anyway, with Umberto out of the fray and their foes given a good bloody nose. They would be back to condottieri sparring for position, laying siege to profitable towns, and looting what they could from the countryside. Given the scale of the Duchy of Milan, Carlo could be back in the city before morning if he wished to be.

Their western attackers had to face crossing the Po or the Ticino rivers, both now in flood with the snow melt, to get to Milan. Attacks from the east could be a little more problematic as Milan's enemies held a crossing of the Mincio River. Of course, the inverse was true as well. There were what had been Visconti lands on the far bank, although two of these had rebelled. Still, Goito, a relatively small town on the Milanese bank, had been held for some generations by Scaliger allies. It was a planned beachhead, Carlo's spies told him. That was borne out by scouts counting the stream of men crossing the bridge and being billeted in the town, and encamped around the fortress there. The strength of the town lay in the bridge, and that the fortress on the Milanese side and the second, smaller fortification on the other bank made it a safe crossing point. The slight elevation of the fort gave a good covering field of fire, and made the bridge relatively safe to cross, even under fire.

The river could be forced elsewhere, boats or pontoons could be used, but right now it was full and fast-flowing, lipping its banks.

"Nearly four thousand men, and not a lot of food or ammunition yet," said the messenger. "Here are the tallies, m'lord. Some of what is in the wagons is hard to guess."

Carlo Sforza had personally seen to the supplying of his troops. He didn't need to look hard at the figures: men, especially on horse, moved faster than wagons on muddy roads. A quick calculation... he rubbed his eyes, fighting off a brief spell of dizziness. At this rate, he would have to consult Francisco. However, even if his body was letting him down, his will was still hard enough to make it focus on the words. At best they had three days' worth of food—barely what the men were carrying in their own kit. The little town would never have enough food for a tenth of the number. It was time to strike again, and strike hard and fast.

That would take an all-night ride. But that, too, was no novelty to Carlo Sforza. What he'd done once, he could do again. And again, if need be.

But by the time he arrived at the hamlet of Cerlongo, some miles from Goito, and just inside the lands held by his troops, to meet his sappers and siege cannon, he was so exhausted he merely gave the orders and went to bed.

He wasn't that surprised to find that his officers had sent for Francisco Turner, who was there on his waking.

"If that explosion didn't wake you, you're sick," said his physician grimly, taking his pulse.

"Did it work?" he asked.

"Took out the center span, the one next to it partially, and damaged the middle piling. They failed to think of a barge full of kegs of black powder and a cross-strut too wide for their bridge," said Francisco, with the ghost of a smile. "The barge jammed under the bridge for a solid couple of minutes before the fuse burned enough to blow the powder kegs. We had sharpshooters keeping them from jumping down onto the barge. Anyway, the siege guns will be in place in the next hour, and the fortress must be bulging at the seams. We've got the infantry in the village, and the encampment has been burned."

"Good. What is wrong with me?"

"Besides doing what two men half your age would be exhausted by, I don't know yet," said the physician.

"I don't get tired, Francisco."

"You don't admit you do. I've seen you gray with exhaustion and still in the saddle."

"Yes, but that was after three days solid, and we'd had no food, and I had the flux."

"I know. I was there, remember? Now lie down, I need to examine you."

He did, leaving few bits unpoked or unprodded and, as usual, asked too many questions.

"When did you last eat?"

"I don't remember. Oh, yes. The boys and I stopped before dawn to change horses and I had some sausage and bread."

"Before that?"

"I had some food at an inn somewhere. It was typical peasant pottage. Too many pease, too little meat, plenty of onions. Bound to give you gas, but I was not feeling too good before we left Fidenza, to be honest."

"It's my opinion that you have been poisoned. Your eyes are yellow, or at least the whites of them are," said Francisco.

"'Swounds, Francisco! If anyone poisoned me, they'd have to have poisoned half my men. It was the same sausage, the same pottage. I ate with the men before we gave Umberto a hiding. You know I always do that, and they like it."

"So do you. But, as Petro Dorma could tell you, not all poisons are administered by food, and not all are quick-acting."

"So what are you going to do to me?" asked Carlo slightly

peevishly. Of all the things he was suspicious about, and disliked most, cupping was very high on the list.

"Restrict your diet. Make sure you use a taster, even for your wine. Shuffle your bodyguards, and order you to take a week's bed rest. A bed back in Milan so you don't get out of bed to shout at your siege masters. We know our trade, too," said Francisco.

"A week! Are you mad?" said Carlo, sitting up and feeling giddy.

"If I order a week, I might get two days," said Francisco. "And now is the best time for it. The Piedmontese troops are not in the field yet, Parma and the Genovese are reeling, and the Scaligeri will be too busy trying to relieve this lot."

"You make a good point," admitted Sforza.

"I do my best. I'll go and arrange a carriage."

"I can't be seen in a damned carriage! They'll be saying I'm nearly dead."

Francisco shrugged. "We'll let you ride out of town."

"I'll inspect the siege first. They expect it of me, and that'll quash any rumors."

"No, you won't," said Francisco.

"Are you telling me what to do? Again? After last time?" demanded Carlo.

"Yes. Because you look like a pallid shadow of yourself, and you'd fall over, and then you'd have worse than rumors. Trust me, I'll go and tell some lies for you. Tell them your new wife is panting for you and the first night left you exhausted. They'll like that, and believe it, too."

"Humph. You should have entered politics. I had no idea physicians were so dishonest," said Carlo, attempting a bit of banter and sensing his man's concern under the joke.

"Doctors have to tell people that they'll recover," said Francisco with a wry smile. "I'll go across to the siege-works. The Scaligeri won't last too long, I don't think, as long as we hold the other bridges."

Carlo Sforza was left trying to think how he could have been poisoned. By whom was harder. It was more a case of which one of his foes would not prefer him dead. Still, he'd planned to go back to Milan in another day or two. Anyway, there was a great deal of planning and coordination that needed doing, and realistically, Milan was far more central and had better resources than some border village did. He'd get reports from the spies he had employed before—a very small select group—and from his predecessors' large and somewhat less select group. Some of them, Carlo suspected, had survived by telling Filippo Maria what he wanted to hear. Those would have to go soon.

He wondered, briefly, how his new wife would take to the news that he had been poisoned. It had seemed very important to her that her child would one day rule Milan. Unless she'd been lucky on their wedding night, that would have to take a lot more wine than Francisco was going to let him have.

Lucia was not surprised to see him brought back to the palace sickly. She feigned concern, of course. He told her to stop it, because their enemies would be given courage by his obviously being ill and dismay by his being seen not to be.

Nothing could be easier.

And while he suspected he'd been poisoned, he had no idea that she, or rather the asp, had done it while he slept. It had seemed fitting revenge, and after all, she had no further use for him after that. He was not to die...not until it was closer to the time of her confinement. So she continued building up her networks of power. She'd paid back those who had slighted her in full already, except for the few whom she was making suffer as long as possible. She'd even made one of them a lady-in-waiting. That was going to be a sweet form of slow torture.

Lucia had also singled out those who had given her suitable deference, too, for advancement. But this gave her a new opportunity. "I think I ought to have my own guards and a taster," she said.

"Certainly. I'll have Francisco Turner choose a few suitable..."

"I shall choose them myself," she said firmly. "I am far more acquainted with the nobility of the court than you are."

Sforza shrugged. "As you wish. But I warn you—most of them could not defend themselves against a man armed with a dried sausage."

He was dismissive of the aristocracy of Milan in private with her, although he avoided it in public. She made sure they knew of his opinions, though, and that she did not share them. She would need some of them, and it was quite pleasant to have them fawn over her. It filled an old need.

"He's quite healthy looking," she said to the asp, disapprovingly.

He is stronger than we knew, said the asp-voice.

"Well, do something. I can't have him dead yet, but I want him weaker so he does not come back to my bed. I do not wish to go through that again."

When darkness falls. In the quiet hours I will prick him again. Just a tiny scratch on the skin. It is much easier just to kill.

"I don't need you to do things the easy way."

Chapter 24

Milan

Francisco had informed his commander that he, too, was staying in Milan. "I cannot be on hand to see to you if I'm seeing to troop deployments in Brescia. Besides, you have better men than me for that. And you really do need to rest, stick to the diet I have prescribed, and take that vile concoction of mine." He pointed to the cordial he had made up. He was not too sure that it would help, just as he was not too sure what poison had been given to Sforza. It was not, at least as yet, a lethal thing. He'd seen a little improvement in Sforza's color and general mien since he had slept all the way back through the jolting to Milan. That he could sleep in the swaying bouncing carriage was worrying enough.

Francisco was a soldier and a physician, not a spymaster. He needed to be the latter to find the poison, the poisoner, or the means of administering it. He did know, both from the prevention and treatment point of view, that it was vital to do so. However, he trusted none of the spies whose proper trade it was, so he would just have to try his best, too. Carlo's bodyguards were all personally loyal and long-term soldiers. He had enlisted their aid in this, and they were being slightly more jumpy than a mouse sneaking though a cat's fur. That was fine by Francisco, but he still felt more needed to be done. So he went for an early morning run to think about it.

That always did his head good, even if it did not entirely solve anything. He stopped for his usual beer afterwards, thinking of his strange aquatic encounter last time, and keeping away from the water.

That resulted in a large lump of decaying lily root hitting him on the back of the neck.

"Stop ignoring me," said the water-woman, whose bare breasts would have been hard to ignore had he been looking that way.

"I have no desire to be drowned, nor am I feeling frolicsome. The water is still too cold, and I have other things on my mind." He wondered if she ever did.

"I've got another message for you. Where have you been? Have you been avoiding me?" she asked, handing him the same bottle, but resealed.

"No. I've been across the Po to a battle, and down to Mincio for a siege," he said, guessing that river names might mean more to her than town names. "And don't you have many admirers of your own kind? I'm surprised you're interested in humans. We're poor swimmers."

She looked at him in surprise. "There are no males among the nyx. We look to humans to breed."

"Oh." Perhaps comments about mules would be less than wise, he thought. "So, um, do you have many children?" he asked out of politeness.

"No, they all die."

She actually seemed quite upset by that, and it was hard to know what to say. So he settled for, "Well, you must have been a child and lived, or you wouldn't be here."

She wrinkled her forehead. "That was long, long ago. So long it has faded in my memory."

That seemed to affront her, too, and she slipped away under the water.

Which left Francisco to take Marco Valdosta's message back to his quarters, and later to his commander. Sforza had chosen his sickroom with some care. It was a tower and had, one hoped, no secret chambers or spying points. It also had a most ingenious conceit which worked very well—on the roof there was a large cistern, which was painstakingly filled every day by men with buckets. That provided the water for a little ornamental fountain. A strange conceit indeed, indoors. But the tinkling splash made overhearing what was said very difficult. It was a fine idea, as long as you were not one of the poor fellows carrying the buckets up the stairs.

Francisco was pleased to see Sforza looking alert and—as he always did when confined indoors too long—looking like a caged lion, considering all ways out of there.

"I have some interesting news from our spies in Venice," said Sforza with a tigerish smile. "Two of them, separately, so I can believe it. We apparently have recruited a powerful and evil magician to our forces. Someone named Count Mindaug, originally from Lithuania. You were quite right. All we had to do was tell them we absolutely had not set out to do so."

"It's amazing how far the imagination can stretch," replied Francisco, chuckling.

"In this case, it appears to be supported by a fellow showing up in Milan with a great many books. I am assured that anyone who arrives with a whole wagon load of books and two foreign servants has to be a magician."

"Yes, I had similar conclusions jumped to about me in Venice. So who is this 'magician'?" asked Francisco, who was naturally curious at the mention of books.

"He claims to be Freiherr Jagr, of Bohemia, who has inherited his father's library and is a traveling bookseller. But he hasn't sold any books. My spies are, frankly, very suspicious."

"I would be, too. It's a fair distance from Bohemia," said Francisco, who had been there twice on horseback.

"But he really does have a vast number of books, according to them. I don't trust their judgment. I want you to investigate. It's an opportunity you are not often offered by me: go and buy a book. We're watching him and can toss him in jail if need be, but sometimes one can find out more before one puts on the thumbscrews than after. Take a few men, in case he tries anything exciting, but don't make him run if you can help it. He's frightening our foes for us."

"I suspect a vast number of books will be ten, and he will be some illiterate mountebank, but yes, I will do that. Now, I have something else that's peculiar, that I wish to bring to your attention, m'lord." He handed Carlo the letter from Marco Valdosta. "There are two things relevant about this. The first is the nature of young Valdosta: he simply isn't any good at duplicity."

"I remember that from him as a child, occasionally attempting, as children do, to deny responsibility for something. It usually wasn't him, of course, it was Benito, and then he'd say it was him, to shelter the brat. Benito could be as clever as a fox about avoiding being caught, but not Marco."

Francisco nodded. "That probably hasn't changed. But the second is that he names the source of this 'plague' story: Thomas Lüber of Baden, who is something unusual. He's a churchman, but he is known across the medical world for his systematic work on medical plants and his blunt outspokenness. He's no mystic or politician dressed in Church clothes. He's a scientist who cares for nothing but his work."

"And to add a third, you and I were both sure this was a rumor set by the Church intent on bringing Milan down," mused Sforza. "There is a faction in Rome that would like to see that happen. But none of my spies have reported it to me. None. That says for a deliberately spread rumor it's being kept very secret. We've had it from precisely two people, and while Cosimo can be as sneaky as a Sicilian"—Carlo Sforza had never forgiven the entire population of Sicily for the fact that one of them had stolen his pilgrim medal—"he appears to only have told you, and only once he knew that he could trust you."

"Which brings us a problem. I don't think it's in our best interests to alienate young Marco. Besides, it would be like kicking a puppy. But there is no real treatment known for the Plague of Justinian. It killed vast numbers across Europe, and then came back more or less every generation. It did seem to get less intense in the numbers killed, but stories of the blue-black buboes are enough to frighten peasants witless centuries later."

"What happened to it?"

Francisco shrugged. "It would run its course, and stop when it ran out of new places to spread. Quarantine did contain it... for a while. And then it just didn't happen anymore. We've had a few centuries since the last outbreak."

"Like fire, it needs to keep spreading. And if you thin the fuel out enough, it'll stop. Well, I agree with you. Let's do our best to keep young Marco sweet. Did you get this message in the same bizarre way?"

Francisco nodded.

"Always good to have...shall we say, alternative channels of communication. Give him some advice on quarantine, and give him an opening which will allow him a chance to tell you how that won't work," said Sforza.

"I'll have to give it some thought, but I will do my best. Now, how are you feeling today?"

After examining his patient, Francisco picked a couple of men—a tough sergeant, and the sort of trooper who would have been a sergeant if he gave up getting drunk and fighting with the sergeants. Both were in Milan because they'd been injured, but both were due to rejoin their troops soon, and anyway, reflected Francisco, half-dead they were still tougher than any so-called magician, or most other forms of life. In that, they were like Sforza, but not as intelligent, or quite as tough.

"Where are we going, Captain?"

"A bookseller. Or so he claims. It should be a new experience for both of you, unless it turns out that he is being a front for a brothel or tavern, and I can't see any sign of anyone keeping those secret," said Francisco.

"He's a spy or up to something," said the trooper.

"Possibly. But you're to behave unless he shows signs of trouble or flight."

Because Francisco was a soldier first and an investigator of dubious booksellers somewhere far below that, they checked the flanks and rear first. Francisco left the sergeant to watch the rear and told him to come running if there was a shout.

He and the trooper knocked at the front door of the unpretentious little house. It was opened almost immediately by a pretty young woman, who was plainly pregnant.

She smiled at them, "Good morning, *úr*," she said, in heavily accented Frankish—and not with the Italian accent, either. Hungarian, by the honorific. Francisco was dressed well enough for the woman to grant him that, and a small bow. She did keep one hand tucked in her apron, and there was a bucket and mop just behind her. A smell of new-baked bread, and . . . gunpowder tickled Francisco's nose.

He bowed politely. "*Jó napot kívánok,*" he said cautiously, expending his entire supply of polite Hungarian.

He was given a huge smile and a positive gale of what was presumably her native language, and a far bigger curtsey—enough to see a glimpse of the hand-cannon she had tucked under her apron.

He held up his hand and shook his head. "I am sorry. That is all I can understand or can say in your language. I am the

Caviliero Francisco Turner. I am a collector of books and I have heard you have some for sale."

She frowned. Realizing she had not understood him, Francisco repeated himself, slowly.

"Ah. Books. So many, so much to dust. I am not to touch some, the master says. I call him. Wait. I call."

As she turned, there was an explosion. Not huge, to a man who had known cannon fire, but still loud. The young woman turned and ran. Francisco and his man ran after her, down a short passage lined with shelves of books, into the kitchen and down a stairs.

Well... partway down the stairs. Smoke and a smallish man with a vast white mustache and rather disheveled hair was coming up it, coughing. Francisco would guess that what she was frantically asking was if he was all right. From a scullery door came another young man, limping and with a bandage still around his head—obviously equally concerned.

"Let me guess," said Francisco. "You're an alchemist."

The fellow with a mustache waved off his servants and stepped forward to meet him. He bowed. "Alas, no, just a man seeking knowledge, and occasionally making some error of judgment."

He looked at the two of them, in an assessing fashion. "What is it that you gentlemen seek in my house?"

His Frankish was impeccable, as if spoken by a gentleman of Mainz. That in itself was a bit odd, combined with the Hungarian servants. Francisco introduced himself and repeated his story about wishing to buy books.

"Ah. The Caviliero Francisco Turner. I had heard you might be my only customer in Milan," said the man. "May I introduce myself? I am Kazimierz Jagr of Bohemia, a visitor to your fair city. What manner of books are you interested in, m'lord? I am afraid I only have a small number of volumes for sale. The rest are for my work."

His eyes were as sharp as gimlets and very alert and, despite the fact that he was not very large, Francisco, who had spent much of his life summing up enemies, had a feeling this man could be dangerous if he chose to be. Still, at the moment he seemed polite and wary. Well, that was wise for a foreigner in any place. "Medical texts, particularly," answered Francisco.

"Aha. You are a physician? I have some texts... and I would like your services."

"I'm a soldier, not a physician for hire."

"A pity. Come with me, good sir. Emma, bring wine"—he sniffed—"and maybe some of the new bread."

He led Francisco and his man to a second room. The furnishing was, at this stage, Spartan: a table and shelving which the fellow with the bandage on his head had perhaps been constructing more of; there were planks and tools, and a pile of oilskin-wrapped bundles. The shelves were in the throes of having books unpacked onto them. Not as many books as Cosimo de' Medici had in his public library—but this was one room. And these books were different. They were old. "I try to collect the original texts. With hand-copying, they become much altered. But the inks do not last forever," said the man. "You are, I gather, a reading man. Are you familiar with the Persian physician and philosopher Avicenna? I have a very early translation, a copy in Cremona's own hand. I have it in Arabic too, but..."

"I do read and speak that."

The look he got from the supposed bookseller said he had gone up in the fellow's estimation. "Then I do have something which will interest you. I do not have the complete work, but I have some of Al-Nafis's writings. Some of the originals."

Francisco's mouth fell open. "Interested! I should say I am. I thought they had all been destroyed. I must...um, I would like to see those."

"It will be my pleasure to allow you to read them. I don't think they have been unpacked yet. Tamas, poor fellow, is suffering quite badly from the effects of an assault we suffered in Scaliger lands just east of Verona. He has been struggling to put up the shelves."

Francisco knew when he'd been outmaneuvered, and it was not unpleasant in discovering one of the rarest and most anatomically accurate of texts. "Let me have a look at him," he said. He dug in his pouch and took out a coin. "Gilotti, go tell Marona I said for you both to go and have a mug of wine. And I mean a mug. One mug. Come back here when you're done. I see that I shall be a while."

The trooper grinned, took the money, saluted and left.

By now, Francisco was sure of three things: the man was not illiterate, he was not a mountebank, and he did have a large number of books.

He just wasn't sure quite what he actually was. He was too well read, too knowledgeable. He was decidedly experimenting with something in his cellar. Did magic involve black powder? Alchemy seemed most likely. On the other hand, his servants plainly worshipped the ground he walked on, and yet there was a peculiar attitude to both of them, as if they were looking after a beloved but slightly abnormal child. The man was investing a level of care in his servant not common among the nobility. That, no matter where he was now, was what this fellow had been raised to be, and amongst.

Francisco examined the servant. "You should have stitched that up," he said of the long, shallow slash down his chest and abdomen. "You have some infection down there. It needs to be kept as clean and dry as possible. You have some spirits of wine in your experimental equipment? Clean it with that. I hold with boiled cloth for dressings myself; there seems some virtue in it from the heat. Clean the wound drawing the swabs away from the wound, like this. You won't believe how many healthy wounds can have the evil humors spread by cleaning up and down them."

Then he examined the patient's head, tapping his teeth, feeling very carefully. "I'll need a razor," he said.

"Er, it requires surgery?"

"No, I just wish to shave a piece of his head. I believe he has a fractured skull, but it is necessary to see if there is any depression of the bone. I don't think so."

A razor was hastily brought. And Francisco noted the bookseller knew very little of medicine, but a great deal about anatomy. The girl was quietly crying and praying. But the bookseller was two things: curious and worried. He did his best not to let either show, but Francisco had dealt with too many men in too many battles.

He examined the shaved skull carefully, gently. "It's unlikely there is large damage. He'd have had worse than headaches. But my experience says as little activity as possible, as little bouncing about as possible—I've lost count as to how many patients got worse after riding. Give it a few weeks. He is to sleep as much as he can, and from my experience keeping troopers from doing stupid things, you should keep him busy doing nonphysical activity when he isn't sleeping. There's no guarantee, but there is a good chance of recovery. It's my finding that narcotics or wine don't help much, and tend to have worse effects later, for all the relief they give now. Sleep is best."

The bookseller translated. The girl let loose with a burst of what Francisco would bet was a severe lecture directed at the poor young man. She was a pretty young thing now, but she'd make a dragon of an older woman one day, he judged. Then she kissed Francisco's hand and, from what he understood, thanked him and the saints and God profusely.

"Take him upstairs and put him to bed, Emma," said the bookseller, putting an end to her recital.

When they'd left, the man said: "And now, Caviliero, maybe you will actually tell me what you want?"

He sounded faintly amused. "I know you are one of the officers of the Protector, Sforza. I have seen you are a well-read man and plainly an experienced physician. You did not come here—accompanied by a soldier, with another outside—merely by chance. I would guess that you want to know who I am and what I am here for. I would guess you act directly for your commander. Am I correct?"

The fellow was all too astute. "You could be. But I want to know what you were doing in that cellar?" asked Francisco.

The bookseller scowled. "Following instructions in a book precisely—and getting an unexpected and very dangerous result. I can only conclude the quantities were willfully recorded wrongly to cause that result. I had used only a tenth part of the recipe, too."

"What book?"

"Your knowledge of Arabic script may be of some value here, Caviliero. Perhaps I made a mistake. It is a Persian translation of a book from China, the *Wujing Zongyao*, a text largely on the construction and use of Chinese imperial weapons. I had thought the weapons described in it might make me of some value to the Protector. If he does not want magical support, that is. I have already had a number of others making enquiries for suitable spells."

"And can you provide those?" asked Francisco, who had reached his own conclusions.

The bookseller looked at him from under heavy-lidded eyes. "Can I make gold from base metal? What do you think, Caviliero? If I could transport magically, would I travel by wagon? If I could conjure ever-filled purses or demons to transport the treasures of the earth to me, would I be down in the cellar grinding charcoal and saltpeter crystals, and adding various other substances to achieve suitable smoke? Would I not have foretold your coming and magically cured my man?"

"A point. As it happens, my master might have employment for someone who was *believed* a great magician," said Francisco. The man was as sharp as a razor and had successfully pointed out the flaws in many a mountebank's tale . . . while enhancing his reputation.

"People will believe anything, especially aided with a suitable trick or two," said the bookseller, cheerfully admitting he was a fraud. "I was experimenting partly for that reason, too. I have a marvelous list of pyrotechnic effects in a treatise by Hakawai, in one of the languages of Hind, which did not agree with those in *Wujing*—which was what I was experimenting with. And, of course," he added sarcastically, "I can write you suitable protective cantrips against diseases of the genitals and for creating lust or fidelity."

As he'd had experience of being asked for those, Francisco understood precisely what he was talking about. "They seem to work, too, when they are believed in."

"Ah, belief. Many strange things may be due to that," said the bookseller-cum-magician-fraud. "It was a concept about which Xenophanes was wrong, and Pythagoras correct. Anyway, come down to the cellar and I will show you one of the devices I have had some success with. I am really in need of a larger and more private place for this. I used to have space . . . back before I was relegated to fleeing with my books. In those days, I never thought of experimenting with these things, and now I regret it."

"You fled your home?"

"Oh, yes. In Hungary, not Bohemia. Politics, you understand." He sighed. "At the time, I cared, I think. But now the farther I get from Hungary and its mad politics, the more I just want a safe place to read my books and experiment a little."

"Milan is not what most would think of as 'safe' these days."

The man shrugged. "I actually wanted to go to Florence, but it seems there is a war in my way."

He led Francisco down to the cellar, which was singularly lacking in pentacles or such arcana, but did have a workbench along one wall with considerable broken glassware—the result of the last experiment, Francisco guessed. There was a little shelter of crates, which had a desk, a journal and a book which plainly had been being referred to, and a stool in it, and in the far corner a second screen—now somewhat splintered.

The journal had careful notes in it, Francisco noticed. The man was obviously systematic and, for what he was doing, careful. He took out a small tube from the drawer. "These are quite successful. I have a larger version which produces a great volume of smoke, too, and considerable noise. But I cannot test those yet. The smoke would be unendurable down here, and the neighbors might become upset. It is a simple mixture of the substances used in gunpowder, ground malachite, and salt and iron filings." He put the little tube in a clamp behind the structure, and then lit a small candle, which he placed under a second little bowl, and a wick on top of that. He retreated to join Francisco. "The second little bowl is made of wax. It takes a little time to melt through and ignite the fuse. This little device appears quite safe—but I am cautious."

They waited and watched. The second wax bowl melted through, the candle flared up, the fuse burned, and the tube began spraying green fire—and then spat, with a small shriek, a fat glowing yellow spark which burst with a loud pop and smell of sulfur.

It was, even knowing what it was, and having seen the muzzle flash of cannon often enough, and even having seen gunpowder sparking and burning, still enough to raise the hair on Francisco's neck.

"So-called 'magic' via gunpowder," said the supposed bookseller, plainly smiling behind the mustache. "Now let us go upstairs before those men of yours come bursting in to rescue you, and I end up on trial for black magic. I can provide you with the precise instructions. There are no demons involved."

"I'll talk to Carlo Sforza about it, and possibly find you a place where the neighbors are less likely to come and haul you out at night and crucify you. You can do other colors?"

"Some. And probably more, with experimentation. The description of rockets that I have read sounds...militarily interesting."

Francisco was thinking of night signals, let alone frightening the hell out of superstitious foes. The trick might be to not frighten their own troops just as badly.

He was actually whistling jauntily when he left there. More so, because the bookseller had given him a gift of the three books attributed to Al-Nafis that he had wanted. So the fellow was a fraud...

All the better. Both Francisco and Carlo Sforza would be

more comfortable with a fraud and a man of science than a real magician. Now all he had to do was compose a letter to Marco Valdosta.

He was a few hundred paces down the street when it struck him that he might just as well ask the bookseller-fraud—obviously a fallen nobleman, but one who had spent his wealth on reading and experimentation rather than drink and fornication—if in his researches he'd ever seen a description of that snake. That would be something to tell Marco, anyway.

So he went back. The man was settling in with a book when he returned, but got up to greet him. "Had you forgotten something, Caviliero?"

"Not directly, no. It struck me as I was walking down the road that you are a well-read and, it seems, a well-traveled man. I have been trying to identify a snake—an extremely poisonous one. It's a plummy blue-black and has a dirty yellow belly, with some brighter yellow about the head. I had never come across such colors in a snake."

The man raised his head and nodded thoughtfully. His cheeks moved indicating a smile beneath that vast mustache. It must be very in the way for eating, thought Francisco.

He cocked his head slightly. "Is this a trick question?

"Not that I am aware of."

"Oh. I thought you were referring to this." He pointed to the book on the table. "A few pages back."

He turned them, carefully. It was a very old book, handwritten and illustrated. "A history of Lombardy. Not very well written, but interesting. Ah. Here it is."

There was a color illustration of a crowned blue-black serpent, with that precise purple shade to it, devouring a red human.

Francisco had seen it often enough. The *biscione* was the heraldic charge of the noble House of Visconti. The modern version he'd always seen, however, had made it far closer to argent than purple, and the figure had been more determinedly male, and the head modified to be more dragonlike.

The bookseller frowned slightly. "I did read something about it in a poem about Theoderic many years ago. I forget the precise details. Something about a knight rescuing a virgin from the wyrm."

"That was what dragons did," said Francisco.

"Ah, but the line between 'dragon' and 'serpent' or 'wyrm' is very small, the further back you go. I'll look for the story. It's still in one of the crates to be unpacked. Such stories and symbols often have a basis in reality, or have become real as a result. Reality, Caviliero, is less easy to understand than I once thought." His sharp eyes were glinting. "Now, is there anything else I can do for you?"

"No. My thanks, although I don't think it can be that serpent... Well, unless reality is more complex than I imagine."

"Oh, it always is," said the bookseller.

Walking back to his quarters, this time Francisco was not whistling. He was deep in thought.

That was true of Count Mindaug, too. He'd lied. He had never forgotten any of the details of anything he had read. It was, of course, court practice, and his in particular, to use that knowledge to outfox and entrap your foes. But there had been something unusual about the caviliero's visit. It had been many months since Mindaug had last had anything to do with people of his own order, and years since he'd had anything to do with men of his own intellect, well-read and with quick minds. And those had been foes, who would rather not give him information unless, as he had done himself, for advancement or as a trap.

This Turner was not of his own order—he was a soldier and an officer, not a nobleman. But the gap was not large, especially in Lithuania. Furthermore, his curiosity and his willingness to explain his field of knowledge, and the fact that he could converse intelligently on other topics and was, it was easy to see, still excited by ideas, had been striking. Turner had briefly made the count forget who and what he was, and take pleasure in the exchange of ideas.

This was a different world, and one which had not been given to the count's prior experience. He thought, slightly wistfully, that it might have been rather pleasant to live like that. It was a bit late in life now, and Lithuania under Jagiellon had been no place for it.

But what was this about the wyrm? That was worrying, and not in his plans at all. He knew how it had been born, and whence the color came from. It was the color of the buboes.

Chapter 25

Corfu

The Venetian fleet, storm-battered and tired, limped into Corfu Harbor, having had to make back under oars most of the distance they'd been blown south. Several of the vessels would have to remain in the little Arsenal for major repairs, and it would be a few days at least before even those which had weathered the storm best could sail on in convoy for Venice. Benito was glad he was going to be leaving the fleet there. Glad to get back to Corfu, glad to get back to his wife and babe.

Maria was not on the quay, nor waving with the others on the walls. Renate Belmondo was not an adequate or welcome substitute. She did bring him a letter from Maria and a letter with the seal of the Doge, as her husband, who was sick again, was not really up to coming down to the quay. He had been wheeled out of retirement to act as governor while Benito—who was himself a temporary appointee—was away with the fleet.

"I am sorry not to see your wife back on the island," said the woman who was the high priestess of the Mother-Goddess cult, as well as the wife of the ex-governor.

She was not entirely sincere, Benito could read that in her tone. Maria might not be aware of it, but he could guess that the old queen bee was enjoying being in sole charge of the hive. Maria being away was good for her, but he was sure Renate would have been a lot happier if it was Benito who hadn't come back.

"Yes, but the letter is reassuring," he said calmly, hiding his worry as he tucked the letters away in a pocket of his doublet. "I am grateful for the messages."

He'd do his level best to get the Venetian Republic to post Renate's husband back to Venice, or somewhere else. On the other hand... that might promote Maria into her shoes.

"Excuse me, I must go and read these," he said. She'd be curious and that would gall her. Benito knew he was nurturing a grudge, but that was what happened when anyone did not take extreme care with his family.

Duty be damned. After he got back to his cabin on the ship, he opened the letter from Maria first. She'd plainly worked on her penmanship since the last letter he had from her.

> *My darling Benito*
> *I am missing you terribly, and so is Alessia. The Doge will not permit me to sail to Corfu to meet you, as they want you in Venice. I have a good surprise for you in that we will not have to be apart again.*

That was wonderful. But... how had she done it?

Benito eased himself onto the chair at his small writing desk, as he pondered the problem. He'd made the bargain with Aidoneus, knowing that two thirds was still better than none at all and that had been his alternative. He'd never been that secure in the Lord of the Dead's ability not to weasel out of his promise, but it seemed that not only had he honored it, but he had also decided to do more. Meeting the Lord of the Dead to thank him for his honorable conduct probably wasn't going to happen, but one never knew. He wondered if Maria had thrown plates at his head. She had a fire of a temper on her!

There was more, news that Katerina was pregnant. That would be good for Marco. News of what Alessia was doing and saying...

Benito stopped himself from rereading it immediately, and opened the letter with the Doge's seal on it. He knew it would be ordering his return to Venice, and indeed it was so. There were scant details, just that he should proceed immediately to Venice, as the Republic had need of his services yet again. They did get around to thanking him for what he'd done, but obviously the willing horse was to be flogged another mile. Well, at least Maria would be there waiting for him. And Venice would have to wait for services until he'd provided them to his wife.

His grandfather came into his cabin, closing the hatch behind him. "Well. So you're to go to Venice."

"Does everyone know? I have just read about it myself," he said, holding up the letter. "Do you know why, seeing as they don't say?"

The Old Fox gave the smile that had earned him his name, as much for his ability as a strategist and his cunning in outsmarting larger foes. "Not yet. But two of my spies were waiting on the quay for me, as well as a considerable number of letters. The joys of governance."

Benito nodded in invitation at the nearby bunk where he slept at night. His cabin was on the small side and that was the only other place to sit besides his writing chair. After his grandfather had taken a seat, Benito shook his head. "Indeed. I'm quite glad not to wade through the mess old Belmondo will have made of my reforms to the Libri del Oro system. They'll have been trying to get at him to reverse the changes. Not so good for Venice."

"It's a smart man who can see the long term," said his grandfather, "and a smarter one who can persuade others to do so. It's one of the joys of absolute rule. Not that you can let go of popularity, just that you allow yourself a little more leeway."

Benito shook his head again, this time in disbelief rather than reproof. The duke of Ferrara, Benito knew, was so popular with his people that it was hard to imagine them turning against him.

He said so.

The duke pulled a wry face and shook his head. "That is something you can never be sure of until you're dead. Remember that. Always remember that. If you have to do something unpopular, you see to it that you make a good show of it making your life less pleasant, too. Let them identify with you—beat iron even if you do it badly. Give them victories, but don't let them get too fat and comfortable."

Benito realized he was getting the *you will take over my principality* talk. He still wasn't at all sure how he felt about that, but instead of debating the point, he merely said: "But if they're fat and comfortable, surely they won't be rebellious?"

"Ah, but if they're too fat and comfortable, the slightest hardship will seem like the world's end and fit to rebel about. It's a balancing act. You should be good at it from climbing around on rooftops."

"They don't move as much as people do. So how did you know I was going to Venice?"

His grandfather looked around, making a pretense of inspecting the cabin. "No Maria here," he said after a few seconds. "But you are not that upset. Therefore, logic states she and your daughter must be in Venice, and you are going there. So: as you have nothing else to do, come and hear my spies reporting to me."

This, too, was a great honor and an exercise in trust, Benito knew. But it was not to happen just then, because no sooner had he and Dell'este gotten back out onto the deck than Manfred came bustling up.

"Ah, Benito! Our friend the Loukoumia just found me on the quayside." He waved his hand more or less in that direction. "He says Erik is across the channel, some miles away, with Iskander Beg. Is there any chance I can prevail upon you to arrange transport and accommodation for him and Bortai before you charge off to Venice?"

Benito scowled. "Does everyone know I'm going to Venice?"

"Of course. It's as obvious as the nose on your face, even if all the crew didn't know it already. Some trouble with Milan apparently. Not war, though—yet, at least."

That was uncomfortable. The last time he'd faced his father, it had been as Carlo Sforza handed him back his daughter, and without Sforza, that entire incident would not have come out well.

"Why do I bother to pay spies? I should just listen to the crewmen," said Dell'este sourly. "Go with Manfred, Benito. I'll tell you all about it later."

So Benito did that. Arranging transport for Bortai and Erik Hakkonsen was not particularly trying. Arranging transport, feed, and sufficient land for the grazing of their herd of horses was another challenge entirely. That involved going to his old offices in the Castel del Mar and seeing the mess that he would have to deal with, if he did not leave for Venice, pretty smartly. It involved old friends, all of whom wanted to talk to him.

On Corfu they understood that talk was a dry, thirsty business, and believed it needed lubricating with wine. So they repaired to a nearby tavern. It took a long time before he got back to his grandfather, who was waiting for him in his cabin, reclined on the bunk and reading a book.

The duke of Ferrara sniffed and said: "Good party?" disapprovingly.

"If you mean the smell of wine, you try talking to the skipper of a fishing vessel without it. It hasn't been a party. More like a mystery of just how they all managed before me and how they managed without me," said Benito, sitting down on the chair at the writing desk. "And, no, thank you. I won't have another glass of wine. I shall have a headache tomorrow anyway."

"They probably did manage to cope just as well as they will manage when you're gone again," said his grandfather. "Some interesting news about Milan for you." And he outlined the fact that Carlo Sforza was now the Protector of Milan, and married to Lucia del Maino. "Who I gather was one of Filippo Maria's by-blows."

"And I didn't even get an invitation to the wedding," said Benito, who had actually had a bit more wine than was wise, or rather, made him think he was wise. "No wonder we're on the brink of war."

"Well, for what it is worth, Venice is not. She's sitting out this one, although it seems there are several other supposed rightful claimants to the ducal throne for whom any excuse will do."

"Venice is sitting out a perfectly good war with Milan? That is surprising."

His grandfather shrugged. "It's one I plan to sit out if they do, at least while I wait to see what is happening, and can see when and where to strike. I have no desire to have Sforza ruling a powerful, wealthy duchy that near to Ferrara, even if I did not have my own axe to grind, but only a fool underestimates the man. And it seems he has a number of fools opposing him. If they attack singly, he can devour any of them, and as I know most of them, each of his foes will consider themselves to be the leader. Especially that ass, Umberto of Parma. Count Andrea is nastier, but at least has the sense to hire professionals and then claim the credit for their skill for himself."

Benito sighed, seeing Sforza in his mind's eye, holding Alessia. "It's a war I hope we can stay out of. Odd, really. I used to dream of finally paying him back. But that was before I knew it was Caesare Aldanto who actually killed Mother."

"Sforza was still to blame," said Enrico tersely. "And now, boy," he said, obviously declaring the matter closed, and subject changed. He sat up in the bunk and swiveled so that his feet were back on the deck. Then, he planted hands on his knees. "When do we leave for Venice? And what happens with Prince Manfred, and Erik and his bride?"

So Benito told him. He was relieved to leave the conflict between Carlo Sforza and his mother, Lorendana, out of it. Enrico Dell'este, as cool and calculating a man about almost any other subject, was still less than rational about that. Some of it, Benito had decided, came down to the fact that his grandfather still felt guilty about it all.

"We sail in six days' time," Benito said. "Venice may command our immediate return, but that will allow the little Arsenal, working nonstop, to repair and refit twelve of the great galleys so we can sail with a safe convoy. The rest will follow in three weeks' time. It has been arranged that some of the vessels, those finished earlier, will ferry Prince Manfred and the Knights, Erik and Bortai and the horse herd to Venice. They'll proceed together on to Mainz, following whichever route seems most feasible. Probably through Trento and Bolzano, but that might change depending on Milan and this war."

"They'll almost certainly have to avoid Lombardy and the Scaligeri territory around Verona, but they should be able to enter the Holy Roman Empire entirely through Venetian lands."

"I hope so, because the only other alternative would be to travel by sea—and finding adequate horse transports for that long a voyage would be difficult and expensive." Benito had just had firsthand experience of that.

"As a reason for peace, saving Erik the cost of horse transport will, I am sure, appeal to the combatants," said Enrico Dell'este with a laugh.

"You never know," said Benito. "He is a handsome fellow, and some of those lords..."

"Go and sleep it off before I throw something at your head."

"I'd rather do that than join Manfred in a last night before Erik returns, exploring the delights of Corfu town. Sometimes I can be quite irritated with Francesca for going off to Alexandria."

Chapter 26

Francisco Turner arrived back at his quarters to find a messenger from Carlo, and a small military matter he had to ride off and attend to for his master. It was the next day before he got to see his commander. Sforza was not looking as well as the previous day, and his pulse was a little faster. Francisco began to wonder if, somehow, despite the precautions, the poisoner had managed to administer another dose.

But Carlo Sforza was as mentally restless as he was feeling physically under the weather. He was on his feet, having chosen to meet Turner in a small chamber—not much more than a pretentious hallway—which had no furniture in it. As if to make up for the bare floor, the walls were covered with portraits of various dignitaries of Milan's past, not one of whom was familiar to Francisco. *Sic transit gloria mundi.*

Despite the haggard look on his face, the new duke was not only on his feet but pacing about. "How was your visit to the bookseller?" he asked brusquely. "One of my spies reports he may have enchanted you."

Francisco smiled. "Then he'll enchant you, too. He's an unashamed fraud who will put on a wonderful show for the spies of our foes, and may actually produce something useful."

"What is he doing here?" asked Sforza.

"A nobleman of some sort, he is evasive about quite what he's fleeing. He's also a very intelligent man, multilingual, with more books than Cosimo de' Medici, and he is widely read, too. Able to debate the merits of Greek and Roman philosophers. I would guess a dilettante at various arts, including some experiments with gunpowder that are truly interesting. They're not magical, but could look that way. But he needs a bigger, more isolated place for his experiments!"

"Men who experiment with gunpowder tend to get killed," said Sforza with a frown, obviously remembering one.

"He's cautious, within the limits of what he has. He has made quite a neat delayed-fuse system. And I could see the use of flares—aside from making the enemy think we have magical weapons. He showed me a green one which spat yellow sparks—very bright. He says he can do various colors. I thought they could be useful both as a way of signaling and possibly for lighting a place to be attacked . . . well, it could have quite an impact on night attacks."

"There is a reason for avoiding those," said Carlo with a grimace, "but yes, I'm interested. What's he likely to cost me?"

Turner shook his head. "I have no idea. A secure comfortable estate, and someone to put up bookshelves would be my opening bid. Maybe a bombardier to help him with his experiments. It's hard to judge, m'lord. He's not easy to read. But he's not a young man, and I get the feeling that he's looking for somewhere quiet to read his books and continue his experiments."

Sforza's eyes seemed to get a little unfocused, as he searched through his memory. After a few seconds, he said: "I've plenty of estates in my gift. Filippo Maria seemed to collect them, killing off the owners on his little whims. Hmm. There's Val di Castellazzo. I was considering turning it into an officer school for the artillery one day, but the villa is really too small for more than twenty men. It's not more than eight miles out, but the woodlands are dense. It's very private. As for money . . . well, let him ask. I have a tight purse right now, so if it is too much, it won't happen. But the joy of it is my foes also are purse-pinched. Let them borrow more from Cosimo to counter my magician . . . whom I don't have, of course."

"Of course. Now, he did bring up something else. You remember the snake that bit the fat girl—Cosimo's niece?" asked Francisco.

"Yes, you said it was the strangest color you'd ever seen on an animal."

"I've seen shades of blue on birds and some fish. Never a snake or frog or any other animal."

"There was a bit of blue on those newts from the streams in the Alps. Remember, we had half a troop claiming they were devil's spawn."

"True. But that sort of bruised purple is not common. But as our future magician pointed out there is one blue snake, which is quite well known. The old picture he showed me was a lot less blue and a lot more purple in color." Francisco pointed at the coat of arms carved into the stone above the doorway in the chamber where they stood.

Sforza looked at the snake. "But . . . it's just a heraldic device. It is not real."

"Yes," said Francisco. "An odd one, thinking about it, and the figure he had being swallowed appeared to have breasts. Anyway, I wondered if I should mention that in my letter to Marco Valdosta. I'm still trying to think of a suitable reply to his request. It may have been based on a historical serpent, and that may just help him. But it does perhaps make it look as if Milan was involved."

"As if the Visconti were involved, not Sforza of Milan. They throw it in my face that I am not one of the Visconti. Let them square that with my somehow training the Visconti snake to kill people. Besides the *biscione* is a grass viper. Not venomous. Tell him. And tell our new fraud magician to come up with a spell that sounds good for you to reply to Valdosta with."

They talked of the reports coming in from the captains on the various fronts. Not surprisingly, the Scaligeri had tried to construct a temporary bridge to Goito's fort. But a little grapeshot had dissuaded them. Then they'd tried to force the bridge at Borghetto. And then sent some troops over by boats.

"Infantry, of course—horses in small boats on a flooding river not being a great success—and their attempt at swimming them over was brave, but sad for the horses. So Captain Pelta waited until they had gotten close to the bank—they'd been watching them set up for hours and his harquebusiers were behind a good solid stone wall—and let them try landing under fire. They plainly planned some kind of suspension or pontoon bridge—but they needed a bridgehead.

"When you have to do that under fire it gets expensive in troops," said Sforza dourly. "They seem now to be trying to send a force over by stealth to capture a bridge. They're not doing very well at stealth. I'm tempted to let them have one—and blow it up when they've got enough men over to be in more trouble than they can cause. But Goito will surrender soon, I think. And if we get through this, we'll have to rebuild the bridges, which is expensive in money."

"And on the other side of the Po?" asked Francisco, taking his commander's pulse. It was faster than it should be. It was easier to keep him talking for as long as possible, while he got the examination under way.

"How am I supposed to wave my hands around if you're holding my wrist?" demanded Sforza, half annoyed, half amused. "So far we're sparring. They advance. We retreat. They assume it is a trap. They retreat. We advance back to where we came from, sometimes a bit further forward, because our logistics and communication is better. We threaten to besiege a town...and they rush to defend it. So we go elsewhere. But I need to get a bit closer to the action."

In Francisco's opinion, what his master had done was move a fraction closer to an early grave. "I'm going to purge you, for the bad news. For the good news, yes, I think you should move at least to Pavia."

"Purge me? For Heaven's sake, Francisco, I have no appetite anyway, and now you want the rest of what's in me out?"

"Yes. You had improved, and now your vital signs are worse. So is your temper. I think, somehow, that they've slipped you some more of whatever they had poisoned you with."

"Hmph. Well, I'll have to exercise that temper of mine by sending you to the East to keep an eye on matters there for me, at least until Goito is resolved. It'll keep you from being a mother hen in Pavia. You know, I despised poisoners even before you thought that I was being poisoned. What is it they've given me?"

"I don't know. If I did, I'd be a little happier because I'd know where to look and what to do," admitted Francisco.

Later, when the examination was over and Francisco had seen the purgative administered, Carlo said, in a quieter voice: "Turner. You know I am sending you to the East because there are few men I regard as highly, and none I trust more. It strikes me, old friend, that I am sending you off to offer a fraud the gift of an estate. When, if, this is all over, my friend, we are going to look for a suitable set of estates for you. It's in my gift, if we survive.

A place where you can run in peace, eh? And titles and suchlike, as I can bestow them, and wealth enough to buy all the books you ever desire. A place at court, and a role in the running of Milan. You need to know that, as do all my loyal men, I think."

"You pay me well," said Francisco gruffly, knowing that his loyalty to the man had been freely given, but was at least appreciated. That made a huge difference, and while Sforza might know this was a good way to make loyal men more so, he was at least genuine about it. "And we trust you. Anyway, what would I do with an estate? I'm no noble."

"Grow old comfortably on it. Not something every mercenary soldier achieves, and something you deserve. And titles, well, you can have those for the asking, friend. It doesn't mean that much."

"I'll put it all off a while," said Francisco. "Especially the growing old part."

He took himself to see the bookseller, who was plainly expecting him. "Signor Jagr," he said, bowing.

"Call me Kazimierz, Caviliero. That is one of my actual names, the latter part being a convenient fiction, which I will maintain."

"Well, Signor. My master says he possibly has use for someone who can convince our foes we have a powerful magician in our employ. He empowered me to ask what you would expect to be paid. It is fair to say he is fighting several wars at the moment, and these are expensive, so he is unlikely to agree to vast sums of money, but he would offer you an estate with some lands, and help with your experiments. I suggested a bombardier, since I have one at the barracks who has lost a leg and an eye, but is still a man with a great knowledge of explosives. It would give you privacy and space to conduct your experiments."

Behind the mustache, there was definitely now a smile. Perhaps the old fellow had bad teeth or something that he wished to hide.

"I would need some money for materials and equipment," he said. "For myself..." he shrugged. "Say the same rate as one of his newest captains. I think he will discover my worth."

"He's good at showing that appreciation. I will speak to him. As for materials, well, I would guess as long as they're not ruinously expensive, he would be willing to agree to reasonable expenditure."

"Oh, I think he will get good value. I have a good assistant in young Tamas. Good with his hands and good with adapting things. I showed him the drawings of the fire-thrower, and he has wasted several good pieces of parchment redesigning it. Keeping him still, as you prescribed, is hard for the boy. Unlike us, he cannot merely read a book."

"Let him learn. He'll make a better assistant that way."

The man blinked. "He's a good worker, but he's a peasant, really. They don't read."

"Not unless you let them learn, no."

"It's a dangerous idea," said the bookseller. "Like giving women guns. Far more dangerous than wars."

Francisco was not sure if he was joking.

Chapter 27

Venice

In Venice, Marco Valdosta was experimenting on his patient. He felt as if he was both losing and gaining ground at the same time. The necrosis around the puncture had halted, and gradually the flesh itself was healing and the wound drawing closed. She would have a nasty scar, but the leg itself now had almost normal circulation. Unfortunately, that was the only real victory he'd had. The wound was healing, yes, though not at the pace a normal healthy person would heal, but with a glacial slowness. And her breathing and heartbeat, too, had gone from fast and weak, to slower...and no less weak. She'd come in fat. She wasn't that anymore.

He was finding that having a pregnant wife was hard on the whole household, and him in particular. A war on the northern borders, even if Venice was not involved...yet. Marco knew there were those on the Council of Ten saying quietly and in the senate calling loudly for Venice to take up arms, to punish its old enemy and make territorial gains while it could.

That was worrying enough, but the very idea of the plague was deeply disturbing—and he hadn't heard back from Francisco. He'd even been to ask the undines if they knew if the message had been delivered...and been told yes, but that Francisco was no longer in Milan. So Marco had decided to try some experiments on the de' Medici girl, before she slipped away completely. Marco, and her attendants, massaged her limbs gently every day. At first, that had been to ensure the circulation of blood, and possibly to keep up a little muscle tone. But he noticed that after the sessions, she stirred slightly. Tiny movements of the fingers, a twitch of the cheek. This would last a few minutes and then she would return to lying like the dead. She did suck weakly and swallow of her own volition. But it could take an hour to get a cup of broth into her.

He'd tried scents, and sounds, and even pricking her with a pin. That was futile. But she did respond to music and smells. She turned her head a bit toward the music, and her nostrils flared slightly with various odors. He'd tried pleasant, and unpleasant. Rosewater and ammonia, burned hartshorn, vinegar, garlic... she had actively sniffed at that.

It still had not woken her.

He'd tried saints' relics and prayers, spells of healing, and small doses of various stimulants.

He was not winning, and felt that there was something he'd missed.

Violetta de' Medici knew she was somehow trapped in a dark and terrible place with a serpent. At first, she had been so full of that paralyzing weakness that she'd been barely able to feel anything at all, not even terror.

She was dimly aware of a lion walking down in the darkness. She was not sure how she knew that it was a lion but was certain of it. She knew that she should have been terrified of the vast and savage beast, but was not.

She wanted, desperately, to warn it of the serpent. But she had no breath or strength to scream.

And somewhere, somehow, she caught the smell of osso busco... at least of the garlic. That was good, and comforting.

Rimini

It was all about sparring for position, Count Andrea Malatesta knew. They'd pushed Sforza's forces back, and even had a minor victory against one of his captains, to make up for the reverses suffered by that idiot Duke Umberto Da Corregio. The big difference, of course, was that Milan was outnumbered and largely surrounded. His allies in Venice assured him that the Republic would join in the war just as soon as the fleet arrived back.

To improve things, and the morale of the troops, was the news via spies out of Milan that Sforza had been taken sick, and had come back to the city with his personal physician. That was sweet music to the ear of Count Andrea, although he was irritated by the fact that his allies and his troops gave such weight to the legend of Sforza, the Wolf of the North. Venice and Ferrara had humbled him in the past, had they not? Surely, with all the allies Malatesta now had and Venice together with Ferrara, they would break him. They greatly outnumbered his troops already. And there was word that a thousand more men would be joining them from Naples. They all wanted a piece of the loot.

Even that coward Cosimo would be there eventually, like a carrion crow after the eagles had made their kill. If Andrea had his way, the Florentines would get precious little. The money grubbers were already owed far too much.

Chapter 28

Francisco rode out that afternoon, having had Kazimierz approved by Sforza, and the matter handed on to various functionaries. *The man who claims the name of Kazimierz*, Francisco cautioned himself. He made a mental note to ask someone familiar with the nobility of Hungary just who the man was sometime.

But that could wait. Right now, Turner had a war to deal with. Both the East and West were fragile—simply because there were two fronts and a limited number of men. If the Holy Roman Empire on the northern border or Venice in the south were drawn in, things could become very ugly very quickly.

But at the moment, there were only four bridges across the Mincio. It was not a huge river, perhaps forty yards wide in the dry season. But now, with spring melt-water, it was wider and deeper and hard to cross, with very few fords. The bridges at Peschiera were protected by Visconti-built fortresses on the island part way over. The bridge at Borghetto, the Ponte Visconteo, was nearly half a mile long, and the obvious place for attack. Because of the braiding of the river in this area, there were several ford-able places and the moraine ridges could hide the troops—but the bridge was fortified with two elderly towers. Goito had been held by the Scaligeri. That left Rivalta—but that bridge was in open country and defended by a fortress on the Milanese side.

From the ruins of the little village that had sprung up around the Scaliger fortress of Goito in more peaceful times, Francisco huddled with Captain Pelta, looking at the walls. They had nothing here but light siege guns. Sforza did not wish to take the fortress in his trademark way. He wanted it to bleed the Scaligeri's capacity to do anything else, at as low a cost as possible. They had to lose expensively here, to surrender, to give over plenty of their nobles and officers to act as bargaining chips, to be ransomed eventually.

Pelta belched, the result of drinking beer, which he plainly rarely quaffed. "Better out than in."

"I think they're saying that," said Francisco, gesturing at the fortress. "A good thing they have no idea how few men you actually have here."

"Judging by the shooting, they're low enough on ammunition to be rationing it, anyway. At first they blazed away at anything that moved out here. So even if they decide to sortie, it might not be too bad."

There was a large camp, with cook fires burning every night, just outside cannon shot, but visible from the walls of the fort. Troops could be seen coming and going from time to time. It was unlikely the men trapped in the fortress—or those on the other side of the river—knew it was all little more than canvas. Pelta had no spare men to sit waiting for the fortress to fall. Even in the initial attack, with the blowing of the bridge, there had been only three thousand of Sforza's men to the nearly four thousand foes who panicked and ran, some back to try and hold the fort. Some of those had fled in the initial fray, but they had nearly three thousand men in that little redoubt, doing nothing. The three eighteen-pounders were aimed at the wall tops, sending masonry flying down into their fortress and discouraging shooting from the walls. The building had been built to withstand old-fashioned sieges, and the Scaligeri had invested nothing in updating the fortress in a trusted ally's borderland. Sforza's heavy guns could have pounded a hole through the walls in a day or less, but instead, they had left their enemy to sit with three thousand of the cream of their army inside a fort which could house five hundred, and had no vast stockpiles of food or ammunition. Water they had, but they'd be tightly packed and hot and hungry. In the panic to flee Sforza's attack to the safety of the fort, most of the supply wagons had been abandoned or burned.

Francisco and Pelta sat on the remains of a half-collapsed stone wall and counted the desultory shots coming from the fortress.

The distance was great enough that they weren't worried about being hit, even if the gunfire had been more vigorous.

As was the Milanese response, which came close to a fusillade. Ammunition was not something Sforza's harquebusiers were short of or had been told to spare. Milan had been buying and stockpiling powder and shot for months. Pelta's men were sitting with three harquebuses each so they could fire off an impressive volley of shots in reply. Of course, with a mere thousand men here, a real sortie could be a problem.

"So: what's next?" asked Francisco.

Pelta pointed northward, in the direction of Lago di Garda. Although the lake was the biggest in Italy, it was still too far away to be seen. "They've been collecting boats just upstream. They're doing their best to do it in secret, bringing them down by wagon—I would guess they plan to try and get some of the more valuable men out. My men have barrels of olive oil and floating barrels with pitch and naptha ready to push into the river. It's tempting to let the stupid bastards get over and be heading back, but the ransom for some of those in there should be handsome. They work on rebuilding the bridge again, but I think even they know all we'll do is send another barge of explosives down."

Just then a runner came to find them. "Scouts spotted something."

They returned to the camp to find the scouts waiting. Two sets of scouts, one from the Ponte Visconteo. Carlo Sforza had men up on the ridge on the Scaliger side, well hidden, who would signal troop numbers to the scouts, so the secret movement of the soldiery was less so than the Scaliger commanders might think. Of course, they might guess, but they had no reputation for it. "They've got around a thousand infantry and six culverins waiting in between the ridges."

Carlo had left them with a reserve of two thousand mounted men and two thousand five hundred infantry. Normally infantry, easier to train and cheaper to arm and equip, made up the bulk. But Sforza had kept his infantry for other purposes, and left them with a small force on each bridge, positioned to respond fast, and a well set-up perimeter of scouts, observers and messengers. Given that they had to guard twenty miles, adequately stationing enough men at any possible crossing would have stretched Sforza's men thin. But so long as those who crossed could not hold their crossing or bring large numbers without a forceful response, the river made a reasonable barrier.

The other scout was from the marshy area near Rivalta. It was his home; he'd grown up shooting ducks on the water there. "They're building a pontoon bridge in the marsh. And there are some men on horses with a local boy marking a trail."

The Rivalta Bridge was actually a series of smaller bridges with a causeway across the swampy ground, and one relatively deep but narrow channel crossed by a stone bridge, fortified with small towers on both sides. Getting cannon to the bridge was just not practical except straight down the causeway. The bridge itself was only six feet wide—too narrow for many carts or wagons, and not easy to get great numbers across in a hurry, if it was under fire. It had not been considered a very likely point of attack for these reasons. Sforza's troops had small outposts and guards at the forward bridges.

"Must be cavalry," said Pelta. "They're keeping them out of sight. Probably a couple of miles off. I suppose this means they plan this for night or dawn."

That was guesswork, of course—scary guesswork, because if they got it wrong, they'd all end up dead. Even if they got it partly wrong, they could end up letting their commander down, and some of their number dead. It was a measure of how much they all trusted and were loyal to Carlo Sforza, that it was the first part that seemed to worry them most.

"I'd guess the attack on Ponte Visconteo will start first and isn't meant to succeed," said Francisco.

Pelta nodded. "Yes, Ponte Visconteo is probably a feint. Not enough cannon, not enough men. I'll still send some more infantry there tonight. It's what they'll try at Rivalta that worries me. If they've half the brains of a rabbit, they'll screen their pontoon bridge with nets to stop us breaking it with a barge or a raft full of explosives. The oil and pitch and naphtha will work at keeping them off it for a while—but may not set fire to it."

"And the river runs faster in the narrows. It'll clear faster."

"I suspect they'll try to get men on this side, to attack the bridge from the flanks, and hit the outposts hard with the cavalry, and hope that in the retreat there'll be enough chaos on the bridge to take the towers. They're not worth much, defensively."

"Well, barring a cannon shot down the causeway."

"They're hundred-year-old relics," said Pelta. "As likely to blow up and kill the users as do anything useful. And they probably know that. That's why Carlo changed the guards here—they seemed very cosy with the Scaligeri. The defensive cannon in Peschiaria and Ponte Visconteo have at least been supplemented, but the only field pieces I have are those here at Goito. Moving anything down there fast enough is just too much. It's going to have to be cavalry and infantry, Francisco."

"Then I think we'll mine the causeway. Let the bastards gallop through mud."

"Well, partly practical. I've got tarred kegs full of powder in place under all the bridges. But the causeway... that'll take too much time and powder. I can't do it. It would be easier to blow up the final bridge."

Turner started tugging at his beard, as he was wont to do when pondering a problem. But he left off after a few seconds. He made it a point to keep his beard very closely trimmed in time of war—that was more in the way of superstition, he'd admit, than anything really needful—and the exercise of beard tugging was more frustrating than helpful.

"It seems odd that they wouldn't anticipate that," he said to Pelta. "What got them at Goito is that they got caught by surprise, hit hard, and were trapped without much ammunition or food, and they lost a lot of their horses. This time... they're not going to be surprised, and they're not going to be unhorsed or out of ammunition."

"To be honest, Francisco," said the young commander, earning him serious respect from his somewhat older fellow captain, "I don't know what best to do. Carlo told me to hold the Mincio, to not try and put a perimeter on every inch, to keep troops in reserve, and to respond hard and fast to any attempt to gain a beachhead—which I will do. But if they press hard on Rivalta, cross in several places with enough men, it'll cost them dear, but I think they can take the crossing. There are at least seven places the river can be forded down there, let alone their pontoon bridge and whatever men they land by boat. They'll try that tonight, for sure."

Francisco shook his head. The gesture was not one of disagreement so much as it was an effort to concentrate his thoughts. "I'm not Carlo Sforza, but I've fought beside him for nearly ten years. I'd say what he'd do would be to respond hard and fast to this attempt, before they gain a foothold. Turn their attack plan against them... Moonrise tonight, if you give me three hundred horse, what I suggest is I'll hit their outposts off the end of the causeway. They're expecting to invade us, and believe that we are on the back foot, being attacked on several fronts, trying to hold our own territory. From what Carlo said, they have no substantive defenses their side of the river."

Pelta grinned sharkishly. "Why you? I'll do that. You can deal with the logistics of watching this side."

"Because the commander put you in charge of it. He sent me to support you. And he gave you the hard task because he knew you could do it. He just sent me here to be out of the way, because he knew I would try to stop him doing too much."

Francisco noted Pelta, who had been looking strained, straighten his shoulders a bit at that. "How is he? I have never seen him show signs of being tired before."

"He hasn't either. He's not handling having to rest well. I am sure he will recover from whatever it was," said Francisco, carefully not saying what he thought it was, or that he thought someone had got to Sforza again, somehow.

"Good to know. Well, you need to get on with this so you can get back to keeping him resting a bit. I like the idea, because they'll be devoting more men to guarding their frontier than invading us. But in the long term it may cause problems when we want to invade their territory. There's going to be quite a reckoning for this, and they'll be paying for it."

"You've got a point, but we'll let Carlo worry about it. Now, what have you got in the way of details, maps and locals for guides? And how many men can you let me have?"

Over the next few minutes, Francisco saw why Carlo Sforza trusted the young man. He was, in terms of his staffwork, very, very good. He had two men from the area—one of them the scout who had grown up shooting ducks in the marshy area across from Rivalta, and the other a runaway from an apprenticeship in Marimolo. The woodland between Marimolo and the little town of Soave di Mantovano, on the border of Scaliger territory, and the land they had lost to Venice and Ferrara around Mantova was the most likely place for the Scaliger army to be massing. The forest would make them invisible to the watch at Rivalta.

It was three miles into Scaliger territory—too close, Francisco reckoned, for them to be comfortable and relaxed about the chance of an attack. But it would overset their plans somewhat, no matter what they planned. Pelta had a reasonable map of the tracks and roads, and he, Francisco, and the two scouts and the three lieutenants that would be going along discussed them.

By sundown they were ready and rode out in the twilight, slowly passing over the narrow Rivalta Bridge, and waiting for moonrise to storm the guardpost on the far side of the last small bridge on the causeway. The duck-hunting scout had taken a boat and twenty pikemen, to flank the outpost. Shooting was to be avoided, unless need drove them hard.

They were waiting, when the duck hunter came out of the dark. "The men are waiting, m'lord," he said to Francisco, "but it seems like there's more than just the usual men there. A pack train of horses with panniers are there, and there's a lot of men moaning they can't light fires and the mosquitos are biting them, in the field just past the outpost. It's wet, and they are cold."

"What is a 'lot' of men. Mario? Are they mounted?"

"No, foot soldiers, m'lord. Harquebusiers. Maybe a hundred men. They are complaining that the pikemen are late."

Pikes, well ordered, could stop a cavalry charge. A bunch of harquebusiers, likely with their weapons not ready, would not. Francisco sent messengers back to Pelta, and then ordered the signal lantern flashed as the moon rose above the trees. The causeway spread into a road here, but the fields were still a few inches deep in water on either side of them—there was no choice but for the mounted men to charge down the causeway. They started at a walk, then accelerated to a trot, and then to a gallop.

There was a startled yell ahead of them, and then a single shot fired and they were onto the small fortified building. There should have been an abatis across the road; they'd been prepared to sweep into the field to get around it, but it was not there. They charged down onto the desperate scatter of harquebusiers with their officer screaming orders, too late and too slow. Francisco's cavalrymen simply cut them to pieces. There were, despite all of it, several shots fired. In the chaos and darkness, many men fled. What failed to flee was the packtrain. Francisco sent ten men back with the string of horses, still loaded with their panniers and saddlebags, and the unfortunate lieutenant who had been supposed to be commanding the harquebusiers.

Horns sounded in the distance. Francisco and his men did not wait to find out what it was about, but instead regrouped and headed deeper in Scaliger lands, leaving the pikemen to deal with the cleanup and retreat. Trotting down the road, scouts out, Francisco soon discovered the flaw in his plan: moonlight or not, a mist was forming in the hollows, spreading across the low-lying fields. You could lose the tail end of the horse in front of you in this, let alone keep the troop in sight.

And into their midst, at a brisk trot, came half a dozen men—and not Francisco's scouts either.

It was hard to say who was more surprised, but on balance, the two Scaliger officers and the troopers they had with them to act as messengers were far less prepared for meeting the three hundred in the mist. Although one of them did manage to flee, he ran straight into the sword of the scout who had been chasing them.

The officers were not talking—not while they were together. But their troopers were much less reticent and quite happy to spill. There were five thousand men en route, nearly two thousand of them cavalry, some from the Carraresi of Padua as well as the Viscount di Scala's forces. The attack was for tonight; the men would be crossing in boats to attack Rivalta, so that it was taken and held. Shots had been heard and reported, and they'd been sent to investigate... and the troops were already on the road.

A frontal meeting, with three hundred-odd men against the full Scaliger relief force could only end badly. And flight now would end up with them jammed on the bridge, with Pelta unable to blow his mines without killing Francisco and his men, as the tail fought the overwhelming numbers. "Back to that track, about a hundred yards back on the right," said Francisco. "Pass it back down the line."

They retreated to the track. Francisco sent an escort of ten with the prisoners and the information gained. They would be, he suspected, the lucky ones.

"Have you any idea where we are?" asked Francisco of their two guides.

"I think this track leads to the Casera farm, just north of Soave di Mantovano," said the one.

"It's in for a very bad night," said Francisco grimly. "How far to it?"

"A quarter mile or so, m'lord."

Francisco re-created the map in his mind's eye. "There's that ford you talked about on the big bend, with the oxbow lake beyond it. Could you find your way there?"

"The track leads through the farm. And then we take the right fork nearly a mile from there, and then, when we get to the Baridi farm, we take the track to the water. That's a bit tricky... we have to cross a stream..."

"How wide? And how deep?"

The man threw up his hands. "There was a bridge, m'lord. Just a log over the water. I never got into the water. The ford's fifty yards wide, maybe sixty. The water hits the stones there, spreads out. The other side will be hard going, swampy ground."

"If we get to the other side, that'll be a good thing."

They rode to the farm. There they caught every person in the place asleep. They were tied up, while the scouts returned to the main road from Rivalta, with enough stakes to make something of an abatis at the junction. Francisco briefed his men.

"The mist is getting thicker. We're going to hit their midtail end and run." He picked on three of the men. "You're lucky. Or unlucky. You're going to ride close to the village. When you hear us shooting, start fires. I want part of Soave di Mantovano burning. And then ride like hell back down this track, then back to the ford. If you're lucky, you'll be there before us, and if you're unlucky, after. There are some of Captain Pelta's infantry on the other side, so be sure you yell 'Sforza' or they might shoot you."

He turned in his saddle to face the main body of his troops. "The rest of us are going to cut a hole in the middle of their column in the mist, fire our horse pistols, and ride back along this track. Now, I'll want the lieutenants and the two sergeants."

The plan was worked through hastily, and soon they were riding back, having made sure that those who might follow would hit a slowing blockade at the farmhouse.

His stomach in that familiar before-combat knot, Francisco edged forward with his men in the wreathing mist. The moon broke through, showing a stark black-and-white tableau of men checking their priming, loosening blades in their sheaths, and patting their horses who, inevitably, were catching the nervous stress from the riders. Then the mist closed in again and a little later they could hear the sound of the Scaliger army moving past, not more than a hundred yards off.

Francisco waited for the moment to tell the trumpeter to sound the call. And then, in the distance came the sound of massed harquebus fire. He tapped his trumpeter. "Sound it."

The man gave the bright sharp shrill call. "Sforza!" yelled Francisco, and the cry echoed from the better part of three hundred voices as they plunged forward. It was impossible to have everyone on the muddy track so they were in the field on either side—barely able to see ahead. The thirty men on the track reached the road first, and Francisco could hear the clash of steel, more yells of "Sforza!" and in the distance yet another volley from the harquebuses. Then the flankers started to reach the road. Those on the left scrambled across the ditch and fired back toward the tail end of the Scaliger column, and headed right to the lanterns the scouts had now put to mark the track, and those on the right did the opposite. In theory, at least, because the wings of Francisco's attack had been well back and had further to go, they would not shoot each other.

Of course in the chaos, screaming, shouting and gunfire, anything could happen. Francisco felt a burn across his shoulder. It could have been one of the panicked Scaligeri, or a latecomer from his own side. He managed to cling to his saddle as his horse suddenly jumped and scrambled over another horse. And there were the lanterns, and dizzy with the shock, he joined the other horsemen streaming down the track. He was glad to leave the process to the horse. It saw better and heard better in the dark than he did. He heard the grenades they had left at the entry to the track explode. The scout had been instructed to light the fuse when Francisco's trumpeter sounded the second call. Francisco could not recall hearing it.

The rest of the ride was something of a blur, which only became somewhat clearer as they hit the icy water of the Mincio ford. As an invasion route, it would have been a failure, as the water was deep enough to wet them from head to boots and force them to swim a little, and then struggle out and through a series of shallow lagoons and glutinous mud . . . but there were some of Pelta's men, waiting.

It was some hours later, back at the camp outside Goito, when Francisco suffered the indignity of having to have his own wound treated, that he was finally able to get some idea of how

well they had done. One of the two lieutenants who had been
with him reported gleefully, "We only lost fifteen men in all.
Well, men who have not returned. Twenty-two wounded, yourself
included, Captain. Three more seriously than you, but mostly they
are minor wounds. The Scaligeri did not succeed in crossing the
Mincio. When Captain Pelta got the captives we sent them—he
got more detail out of them, sent a tercio of harbquebus and
pike forward along the road to meet them, and to conduct a slow
retreat onto the bridge. It's been a busy night. They tried to sortie
out of Goito fortress when they heard the shooting. That didn't
end well for them. They got a ball from the cannon right in the
middle of their mass, and then got blown up by the mine that
Captain Pelta had us dig. I thought he was wasting the men's
time making them dig that tunnel. I thought it was heading for
the fortress. I didn't realize it was under the road out, and that
Pelta had had the sappers fill it with explosives."

While what losses the Scaligeri had suffered on the other side
of the river was not something they could know, it appeared that
the men trapped in the fortress of Goito had had enough. They
had used what little reserve they had in their attempted sortie.
They asked for terms, later that day.

And that night, six more of the troop that had taken part in
Francisco's raid made it back across the Mincio, bringing news of
mayhem on the opposite bank. It appeared that the rear had been
made up of troops from Padua, and when the Scaliger troops were
attacked in the mist, the Scaliger commander concluded they had
been betrayed by the allies behind him. The fight had been raging
on for most of the next day apparently. The surviving Carraresi
troops had fled back to Padua, and the men who had hidden in
Scaliger territory had heard distant shooting, further east.

Chapter 29

The Duchy of Milan

Francisco and an escort of a hundred men left the next day to take the valuable captives—nobility and gentry who had been part of the Scaliger army assembling in Goito—to Milan. For Carlo Sforza's soldiery, they represented the potential of a handsome profit, as they would be ransomed when the conflict was over, unless Milan was overrun.

Francisco was still moving a little gingerly after his wounding, but giving himself a professional assessment, there was no reason that he shouldn't ride. He also wanted to get across to Pavia and see how Carlo was doing. At a guess, the Mincio border was quite secure for now, and young Captain Pelta seemed to have it all well in hand.

Passing over the Naviglio Grande, Francisco had a twinge of guilt to add to the ache in his shoulder. He needed to send a message to Marco. He decided that, once the prisoners were safely bestowed, he'd go to see the bookseller and ask if he had a cantrip that sounded plausible enough. Valdosta, much deeper into researches of the magical, would probably laugh at it and at him, but that was what you got for attempting deceit.

He found "Master Kazimierz" ensconced and comfortable in the large house at Val di Castellazzo, and his two servants rather bewildered by it all. A number of salons had been extensively shelved by workmen, and the men were now engaged in carrying in crates and bales. Emma was overseeing them with a rod of iron, no less effectively wielded because she couldn't speak much of their language. Master Kazimierz was in fact out in the workshop with his bombardier, she informed him. Francisco was plainly an honored visitor by the low curtsey he got. She would have him called immediately.

"Please to come in to the green salon, sit. There would be wine brought immediately."

"And how is your man?" he asked.

"Muddling his brains with reading! As if a blow on the head was not enough!" She dimpled, her pride enormously obvious. "He spends all day looking at the books. He showed me some of the words and what they mean. The master encourages him. Our master is too kind and too clever."

Kazimierz arrived a few minutes later, smelling strongly of burned powder. "Ah. Caviliero. An excellent man you have sent me. He'll be the death of me yet. I am joking, Emma," he said hastily to the woman bringing the wine and sweet almond biscotti.

"She is very protective," he explained in an amused tone to Francisco, after the young woman left. "I don't know how I survived without them, for so many years."

"They haven't been with you long?" asked Francisco.

"No," said Master Kazimierz. "A few months, although it does seem much longer. I picked them up on my travels."

"Oh. They behave like hereditary family retainers. Grown up in your service or something. Normally, the ones like that are old and wrinkled, loyal to the death and can tell you about Master so-and-so's first steps, and every wonderful thing he's done since—and will, if they are given half a chance."

Master Kazimierz snorted. "Not in this case."

"Well, she just told me that you were too kind and too clever," said Francisco, smiling. "But actually I didn't come to discuss your servants or the bombardier, although I am amused to hear your man is trying to read."

"I showed him a Chinese book of war contrivances with pictures in it, which fascinated the boy. You said to keep him from doing physical exertion for a while, and I wanted a device to launch something into the sky at night without making it obvious from whence it came. I had another book on mechanical contrivances—even a water mill, with which he was familiar. For some reason, the author had actually written it in Hungarian, not Latin or Greek or something sensible. I showed him the diagram of a trebuchet, asking about the practicalities of building such a device, at least on a small scale. The pictures were to him like some vastly addictive drug. He's not a fool, just uneducated. I think it may be of value to me if he learns a little."

He leaned forward a little in his chair. "But what can I do for you, Caviliero? A discussion of Plato's noble lies to advance Milan?"

"I need a spell."

Kazimierz blinked, and Francisco continued. "You said you could write a plausible cantrip. I need something which will convince a genuine practitioner of the magical arts that I had been fooled."

"You intrigue me, Caviliero. What manner of cantrip do you desire? A charm to lure maidens to bed, or to strike one's foes with bolts of lightning? And who is this practitioner of the arts? All too many of them are frauds...like me, of course."

"Oh, I think he's genuine enough. He doesn't exactly advertise the fact, but I know Marco Valdosta has had some instruction from Eneko Lopez, and he's beyond any doubt a real master."

"You know Signor Marco Valdosta?" exclaimed Kazimierz, sounding more than a little surprised.

"Quite well, yes. Do we share the acquaintance?" asked Francisco, prickling with alarm. Was this man a Venetian spy?

Kazimierz shook his head. "No, but I have heard of him... he is a nobleman of Venice, I believe."

"And a physician."

"Aha! Now I make the connection. Forgive me, Caviliero. I was puzzled as to what you had to do with a student of Eneko Lopez. Lopez is an ecclesiastical magician"—he spread his left hand, as if bestowing a gift—"and, as you say, a genuine one. Not, alas, like me. I could not fool him for an instant."

"Yes, but it only needs to appear to have fooled me. I don't expect Marco to be taken in. I, um, said something foolish, as I thought he was being used as a cat's-paw by others. And now, without ruining the friendship, I need to look as if I was the one being made a fool of."

"A web of deceits, growing ever more tangled," said Master Kazimierz.

"Italian politics is like that."

"Oh, it's not just Italian. And it can be far more than a

friendship ruined. So: what manner of spell is this you require? I have a few books which purport to be grimoires. Who knows, some of the spells in them might even work."

Count Kazimierz Mindaug thought on his feet. He had always been glib, quick to adapt and not easily caught off-guard or unbalanced. At least, once that had been true. He was finding life in the West difficult to adapt his thinking to, accustomed as he was to the patterns of monomania of Lithuania and Elizabeth Bartholdy and Emeric. This Francisco the physician had nearly knocked his feet out from under him with his casual reference to Marco Valdosta. And then to Eneko Lopez! The world was indeed a smaller and more interconnected place than most people realized. There were levels of fate and links in the other worlds that made these things more likely, but still he was amazed.

He was still not sufficiently braced for Francisco's next words. "Well, what I need is a spell to deal with Justinian's Plague."

Ever since he had been asked about the snake, that had niggled at him, and he had wondered if it was going to resurface. He wanted no part of it, none at all, and he had coped with demons and ancient monsters. "There is no cure for the plague," he said, his voice harsh. "Do not go there. People have tried to control it magically before, but instead it controls them."

Francisco wondered quite what had upset the old fellow. He was visibly disturbed by it all. "I was hoping merely for one of the supposed preventive spells. There are plenty of medical prophylaxis methods described, vinaigrettes, mixtures of vervain comfrey and rue, silver and arsenic worn at the throat—and there is no indication that any of them worked in the least."

"They did not. Neither did magic. Neither did...appeasement. I have read about it at length. It was a field of study I pursued many years ago." He pulled himself together visibly. "I will take a few of the elements of the supposed preventive spells. The disease came to Constantinople out of Egypt, but appears to have ravaged many other countries to the east wherever men gathered together in towns or cities."

"It doesn't have to work, Master Kazimierz. It just has to look like I might have believed it could."

Kazimierz shook his head as if to clear it. "Very well. If you will come with me to the testing field, I have some things to show you that I wish you to tell Protector Sforza about. Klaus should have the next rocket ready to fire by now. And I can show you the flying star that he and young Tamas have built. I shall take a piece of parchment with me and write down some doggerel for you to send."

So they walked together to the outbuildings off to the side, which were separated from the house by a row of Italian cypresses. The tall and narrow trees were planted together closely enough to obscure vision. Once they got past the trees and into the little courtyard formed by the outbuildings, they found the bombardier who had once been one of Francisco's patients busily grinding powders.

The sound of their footsteps drew his attention. "Captain Turner!" he exclaimed, coming to his feet. He bowed respectfully to Francisco before clasping his hand in the ruined remains of his own. "I cannot thank you enough!"

"You are enjoying your work?" Francisco knew that, as a secondary task, the fellow was to report to Sforza's spymaster. But he was a good craftsman and seemed to have loved his cannon.

"I could not ask for better," said the man gruffly, with genuine emotion. "I thought... I thought I'd be being bored out of my wits, using my pension to buy a tavern, and drinking away the anger at seeing all the fit bodies around me." He looked at the vast workbench, which showed signs of various projects and which, although new, already had several burns. "It's not that I wouldn't give anything to be hale again but..."

"It's work that suits you."

The fellow nodded. "Ideas that I couldn't have tried as an artilleryman. Things which will change the face of war, I think. Master Kazimierz has some unusual books. And he allows me to experiment."

"Within limits," said Kazimierz. "We have a small fortification that I am sure mystifies the Protector's spies. But I know we deal with dangerous things. Klaus, despite reasons to know otherwise, I sometimes think does not. Klaus, show him the flying star, while I write something for the caviliero."

The flying star proved to be nothing more than an oversized crossbow. It was nothing like the size of a ballista, but was a similar device, loaded with a windlass and aimed in a steep trajectory skyward. The arrow, however, was something very different. "The master wanted to give it a pair of wings to keep it aloft for as long as possible—but those tore off when I fired them, or stopped it going very far, and anyway, it didn't stay aloft for long. But young Tamas had the bright idea of making it like a pine seed. So you've got the head there—and it's bright enough in daylight and startling at night."

He put the arrow in place, wound the windlass down, lit the wick and fired the arrow upward. "Look up there." He pointed, and Francisco could see first a puff of smoke, and then a slow-spinning star burning.

"We're working on the wing and the weight of the star—but it's up to a minute and a half aloft now. Think, Captain. You're sneaking a bunch of sappers or infantry close to a fort, safe and hidden in the dark. If they light torches on the walls, it blinds 'em to the dark, makes men on the wall easy targets, and doesn't light much past maybe fifty paces. You're safe... until someone fires one of those up in the air. That'd have half the men running home to hide behind their mothers' skirts screaming witchcraft. We... Tamas and the master and I, were talking of different heads for the arrows—one that'll explode and send down burning sparks to start fires, and one that'll burst into a rain of flechettes. From high enough, those'll go through armor. It's like working with a lot of gunpowder flakes—one of us burning up an idea seems to set the others off. I know guns and black powder, and Tamas is a natural with mechanical contrivance and doesn't know what can't be done. And the master, well, he knows something about everything."

"Well, I can see some use for it. But it's just one more piece of equipment to go wrong and cost a great deal, like all of it," said Francisco. "How is the development of those colored flares? I could have used those a few nights ago."

The bombardier's expression got very cheery. "Well, Captain, that's the joy of Master Kazimierz's ideas so far. It's the knowing how that counts. It's not like a harquebus, or armor that'll take a life of learning to make and some skill to use. I could make most of the devices for a few coppers, in a shed. Most of it is beeswax, paper, black powder, and bits of willow or cheap cloth. I've a batch of the flares in different colors and a smoker ready to send off to the commander." He moved over a few paces, gesturing as he went. "Now, this rocket. I think they're too inaccurate still, but they're showy. Come over to the fort."

Francisco walked beside the limping ex-bombardier to an earth-walled dugout, with a bench and a stool...and, on posts beyond, a mirror. "The master says the demons struggle to control you if they only see you in the mirror. They do everything backwards. His jokes are sometimes...strange. But it does reduce the chances of flying shrapnel. Mind you, we've hardly had any rockets explode." He pushed a wick through a piece of curved pipe which took it through the wall and attached it to the device, which was a long tube with a conical head. It was pushed in between four bow staves, which in turn had a barrel hoop holding them together, which were lashed to four stout posts in the ground.

"We're still working on the best way to do this, Captain Turner. It should hit the hillock over there." He pointed at a mound some three hundred yards off. "I'm all for a cannon tube, but Master Kazimierz says it's confining powder too tight that makes it explode, and we want it to burn fast, not explode. Come and sit you down in the fort and look in the mirror and we'll set her off."

The bombardier lit the fuse when they were ready. Francisco noticed he had an almost beatific expression on his face as he did so, and then stared intently at the mirror.

The rocket did not explode, but it did make quite a roar. It shot off in a huge trail of smoke, fire and sparks, and then flew rather erratically toward the hillock. It didn't hit it, but did explode quite closely, though.

"Still need to work more on the fuses," said the bombardier. "It's supposed to explode on impact."

Kazimierz was frowning a little. "It did not fly straight. I wonder if fletching as on an arrow would make it fly more true?"

Kazimierz excused himself at that point. Turner remained behind and spent considerable time discussing the possible uses of various weaponry with the bombardier. When he finally arrived back at the main house, Kazimierz greeted him with a piece of parchment in his hand that had lines of odd wriggly symbols on it.

"Demotic, I think from the first century," he said. "It's based on a document I have with some Latin in it, which I think is original. There are a few experts in Rome who would be able to read it. It is an invocation of the divine—probably the Christian God of the Copts—to watch and guard against disease. It will require your friend to get it translated and while I very much doubt it will help, it is a real prayer spell. There are instructions for the placing of colors and candles in it."

Francisco was left wondering just what, or rather who, this scholar was that they'd hired to pretend to be a magic worker. The world of scholarship must know him and it would be a good idea to track him down at some stage. Still, right now, when they faced foes, he was quite an asset to have on their side. And, yes, this would make an ideal document to send Marco. He thanked Master Kazimierz for it, declined an invitation to eat with them.

"You're missing something, Captain Turner. Emma sets a good table," said the bombardier. "And we have taken to talking the day's experiments over at the table. You'd be amazed at the ideas that come out of it. Tamas wanted to put rockets on a cart instead of horses last night. Ideal for driving a ram at a city gate, he thought. And faster than horses. We had star lights on kites the night before."

"I'll ask the commander if you can found a military academy, or rather a place where like minds can gather to invent new ways to blow things up, instead of merely studying the arts or religion." said Francisco. "But I wish to get on to Pavia, to report to him how things have gone against the Scaligeri and their allies to the east."

"And how does it go, if I might ask?" asked Kazimierz warily.

It was no secret. "Goito fortress fell. We hold the Mincio as a border. It's been a successful campaign there so far." Of course, the real difficulty would come from the south and west, but there was no need to point that out. To the west, there was no convenient natural barrier, and the borders would have to be held by battle and men-at-arms, with a constant shift of strategy and conflict. That was the hard front to hold, that and the south. At least, right now, they weren't fighting there yet.

Soon Francisco and his escort were en route to Pavia, with a box of varicolored flares and smoke producers, and two of the flying star arrows. They reached the town well after dark. Francisco was dead tired, but he still made his way immediately to see Sforza. He was pleased to find that his commander was in town—sitting at a table in a good tavern, to make things still better—and not off on a horse somewhere. Francisco was not pleased to see him looking exhausted, having just gotten in from the ride some minutes before.

Carlo read his expression well enough. He leaned back in his chair and sighed, as he pushed away a half-eaten plate of food. "Yes. I feel like I'm carrying a hundred-weight of cannonballs. Yes, my back hurts. No, I haven't much appetite, even though"—he gestured at the plate he'd shoved aside—"the food is quite good."

He sat up a little straighter. "But we are in a crucial phase, Francisco. I've just been reading young Pelta's report, which pleased me, except that I don't recall giving you leave to stick your head into a hornet's nest."

"I'm carrying a bullet burn in repayment for that," said Francisco, wincing a little. "But generally speaking I thought working for you came with an automatic permission to risk our lives. Young Pelta's doing well."

"He should have taken some of their territory, while they were running around like chickens with their heads cut off. But, yes. It's a weight off my mind, especially if Padua and the Scaligeri fight bitterly and keep each other occupied and broke for a while. One of the downsides of being the paymaster: war is expensive. At least the nobility from Goito will bring us some rewards."

Carlo was tired, but the utter exhaustion that had so badly worried Francisco was not evident. "You may have been right to treat me with that purgative. I felt like a weak half-drowned kitten, but I am a little better now."

Taking his pulse, Francisco was not that convinced. "I still think you were poisoned again. Arsenic was my first suspicion, but I think it may be something more exotic. Who did you see? And who did you touch or eat or drink with?"

"Touch? Besides you prodding me all over? Or my dear now-wife allowing me to kiss her perfumed cheek? No one. And I neither drank nor ate anything that old Hellbore or you didn't give me. And if I can't trust Hellbore, I can't trust you either."

Hellbore was Sforza's orderly and had been with the condottiere since he'd been a lowly lieutenant. He could swear the devil out of hell and had no real interest in making his master look like one of the nobility, could get a drink for a thirsty officer at the drop of a hat, always had some spare rations tucked away... and would no more deliberately poison his master than he would give up drinking, which was very unlikely this side of the grave. Of course, there were other possibilities—poisoned clothes, bed sheets, a thin-bladed knife, poisoned air. "I suppose you'd better give up kissing her perfumed cheek," said Francisco, in jest.

"A hardship. But she, of all people, should wish me to stay alive. I'm all that is defending the throne she sits on, and she has this dream that a Visconti will sit on the ducal throne via her loins. And she needs to make sure she's pregnant first before that happens."

"She probably has no idea how fragile Milan is, or what onslaught it faces. And besides, wouldn't she still be the ruler with you out of the way? The other claimants are all dead, or as good as dead."

"I'd agree about the first part. After my experience with Lorendana, and the women of the various courts I have been in, most of them have no grasp of war or what it means, even if they thrive on intrigue. But the second... It's only the female claimants who were closer. I wasn't going to marry Andrea Malatesta or Viscount Palacio of Naples. Milan should thank its lucky stars that it has me instead. But her face powder was not something I ate, and if it poisoned through the skin, she'd be dead. So tell me about your adventures—from your point of view, not Captain Pelta's. He thinks you are a hero. I think you are a lucky fool."

Francisco planted his hands on his hips and tried to look as stern as possible. "Just because you are right does not mean I do not think you need to rest, and can hear about it tomorrow."

"Tomorrow, I need you to go back to Milan. There are some matters I can trust no other with, for the defense of the city. You will handle that sensibly. Others would cause panic."

"Well, you've heard most of it from Pelta. The rest will wait. But I will show you some of the devices that your new 'magician' has sent. I want to see them in the dark myself, and hear your opinion of them."

In the darkness just outside the encampment where Carlo had chosen to make his resting place, rather than a villa he could have demanded, the flares were very impressive. They came in a distinct green fountain, a red fountain, and a bright yellow one.

Carlo, sitting next to him, squeezed his sore arm. "Excellent! Your bookseller has proved his worth already. Compared to fires or lamps, you'll see a lot easier and can signal more. And it doesn't make the betraying noise of cannon. Those are good enough signals, but rather hard for an enemy to miss," he said dryly.

"Well, his other device takes a big crossbow. I asked one of my sergeants to hunt one up for me, but we might do better to save the display for a time when it's not as easily seen. He tells me he tested them several hours after midnight. Once only, because his servants brought tales from the local village."

"I could use a few tales. Let's see it."

So they fired one of the stars up . . .

In the dark, they could just see the burning wick rise to the height of two cathedral steeples and then blossom into a sparking yellow light, which eerily spiraled slowly toward the earth.

The dark was full of the gasps of the watchers. The light was less bright than Francisco had hoped, but it seemed he was the only one who had had such expectations.

"A lamp aloft! How to wreck a perfectly good sneak attack on a fortification," said Carlo Sforza, "or to spot an ambush. I see why you said it might be better to do this when there were fewer watchers. I expect there'll be claims of a virgin birth at best, and witchcraft at worst. And they must have seen that for five miles around in this flat country."

"You'd better set it about that you prayed for a sign to ensure that God felt you had just cause to pursue this war."

"I think they'd be more inclined to believe in the witchcraft theory. But this bookseller seems to be a man of some ingenuity."

"I'd say so. Although he seems to be both bemused and amused by his assistants, it's their combined effort that produces these contrivances. He has a device called a rocket which could be very intimidating. He talked of a thrower of gouts of Greek fire, and dozens more murderous and strange ideas. They are not magic but they'll be believed to be that. And I'd say he knows a little more about magic than he lets on. We need to establish who he was. No minor noble, in my opinion."

"My spies are supposed to be working on it. That means I may know tomorrow, or never. Most of them are Visconti's old agents, and I need to get rid of half of them, but I can't do it right now. If anyone was poisoning me, I'd suspect that lot." He yawned. "I'll still sleep better knowing that we've some fear and tricks up our sleeve. It strikes me that when you go back to Milan you'd better see this asset well guarded. I wouldn't put it past someone to kidnap him, poison him, or make him a better offer."

"I'll do that. How many men do you think it justifies?"

"Get your sergeant to count how many of my men ran away from that flying star. He's worth that many men to me," said

Sforza, with a wry smile. "Seriously, how many more of these toys do you think he knows of, and why haven't we heard of him and them before?"

"I think it's been a happy accident. We've got a gunpowder man, an ingenious young artificer who doesn't know what is impossible, and an old man with a great deal of knowledge in many fields. I said I would tell you they ought to start an aca-demia where it was not the usual languages and arts studied, but how to make the tools of war. I suppose they'd have other applications, too."

"Let us get through this conflict with both the territory of Milan and ourselves intact, and I'll do so," said Sforza. "But now I am going to sleep."

Chapter 30

Milan

The next morning Francisco rode back to Milan to go and begin the preparations his commander had wished on him. En route he stopped with Master Kazimierz, who came out of the villa to greet him.

Francisco did not dismount, since he didn't want to spend much time there. "Protector Sforza liked your devices. He wants twenty of the green and red ones, for a start. And a lot of the whirling star ones. And I am to put a guard of some fifty men on you and the estate, in shifts, of course. In times like these, that says he values your devices."

The man blinked. "I had not thought of someone trying an actual physical attack on me. I suppose that guards might be wise. What you ask for is quite a lot of time-consuming labor." He frowned, and then looked around. "There's plenty of space here for soldiers to make camp. I would rather I and my men were occupied in developing new things. Can I use some of these troops for the mundane tasks? Under supervision, of course."

"I'll get my sergeant to arrange it appropriately. He'll get you the right sort of men for the work."

He had then gone to his quarters in the palazzo—and regretted it. It seemed that Lucia Sforza had not merely settled for ensuring her putative offspring sat as a ruling duke, but had issued orders that, on pain of . . . well, pain, she would be addressed as "Your Grace." Overnight, the place seemed to have filled up with her eager toadies. There were courtiers all over the place, demanding to know what soldiers on errands or carrying dispatches were doing. Francisco had a list of tasks to achieve that he really did not want these people to gossip about, so he gave orders to that effect.

What he hadn't expected was the descent of the new duchess from on high, as a result.

"Good evening, m'lady." He bowed as she, and a wave of strong scent, and two large bodyguards stormed into the rooms Carlo had given him, where he had set up something of an office.

She looked down her nose at him, not acknowledging his bow by as much as a slight nod of the head. "If you fail to address me as 'Your Grace,' I will have my men flog you. In fact, when I have done with speaking to you, that will happen anyway. I need to constantly make examples, it seems. I have come to tell you that your men have been showing insufficient respect for authority. If they are asked just what they're up to by one of the nobles of this court, they must answer with speed and precision. I will not tolerate anything else."

"I was unaware that I was to use that title, Your Grace. I apologize for the oversight," said Francisco, who had no intention of being flogged. "I do suggest that, before any flogging is done, the importance of my work be considered, and the displeasure that work being interrupted would cause to the Protector, Carlo Sforza. I am here on his direct, personal orders, Your Grace, doing tasks on the explicit command of your husband, not by my own authority."

He left out "or by yours." Possibly the implication that she was subject to the authority of her husband was less than clever, even if it was true. However, he saw how the two bullyboys looked at each other. Their smug brutal complacency was replaced by a *how can I make it you who has to do the dirty work?* look at their fellow. Left to them, a hasty retreat would have been in order.

That did not stop their mistress, but it did give her pause. Not for long, however. "Bah. What work? I manage the affairs of M— of the court in his absence. Do not attempt to usurp one ounce of my authority . . . you."

"My task has nothing to do with the court, Your Grace, but with matters beyond it."

"What matters? I cannot have trivia disturbing the smooth running of the palazzo. I should be organizing a musical soiree and I am wasting my time on the likes of you."

That was outside of enough. She was young, vain, stupid, and in need of personal hygiene, but surely she could not know in an Italian court what was happening? "It doesn't seem to have occurred to Your Grace that we are fighting a war on several fronts," he said.

She shrugged. "There are always wars being fought. It's no excuse for unacceptable behavior in my court. I will not have your men telling my gentlemen of the court that what they are doing is none of their business. It engenders a lack of respect. Do I make myself clear?"

Francisco prided himself on keeping his temper in tough situations, but this was going beyond that breaking point. He could not back down now. "I have orders from your husband to do what I am doing. And that includes having his soldiers maintain secrecy. There are spies everywhere."

She stared furiously at him, gathering her bile to spew in a tirade that could well end in *off with his head!*

"You do understand," said Francisco in the gap, "that if our foes win, they will put your head on a pike at the gates of Milan for the crime of marrying Carlo Sforza. They want you dead, m— Your Grace. That is what I have been sent here to prevent."

For a moment, Francisco thought that would not be enough. But she swallowed. "You speak nonsense."

He shrugged, trying to keep as calm as possible. "Send a message to Carlo. He is only in Pavia and could be here in the space of a few hours, and I promise he will confirm my authority and the importance of my task, and the danger to yourself."

He used the first name with deliberate intent to stress that he was one of the few people who were on first-name terms with the Wolf of the North. "Or wait until he comes to Milan and ask him then. I speak nothing but the truth, Your Grace. I am sorry to be so blunt. I had assumed you would know, but if you think about it, it cannot be otherwise."

She was finally silenced. Almost shrunken, she stood there, looking not like an arrogant duchess but like a frightened, inse-cure girl. "But why would they want to kill me?" she complained finally, almost plaintively. "I *am* a Visconti. That was why Sforza married me. There are no other claimants remotely close in the noble linage of Visconti."

"He couldn't have married the male claimants, could he?" said Francisco.

Her mouth literally fell open. Then she recovered herself. "They must be killed. They must be killed immediately!" she snapped.

"Your Grace, I am afraid they feel the same way about you. That is why we have a war, and why I am taking some preventative measures."

"Have my father's assassins been told to kill them? Who are they?" Lucia demanded.

"I only recall that Viscount Palacio of Naples is one. I am not privy to what the spies and assassins are doing, Your Grace. I am a military man, dealing with military problems and issues, not that. You'll have to talk to Carlo about that. But he is trying to fight a war to prevent them from doing by main force to you, what you would do to them by stealth. It is no easy task."

She looked narrowly at him. "How close are these enemies? Will they take Milan?"

"Not while we have the Wolf of the North at our head," said Francisco, with as much confidence as he could inject, avoiding even hinting that part of his work was to make sure that Milan could face a siege. "But he wins by being prepared, Your Grace. And that is what he sent me to do, and what your courtiers are getting in the way of. What he prepares is not for anyone to know. I myself only know the scope of my own orders, and I may not speak of those. Spies are everywhere. Even listening to us, probably."

"I will speak to him."

"I would appreciate that, Your Grace," said Francisco. He had a grasp of her character by now, and was sure that it would include her telling Carlo what an insolent pig he was, and she would follow that with demands for appropriate punishment. But she would not confront him directly again. However, he wasn't going to give her the chance. She turned and swept out without so much as a word.

As soon as she had gone, Francisco called his sergeant. "Get my kit and tell all of the men we're moving to the central barracks." It would be less comfortable, less convenient, and a lot more pleasant.

"Good," said the sergeant, which was quite a long speech for him.

Lucia walked away from the rooms of the officer whose name eluded her. One of Sforza's mercenary scum...but he had said things which had shocked and surprised her. She'd always regarded Sforza as a mere key to the ducal throne, to die as soon as was convenient and unobtrusive. The idea that the boorish oaf could have any real value otherwise had never really occurred to her. He was a soldier. They were ten to the copper.

On impulse, she stopped to speak to an elderly courtier, one of her father's cronies, Lord Miletti. He, too, had been a general and had commanded an army somewhere. Not too successfully, if she recalled correctly, but he was a good man at court.

"Miletti," she said. "As a military commander, how does Carlo Sforza rank?"

He blinked, trying to work out what this was all about. "Oh, he's a genius, beyond peer, magnificent, Your Grace. A nonpareil. Superb. Brilliant."

She knew, all too well, the exaggerated flattery of the court. "Really? As good as you, my lord? Say it without hyperbole now. I wish to know, not to inflate his importance. My father never said much complimentary about him."

Miletti tugged at his neat beard. "Well, that is to say . . . he's had lots of victories, although the genius was really your father, of course. But the common soldiers love him and believe in him. They're very loyal to him, not to Milan, which your father found difficult. He was paying Sforza, after all."

That, to her, made sense. But the fact remained that his troops were a substantial force and the duchy was, unless she read that obnoxious captain wrong, facing a real danger of an attack overrunning her Milan. That would deprive her of her birthright, and made him more valuable alive than dead, as his troops gave their loyalty to him.

The snake stirred in her bosom. *He is dying. Slowly.*

She ignored it for now. She went to her chamber and sat, queenly, waited on by the ladies of the chamber, which was pleasant and helped her to relax. She liked them in their subservient roles. Presently she sent for her father's old spymaster. She had no idea if he still fulfilled the same role, but it was probable. She banished all but Helena, who had broken one of her hairbrushes and was, therefore, going to receive a bite from the asp.

The spymaster bowed, said all the correct courtly things, and indulged her in some idle gossip. "It is good to see you taking up your father's reins, Your Grace, with his touch."

His touch . . . that made her feel faintly revolted, but she appreciated the intent of the compliment. "Yes," she said. "I would appreciate it if you reported to me as well. Sforza may be a military man, but he was not brought up in the court, and fails to grasp its subtleties."

"Quite. A man whose strategy is mirrored by his name. Very effective on the battlefield, but not so experienced in matters of, shall we say, state. He has hired a man to be his magical advisor without even consulting me."

That made Lucia nervous. Magical power...that was hers through the serpent. She did not need competition, or threats. "Whom?"

"He goes by the name of Master Kazimierz. He arrived from Verona perhaps a month ago. He is now living on an estate out at Val di Castellazzo. I am pursuing enquiries, but the man should have been investigated first. Out of Venice comes the belief that he's a powerful, evil sorcerer."

Lucia wondered if he was a threat, or whether he could be recruited.

You have me, said the voice in her bosom.

But she wanted more.

She continued her work, using the asp to hypnotize some and, where they might prove an obstruction to her rule, to kill them.

She'd leave defense to Sforza, for now.

Francisco finally got around to the task of sending Marco a message.

> *My dear friend in Medicine,*
> *I apologize for being so long in replying to you, but I have been away on our successful campaign against the Scaligeri, where I suffered a minor wound.*

No harm in doing a bit of propaganda, although Venice would already have reports of what had happened.

> *I include a copy of the magical protection we obtained from our advisor in these matters, which we have been assured may be effective against the disease. I am not knowledgeable in these matters, and the language is strange to me. I know you have access to greater resources than I do, so I would appreciate knowing if it will work. The practical measures I suggest are obviously a strictly enforced quarantine. The*

*records seem to show that not every person is affected, and
a few survive, but that the disease has a short duration of
being infected—troops have invaded territory a mere two
months after an outbreak and been unaffected. This scenario
happened during the Gothic invasions of Italy under Theoderic. Cleanliness, both of person and of the environment,
seems to also affect its spread. It is possible, as thought by
some physicians, that it is an evil humor contained in the
malodors of putrefaction, which may account for outbreaks
usually beginning among the poor, and often in harbor areas.
The disease has apparently its origins in Egypt or in places
east of it.*

*On the subject of the snake, I have had it pointed out to
me that it bears some resemblance to the older versions of
the heraldic emblem of the House Visconti. I discussed this
with my commander, and he said I should tell you of it, and
remind you that he is responsible for the demise of the last
ruling member of that house, but that there are others. It is
possible that the heraldic snake is somehow a folk memory
of such a creature.*

Francisco signed the letter, sealed it up in a bottle and set out
for his usual aquatic meeting place in the twilight. He wondered
if the nyx would be there. He preferred his women not to be
naked pond dwellers. They'd probably wet the bed.

Sitting by the water, his doubt at whether Rhene would be
there was erased. "He's been asking after you, you know," she said.

"I've been busy. Doing things humans do: fighting a war," he
said, handing her the bottle with the message in it.

"I remember that," she said in an odd voice, sad and poignant,
quite unlike her usual coquettish tone. "You made me remember
things that I want to forget. Where I came from. And why I
dream of a child. I was human, like you, once. I had a lover, a
tall, handsome, strong, lusty lover. I could not tell him no. And
he went to war and never came back."

She disappeared under the water, with barely a ripple.

Francisco was left looking at the canal with the last light of
the day reflected in it. He shook himself, took a deep breath and
went back to the inn and had a beer. He probably didn't want to
think too much about the implications of what she'd just said.

Chapter 31

Venice

Marco Valdosta was relieved to find things finally turning his way. There was news that the fleet, with his brother on it, was finally in Corfu, refitting after storm damage. That news, via a small coaster, seemed to have had a calming influence on Maria.

Secondly, he had had news from Francisco in Milan. He had taken the spell contained in the bottle with him to visit Patriarch Michael. Someone in Rome could certainly translate it, assess it, say how it best could be used. He also wanted to send the rest of Francisco's comments about dealing with plague on to Father Thomas Lüber. The only worrying thing was this war. War could destabilize everything and allow the disease to spread beyond any chance of containment.

The patriarch, ever his humble self, in the quiet of his inner sanctum had stared at the piece of parchment for a long time. "Alas," he said finally, "it is Demotic Egyptian script. I do understand a few words, but not enough to begin to know quite what it is about."

He smiled apologetically. "Hebrew I read, and Greek, from my wishful desire to read the Bible in as much of the original form as possible. We humans are such frail implements of God's grace. But, with your permission, I have a guest, Archimandrite von Stebbens, whose knowledge of things magical far exceeds mine. I happen to know he is an expert in several languages, and I recall him speaking of the Coptic translations of the Bible. We could ask him to come and have a look. He is one of the

Knights of the Holy Trinity, and I believe is to be trusted in the confidentiality of this matter. The Holy Roman Emperor has been informed, so there are no secrets at the state level for this, and nor should there be."

"I think we have to take what steps we can. Let us ask him. The worst he could say is 'send it to Rome,' which was what I was going to ask you to do for me anyway."

So a few minutes later, a tall, somber-looking Knight came down to the sanctum. He had a curiously deep, resonant voice and a very intense gaze that reminded Marco somewhat of Eneko Lopez.

The patriarch explained: "We find ourselves in something of a quandary in our dealings with the Duchy of Milan, and the forecast of medical disaster. Given that the Church has decided not to recognize Sforza, due to considerable pressure from various factions, it was very awkward to ask for their assistance. So I asked young Signor Valdosta here for his help. He had already been recruited by Father Thomas Lüber to assist in dealing with the possibility of the plague... and he has a contact in Milan."

"My friend Francisco Turner," explained Marco. "He is a physician, a scholar and is also attached to the service of Carlo Sforza. I felt I could turn to him, in confidence. He assisted in rescuing my niece and is a very honorable man. I let him know what we knew. To my surprise, he said they'd received similar warnings, but that they had some form of magical protection. In this matter, all men of medicine are allies. I asked him to share this information with us. He sent me this, which he says they got from their magical advisor, and asked me to find out more about the efficacy of it. He is a physician, not a worker of magic"—Marco could not help smiling—"although the two do get confused from time to time."

The Knight took the parchment, and quickly and carefully turned it over, so he could not see the writing. "He got this from the magical advisor to Carlo Sforza, you say? My young friend, this may be the most deadly of traps. There is a particularly evil magician who, we believe, has insinuated himself into that position. We know he plans something. May my brother Knights and I examine this under suitable magical protection? You would be welcome to attend while we did so. Sometimes, even reading such a spell is enough to trigger it."

Of course Marco had to agree. A little later, in a prepared and warded chapel, within a multicolored nine-circle chalked ring, the candles and prayers of invocation said, the parchment was turned over with a piece of consecrated olive wood. The wood did not catch flame, nor did demons rage up from the parchment to be trapped. There was strange squiggly writing on it, but that had been there when Marco looked at it originally. The Lion stirred within him ... and perceived no magic.

"It ... er, seems innocent. We will test it further ..."

"What does it say?" asked Patriarch Michael with just a tiniest touch of exasperation. "You said you could read Demotic. My own ability is poor, but I read it without such protections, and what I could understand seemed innocent enough. I read 'Emmanuel,' and the Tetragrammaton, neither of which I associate with evil. In fact, I thought evil could abide neither, let alone name them."

"Well, on the surface, on first examination, it appears to be ... um, a prayer. Possibly used as protection against disease," said the archimandrite. "But the source ... You understand, Count Mindaug is as devious as a serpent. Nothing about him is to be trusted."

"Yes, but would it work as a spell against the plague?" asked Marco. "My friend believes it would and he is not an evil or devious man. He's just a physician, a soldier, and a scholar. A very good man, really. Our Doge owes his life to his wisdom and care. So does a young lady in my care at the moment."

"Prayer is always valuable. But, to be honest, it is merely a prayer written in Demotic script. I cannot say it would protect the body against plague. It might. It calls on God to bless and protect, but I can't say whether it would."

"That is God's decision," said the patriarch.

"Would the language have any virtue besides, well, looking magical?" asked Marco.

"A difficult question. Some languages have layers of meaning, and what appears a blessing can be a curse, or the inverse. But no, unless its virtue was dictated by belief. We know faith can move mountains, it is just hard to come by."

"Well, it is worth trying, I suppose," said Marco with a sigh. "I was quite hopeful."

"Prayer is always worth trying," said the patriarch.

Which was something, Marco thought grumpily, he would say.

He did not discuss the matter of the snake with them, although he brought it up later, when talking to Petro Dorma.

"If the Visconti had had a secret stock of well-trained deadly vipers, Filippo Maria would have used it on me and half the nobles of Italy," said Petro. "He could never have resisted the temptation to use it as often as possible."

Marco told Petro about the "spell" he'd gotten from Francisco, and about the Knights and their reaction to it, and the fact that it was merely an old prayer in a foreign language. "They were very put out about it. You'd have thought they'd be glad," he said, amused.

"Yes, the archimandrite has been to see me. I've even had a communication with the Emperor about this fellow. After pressuring the archimandrite, he finally admitted that they're monitoring magical use by this fellow. And so far either he's managed to hide it, or he's not intervened with magic use at all. They want to go and capture, or better still, kill him. That's awkward in the middle of a war. Speaking of which, it seems your friend—the man to whom I owe some of my survival—is quite a military man. And quite a diplomat."

"Really?"

"Yes, it appears it was he who invaded Scaliger lands at the head of ten thousand horse, according to my spies on the other side of the border's reports—which may be a little exaggerated. He then administered, with the help of a secret alliance he'd made with the Carraresi of Padua, a sound drubbing to their condottieri's forces, aimed for the relief of Goito. A soldier and a physician, as well as informed about snakes on coats of arms."

Von Stebbens, suspicious as always of anyone who had any possible contact with Mindaug, asked their host, the patriarch Michael, about him. "This Signor Marco Valdosta, he seems a pleasant young man, and obviously one Father Thomas Lüber of Baden trusted enough to confide in . . . but, well, evil communications. I worry. What can you tell me of him, Your Reverence?

The laughter from the old man was kindly, but it was still laughter. Von Stebbens was not used to being laughed at. "You are a student of magic. A learned man. What do you know of the names of the families of the four who originally made the pact with the Lion of St. Mark, the Lion of Etruria, the guardian of Venice?"

Von Stebbens knew the story. And the names associated with it. "*That* Valdosta?"

"By blood, the last man of that line, married to the last woman of the Montescue line. According to my friend Eneko Lopez—who married them, by the way—he's one of the bastions of light in the West. Eneko was both awed and comforted by the power and goodness of that young man. He said to me that young Marco was possessed of natural gifts of magic of a high order. With those and because of his relationship with the Lion, he was able to withstand Chernobog. We know, privately, that Marco is a man who shares his being with the city's guardian, and that it is a mutual relationship of love, both for the people and the place. So I doubt somehow, that a mere mortal magician like this Mindaug could contaminate Marco and the Lion of St. Mark. I know he is aware of the use of any dark magic within his demesnes. I don't think you have anything to fear."

Von Stebbens, who had met and been awed by Eneko Lopez himself—who was also a humble fellow, now that he thought about it—swallowed. "He simply seemed a nice young man."

"He is. It is possible to be both, you know. You may trust him completely, and if you can enlist him, he would be an ally against which your cunning magician might fail."

That evening Marco sat talking with Kat, Maria, and Lodovico. He might have had a glass too many. Not far too many, but enough to loosen his tongue a little. "Francisco says it looks like the snake on the old Visconti coat of arms. I am convinced there was something magical involved. But as Petro says, if the Visconti had such a magical viper, they'd have used it."

"Unless the price was too high," said Maria. "There is always a price on using such things."

"Or they have only just found out how to do it again. As if it was a part of their magical armory back when the house acquired the coat of arms. But they lost the skill..."

Marco snapped his fingers. "I think you may have it. Sforza just got a new magician, who may know how to use an old Visconti magic."

"But, Sforza...he's not a Visconti. And the sick girl you have at the palace is," said Lodovico.

"That's true. But I will go and see that archimandrite first thing in the morning, and take him to Violetta, and see if he can detect any sign of this magician of theirs."

"It still makes no sense to me," said Lodovico stubbornly. "It's more likely to be one of Sforza's enemies, or a claimant to the ducal throne that would kill all his rivals. I wouldn't put anything past Andrea Malatesta, for all that he is only a second cousin."

"It might also be that this magician is using Sforza, either for his own or someone else's ends. It's worth investigating."

The next morning, Marco had a message sent to Archimandrite von Stebbens, asking if he could come to the Doge's palace, to the rooms where Violetta de' Medici was being cared for, and meet Marco there. The Knight arrived shortly after Marco had done his morning examination of the patient. She continued her depressing course—physically healing, but slowly creeping toward death.

After greetings had been exchanged, and while the Knight had not been disrespectful in any way the day before, Marco got the feeling that his status had been elevated hugely since. There was almost deference in the Knight's speech now as he explained: "Further examination of your parchment showed no evil communications. It appears to be exactly what it looks like, a copy of an old prayer, possibly from one of the Gnostic heresies, but at least it is calling on the one true God. It was surprising that Mindaug dared to use such a thing."

"Well, I asked you to come here on a separate but possibly related matter. Would it be possible for you to detect traces of magic having been used on a person? You see, I have this young woman here...apparently bitten by a very strange serpent, and I begin to suspect that some form of magic was involved."

"It would be possible, yes," said Von Stebbens. "Powerful magework leaves traces. It is why whatever Mindaug is up to is so worrying. He appears to have barely used any of his vast power. At first we thought that was merely a desire to hide, but we realized that he had outsmarted us with the snowstorm that he used to give us the slip."

Marco nodded. "So he may have a way of not leaving a trace. These levels of magic are still far beyond me. I've been so occupied in my medical studies that I have not really given it much concentration."

"Given that which you have to help you, and quite possibly your natural aptitude, you would not need it to do things which are beyond our power," said the Knight, confirming what Marco had suspected. Someone had been talking about him. "If I might call on three of my companions, we will attempt to discover this for you."

"I'd be grateful."

The Knight nodded. "I will send a message, and then begin to prepare the room. It is not without danger, M'lord Valdosta. If you could remain...and grant us your protection, too."

"I am quite unschooled in this kind of magic. I can scry within the lagoon, and defend it. But these subtleties—I don't know much about them."

"Defense would be our need. I suspect demons."

Something within Marco said, "I would rend such creatures into gobbets if they dared," and there was something of a roar in his voice.

The Knight nodded, slowly. "The danger, of course, is also to the poor young lady. We may summon back what injured her in the first place."

Marco sighed and said aloud what he had known for some time. "She's dying anyway. Day by day, hour by hour, something draws her life away." He knew this as the Lion, not as Marco Valdosta, the physician.

A little later the room was prepared, the girl was lying in the center of a cross drawn onto the floor in the elemental colors, and inscribed with symbols traced out and framed in sulfur, mercury (in a curved wooden platter) and salt. The ward candles were lit, the chants of invocative prayer sung.

A soft halo of light formed above Violetta, and in it something like a watercolor scene appeared, washes of color resolving into forms, tall sycamores and a scythed lawn, and laurel bushes fringing the rose garden...and two figures, patterns of movement, rather than distinct...and the blue wash of the sky was suddenly flushed with something dark rising from the earth, a blueish-purple apparition that crawled with sickly yellow lightnings.

It was, of course, just a recreation, an illusion, a picture taken from the mind of the woman. Marco knew that.

The warding candles flared and burned like torches, but the purple serpentine darkness rose and swayed, no mere illusion now, scattering the symbols and brushing the Knights aside.

The morning air was suddenly darkened, dank and full of the stench of putrefaction.

Violetta made the first large movement that Marco had seen, and made the first real sound he'd heard out of her since she'd arrived in his care. Her back arched and she clutched at her now healed leg and screamed. A scream of both pain and fear, but especially pain.

Marco stepped forward and swiped his arm through the air and he reached to take her hand, to stop her clawing at the newly healed flesh. Golden light slashed through the purple darkness, scattering it.

"*Begone!*" he roared.

The walls shook and windows rattled across Venice, but the dark force was strong with pain and fear. Marco knew that that was its food, what it sought endlessly, relentlessly. But in the realms of the spirit, here within the bounds of the ancient marsh where the belief and trust of generations was vested in him, it could not prevail. He knew it now. He'd fought it before, when men fleeing from its purple buboes had fled into the marshes. Some had carried the killer disease. He had not been able to save them as individuals, but he had kept them apart, and had kept the serpent out.

He could stop the creature drawing them down into the dark, and could still their pain. And some of them had recovered. So too, now, he stilled her pain, and banished the thing that had been drawing her down into screaming death.

The candles, mere wicks in puddles of wax, still burned. The morning light streamed in through the broken window and the wind brought them the fresh clean smell of the sea across the lagoon bar.

A little later, with the room warded as well as the Knights could—not that it mattered anyway, Marco knew—Von Stebbens turned respectfully to Marco. "M'lord Valdosta...well, I am afraid we know now that there was magic involved in that 'snake bite' and it was very evil and dark. This, I think, is without a doubt the power that Mindaug wields. I don't know quite what it is..."

"I do. It is a serpent, and its power lies in suffering and death. It is also, somehow, the plague."

"So—this Mindaug has come to Milan and somehow awakened this ancient monster."

"It is not ancient," said Marco, with the certainty that was the Lion speaking through him. "I know it now. It is, as magical beings go, barely adolescent, and merely beginning to gather its power. It lurked in caverns near Arona digesting its last meals and waiting to be called out. But it not old. It is new, by the standards of the powers, and all fear it. Even Chernobog. It kills all it can reach, and gathers power from each death. Enough deaths and it will be unstoppable, until it runs out of lives. It will eventually devour the person who tries to control it, too."

The Knight shook his head. "He has been there barely a month. To free such evil on the world..."

"She was poisoned six weeks ago, near Florence."

"But Mindaug was in Tyrol then. We saw no signs of spell-working..."

"Yet...Tyrol is important. I feel this. And it is not as a place of evil," said the Lion-Marco.

"He must have been up to something. Perhaps thwarting something good there. There must be a reason, and I am very afraid of what it could be."

Marco—and the Lion—were troubled, not really wanting to talk to the archimandrite, or anyone, but needing to digest this situation. Marco the healer, faced with the news of an outbreak of the plague, had not made the connection with the wyrm and the disease that had gone with it. There had been five recorded outbreaks. And then it had stopped. Or had it *been* stopped?

One thing he knew: he would make this Count Mindaug tell him everything.

He wondered about Francisco, if anything could be done to save him. Probably not, he realized, with a heavy heart.

Violetta, from her sleep of tangled and terrified dreams, had suddenly found herself rushing to her mother's rescue, in between the bay trees and laurel bushes, with the snake rearing and striking at her. The pruning scissors in her hand had not been enough; she needed a sword: a sword to save a maiden from the great wyrm that would devour her slowly otherwise. A some-what divorced part of her mind said she was the maiden and it couldn't possibly swallow her. But then she saw the bruise-purple and pus-yellow enormity of it. The terror was nearly as bad as the pain. And then, roaring his challenge and blazing golden, there was the Lion. And behind him, the rose garden. Soon she would enter the rose garden.

Why a rose garden? part of her mind wanted to know. She had never been particularly fond of that flower.

Chapter 32

Milan and environs

Count Kazimierz Mindaug had been thinking for some days now. He had begun to wonder if he should essay at least some scrying. He had prepared a few careful traps that required no magic at all in laying out—but at a word, they would no longer be inert and harmless. That was his only step towards defense. He knew—none better—how vast the world was to try to search, magically, for something that gave no sign of its presence.

But the plague, and the great wyrm—those were worrying enough to make him begin to consider the problem. It was, he admitted wryly, a strange thing to discover about yourself, that you were like other humans. And, when faced with the most horrible danger, you could still bury your head and try to pretend it wasn't there.

The problem was that the count had discovered, late in life— probably too late, he admitted—some degree of pleasure and contentment. Yes, there had been satisfaction, deeply hidden, at his cunning plot to destroy Chernobog and Jagiellon. There had also been some pleasure in setting the trap that he had foreseen would probably end the evil power of Elizabeth Bartholdy. But he had never sat with a group of men who, rather than pull him down for their own advancement, seemed to revel in his ideas and delight in his leadership.

It was strange and . . . heady.

He did not wish to give it up. But he had come to realize

that with their loyalty he had also acquired responsibility. Most inconvenient that was!

So, he had been looking for a way that would allow him to continue to avoid magic, and also to continue his present life, when it presented itself to him in the form of Francisco Turner, and his friendship and contact with Marco Valdosta. Let the Lion of Etruria deal with the great wyrm. Mindaug would help it along, with a little information.

"Ah, Caviliero," he said, smiling, once Turner had dismounted and tethered his horse to a hitching post. To his inner surprise, that was a smile of genuine pleasure. He found enjoyment in the visits of the man. He was well-read and acerbic from time to time, which provided a counterpoint to Tamas, Emma, and Klaus and their hero worship. They had their forms of intellect, too, but this was different. The question now was how to feed the information to him, and to be sure he would pass it on to Valdosta.

Mindaug just needed an opening, and after talking military matters for a while in the comfortable chairs in the green salon, Francisco Turner gave it to him. "I've a question, seeing as I gather your reading has taken you far from just the sciences. Magical creatures...a water-nyx to be precise. Is it possible that she was once human?"

"The origin of such creatures is not simple or monophyletic," replied Mindaug, shaking his head. "Some could once have been human. There are elemental creatures and those created by the divine. We do not begin to understand the nature of magic, or of ritual and the innate. But circumstances, place, power and belief all come into it." He shrugged. "I don't pretend to understand half of it, but some things have power from being conferred on them by belief. A stream may once have been a mere flow of water, but if enough people possessed of enough belief think it to be an aspect of a naiad...there may indeed be a naiad there. And once she is there, or thought to be there, belief will be strengthened. It becomes its own fulfilment."

"So...a drowned pregnant girl could somehow become a nyx, desperate to have that child?"

Mindaug waggled his hand back and forth, indicating a range of possibilities. "Or some part of that girl's spirit could shape the nyx, which was once merely a drift of waterweed that recalled her face."

Turner made a face. "That's quite terrifying. I think I will stick to medicine."

"Well, it, and medicine, bring up something I have been wanting to pass on to your friend Marco Valdosta," said Mindaug. "I am a mere scholar, not a man of medicine or magecraft, but I have been thinking about your snake. You recall I said that I thought I had read something about it. Well, I had and I have found it. And it is worrying me, especially in the light of your questions about a magical protection against the plague. I think I now know what your snake was, or was a sendling of. I believe the plague your friend seeks to prevent and the snake may be one and same, raised by the same means as the nyx was."

Francisco's eyes widened with surprise. "*What*?"

"When the plague swept Europe for the first time, the people facing it did not know what it was, or how to deal with it. So they did the same as they did with lightning or a stream. They personified it, gave it form, and made it into a being: a being with a nature like the disease. They had seen and smelled the death from the kind of snake venom that rots the flesh. And somewhere in northern Italy that took the form they believed it had. The wyrm came to be, came into existence. They tried to appease it, made sacrifices to it, to make it spare them and theirs. And, because they were human, they tried to turn it on their foes. But the thing they'd given life to was not the spirit of a woman. It was a disease, which they themselves had made into a magical creature. They had given it form and they had given it life, and they tried to control it. It has those attributes they gave to it, now. But it remains a disease. It is a new god, and with time and belief they become more like the humans who believe in them."

Now Francisco's expression was skeptical. "Quite honestly, it sounds like a myth to me."

"We humans are bad at inventing completely new things. It is a myth, but like most myths has its origin in the truth. And the myth has grown stronger because people believe in it. It has grown other aspects and other abilities, like the snake sendling to this person. They die, because although you harness the disease and give it a name, death is really all it can do in the end."

"She's still alive."

It was Kazimierz Mindaug's turn to look surprised. "As far as I knew only one man had ever resisted it, freed the sacrifice from the devourer, and banished it. And he was a legendary knight of his age and had the fruits of his previous adventures."

"Quite a few people survived the plague. Around one in ten, I recall. Justinian himself did."

"They survive the plague, but not the wyrm. But that is irrelevant. I have here a book for your friend Valdosta." He reached down to a shelf below the top of the side table he was sitting beside and withdrew a slim volume. Then, leaning forward, he handed it to Turner.

"It's a compilation of the tales of Diderich—or Theoderic, as the Goths called him," Mindaug explained. "They're popular still in song and story. You would both have heard some of them, but this is an old book, not changed by storytellers and bards. This copy comes from a bare hundred years after his death and is nearly nine hundred years old. There is a marker at the page describing Theoderic's rescue of a maiden from the wyrm. Later versions made the wyrm into a dragon. The description is precise, and I think you will recognize it. It also speaks of the treatment he administered, which will be beyond your friend."

The moment he heard the book was almost a millennium old, Francisco set it down on his lap, as if afraid the oils in the skin of his hands—anything—might damage the precious thing. "What treatment?" he asked.

"An attar of rose petals from the garden of the dwarf Laurin."

Francisco looked up. "Ah. There are some Arabic texts on the use of scents, but I've yet to see it proved."

"Still...you will send this book to him. Please? I ask it as a boon."

"Well, certainly. That is, if I can get the nyx to deliver it. She carries the messages in a bottle—it would need to be waterproofed."

"I have a glass canister for my experiments which will hold it. It can be sealed."

Lucia was pleased at how the reins of power had fallen into her hands at the Palazzo Ducale. It was relatively simple: those who did not do her bidding had a visit from the asp. Those few who did not fall under its hypnotic spell...died.

And word, it seemed, still got around. Someone had tried

to poison her. But the asp detected it. *Not that it matters. You have the great wyrm's own poison in your veins. That poison will drive out lesser ones.*

"It never bit me! Never. I did not permit it to do so."

The tooth of the great wyrm is so keen that all you would feel is barely as much as a fleabite. But it does not matter, mistress. The wyrm is yours to command. I scent his magnificence about you.

She was not pleased or soothed. "Who tried to kill me? Who dared?"

The asp slithered out from her bosom and let its black forked tongue flicker across the sweetmeats. *One of your ladies-in-waiting. The one with the blonde hair.*

Lucia knew who and knew why. The fool girl was wrong, of course, for her lover had no appeal to the duchess. His flowery talk was amusing, no more. But she did like to have the handsome men of the court dangle after her. It would be amusing to flirt with him in her presence . . . and then to make him feed her one of her own sweetmeats. Lucia was mildly annoyed at the choice of delicacy. She liked marzipan flowers both for their artistry and their taste.

Then her footman came to politely inform her that Lord Palmeri craved an audience.

After making his entrance into the chamber she used for her dealings with courtiers, the spymaster brought news of the war. This was not of vast interest to Lucia, but after the possibilities that that lowborn scum captain of Sforza's—she refused to think of him as "husband"—had pointed out, she did need to pay it some attention.

The news wasn't exactly what she wanted to hear—which was that it was all over, and Sforza could get on with dying. "It's very balanced, Your Grace. But the balance has shifted now to Sforza. He wins battles against the odds, or I would say it was not. I think victory for Milan assured. He's not been well, but his men fight well for him. He is due back in town tomorrow." He smiled coyly. "They say he longs for the sweet embraces of his beautiful wife."

It might be time for yet more poison, if that happened. And if he had defeated the military threat . . . well, he would be less needed then. It would be nice if he could be rendered witless and compliant, like her mother, to frighten foes. But the asp said that was not possible.

"And did you track down the one of his soldiers, the captain who was in my palazzo sending his soldiers scurrying about?"

Lucia had thought it over. He had to be taught a lesson, and if not killed outright and openly, he was still overdue a good flogging. She always remembered her grievances and settled them.

"Yes, indeed. He is Captain Caviliero Francisco Turner. He is Carlo Sforza's personal physician, and I gather also a military man of some note. He played a great role in the conflict with our old allies, the Scaligeri. He has removed from the palace to the central barracks, and spends some time with a man that Venice believes is our new and highly dangerous magician, out at Val di Castellazzo. A man who goes by the name 'Master Kazimierz' and is under heavy guard."

A magician? Yes, he had mentioned that and the Val di Castellazzo before. What would Sforza be doing with one of those? Could he be useful? They were reputed to be good with curses to make foes fail to prosper—that she and the asp could see to themselves. They provided potions to inflame lusts and solve unwanted pregnancies. Hers was not unwanted...by her. Not anymore. Uncomfortable and unpleasant, yes, because it spoiled the fit of her dresses and took up space in her abdomen. But it could be that Sforza would not want her child to take the ducal throne of Milan. He had a by-blow child in Benito Valdosta, whom, Lucia realized, she'd better see to getting killed as well. Inflame lusts? She would have none of that. She'd seen and experienced what it had done to her father.

"I shall need to go and see this so-called magician. Arrange it." This Caviliero Turner would just have to wait a little... On the other hand, did he have to? And it might just be better to have the physician out of the way. "This man Turner. I want him dead. See to it."

The spymaster, who had, she knew, taken care of many deaths for her father, knew better than to pause. But his face betrayed him. He blanched, but nodded. "It may take a little time. He is away quite a lot."

She just looked at him.

"He's, um, known to go running in the morning."

"Running?" Lucia wondered if she'd heard right.

"Yes. A very strange act. We thought it must be a cover for some deviant behavior, so I had men follow him and observe. They complained a great deal. He typically runs along the towpath. But I gather he also runs elsewhere."

"It sounds unhealthy. Anyway, see to his death."

He nodded. "When would it be convenient for Your Grace to see this magician?"

"Within the hour. My father always said to strike as soon as possible."

He bowed and scurried off.

Lucia wondered if he was even aware that she had his hat, secreted and ready, in case he had to die. Her father had also believed in being prepared.

Within the hour she was in her grand carriage, sprung on leather straps, ornate and liberally decorated with gilt. She and the outriders and escort were rolling out of Milan towards Val di Castellazzo. Looking out of the window onto the green fields she realized she'd forgotten how much she despised the countryside, and drew the blind.

When she arrived there and was ushered through the guarded gates and arrived at the small villa—barely twelve rooms, hardly worth calling a house—she realized rapidly that it had been a waste of time. Other than a large mustache and an impeccable Mainz-Frankish, the man was a very ordinary elderly fraud, poorly dressed. He had a lot of books apparently, which were grounds for suspicion. He also had suitable court manners, but showed no obvious signs of arcane knowledge or skill. Nonetheless, she had a private interview with him.

"What may I do for you, Your Grace?" he asked, bowing respectfully again. "I am entirely at your service."

"I've been informed that you're a magician. A worker of spells and curses, potions...and poisons."

"Alas. You have been gravely misinformed, Your Grace. I wish I was, but I am a simple scholar. I work on weapons for the Protector, for the great Duchy of Milan."

Still, there was something about him that made the asp stir. "Why all the guards?"

He shrugged. "My previous employer does not like the fact that I am making cannon that fire further and shoot straighter—for someone else."

Count Kazimierz Mindaug had dealt with murder, foulness, and Jagiellon's lack of hygiene. He knew a great deal about poisons, spells and curses. He maintained his cool demeanor, showing, he hoped, no indication of the fact that he was weighing his chances with the misericorde in his sleeve.

He thought, he certainly hoped—and if he could find a divinity that would accept prayer from him, he would have prayed—that she had no idea what or who he was. His little spell traps would not affect her, and unless he was very much mistaken, she was probably carrying a serpent, a part of the great wyrm. He saw the tiny unblinking eyes in the mirror as it peered out of her corsage. People always thought of mirrors as vanity. Mindaug thought of them as eyes behind his back and had positioned them accordingly. Emma thought he was mad, but he was allowed to be that.

So: this was whom the wyrm had entrapped. Logic said it was probable that his employer, Carlo Sforza, was also given to the serpent. Did they not know what it was?

The answer was "no," for no sane person would agree to that. No insane person, for that matter. They had deceived themselves that it was merely a key to power. They always did.

"So you do not have any appropriate curses or poisons for our foes. How disappointing." The expression on the young duchess's face was not pleasant. "My spymaster tells me our enemies believe you do. I have no use for you in the service of Milan. I need a real magician."

Her hands twitched convulsively, her voice rising as she said it. The count knew this behavior, knew the signs, and had seen it in Elizabeth Bartholdy. She was moody and going to kill someone, simply because her monomania was mildly obstructed. With the insane, logic did not work, and the best he could do would be to appease her, to buy time.

"I don't have any curses, I'm afraid. Poisons of various sorts, yes; I do experiment with those."

That worked. She was interested and no longer displaying signs of that angry petulance. "Ones which kill without trace?"

"Sadly, such things are rare. I can provide one which kills slowly and with the victim losing their mental faculty over several months. There is no trace to that."

He saw by the glittering eye that he'd scored a hit. And that his own death would follow shortly if he had the folly to stay where she could reach him. "That could be useful. Give me some."

"It will take a few days to prepare, Your Grace. I could have it sent to the Protector."

And that surprised him afresh. The expression betrayed her to Mindaug—he had dealt with treachery so often, he knew those signs too well. "Ah. No. It is not a military matter. I will have one of my men fetch it. Tomorrow. You must do it by then."

He bowed. "I shall work through the night. How will I recognize your man, Your Grace? Secrecy is paramount with such things, of course. I do not wish to accidentally betray your great trust in me."

She showed him a signet on her hand. It bore the Visconti coat of arms. "He will bear this. You are to give it to him, in here, alone."

And he will then kill me and leave, thought Mindaug, to whom she was quite transparent. "Of course," he assured her.

"You are to tell no one of this. How is it administered?"

"Approximately seven drops a day, for at least three days. In the evening, in wine is best. It will work slowly over the next week. Even a single dose works, but takes much longer. The victims gradually lose their wits."

"Good. See that it is done and I will have Sforza reward you richly."

And she thought that so funny and so clever! Mentally, Mindaug shook his head. She wouldn't have lasted long in Lithuania.

Well, not without the wyrm, at any rate.

When she had left, Count Kazimierz Mindaug fell into one of his new comfortable chairs and sighed. Emma came out from where she'd plainly been watching through the keyhole. "Can I get you some wine, master? Maybe some of my sweet cakes? What did she want here?"

"Nothing good." He bit his lip, and then suddenly decided. "Emma, you and Tamas...ready any small precious things. Nothing heavy, nothing bulky. We may have to flee from here. Can you ride?"

She shook her head in alarm. "What is that smelly bitch going to try to do to you, master? I should have shot her."

She had the hand-cannon ready and primed in her apron, the count observed. He also observed she was patting his shoulder and looking militantly defensive. He couldn't help but see some humor in that.

"What are you laughing at, master?" she asked.

"Ah, Emma. I laugh partly at myself, and partly because I realize that I still have much to learn about people."

"We'll take care of you, master. You have been very good to us."

The idea was still foreign to Count Mindaug, but he knew that in exchange, he was obliged to do his best to take care of them. Their power to do this was far below his, but in terms of their ability, they would give all. It was a loyalty worth keeping. That was the first time he'd come to admit it openly to himself. The peasants of Braclaw and Zwinogrodek would have been amazed. His late relations, more so.

But then, so was he.

"Did that woman—I know you only saw her in passing—did you notice anything odd about her?"

"She's carrying awkwardly. And that scent of hers!" Emma waved her hand in front of her nose.

"Carrying awkwardly?"

"She's pregnant. You can see it in the way she walks, even in those funny shoes of hers. I'd say she is nearly as far gone as me." Emma blushed. "Master...would you, before we have to leave, give Tamas and me permission to marry?"

Mindaug knew that they were rural peasants. He had also never really given their marriage—or lack of it—a single thought. By the look on her face, it was something she desired, though.

"But why not? I will have to provide you with a suitable trousseau," he said as a joke.

He was not prepared for her to burst into tears and kneel and kiss his hand. "You are like a father to me, master. Better than a father! God truly blessed us when he sent us to you that day. I pray for you every night, and thank God for you being there to save us, but there will be special prayers of thanks tonight, and every night from now onward."

The count knew how to deal with demon-possessed princes, duchesses who had made deals with the devil, and even someone who had sacrificed to the serpent. This, however, was new to him.

"There, there," he said awkwardly, and patted her head. A trousseau must be important to a peasant girl, especially one marrying up to a miller. He'd have to see she had one worthy of a princess. He'd met a few of those, and this child was worth more than most of them.

He wondered how her God felt about her prayers. Deities probably had a sense of humor, if you believed man was made in their image. And he wondered if Carlo Sforza knew his wife was at least four months pregnant. He knew that she hadn't been in court that long. The man Sforza had usurped had barely been dead that long. Interesting... and right now a boring life had great appeal.

The night was not spent preparing a potion that he already had, and which would disappoint her, but in far more constructive preparations to flee. That was going to be a difficult task, without killing too many of Sforza's men. Even with killing them all, he would still have to cross considerable hostile country before taking an uncertain refuge in Venetian territory. Mindaug was not too sure of the reception he might get there, but they shared a common enemy, and he could be of value. He would have to trade on that.

The difficult part was going to be transporting his books. The wagon would not be practical this time. It would have to be the method by which he had snatched them from Lithuania. Some preparatory workings had to be done. And those did involve very small magics. Well, it was a risk he would have to take.

While he was at it, he set up a further trap or two, ones designed to remove the strength and magical ability of any caught within. He had no idea if they would work on the serpent, but something was better than nothing.

And then, rather late, he went to bed, because sleep, too, was necessary. It stopped one from making mistakes. And the one thing about having fled Lithuania and Hungary: he didn't have to be eternally watchful and set magical and physical traps every time he wanted to take as much as a nap.

Venice

In their quarters in the patriarch's palace in Venice, Von Stebbens knew some triumph and some fear. Finally there were some signs of magical working, bearing the resonance of Count Mindaug. The exact nature of the spells was something that he was unable to discern, however. No blood magic or sacrifice, but something possibly to do with elemental life-forms, the spirits of air, and wood and water.

Chapter 33

Milan

On returning to the barracks, Francisco found a message from Kazimierz awaiting him. There was an awkward matter he did not know how to deal with. Could he see Francisco as a matter of urgency?'

Francisco decided he could wait until morning, after his run. He had put off trying to send the small book Master Kazimierz wanted to get to Marco Valdosta, and he would prefer to have that done before seeing the old fellow. He wasn't sure the nyx would be there—or willing—but he hoped so. Besides messages to be carried he had questions to ask.

He also had worries and doubts about this "Master Kazimierz." The man had, at first, seemed a noble dilettante who had a healthy curiosity about the sciences, and would certainly satisfy the gullible that he was some kind of magician. But it seemed that the fellow had stretched his curiosity into the esoteric and arcane. And actually believed some of it!

A disease personified? Made into a serpent to be worshipped and sacrificed to?

Nonsense...

On the other hand, Francisco himself was about to go and talk to a nyx, who could be said to embody the spirit of drowned girl. He'd written quite an extensive covering letter to Marco about Kazimierz, some of which he hoped Carlo would not object to him revealing.

He was aware of someone running down the trail behind

him, so he increased his pace a little. Occasionally, people would decide to ask why he was running or try to talk to him. He didn't mind, usually, but they simply did not have the breath for it. Today he wanted to think, so he just ran faster. If they were running after him for any real reason, they could call out. They didn't, so he just kept going. He was close to the end of his run anyway.

He decided he'd see if Rhene was there, before getting himself a beer. He stopped at the usual stump bollard, where the barges would tie up for the bargee to get a mug or two from the Grosso Luccio. The tree on the other side of the towpath provided shade. It also had the second bonus of making this a quieter and more private spot to drink beer and converse with nyxes.

And that, as he bent to wash his hands and face, was also its disadvantage, as it turned out. In the dawn, there was no one about, except the knifemen who leapt out from behind the tree and, a few seconds later, their panting red-faced friend.

If it hadn't been for the panting, and the knapsack with the bottled book in it, Francisco might have been knifed in the back before he knew someone was trying to kill him. As it was, either the panting or the sudden footfalls behind him made Francisco turn slightly. The knife, instead of going into his back, ripped into the knapsack, skittered off the glass, and then glanced across Francisco's shoulder.

The force of the blow was enough to turn Francisco, and have the knifeman stumble and fall. The fellow's outthrust left hand missed the edge of the canal and he went into the water, his face smacking into the muddy grass. But his knife was still held in his right hand. Francisco rolled and kicked the elbow of the knife arm. The blade went flying, as his behind-the-tree companion dived forward, stabbing. That narrowly missed, too, as Francisco jerked away and managed to grab the front of his second attacker's doublet, and pull the man over him.

Francisco was on the ground and his attacker stooped, looking for his knife lost in the turf. Francisco hauled forward with frantic strength. The attacker only had one way and one place to go: over Francisco and into the canal with a yell and a splash. Francisco scrambled to his feet to meet the third man, drawing his main gauche as he stood up. The third fellow, red-faced and panting, also had his knife out.

Francisco didn't waste any time. He feinted a wide thrust, and as the man tried to block it, he lunged hard, thrusting the blade under the rib cage. The man gasped, his arms going wide, and he fell backwards off the blade, collapsing onto his knees at the water's edge, clutching his chest. Francisco turned hastily to see if there were any more. The first stabber was on his knees reaching for the second man's turf-imbedded knife. A slim white hand from the canal grabbed him by the ankle and hauled him into the water as, with a brief shriek of terror, he looked at what had grabbed him.

Knife in hand, Francisco looked around. The one who had tried to follow him running, whom he had stabbed, had fallen face forward. He was plainly dying, and there was no help for him, and no threat from him, either. There was no one else on the land side...and in the water was Rhene, with two men, far bigger than her slight self. She held their wrists in those slim hands of hers, and her face was full of a rather nasty delight.

The two in the water looked at her, and at each other, and thrashed and both drew breath to scream. She pulled them underwater in a swirl of greenish hair.

Francisco stood there, panting himself from the shock and sudden exertion, watching the water as a few bubbles came up. She kept them down a good while. Eventually, she popped up, still holding the two men, now thrashing rather weakly, spluttering and gasping.

"Two," she said. "I've never tried it with two." She licked her upper lip—rather like a cat contemplating a bowl of cream. "Do you think that might give me a child?"

Francisco looked at the two terrified half-drowned men and suppressed a desire to laugh hysterically. "I think that might be part of the problem, Rhene. Neither of them would make what I would think of as a good father, as even between the two of them that wouldn't add up to one."

"Oh. They are quite large. Bigger than you. The equipment is usually somewhat proportional. I know. I've looked at a lot. I wondered if that had something to do with it."

"Nothing at all, I am afraid. You've got to choose good bloodlines. Humans, and I should think nyxes, are no different from breeding horses."

She frowned, and then grasped what she thought was his meaning. "Ah. Like stallions. I was right then. I'll look."

He held up his hand. "That's not what I meant. A good stallion in the wild looks after and guards his mares, and protects them and the foals. Those are the stallions whose mares have many foals, and the foals live. These men couldn't even protect themselves, let alone stick around to help to look after the little ones."

"A point," she said, nodding. "I'll drown them then."

"I'd like to ask them a few questions. And then perhaps I can help you."

"Ooh. That sounds interesting. Are you a good stallion?"

"That isn't quite what I meant either. But we'll talk about it when I've got some answers."

"Let us go or it'll be worse for you," said the bigger bald-headed man. "We've got friends." The other said nothing. He was still coughing weakly.

Francisco pointed at the bald-headed one. "Please take that one down for a little, Rhene. He doesn't understand, and that'll help him to do so."

Bald-head had time for a brief scream before she twitched him under, pushing his head down.

"You're probably a good judge of when they're nearly drowned, Rhene. Let him up when he starts to suck water," said Francisco, not at all sympathetic. He turned his attention to the coughing terrified man who was still on the surface, trying to paddle rather feebly for the bank. "I wouldn't try to escape the water. I'll kick you back in and she'll kill you then. You talk, and you might have a chance. I'm not promising though. Who sent you?"

They were too well dressed, and too well fed to be anything but professional hirelings. Also, no bunch of cutthroat thieves was going to be waiting about here on the lonely canal path before Matins bell on the off chance of a victim. They'd been here for him, and on orders.

"Lord Palmeri." Cough. "His orders."

Palmeri was one of Filippo Maria's relics that Sforza planned to get rid of. He'd been slowly easing the man out of arranging Milan's spying and assassinations. It was difficult, because Palmeri knew a great deal and had many contacts, and so Carlo had been running a parallel agency and had several of his own men put across. Francisco had disliked the fellow even before he'd tried to murder him. He was a toady to those above and a thankless martinet to those below—what Carlo described as the perfect example of a bad officer.

Rhene let the other one up. He was gasping and spitting water. When he could talk, which took a little while, he confirmed who the order, the money and the information about where to find him had come from. Francisco was mildly disgusted at the price. He was worth more than that. On the other hand, had Palmeri not skimped on paying for proper help, he might have gotten better quality, and then Francisco would be dead. If they'd been able to afford crossbows instead of knives, he might well have been floating facedown in the canal right now.

"I need these two for a long talk with my commander, Rhene. Or at least one of them. Either of you two not want to cooperate? I can leave you here."

Francisco was fairly sure that Carlo Sforza was going to provide summary justice to both, and if they had any brains, the muscles knew that—but certain death by drowning now might make the probability of being shot or hanged later seem attractive. And they might hope their boss could get them out alive. By the way they hastily assured him of their willingness to talk, they both preferred that option.

Rhene did not look pleased. "I don't like to let them live after seeing me," she said.

"They're not that likely to tell of you," he said. Since both men were within hearing range, he didn't add *because they'll be dead soon.* He left it at: "Let me tie them up and take them away, Rhene. I have a small gift for you as well as, I hope, some way to help you with your heart's desire. And a small gift for my friend Marco Valdosta, too."

She clapped her hands, letting go of both prisoners, who began to struggle towards the verge of the canal. "Not so fast," said Francisco. "Keep them there, Rhene. I want to get some beer out of the taverna, and fetch some rope."

"Don't drink the beer!" said the bald-headed man. "It's poisoned. We don't want to die here."

Francisco stopped. "You poisoned the beer?" he exclaimed in horror, staring at them in newfound fury.

"Yes. But then you came straight to the waterside and we weren't sure if you'd go in the taverna."

"The whole keg?!"

He nodded. "Yes. Lord Palmeri said it was probably better if a lot of people died, and not just you."

"You'd better hope that Carlo either shoots you or puts you in jail for life," he said grimly. "If Old Capra the barman gets hold of you, you're in for a hard death."

He walked over to the taverna where, just around the corner, his sergeant had sat down on the bench against the wall in the first sunlight. He had a mug of beer in his hand, raising it to his lips. "Drop it!" barked Francisco.

Sergeant Balco did, on his trousers. "You haven't drunk any of that?" demanded Francisco.

"No, Captain Turner. The old man just got up. I thought I'd quaff one while I waited for you."

"It's poisoned."

"You're bleeding, Captain."

"You should see the other fellow," said Francisco, going into the tap room.

The old taverna-owner was polishing his bar. "Morning, Captain. A mug of yer usual?" he asked, turning to draw it.

"No. And don't you drink any either. Some bastard poisoned it."

"Oh, it's not that bad. I always use clean water from the canal and a clean barrel..."

"I'll be back in two minutes. Don't you touch a drop of that brew. Wait!"

They had some picket ropes on the horses, and Francisco took them. "Wait here, Sergeant. And keep a gun on hand."

He returned to the canal. "You keep a hold on his foot while I tie him up, Rhene. We don't take chances with beer poisoners." He hauled the man half up the bank and tied his hands behind his back. Then he cut his belt.

"Pull his trousers down, Rhene," said Francisco.

"No!" squalled the prisoner, writhing desperately.

"Shut up. I'm not about to geld you. You'll just waddle with them around your ankles. You can't run like that, and before you can pull them up or kick them off, I'll stick a knife in your kidneys."

Once the first fellow had been handed to Sergeant Balco, Francisco repeated the process with the second. "Tie their feet, too, Sergeant. Then take them in there and offer them some of that beer, until they tell you what's poisoned. Make sure the bastards drink some of what they say isn't. I want them alive, so Old Capra isn't to kill them. I'll be back, I just have some business to transact."

He went back to the waiting Rhene. "A bottle of the Pelaverga wine for the lady." He handed her a bottle of the rare peppery red. "I suppose you do know it's supposed to be aphrodisiacal?"

"Of course," she said. "Would you like some?"

"I am a beer man myself. But I have here a little ruby pendant I picked up somewhere. I didn't think you'd be much on silks or furs, or that perfume would stay on you too well, but I thought: jewelry, now, that's something most ladies like."

She looked at him with faint puzzlement in her foxy smile, but did not reach out to take it. "Are you trying to seduce me?"

"No, actually, I wasn't. I'm committed, you might say. But I thought some gift of thanks was called for, and after your help with these men even more so."

"You're a nice man. All the good ones are taken. Have you got any brothers?" she said in a slightly wistful voice, taking the little pendant from his fingers. It had been a piece of loot taken on one of his earliest battles at Carlo Sforza's side, and he'd no use for it, but had never got around to selling it. She admired it. "Fasten it for me?" she asked, clasping it around her neck and turning her back to him, where he squatted on the edge of the water.

He did. She slipped up onto the bank, with her feet still in the water, naked as a newborn, and leaned over to look at her reflection in the water and admire her new acquisition.

Then she slipped back into the water. "Thank you. There is plenty of jewelry in the river, but I have never been given any."

"My pleasure. It looks well on you. Brings out your hair's color." Flattery was not his natural métier, but he had enough tact to realize that there was a time and place for it. "Now, as a physician, I wanted to ask you a personal question, Rhene. Have you ever been pregnant?"

She looked at him strangely. "Yes, of course, often. That is what happens after lovemaking. I have had many lovers. Lusty young men not afraid of the water like you."

"Ah. Have you ever carried the child to term?"

"Yes, but they all die."

"I think that is the problem. The child is too human. You can swim around in the canals and rivers. Cold does not affect you and you do not seem to need to breathe. But your baby does."

She absorbed this for a thoughtful moment or two. "But how, then, am I to have a child? I cannot leave the water for very long. I am it and it is me. And I will not give up my child."

"A difficult question. Let us both think about it," he said, seeing an answer, but not wanting to push her too far. She hadn't
complained about letting the two thugs live yet. Maybe she could
get her head around a fisherman or bargee father for the child,
being allowed to live, who could then keep the child warm on
the boat, and still let the mother be close. "Now, if that stabbing
beer poisoner has not damaged the container...ah, it seems fine,
just a scratch—heavy glass, but I am afraid my bag is going to
need some sewing." He handed her the glass jar with the book
in it. "If you could give that to Valdosta, I would be glad."

"Which one of the Valdostas? The Lion or the fire?" she asked.

It didn't take a big stretch to get Benito out of "fire." He was
a bit like one. "I didn't know the other one was back."

"He has had contrary winds all the way. But the tritons say they
will cross the Lido bar soon. His daughter is water-blessed, so we
keep track," said the nyx. "Our kind can communicate over long
distances in the water. Sound carries there as it does not in the air."

Francisco wondered if the merpeople had seen fit to share
this information with Marco. He knew that Marco had expended
a lot of anxiety about his wild brother. It probably just never
occurred to Marco to ask them, or to them to tell him. "The
Lion. But give my best to the other one's daughter if you see
her. She's a sweet child."

Back in the taverna, Francisco was not surprised to find the
two thugs had taken some further damage, besides their half
drowning. They were even wetter, having been dunked headfirst
into the poisoned beer and told to hold their breath or be poisoned
or drown. And they were sporting a pair of magnificent black
eyes and a bloody nose, and the outraged innkeeper wouldn't
have stopped there, if Sergeant Balco hadn't intervened. Once
the innkeeper figured out it would have killed half his customers, if not himself, and worse, would have ruined his trade and
reputation, the man had been more than incandescently angry.

"Pour the beer out, take what's in their pockets and pouches,
and there's another dead one out on the towpath," said Francisco.
"I'll make good the difference."

The innkeeper shook his head. "Oh, no, Captain, you will
not. You won't pay for another drop of beer. Not if you keep
up your crazy running along that path and drinking it after, not
until I'm ninety."

"We'll argue about that next time. But I would get rid of the beer quietly, and also that body out there. Their boss and friends probably won't be in any state to look for them, or to pay you back, and these ones certainly aren't getting loose to tell them, but there's no sense in taking chances. Now, have you got a spare nag I can buy or hire to tie these two to? I'm thinking that we'll take them somewhere other than the central barracks. They may have friends around there, and I want them talking to Sforza before those friends get wind of it."

The old mule was a sorry one indeed, but then given the alternative, the two thugs would probably also have voted for being tied on like saddle bags, rather than remain at the taverna.

"Where are you going, Captain?" asked the sergeant, once Francisco had bandaged his arm, and got into the saddle.

"Out to Val di Castellazzo. It'll be away from their friends and contacts, I was going there anyway, and there's plenty of space, spare troops to guard them, and I can send a message to the commander. If he's fighting, he doesn't need to be bothered, but if he's not, this boil needs to be lanced."

The sergeant nodded. "Fair enough, Captain Turner. But I think we better pick up some men first. We can go by the west gate and get a small troop. If they're out to kill you, the sooner I've got you in the middle of a bunch of our men, good fighting men, the happier I'll be, and the less likely the commander will be to bite my head off. And if anything goes down," he said, loosening his sabre, "I'll kill them first while you run, Captain. And you keep running. It's not me they're trying to kill."

That was a vast speech from him. He must be deeply worried—as a sergeant—to tell his captain what to do. Or to say that much, Francisco knew. Francisco also knew that an officer who didn't listen when a sergeant was thus moved was an idiot, usually a dead idiot.

So they rode to the west gate barracks—in the wrong direction for Val di Castellazzo—which was not more than half a mile off, with the sergeant looking like a cat tiptoeing through a sleeping pack of hounds. He was ready to make them run and scratch some wounds to make sure that Francisco got away.

But it was unnecessary and, relatively soon, they rode out from the barracks with twenty men, which the sergeant thought too few, and Francisco, too many.

Chapter 34

Val di Castellazzo, Duchy of Milan

Carlo Sforza had never known a victory to give him less. Not pleasure, not satisfaction, not security. He was just too tired and feeling too wretched to care that his neat scissors had worked a masterstroke. Or even to care that the flying star had exposed Malatesta's condottiere Di Sallieri's sneak attack on Correggio castle and turned it into an utter rout. Some of the troops might stop running before they got to Sicily, but as a force, Di Sallieri's company was broken, and he himself was a prisoner. But now there were three fortresses between him and Pisa, and two of them were under siege.

And he was going back to Milan to find Francisco and ask him for two things: first, another purgative, and second, to just keep things rolling while he had a decent rest.

He had other captains, but none who saw the broad picture—or who were as loyal. Or, perhaps most important, were as willing to tell him "no."

Carlo had quietly ordered a carriage to meet him just outside Pavia. He had a feeling he might fall off a horse. And bumping and swaying or not, he could sleep in the dratted thing. All he wanted to do was to sleep. To a man who had spent his life thinking five hours rest was enough, this was purgatory.

He'd go to Milan, but on the way, he'd stop and reward that fellow for Di Sallieri's defeat.

❖   ❖   ❖

Count Kazimierz Mindaug overslept, which was a novel experience for him. If he'd had to rationalize it, it was that he did not wish to wake, and that something within him wished to maintain the illusion of comfort, safety and, yes, the happiness that he'd been enjoying.

On waking, he lay in bed for a while. Fear, flight and starting all over again had no appeal at all.

He liked this place, he liked the people—which was bizarre. He had found himself really enjoying the non-magical work, the cooperative and excited exchange of ideas. He'd do his best to take the boy and girl with him... although perhaps they'd be better safely bestowed somewhere. That thought had him shake his head at himself. He was going soft in the head. They were his servants!

But he knew that, too, was a lie. He'd used enough lies in his life to recognize them, he thought.

This was not Lithuania, and he was not Count Mindaug of Braclaw and the voivode of Zwinogrodek anymore. He was Master Kazimierz, who was quite a different fellow.

He got up and took himself downstairs, determined to enjoy a last good breakfast, a last good discussion of Tamas's latest brain ferment with the acerbic common sense of the bombardier, who would inevitably end up being infected by it and add more ideas. Even Emma, with her solid peasant practicality, would get caught up in it.

He was taken aback to find they'd all eaten, something like an hour ago, and were all beside themselves with worry about him, as Emma sent a footman scurrying off with the news that Master was awake and about to have breakfast. It was bizarre to find out that even the new footmen, who had come with the house, appeared genuinely concerned. One asked if he could go and fetch a physician.

"I overslept," he said grumpily. "That is all."

Food to break his fast arrived rapidly. It was, however, a solitary meal, which was just not the same. And a little later, a messenger came. "He says he has something to show only you, Master Kazimierz. I don't trust him, he's a shifty-looking piece of work," the footman who had offered to fetch a physician told him. "I can't think why the guards let him in."

It turned out that the shifty-looking piece of work was very annoyed that he'd had to produce Lucia Sforza's signet, to be finally let in. "My presence and who sent me was supposed to be secret," he said angrily. "Now, let us go into a private salon. Tell your servants not to disturb you for at least an hour."

"Certainly," said the count. To the footman, he said: "This gentleman says we are not to be disturbed for an hour. Step this way, sir."

He recognized the inept effort of a nobleman to dress himself as an ordinary fellow and was amused by it. He waved him through the door, and the fool stepped in, in front of him, as if it was his natural right. That was, of course, his behavior at home. Mindaug stepped smartly in behind him, and closed the door with one hand, after pulling the misericorde from his sleeve with the other. The man didn't even start to turn before the knife was at his throat.

He gasped. "*What are you doing?* I am from Duchess Lucia. She'll have you killed!"

"No doubt," said Count Mindaug. "But you won't be the one doing it. Now, stand very still." He removed the man's dagger and a second misericorde from inside the man's cotte. He tossed them in a corner. The misericorde was poisoned, by the look of it. Then he pushed the man away. The nobleman-messenger eyed him warily. Mindaug took the prepared little bottle out of his pouch and tossed it to the man. "This is what you came to fetch."

The fellow gawped at him as if he'd never held a vial of poison before. "I wouldn't drink it," said Mindaug dryly. "It would be terminal. I think you should put it in your pouch and leave."

"Uh. My knives..."

"I am sure we both understand that I want to live," said the count. "Personally, I suggest you tell your mistress that the guards disarmed you, and I constantly had a bellpull in hand and refused to allow you closer than ten paces. When you come to fetch more, that will be the case."

"Fetch more?"

"One poisoning is never enough," said the count. "See yourself out, as you planned."

Mindaug was amused to note that the fellow could not have been out of the front door before Emma peeped in. "I just thought that Lord Laglissio might want some wine," she said.

"Ah. Is that who he was?"

She nodded. "Mario, the stableman, he knew his horse. He says he is not a good man."

"Tell Mario he is not to tell anyone he knew who the fellow was, unless I tell him to tell them. And don't go and pick those knives up, Emma. Let them be untidy until I get a gauntlet and go and burn them and the gauntlet. They're poisoned."

She was quick thinking. She turned on her heel, reaching into her large apron pocket and yelling out: "Stop him!"

"No, Emma, you cannot shoot him," said Mindaug, amused. He was beginning to wonder about having introduced her to firearms. He knew she'd been practicing with Klaus, who seemed to find her shooting both a source of pride and amusement.

"But he came to poison you," protested Emma. "To kill you, to stab you with a knife. I will shoot him and he will not try it again."

"I doubt he will," said Mindaug.

"It's like rats," she said firmly. "You do not take a chance that they will not come back."

"Oh, if he does, there will be a big rattrap waiting for him. Now...I think you had better call Tamas...and Klaus, too. I need to tell you what I have planned. It is possible that you will not wish to go with me. And I think that Klaus can be trusted to help you."

"Master, if you go, we go. Klaus, too, I think. Last night he said to me he has never found a man he's enjoyed working for more. And as for Tamas and me, there is never a question. We will follow you anywhere."

"Even Lithuania?" It had a reputation to make peasants blench.

"Anywhere. Even there," she said calmly.

"Well, at the moment I only plan on Venice."

He was left alone for a few minutes, in a brown study. If this had gone on for too much longer, he'd be taking the footmen, stableboy, gardener, and even Sforza's soldiers with him, he reflected sardonically.

But Klaus was actually not for going with him. "I don't care who this jackass was, Master Kazimierz. Emma was right, she should have shot him. The commander will not be pleased. And it won't be happening again. I'll have a word with Sergeant Dello."

"The man came from Sforza's wife, the new duchess," said Mindaug, not explaining what she was involved in. He knew that would not be believed or understood.

"So? She's just a woman he married to let him rule the duchy, master," said the one-eyed ex-soldier. "You are a man who makes things that will win him wars. I served under the commander. I know what he values, and it isn't her."

The question became moot because they heard the sound of trumpets. They all stood up, and on the carriage drive outside the windows was an advancing troop of cavalry, and a coach.

"It's the commander himself!" said Klaus the bombardier, reverently, and then, "In a coach!" That was said with almost disgust. Shock, at least.

It was indeed Sforza, in person. In his famous battered campaign cap. It had once been red and was now a faded pink.

That did not detract from the man underneath the cap, as he came up the stair behind his guards. The footman had hastily opened the doors, and Count Mindaug made his way forward to greet the man. He bowed. "Good morning, Lord Protector Sforza. Welcome."

He expected the taint of the wyrm. He had wondered if this meant that the wyrm had discovered who he was, after all, or suspected who he might be. He prepared himself for flight, and spells.

He met neither the wyrm nor a need to flee. He did meet a gargantuan yawn. "Forgive me," said Sforza, in the slightly gravelly voice of someone who has been deeply asleep. "I am not bored by your greeting. I am just very tired. You would be 'Master Kazimierz,' the man my spies tell me that Venice's masters believe to be a powerful and evil magician." He was smiling as he said it, which robbed it of offense.

There were two ways to take this. Mindaug chose the high path. "I do my best," he said, "but it is a hard task, Lord Protector." His keen eye was taking in details of the man. He was a big, solid fellow, not of the order of the size of Jagiellon, but not carrying Jagiellon's weight either. Sforza's wife's garb had been the height of fashion and expense, liberally spattered with seed pearls, and she could have restocked a jewelry seller with the gold she had about her person. He was, by contrast, very plainly dressed. Rich cloth, yes, but cut to allow movement. He wore a sword in a gold-embossed sheath—but it had a workmanlike hilt, unadorned by anything.

He was plainly usually a swarthy-faced man, who spent a lot of time outdoors, with the small lines of being out in the weather around the eyes and mouth. But he looked a little pale now, and his eyes were bloodshot and tired. There was still a force in them, and a penetrating gaze. He had a solid broad chin with a small sinus in it, and curly dark hair that was just going to gray on the temples. It was not clothes or display that made Sforza a man to be noticed.

And he, in turn, was studying Mindaug. "Well, that flying star of yours just made keeping your reputation a great deal easier," said Sforza. "Another bit of 'magic' like that and I wouldn't have a war to fight. I must see that you are well rewarded for that. Especially if you have some more surprises for my enemies."

Mindaug saw this as a sudden opportunity to take care of his odd pets. "I'd like to take the credit, my lord, but it is due to the genius of young Tamas, my artificer. And I would be glad to show you what we've been working on. But perhaps a glass of wine first?"

"That would be good. If your people will see to the same for my men and horses, well, water for the horses, and water and wine for me. My physician has instructed it."

"If Caviliero Turner commends it, my lord, unpleasant though it may be, it is probably wise. I shall have my people see to it at once."

"Ah. You trust my friend Francisco, do you?" observed Sforza.

"Yes. I think I do, my lord." It was a genuine observation, which surprised Mindaug.

Carlo Sforza had spent more time with the nobles of the various courts than his physician. Francisco was absolutely correct. This was a nobleman—one who was accustomed to near absolute power and would not be in the least intimidated by having the Emperor himself drop in. The man who called himself Kazimierz was not discomforted by the fact that he was wearing the sort of clothes a mildly prosperous artisan might wear for work, and not court finery, when his overlord suddenly arrived on his doorstep. Carlo got the feeling that this Kazimierz really cared neither about his surroundings nor his dress. He was used to being respected for who or what he was.

That appealed to Sforza. But such men were not common—nor did they suddenly show up in your backyard without reason.

On the other hand...he could be useful. He already had been. And Carlo had to like the way he gave credit to his worker... and the way he brought the boy forward. "His Frankish is not very good, my Lord Protector. I hope you will pardon his rough manners—but let him show you his drawings and ideas."

The boy was a peasant. And probably not much more than eighteen years old. Incoherent when talking politely to this great lord, he lost his fear and became animated when asked to explain his drawings, gently prodded by his master. It was interesting, the almost paternal attitude taken. The big boy looked nothing like the slightly stoop-shouldered, white-haired and massively mustachioed Kazimierz. He probably wasn't a son, Carlo decided, it was just the man's manner.

The boy's drawings were very good, careful and proportional. Drawn from all sides as a man who would wish to build the device might draw, rather than works of art, and yet in themselves, they were works of art. Some of them Carlo judged would not work... but: "I can see why my friend Francisco thought I should create a university, not of the arts, but of the military, engineering and the artifice, and gather your type of minds together."

Carlo was quick at noticing expressions. He picked up the wistful look in the tilt of the head of this former nobleman. "It would be pleasant."

The man patted the boy on the shoulder. "Go and get Klaus to ready the new rocket and a few other devices. We will be along presently."

When the lad had gone, Sforza said: "A great deal of promise there."

"He has surprised me, my lord. He was just a miller," said Kazimierz. "He's now learning to read and write, and took to constructing rockets like a duck to water. There's a lot of talents buried, my lord. Some of them best left that way, not worth digging up. That one... I was lucky. The boy is about to be married, and as he and the girl are both of peasant origin, they have very little. So if his device really was useful, a reward would help them. How did it work?"

"More by superstition than by craft, but it was terribly effective," said Sforza, who had wondered, earlier, if the man was one of those who liked younger men, and not women. Probably not, it seemed.

"The best condottieri among our foes' armies had planned a surprise attack on the fortified town of Correggio. As it happened, quite a few of my troops were garrisoned there. The gates were closed, sentries posted on the walls... and traitors in the gatehouse."

"More castles fall by treachery than by siege."

"Yes, but this one had a watchful guard on a tower, with several of your new flying stars. I knew Di Sallieri was massing his troops in the area, and so the guards had been issued with them.

I assumed there'd be attempts to put explosives against the walls or gates. I should have known better. Anyway, this likely lad, and he's now the proud owner of an estate of his own, thought he saw or heard something. Myself, I think he just wanted to try one of these new devices. It was a very dark night and moonless. So he fired it up in the air—and there was Di Sallieri and his company. They had sneaked up with cloth bound over their horses' hooves, their armor dulled with charcoal, waiting for the gate to open, not a hundred yards off. The horses didn't like the sudden light...and our lad on the wall got nearly as big a fright as they did.

"He probably should have yelled for the guards—half of them were dead in the gatehouse—but instead he cranked that big cross-bow and fired a second one of those starlight arrows. Only the young man admits he was a bit rattled and he didn't fire it up in the air, but straight at the fellows trying to hold their horses. As luck would have it, it hit Di Sallieri's bodyguard just after it flared, and then ricocheted onto the man himself, and bounced around like a jackrabbit amongst the enemy. And I believe he yelled, 'Take that, you Godless bastards!' at the top of his lungs too. I don't know myself, I was fast asleep at the time."

"You were there?"

"Yes. And possibly Di Sallieri knew that from his traitor. However, he's not saying and the traitor is dead. But, by this time, the gate was open. My men were scrambling to action and half of Di Sallieri's company was running for the hills; the other half wasn't because they were off their horses. His pikes had either run or been flattened by their own cavalry. Cannon might have stopped them just as well, but that star device frightened half of them into monasteries, and soiled a lot of armor, and put them off sneak attacks on our fortresses, towns and castles for a while. So, you see, your reputation as a magician is being cemented from here to Sicily by now. I took Di Sallieri and half a dozen of his officers prisoner; they're minor nobles and will be ransomed. So, yes, your young Master Tamas will get his reward. And so will you. And I agree with Francisco. It'll be a different type of university. The Duchy of Milan will steal a march on them with it. They can have their poisons and assassins. We'll walk all over them on the field of battle."

One of the footmen came to the door and coughed. "My lord, Master Kazimierz. The Caviliero Turner has just arrived."

"Excellent," said Sforza. "Just the man I need to see."

Chapter 35

Val di Castellazzo, Duchy of Milan

Kazimierz Mindaug had been debating internally just how he could tell the duke of Milan that his new wife was planning to kill him—had already started, actually. That she was in the thrall of a disease god and was, in his judgment, suffering from monomaniacal insanity. That if Sforza challenged her directly, she was far more likely to be able to kill him, than he her. And that, worst of all, killing her would take the only possible leash on the disease, off it. The situation was equivalent to having a murderous madman—madwoman, in this case—holding the leash of an unkillable rabid dog. The lunatic might set the dog on anyone, but while they held the leash, one needed to humor them.

Francisco's arrival at least allowed him to put that off a little, to try to work around it . . . because he realized he liked this bluff soldier, too, and he liked the university idea vastly. Somehow, some way, this disease monster-god had to be destroyed and contained.

"Bring him in, Mario," said Kazimierz.

Neither of them missed the fact that the caviliero winced slightly as he bowed. "Ah, Francisco. Is that shoulder still troubling you?" said Sforza, in what was plainly concern. Mindaug was learning to judge these things. Sforza cared for his physician, as much as the physician plainly was loyal to him.

"It's the other shoulder. That one has healed beautifully. Three of Palmeri's hirelings tried to kill me this morning when I went for my run," said Francisco.

"What?" snarled Sforza furiously. "I'll have the snake's balls shoved down his throat! Are you sure it was Palmeri?"

"Sure enough. I have two of his men outside, very much the worse for wear, but still alive. I thought you might want to have them put to the question. Not that I think they can sing much more than they have. They tried to knife me and poison my beer."

"You should have made the *testa di cazzo* drink it," said Sforza. "I'm going to have to come up with some special and nasty death for poisoners. A man with a knife at least has to face his victim and do the deed."

"These ones were set on stabbing me in the back," said Francisco. "My lord, would you forgive me if I asked our host to get his servants to get me a glass... preferably of beer. I missed my beer after the run, and have had a fight and a long ride. I feel as if I'll fall over any moment."

"Of course. Sit down. Do you need the shoulder seen to? How did you know I was here?"

Francisco dropped into a chair. "It's only an annoying scratch. I cleaned it with some grappa and bound it up. And I did *not* know you were here, my lord. I just knew there was a decent garrison of men here, and I didn't want the prisoners in Milan, where news of their failure and the fact that they were still alive and talking would alert Palmeri. He'd see them dead. This way, they could at least tell you what they know before they die."

"Very wise," said Sforza. Turning to Kazimierz, he said: "And he plays a good game of chess, too. Tell us about this attempt on your life? The people of Milan are going to learn that I will not tolerate the murder of my men."

As Francisco was doing so, Emma came in, bearing a huge tray, which she was balancing partly on her stomach. She had a pitcher of beer, foaming over the top edge, and a platter set with fresh bread and newly cut cheese, slices of salami, and fresh figs. She struggled to balance the tray and try to curtsey, and settled for putting the tray down while she bowed. "Does the noble sir need anything else?" she asked in her best Frankish, managing a proper curtsey—to Francisco.

"I can tell who is the honored and familiar guest here," said Sforza, sounding both amused and more at ease.

She turned awkwardly and curtseyed to Sforza. "I am not knowing what to say to you, Lord," she said awkwardly.

Sforza laughed. "Nothing, young woman, except 'can I bring you a tankard too.'"

"And how is young Tamas?" asked Francisco, pouring himself beer.

"Much better, noble sir. He is reading too much, though. Will it hurt his brain?"

"No," said Francisco seriously. "But go and get Lord Sforza a small tankard. He has already had wine."

"But beer is much better for you than wine," she said seriously, and then hurried out.

"This is the young woman who will be marrying your artificer?" said Sforza. "I think the size of the estate I'll grant him just increased."

"She's a Hungarian peasant," said Mindaug, feeling mildly awkward. "Francisco helped with Tamas's injury, so she feels food and drink for him must come from her own hand. And food is her way..."

"Oh, it's a gesture of love and respect," said Sforza. "I am not offended, and he'll become a well-fed man by the looks of it. He will need the estate to feed him and a pack of children, by the looks of that, too. Now, continue your story, Francisco."

"And she's right about the beer," said Francisco, smiling and drinking some.

"Eat. You need that, too. It smells almost good enough to make me hungry. My lack of appetite is appalling."

Mindaug noticed that plainly worried Francisco.

One of the footmen came in to say that the rockets were now ready to be shown to the noble lords. So off they all trooped to the testing ground, where someone had put down a folded blanket on the bench. "Luxury," said Francisco, pointing to it. "They're attempting to curry favor with you. I had to sit on the bare boards."

"Most ingenious," said Carlo, looking at the mirror, "but very impractical for the battlefield."

"It's really intended for testing new devices," explained Kazimierz. "They have a distressing tendency to explode when you least expect it. So I try to expect it all of the time."

"It's amazing how like dealing with normal military operations this is," said Carlo, obviously amused. Francisco could tell that he had taken to Kazimierz. "In any given situation, anything that can go wrong will, usually when you least expect it to."

"Can I light the fuses, master?" asked the one-eyed Klaus.

"Oh, you can, but should you?" said Francisco, much cheered by some beer and food, and the fact that his commander was here and had had considerable success at containing and defeating their foes...though he was still concerned about the man's health.

"Now that I am sitting down, I can see no reason why not, Bombardier," said Carlo. "It is merely you and Master Kazimierz who may have their heads blown off."

They sat down hastily, and Klaus lit the fuses. A few seconds later, with a mighty hissing roar, the rocket accelerated out of its launcher and raced toward the two scarecrows set up against the hillock. It exploded spectacularly just short of them, off to the one side. Still, there was nothing left of the scarecrows, except for some burning rags and half a stick.

"The timing on those fuses is still not what it needs to be," said Master Kazimierz, "and neither is the accuracy, I am afraid. But the idea is that the rocket transports a grenade, which has a timed fuse, meaning it explodes in the air above the enemy. As the bombardier Klaus pointed out to me, it is far more deadly to have a grenade explode above them or among them, than on the ground, especially if they are behind walls or in ditches. It is possible to do something like this with a cannonball, but there is considerable risk to it exploding in the barrel. While our first experiments were actually fairly dangerous, with the grenade exploding a great deal too close and too soon, we've got it a lot better now."

"How hard is it to make one of these devices?" asked Carlo, with that particular intensity that Francisco had come to recognize.

"Once one knows precisely what one is doing, any relatively competent artisan could do it. Of course, there is some danger, as there always is when working with black powder. But it is no harder than making a grenade. Making fuses that will burn at a constant rate is a lot more difficult. But, I believe that Klaus and Tamas have some ideas on how to do that quite easily."

"It is rather like the old trebuchet, into which they would put a fused bomb made of clay and filled with shrapnel. The advantage being that these are easier to prepare than making or transporting a trebuchet. They take less training to use or to make reasonably accurate."

"And the cost of these?"

Kazimierz shrugged. "It's a cheap tube. It does not have to contain the force of the explosion, it just serves to aim the rocket. It can be made of almost anything, from wooden staves, with barrel hoops, to clay pipes. The rocket itself, well, at the moment we are using reeds and paper and wire, and a small baked-clay cone. We would get a far greater range and speed out of an iron casing as they do in Hind. The cost is mostly that of the black powder, the men and time. I have not worked it out, but perhaps five silver pennies. The tubes can be used over and over, but the rocket is debris."

"I see. How soon can I have two hundred?"

"It takes Klaus and Tamas a few hours to make one. So, for the two of them, it would take a month. They would get faster, but to be honest with you, it would be better for them to teach some of the soldiers who are making the flying stars how to do it, which would leave them free to continue experimenting. Then it would depend on just how many men you set to the task."

Carlo laughed. "Both a good point and an evasive answer. Two more questions: how many people know of this rocket, and just how big do you want this university to be? You have the potential to be of great value to me, and to Milan, although I suspect generations of widows will curse you."

"The soldiers stationed here know something of it. The villagers nearby know we work on something for the army and probably know it means explosions. Well, they could hardly not know, but precise details, no. As for the university—it remains a good daydream, Lord Protector."

"I'll get Francisco to handpick a few more men to guard you and this place. And daydreams are something to strive for. Now, I'd best get on to Milan. I want to call on Lord Palmeri and ask him a few awkward questions, before he is aware Francisco is alive. I will ask Francisco to remain here for a few hours before bringing his prisoners to town."

Francisco wished that he could simply persuade his commander to go and occupy one of the beds at the Val di Castellazzo. He had been quite animated, quite like his normal self for a while, watching the rocket and thinking about the possibilities. He plainly had become exhausted very suddenly again, but the man was driven by an iron will. Francisco was quite relieved to hear him say: "I never thought that I could get used to sleeping in a carriage, but now I seem to fall asleep the minute I get into one. Francisco, come with me to my carriage. I have some documents that I wish to give you, including an order for Lord Palmeri's head that I'm going to write out, and several signed warrants I had prepared for you. I've left the names out."

That was even more worrying. "Palmeri is a man I expect you to take pleasure in executing yourself, my lord."

"So do I, but I think it may distract him from anything foolish, knowing you're after his head. He might prefer my justice. He won't like it any more, when he gets it, and the other documents will enable you to deal with anyone who gives you trouble or questions your authority."

Francisco accompanied Sforza back to the carriage. "Now that we're alone, I'm feeling like I'm half dead. All I want to do is sleep, and I'm even willing to take another purgative. The war is likely to go cool for a few weeks, while they regroup. I had a bad experience with Captain Reynald selling out, Francisco. I want a man I can trust looking after operations while I rest. I'm going to Milan today and then up towards Lake Como, either tomorrow or the day after, to that castle near Cantu. It's cooler, and secure, and I'll try to regain my strength. I don't know what is wrong with me, but I am sick of it. I am beginning to think you must be right again, and I have been poisoned."

"I do think it. I want their guts for a rope, while they're alive, and Palmeri is a good place to start. But rest, good light food, well, that is the best I can offer. I will make up a tonic for you, too. So who will be in charge while you're recovering? Di Nebbiolo?"

"You. That's what the letters are for in case anyone questions it. The warrants are for anyone who questions it twice. Use them in need, Francisco. You will only need to do it once."

"Nebbiolo's a better soldier."

"So use him as one. It's not soldiering I need, it is trust, and a view of the bigger picture. I trust you, Francisco. I feel wretched, but I am damned if I will just lie down and die. Damn me, I hate all poisoners. I'll find and kill a few first."

"Likewise. And beer poisoners are almost on a level with those who poison you, my commander."

Chapter 36

Marco got a message from the old Hypatian, Brother Mascoli, that there was a message waiting for him down in the water-chapel, and he went in haste. He still retained enormous faith in Francisco, and had been meaning to tell him about the fact that the snake was undoubtably magical... and that this magician he had consulted was thought to be the source of it all. It was an awkward letter, knowing that Francisco was fairly skeptical about magic, from years of being assumed to be a magician just because he had books.

Rhene was there, waiting for him. She turned her head and stuck out her chest. He'd grown accustomed to the fact that the undines and nyxes like to show off their breasts, and it no longer embarrassed or even worried him. By comparison to the larger undines, Rhene was quite petite. "See," she said, and Marco was astute enough to realize that it was the small pendant trembling with a little red jewel between those pert breasts that she actually wanted him to look at.

"How beautiful," he said. That was a fairly safe thing to say.

"Francisco gave it to me. I like it. He is going to help me to have a baby."

This was not quite what Marco had intended for his friend when he had sent the nyx to him with a message. He swallowed and said: "Erhm."

"He says that my babies all die because the water is too cold for them. Can that be true?"

"Possibly...yes. Babies, at least human ones, are a lot more sensitive to temperature than adults. You don't find the water too cold, do you?"

She looked at him with innocent puzzlement. "Of course not, it is the perfect temperature! But humans seem to find it cold. Maybe the children take after their fathers. He said this was for you," she said, handing him a glass canister. Through the glass, he could see a book and paper.

"Thank you. I must send a message back to him."

She clapped her hands. "Oh, good! Last time he gave me this pendant, and two men to play with. And a bottle of aphrodisiac wine."

Marco wondered whether he was doing his friend a disservice or not.

"I will come back when I have looked at these," he said.

My good friend in medicine,

I find myself very troubled sending this letter to you. Master Kazimierz, who acts as our advisor on magical matters, was very insistent. He is a scholar and has begged me to send this very old book to you. He has marked certain passages that he feels may be relevant in treating the snakebite victim. I am afraid he has a great deal more belief in mystical matters than I do. If I understand him correctly, he believes that the serpent is part of a personification of the disease we know as Justinian's Plague, and that any treatment will need to be magical. The book he feels will be valuable in dealing with the plague, too, although we know that is not something that there is any record of. He also recommends an attar of roses for snakebite, and although I cannot think it will be effective, you could try it.

The Lion part of Marco Valdosta knew that his friend Francisco was wrong, and that this Kazimierz was right. But if this Von Stebbens was right about the advisor, what the message and book contained might be a far-from-innocent trap. He did not look in the book, but instead packed it up and went in haste to see the patriarch Michael.

Here he was greeted by the news that Archimandrite von Stebbens and his fellow Knights had left for Florence on the previous day, to see if Cosimo de' Medici could intervene with Sforza to allow them to close on Mindaug.

The patriarch Michael asked Marco if he could help. So Marco explained.

The old man said: "I have no magical ability, Marco Valdosta, but I suggest we take these to the chapel, and I shall bless them. Demons do not endure that well. And then, suitable protections or no, I think you should risk the strength of the Lion against any of the dark arts. You will be aware of any magic, will you not?"

"Here within the marshes of ancient Etruria, it would be very hard to bespell me, and within my demesne I would be aware of their working. I might not be able to find them when they are still, but I could follow and destroy them if they tried that. Anything but the briefest and smallest evil working, I am aware of. It keeps the magic workers here from temptations. Of course, my idea of evil, and the Church's idea, are not always the same."

"In this area at least," said the patriarch, with quiet smile, "I feel I will trust your judgment. Come, let us do this thing."

There were no evil emanations or sudden appearances of demons boiling up from the book. It remained a book. The patriarch looked at it. "Ah. The sagas of Diderich. I know them well. Goldemar, Virginal, the Small Rose Garden. Of course, they are incomplete and fragmented. They were somewhat fancifully based on the Gothic king, Theoderic the Great, who ruled Italy in the sixth century."

"I suspect we will find that this is not fragmented."

"What a treasure that would be!"

Marco hoped so, too, but had a feeling that the treasure would not be one to the world of literature. He opened the book to discover that it was in Latin. Like any medical scholar he had some grasp of the language, but not to the extent of reading it fast or easily. A small slip of paper protruded. He opened it there. It was a note, in a neat, precise hand.

To the Lion, greeting
  This is as near to the original tale of Orkise the wyrm, to whom maidens were sacrificed, and the rescue of Sintram's soul, a man who was possibly the child of the original Visconti lord, from being devoured by this evil. According to this, its

lair is somewhere near Arona. The maiden is revived by an
attar of petals made from Laurin's garden.
  I cannot counter this creature. You have greater means.

                                                                K

"He knows who I am. I think that confirms what Von Stebbens said. And that this could be a trap."

"He also knows the story, but that is not quite as I remember
it," said the patriarch. "I see you frowning at the text, my young
friend. I read Latin easily and fluently. Allow me to have a look
at the book, please? I shall read it and translate."

Marco handed him the book, and the old man held it out at
arm's length and read it to himself. Then he said: "It is recognizably
the story as I had read it, although it is not as poetic and there is
a great deal of extra material." In the slightly singsong voice of a
man reading text aloud, he continued: "The wyrm Orkise had come
to the mountains and was devouring all of the peoples there. Its
fang was as sharp as the finest needle, and it left no more mark
than the bite of a flea, but the terrible poison was such that their
flesh broke into mulberry swellings and they died. And the people
appeased it with the sacrifice of their maiden daughters."

He lowered the book, now that he had stopped reading from
it directly. "Then it tells how Diderich and his knight go to the
rescue. Diderich is separated from his companion Hildebrand and
must fight off the armies of Orkise, heathens who fear he will
break their pact with their god. Hildebrand rescues the young
woman, revives her, and defeats Orkise because he has the scent
of heaven about him which prevents the poison of Orkise, and
does not look in the eyes of the wyrm but in his bright shield.
His lance bears the burning bush. That may be a reference to
the burning bush in which God appeared to Moses."

"Or just a burning bush," said Marco. "What else?"

"Let me read on."

A little later he said, "Well, broadly it is the same story. They
celebrate, and then save the soul of Sintram the son of Hilfrich
of Arone who was being swallowed by Orkise, and Orkise is banished as a result. Hilfrich is rewarded by having his sons made
nobles of Diderich's realm. That's more or less what it means,
anyway. It reads 'and thus Sintram's father's seed will hold the
lands of Arone.'"

"I thought Orkise had been killed?"

"The word is defeated. And one of the books I read did have a whole section on a war with the son of Orkise. So it could be . . . a title, perhaps."

"And what exactly is this Orkise?"

"The wyrm, a sort of early German word for dragon, but more like a gigantic snake than what we regard as a dragon. It says here it stinks of what it feeds on, death and rats. The rats are its kine, it uses them to give it the milk of dying souls."

"Charming! But I don't see how it helps us."

"There are several other markers."

"Read on," said Marco.

The patriarch turned to another passage—an earlier one. "Ah. This is part of the Small Rose Garden of the dwarf, Laurin. The most perfect and beautiful of gardens, which Diderich did not wish to damage, seen only in the light of dawn. Surrounded by the thread which must be broken for anyone to enter. There is a great deal more about the heavenly scent of the roses. And this I had not read before: after Laurin was defeated and then being spared by Diderich, the dwarf allowed him to gather the petals of flowers broken by Witege—Diderich's treacherous companion, who charged in where angels fear to tread. Hmm. It actually says he went foolishly where only angels tread, breaking the thread. I think it may be a reference to the afterworld in some way. Laurin is a heathen dwarf king who is married to the sister of one of Diderich's heroes. As I recall, her death is lamented in the tale of Diderich and Wenzlan. They free her. It says Diderich rewarded his heroes with pomander bags of the petals, which they wore around their necks so the wondrous scent could protect them from all ills."

That, to Marco, did bring in his brother, his brother's wife, and how he, too, got her back. He would ask Maria—or maybe ask Benito, if he got back soon, to ask Maria; she was so moody right now. But that wasn't a tale the patriarch was privy to.

The other marker proved to be a reference to the battle for Ravenna, which said that the land had been devastated by the minions of Orkise. "That does fit in with the history of the land and the history of the plague."

"I just don't see what I can do about it, or how this helps. We know this Orkise doesn't like fire, and that the scent of heaven cures. We haven't met Orkise, and we don't have the scent of heaven."

Marco took the book with him, while the patriarch promised to send messages on to the archimandrite saying they had more communications with the magician, and to Father Thomas Lüber.

Marco also wrote a letter to Francisco.

"The—I don't know what to call it—god-demon your magician referred to is definitely real and was involved in the snakebite incident. I have placed various magical protections on the woman, but I fear the worst. I must beg you to be careful, Francisco, with this Kazimierz. The Knights of the Holy Trinity seek him and they do not do so for no reason. I fear he may seek to entrap you, and Sforza, in his plots."

Chapter 37

Val di Castellazzo, Duchy of Milan

"Now," said Francisco, after he had been ushered into the main house of the villa and provided with a seat. The chair felt almost uncomfortably soft, after hours in a saddle. "You sent an urgent message saying you needed to see me, Master Kazimierz. Or did you deal with the matter with my commander?"

Before he could reply, Klaus spoke up: "Please, Captain, can you tell Master Kazimierz that his inventions are worth more to the commander than that poncy new wife of his?"

The bombardier, looking apprehensive, was standing in one of the open doorways to the salon, flanked by portraits on either side. As usual, Francisco had no idea who the paintings represented.

Kazimierz spoke up. "This is, in part, what I wished to discuss with you, Captain. We had a visit from the Lord Protector's wife yesterday: she wanted poison. Demanded it, in fact, and because of her rank, well, I was in a difficult position. She promised me that the Lord Protector would reward me appropriately."

Francisco looked over at him, frowning. "Sforza would probably impale you for supplying poison to anyone. He disapproves of it, in the strongest sense. You should have told him."

Master Kazimierz's dark eyes gleamed. "How satisfying. So I had heard, and it was to some extent confirmed by his comments about the poisoned beer. Thus it is a good thing that the substance which I supplied to her lackey this morning, was not poison. You may ask my guards about the man, and what token he displayed. My stableman recognized his horse, so we know who he is. He came with the intent to kill me after getting the poison. I disarmed him, and did not give him poison, but a substance which was more awkward. It does have an effect, which may be of some value to Carlo Sforza—it was used to catch wine thieves, because even the smallest amount turns the urine red, as beetroot juice will. It has no other particular effects. But I anticipate a problem when she finds out."

It was Francisco's turn to try to find speech . . . and to find no answer but a laugh of sheer delight. "Oh, dear. I can see how it might worry you, Kazimierz. But it is a marriage of convenience for Carlo. She has no particular power . . ."

"I beg of you, do not underestimate this woman. She is extremely dangerous. I would check the color of my own urine and that of your master. She reminds me of Elizabeth Bartholdy."

Bartholdy? This man had plainly moved in very rarified circles in Hungary—not to mention dangerous ones! Once again, Francisco resolved to find out more about the mysterious man behind the huge mustache.

"I thought she was supposed to be very beautiful? Lucia is too much like her father to be beautiful," said Francisco.

"Bartholdy," said Kazimierz grimly, "paid a terrible price for that beauty, in the end—and many girls paid a bad one along the way, if not as bad as hers. This woman Lucia Maria del Maino . . . Please, Francisco. If you discover the sign of the poison, take it as a warning. Do not confront her, just leave quietly."

"She really did frighten you. Don't worry, Carlo will deal with her."

The man said nothing, but he did not seem comforted. "So who was this lackey?" asked Francisco.

"One 'Lord Laglissio' according to the stableman. He was extremely angry to have needed to have shown her token to the troops in order to get through to me. He is nothing. Merely an errand boy and killer . . . She . . . is far more. Do not confront her, I beg you."

"She'll find out just what she is if she tries to cross Sforza. I suspect he has been poisoned. If I find out it's her, I will kill her myself, and the devil take the consequences," said Francisco grimly.

"My fear is the devil already has, and killing her will actually make it worse. Did you send that book to your friend Marco Valdosta?"

"Yes. I was in the throes of getting it to my messenger when they tried to kill me. My messenger intervened. Now there's a woman, if you can call her that, you wouldn't want to get on the wrong side of," said Francisco, recollecting the ease with which Rhene had dealt with two men.

Kazimierz sighed. "That was why they tried to kill you. If she knew that much, then I am afraid your message was your messenger's death warrant. Mine too, if she catches up with me."

"Not likely, Kazimierz. My messenger is the magical creature Marco uses. A water-woman."

"Ah," said Kazimierz, tugging at his mustache. "The nyx of which you had asked. That is, indeed, a little more likely than most messengers to evade her. They do have the advantage of having died once already. Does this one yearn for her lover?"

"She seems ready to take on any possible one. But she kills them, so I'd advise against it," said Francisco.

"Aha, an old one!" said Kazimierz. "They are the strongest. Well, we will just have to hope your friend can take the right action."

"Well, I know I am going to go to Carlo Sforza right now and will tell him to watch his dear wife. Don't worry too much about it. You'll be safe," said Francisco.

"I may well be. Oddly, these days I find myself worrying about others." The man frowned. "A bad Western habit I have gotten into."

Francisco Turner rode off with his escort, having no way of knowing that he'd effectively set Count Kazimierz Mindaug's departure time for sooner rather than later that week. The attempted poisoning of Sforza was unlikely to result in his excellent advice being followed. Personally, cannon, or a large amount of gunpowder followed by arson, would be the best way of dealing with the woman—but the trouble with that was that she was the only real way of restricting the monster.

He could only hope that the Lion had grasped the import of the last piece about Sintram. The son had had to die—but he'd died with his soul saved and the monster under his control banished. The price he had demanded for this was cheap, compared to the disease ravaging Europe.

Now, the count needed to get a bespelled mirror to the edge of Venetian territory. A bird would have to do. The serpent could not control the air. Mindaug had always liked owls for some reason that went beyond logic, so he had a plan to use one that night.

Francisco arrived in Milan with his prisoners . . . and soon found himself with a dying Lord Palmeri as a patient. The man was not going to be telling any deathbed secrets: he was dying as Violetta de' Medici's mother had died, but faster. He'd gotten the full venom of both fangs.

"We saw the snake, but too late. It was a sort of mulberry-stain color with a yellow pattern on its head," said Carlo Sforza, looking as shaken as Francisco had seen him. "Fast as a whip, it was. The jackass had just told me in fear and trembling that he had honestly believed the order to kill you had come from me. He'd lied like a flatfish at first but when I told him we had two bullyboys locked up safely, and I'd talked to them . . . well, he folded up, very quickly."

"I think someone is using the snake to kill," said Francisco. "There is magic associated with all of this, and I don't like it."

"I don't either. Is Venice right? Is this new 'magician' of ours playing a clever double game, Francisco?"

"As he asked me to warn you that your wife is procuring poison, it would be a complicated game indeed. Especially as he says that what he gave her won't kill, but will have an interesting effect on the color of the victim's urine. It'll turn it red."

"She was here earlier, wishing to bill and coo, insisting on drinking a glass of wine with me. I suspect she's just discovered that you do not always get pregnant the first time, for this Visconti offspring she dreams of having on the ducal throne. She's putting on weight, though."

"I trust you had your taster taste it."

Sforza rolled his eyes. "Yes, Francisco. And she was offended."

"That's too bad. Now, I'd better go on trying to save Palmeri's life."

"It doesn't seem worth bothering, does it?" said Carlo. "If you revive him, I'll kill him in a particularly cruel and unusual way, to make the point that I disapprove of poisoners and disapprove of men trying to kill my officers."

"I like them to die at my or your choosing . . . and to tell me who had set them to trying to kill me."

But this time, he was doomed to fail.

❀   ❀   ❀

Lucia had not been pleased by the fact that Laglissio had failed to kill the "magician." She'd almost killed him instead as punishment. Now it looked like it was just as well she hadn't, as she'd need someone for Lord Palmeri's job who had some grasp of his network and some experience. Laglissio was one of his senior men.

She'd successfully administered the first dose of poison. It was a question of time before that pig Sforza lost his wits and left her to govern, and would be unable to tell that his "son" was born four months too early.

And then...he'd excused himself saying he had to question Lord Palmeri, that the man had tried to have one of his best men killed. Lucia had no faith in Palmeri's ability to lie under the torture that would certainly follow. She wasted no time in getting back to her chambers and giving his hat, with the scent, to the asp and saying he needed to die—now.

I like to kill. But one death is not enough for the serpent. It needs more. Soon.

"Go, and I'll give you some more. Plenty."

Chapter 38

Milan

Francisco had returned to his quarters in the barracks that night. Sheer bloody-mindness made him go for a run the next morning. It did not make him stupid, however. He took a troop down the canal path first, leaving men at fifty-yard intervals, with instructions that they were to mount and follow once he was past. Yes, it was a complete overkill, but it was his way of telling the world he would continue to enjoy his runs, no matter who watched. It would give him quite a beer bill at the end of his run, but then he felt he owed his host Capra of the Grosso Luccio a little profit.

It was a little misty at the tail end of his run and he nearly fell over the glass canister, lying there in the middle of his path in a puddle of water. He was quick-witted enough to realize that it meant a message had come from Marco. He picked it up, and went on. There was no point in stopping, not with fifty troopers behind him. He was relatively close to the Grosso Luccio, so he went in, ordered beer, and sank a mug of it himself while holding the canister. Opening and reading would have to wait for him to return to the barracks. He had just put the canister in a saddlebag and mounted when a man riding at a flat gallop came and wrenched his horse to a halt.

"Captain Turner!" he shouted. "Thank God I have found you! The Lord Protector is sick! The duchess sent us out, hunting for you!"

Francisco swung up into the saddle. "Where?"

"The palazzo. In the duchess's rooms."

They rode hard, and Francisco finished his run with a sprint through the palace, followed by his troopers. He was met at the head of the stairs by several of Sforza's men. "He's been carried back to his bed. The duchess gave orders."

Francisco rushed there. The powerful Sforza was lying on the bed, still dressed, while his man—who had been in his master's service as a soldier for a good many years—stood as if frozen holding his master's hand. He looked up at Francisco. "Thank heavens you're here, Captain."

Francisco felt for the pulse. It was there, which was his one item of relief. "What happened?" he asked, loosening the collar.

Sforza's man Hellbore answered "He stormed out of here . . . he'd been fine, quite cheerful. And then he used his chamber pot and . . ."

Several more men came in to the room, followed by the woman Sforza had married. "Will he recover?" she asked imperiously.

Lucia did not look the part of the distraught wife. Francisco opened his mouth to speak, and then caught his wits. He had no intention of telling this woman anything of substance. "I still need to examine him, Your Grace. If you could tell me what happened, it may help?"

"He came to my bedchamber. He is, after all, my husband. And, alas, he had what I can only think was some kind of fainting spell. I ordered my maids to have a physician called. His guards then sent off for someone they assured me was his personal physician."

"I am indeed his physician," said Francisco, with a calm assurance he did not feel. Master Kazimierz had been correct, and he wondered if he could kill her before the guards intervened. And then it occurred to him that that, too, had been what Kazimierz had cautioned about. At the moment, Carlo was alive. Could he be kept that way?

"Thank you, Your Grace. Now I am afraid I will be removing some of his clothing and cupping him. The process will take some time. I will send a messenger to let you know how successful the process is." He coughed. "If I might say, Your Grace, I think we need to downplay his illness, so as not to give Milan's enemies comfort. He was planning to go to his villa near Lake Como for a period of rest. I would suggest we could inform people that that is where he is."

"A good suggestion," she said coolly. "See his mercenaries are suitably informed. I shall deal with the court."

"I shall do so, Your Grace. Now, excuse me. I must see to him." He went and knelt next to his commander, hoping his rage-shake had not betrayed him.

"Quite. To your work, bleed him well," she said. He did not look up. He kept his calm, somehow.

The door closed.

"Do you want cupping bowls or your instruments, Captain?" asked one of Sforza's men.

"Don't be a fool," growled Francisco. "You. Sergeant Nils." He picked out one of the Swedish bodyguards, a man known for being effective and hard. "We need to get the commander out of here immediately. Get my troops, organize a clear path to a carriage with as little noise and fuss as possible, but they're to kill any of these bastards who try to stop them. Sword or knifework preferably, no shooting if they can help it." He pointed to two of the others. "On the door. No one but Nils and his boys comes in. Make excuses to the duchess. Just tell the others if they try, I said to kill them. You three—we will need a stretcher. He's still a heavy man."

A few minutes later, a hundred-strong group of Sforza's men formed a shield around Francisco and the three men who carried Sforza out to the waiting carriage.

Once inside the carriage, Francisco beckoned to one of the men who had served Sforza even longer than he had. "Galeazzo, go find a courtier. Any one of the useless bastards will do for the purpose. Tell him to tell Her Grace"—he all but spat out the title—"that we've rushed the commander to Cantu Castle near Como. We'll take the right gate out of the city. I'm not telling you where we're actually going in case you get caught and questioned. Rejoin any one of the commander's units, and I'll see you well rewarded for this."

The man didn't move. "Is the commander going to be all right?"

"If I can get him to safety, I hope and pray so. But he needs to get away from here, fast."

Galeazzo saluted, turned on his heel, and was gone within seconds.

Francisco opened the small window that allowed him to address the man on the box. "Val di Castellazzo. Spring 'em."

Inside the carriage, he did the things a good physician should do and kept his calm. But he knew, had from the moment that Sforza's man told him of the red urine, even before he saw the two puncture marks on Carlo's hand, that his greatest friend had been poisoned by Lucia. The woman who called herself his wife was the same woman who had orchestrated the murder of any others who might have taken her place. It was obvious now. He doubted there was much Kazimierz could do to help, although he wished that he'd listened earlier. But there were two hundred men there, and he needed to organize to get his master to Venice.

Back in her chambers, Lucia considered what the physician had said.

"How long," she asked the asp, "until he dies?"

Weeks. Maybe a month. He is stronger than most men. I could have killed him outright, but I thought that you did not wish that.

Sforza had terrified her with his sarcasm and rage, when he'd come in to tell her he'd found that she'd poisoned him. His threat to put her in a tower somewhere and keep her there to trot out to show that he still had a living claim to be the Lord Protector of her duchy had been the final straw. The asp had struck. He deserved to die, slowly and horribly.

But slowly, and then without telling anyone he was dead, until she had all secure. That fool physician could go on trying to keep him alive. She would tell him to remove the piece of filth to Cantu Castle.

So when one of her courtiers brought word that he had done so, she was actually quite pleased with him. It was just as well Palmeri had been such a hopeless, hapless failure.

Francisco found himself relieved to arrive at the Val di Castellazzo. Master Kazimierz looked somewhat taken aback to see them. But then, having a second visit from the Lord Protector in two days did suggest something to worry about.

He got out of the carriage and said grimly: "I should have given Carlo your advice. But he wouldn't have listened anyway, any more than I did."

"Is he dead?" asked Kazimierz.

"No, just comatose. I have no idea if he'll recover."

"You need to get him to Venice, to your friend Marco Valdosta, as soon as possible. He is the only possibility of your obtaining the only cure we know of. And, also, he is the only creature of reasonably goodwill powerful enough to repel the serpent Orkise, so long as he is in his own territory."

"That was exactly what I had planned. I wanted him out of Milan first, and then away as quick as possible with as strong and secret an escort as we can manage. Some men and this carriage must proceed to Cantu above Lake Como. I am going to steal some of your guards and use this as a base to arrange transport. I wish I could have arranged this in advance. The Venetians might not take kindly to Sforza arriving with an armed escort, and it will be hard to keep quiet."

"Use your nyx friend and a boat. They can make a mist on the water that will hide you by night. You could be in Venice by morning," said Kazimierz.

"I would be tempted if I could. She comes to talk to me in one place in Milan. I suppose I could go back."

"Most unnecessary. Water carries sounds well. I have a device which can be used to summon their kind"—the man's cheeks betrayed a smile that the mustache hid—"and I have protection against them. There is a fair-sized river close by. Give me a few minutes to prepare, while you see him comfortably bestowed in the house, and we will send the carriage and some guards onwards."

It was rapidly enough done, but not before Francisco had had a confrontation with Captain di Nebbiolo and Lieutenant de Malarde. "Yes, I see the need for a suitable decoy, and I'll see no human gets in to see him, no matter what," said the lieutenant. "But what are you going to do, Captain Turner?"

"Get him to the best help I can. A young physician in Venice, whom I rate as having the best chance of helping him to recover. He was poisoned, but apparently there is some kind of magical antidote. I need to go in person to make sure he gets there, and in as good a health as possible, and then I shall do my best to see him recover."

Di Nebbiolo, who had known Francisco a long time, shook his head. "Get him there, see him safely bestowed, Captain Turner. And then get back here as fast as possible. He gave you orders to see to things while he was recovering."

"Yes, but that was . . ."

"No buts," said Di Nebbiolo. "If you trust this physician, that's good enough for me. For all of us. You, too. The commander gave orders, he wants it done, and it will be done as he wished. I'll keep you and him here if need be, Turner. I'll start getting things ready, but we're going to have a fight on our hands when this gets out—and it will."

"The commander does not abandon his men," said the lieutenant. "That's why we stand by him."

Francisco ground his teeth. They had a point: Carlo would not thank him, or forgive him, for abandoning his task. Eventually he nodded in reluctant agreement. "Very well. I'll need an escort waiting near the Venetian Republic's border. At San Penti."

Di Nebbiolo nodded. "It will be there. Now, jump to it, Lieutenant. You'll want Captain Turner's hat for whomever you put in the carriage.

"Hmph. When all of this is over," said Francisco, "I want it back. I like that hat."

A little later, he and Master Kazimierz, and some ten guards, set out for the river. When they got there, Kazimierz said: "Send them off to buy you a boat. The water-women have no liking for admiring crowds...that leave alive."

He plainly knew them. So Francisco did as he was bid. He wanted to get this done, and to get back to Sforza's bedside.

There was no mistaking the calm professionalism of the man preparing his ritual. He might be a scholar, an experimenter with gunpowder and other devices, but he was a competent practitioner of magic, too. He handed a long horn to Francisco. "I place myself at some risk doing this, Caviliero. I trust you will remember, when I need your help."

"If I get Carlo to help...I'll be deep in your debt. If he survives, Milan, he and I will be in your debt forever."

"I'll settle for life, and hopefully that's longer than a few months," said Kazimierz. "Now, allow me to concentrate. A mistake and I could get a river monster less amenable to conversation. She is closely related to that."

He began walking widdershins, tingling a bell with one hand, dribbling river water from a wooden goblet in the other, and muttering a string of words too fast for Francisco to recognize any more than the fact that they were not Frankish. "Put the horn mouth in the water and call her name down it," he instructed.

So Francisco did. And again. Several times.

"It may take a while. But if she is within twenty miles, she heard you," said Kazimierz.

They waited. It wasn't easy.

Suddenly the still water rippled, and Rhene thrust up from the depths.

"Hello. I was hoping you'd call," she said, artfully flicking back her hair. Then she saw Kazimierz. "Who is he? He has all sorts of nasty protections about him," she said crossly.

Master Kazimierz bowed. "I am merely the fellow he used to make the call. You need to teach him. And yes, I am protected, and yes, I could compel you to do my will. But I will not, since the caviliero has assured me he has no need or desire for me to do so."

Francisco spoke up: "I won't let him compel you to do anything. I just have a huge favor to ask. I need to get a . . . a very dear friend to Marco Valdosta in a hurry, in secret. I was hoping, if we got a boat, you might help us."

"It's not a very dear female friend, is it?" she asked, eyes sharp.

"Good gracious me, no," answered Francisco. "He's my commanding officer, and the man to whom I owe my life and liberty."

"Oh, then, nothing easier. But only the two of you. I can hide you and move your boat easily. You would be there by midnight, I would guess. Are you ready right now?"

There was a risk to just the two of them. There would normally be bodyguards. But this would be fast, far faster than he had dreamed of. "I need to get the boat and the commander safely bestowed in it. I hope within the hour?"

"I'll be waiting for you," she said.

On the ride to the nearby village, Kazimierz said: "You have indeed snagged a very old one there."

"It doesn't show," said Francisco, thinking of the smooth skin.

"Old and powerful. The older they are, the more they forget, and yet the more human they become. A sort of full circle. Now, I do have a small favor to ask. If you would take this mirror with you to Venice? I was going to use a bird, but that would only be to the borders of the Lion of Etruria's demesne. You see, if we have to flee, I can use it to magically transport myself and Tamas and Emma to where the mirror is. I think you would be able to ask if they would take me as a refugee, if Orkise or the woman come hunting me. A cell would be acceptable," he said wryly. "It would mean that I thought it would be safer than here."

"You think they might want you in a cell?" asked Francisco.

"I don't know. We have a common enemy—in fact, common enemies. I am no threat to them, and they have nothing to gain by imprisoning me. But I was once in the employ of a deadly enemy of Venice, the demon Chernobog, who had possessed my prince. I tried to kill that employer, for my own safety, for what that is worth."

He looked at Francisco's face. "No, I had nothing to do with your master—my current employer's—present state. The opposite is true, and I would like to see his fortunes revive. This place and situation suit me. I am getting old," he said, mildly plaintive. "All I want are my books and a reasonable degree of comfort. Tell the Lion, from me, that Lucia needs to be captured and, at all costs, not killed. She is the only one who can restrain the wyrm, and it cannot be killed by ordinary means."

The man sighed. "The university idea...is something I can daydream about. It has been very pleasurable doing this work, to my surprise."

They caught sight of the troopers, and confidences were at an end. The men had located and bought a boat. "Bit smaller than we'd like, Captain. It won't take more than about six people."

"There will only be two of us in it."

There was a silence. Then one of the older men cleared his throat. "That's not wise, Captain."

"I know. But it's what we have to do. This will get the commander to help in the fastest and, oddly, I think the safest way possible. You all know he trusted me with his life, and has on many occasions in the past—so you will have to do the same this time. Let's get to it."

And so, less than an hour later, the boat was pushed out into the stream with Francisco at the oars, and Carlo Sforza lying on a stretcher, and a mirror in Francisco's hastily gathered gear.

A few yards from the shore, the boat began to move a lot faster than Francisco could paddle. He shipped the oars and looked over the gunwale, where he could see the fish all around it. They moved very fast and, oddly, the villages on the bank seemed lost in a forest, a huge, ancient forest. In the twilight, they moved on into a country of rattling marshes, alive with mosquitos and the song of frogs. Francisco had no conversation except for the stentorian breathing of Carlo Sforza. That suited him, although he would have liked to know where he was, especially when he heard what sounded very like a lion's roar somewhere in the distance, as they sailed on into the darkness.

And then there were lights. And the characteristic smell of Venice's canals.

"It was quite different, back then," said Rhene dreamily. "I still have it within me though. He was a soldier, too, and just as loyal to our chieftain. Do you wish to go to the chapel where we usually meet Marco, or to his home? He is at his home at the moment, according to the others."

"His home, please. You are a marvel, Rhene!"

"I am? Why, thank you." She preened.

A few minutes later, the door to *Casa* Montescue was opened by a sleepy-looking servant. Fortunately, he was one who recognized Francisco, and agreed to call Master Marco immediately.

Chapter 39

Venice

Marco Valdosta looked incredulously at the travel-stained, tired-looking Francisco Turner, who had insisted on staying on the doorstep, rather than waiting in one of parlors.

"Forgive me for intruding and for not coming inside, but I have my commander, critically ill, on the boat." He pointed behind him, to a boat tied in front of the mansion. "He's been poisoned, just like Violetta de' Medici, and I think you are the only man who could possibly save him, Marco. Or at least that's what Kazimierz says. I don't know any more."

Marco was surprised to see a tear on the tough mercenary's cheek.

He did not waste time talking, but went out and got down into the boat. Even in the light of the house windows, Sforza's pallor was obvious. Sforza had aged since the last time Marco had seen him, but he would still have recognized his tough sort-of-stepfather. Marco wondered if the hard man had ever realized that he'd hero-worshipped him for a while, until Carlo and Mama's fights had drawn him away to her side. He looked very odd and still now, but he was still breathing, and his pulse was still beating.

"The snake that poisoned Violetta de' Medici got him, too," said Francisco, his voice low, gruff, and angry. "I found the bite on his left forearm. And I know where it is coming from now. It's that hell-bitch Carlo married—Lucia Maria del Maino. I wish to God she'd stayed in that castle in Arona and never come to Milan."

Arona. Marco thought about the words from the book that had been brought to him.

Francisco's voice cracked. "Please, Marco. I don't ask this lightly... but I will be forever in your debt if you can help him. It needs magic, and I have no knowledge or skill with that."

Marco felt the weight of the request. He also wondered if, magical skill or not, he could do anything for the man. But he had not been reared in Venice and on her intrigues for nothing. He also knew that this was a political deathtrap, possibly for Venice, certainly for Milan, and would have far wider repercussions. Even here and now, there was probably a spy edging closer. He was Marco Valdosta; he was watched.

He took a firm grip on Francisco's arm, squeezed, and said loudly: "Yes. Undoubtedly an infectious complaint! He must be isolated at once. I believe the infection is carried through the air at this time of year. You will have to be isolated with him, Signor. Now, you say his name is Captain Parolo and he came all the way from Verona. We have special quarters for the infectiously unwell: the lazaretto on the Isla Santa Maria di Nazareth. I will instruct your boatman to take you there."

"Rhene brought us," said Francisco quietly.

"Excellent," said Marco, equally quietly. "I need him taken to the Doge's palace unseen. To the water door on the Rio di Palazzo. She can use her power to hide you, I think." He handed his signet to Francisco. "Give that to the door guard. I will be there within minutes."

He got out of the boat, waving his hand in front of his face. "Off to the lazaretto with you. I pray to God you have not spread the contagion to me," he said loudly.

To the doorman, just in case, he said: "Do not admit him again. It was some kind of skin complaint the fellow had. Thank heavens it was not necessary to touch him. I will go to bathe."

Marco didn't have his brother's skill on the rooftops. But he did have enough skill to drop himself off the roof of the *casa*, to the water door of the adjoining house where, by long-standing arrangement, a paddle was hidden, and there were, as anywhere in Venice, a selection of small boats. Now he let the Lion within guide him, down quiet waters. He might not be quite unobserved, but his identity would not be known. Francisco and his cargo were there before him, and Marco found the man pacing.

"Violetta's decline has effectively been halted by the magical wards. I will try the same on Carlo Sforza. Otherwise...I still don't know quite what to do. The leads your magician sent us don't help enough. Did you get my message about him?"

Francisco laughed tersely. "I got the message, or at least I assume so, but before I got to read it, I was called to Carlo. Kazimierz was the one who managed to get Rhene and organize the trip here. Your message is sitting with my kit, quite possibly at his house, Val di Castellazzo. So you'll just have to tell me about it, but later, when the commander is safely inside these wards of yours."

It was some hours later that they finally got that chance to talk, and even that was interrupted by a call from Petro Dorma, summoning them both to an audience in one of the small salons. It was not quite dawn yet.

"I hear my physician was called on, and directed a sick person to the lazaretto. The boat has been reported tied up there. A vessel from the upper Po, my experts tell me, and would you still like beer to drink, even at this time of morning, Caviliero?"

"For me, it is a late night and not an early morning, Your Grace. I would love beer."

"I have not forgotten that we owe you a debt, but I suspect you have brought me a problem. Would you like to explain, Caviliero?"

"How many ears do we have listening, Your Grace?"

"Certain select members of the Council of Ten. No other. And what you say would be told to them anyway, even if they were not listening."

Francisco nodded. "I understand. Your Grace, Carlo Sforza was poisoned using a magical serpent, just as Violetta de' Medici was poisoned. The poisoner is Duke Visconti's bastard daughter, Lucia, who is now married to Carlo Sforza. She is her father again, but far worse. There is no length that she will not go to. She killed all the potential rivals for her position—or tried to, at least, since thus far the de' Medici girl still lives. I have pretended to take Sforza to Cantu Castle to recover, and brought him here in secret, to the only physician I thought might cure him."

"Very secretly indeed," said Petro, "which was good, although the possibility of that does not please me. Mind you, I'm not sure if the cover of a rumor of a plague of dread disease was worth the cover-up, Marco."

"It's not a route the Lion of St. Mark is unaware of, or that Venice has anything to fear from," said Marco, his voice deep and full of the power of the Lion within him. "But we do have a great deal to fear from Lucia. She has awoken Orkise so that she could gain her goal, and Orkise is the danger the seer of Rome detected. She must be killed because Orkise is the plague. The great plague, the Black Death, which could, as it did the last time it was loosed, devour most of the human population, only stopping when it runs out of victims. At its worst, nine people out of ten die, and even the mildest wave took two in every five souls. Those who survive starve as food rots in the fields for lack of workers, and hide in fear from contagion. Last time, people were more scattered, and some escaped the wave, until the disease was banished. Banished but not destroyed. She has roused it again. We need to destroy her, now."

There was a silence. And then Francisco spoke up. "Kazimierz said I was to tell you that, at all cost, you must not kill Lucia because she is the only one who can restrain Orkise, the monster she has woken. It cannot be killed by other means, just restrained."

"And who is this Kazimierz?" asked Petro Dorma softly, dangerously.

"A magician," answered Francisco. "A very powerful one, at a guess, who was working for Carlo. He tried to warn me and, when she had poisoned Carlo, he helped us escape."

Francisco stuck his hand in his pocket and pulled out the mirror. "He asked me to bring this to you. He said he could use it as a magical means of escape, and to ask if you would give him refuge. He said to put it in a cell if you so wished, because in a cell in Venice, he would still be safer than where he is now."

"Is he an enemy of ours?" asked Dorma.

"He says not, Your Grace. He's very clever, powerful...and, in my opinion, worth helping. But I freely admit that he has fooled both Carlo and myself before, for his own ends."

"What did he do?" asked Petro Dorma, plainly curious as to how this had been done.

"Convinced us—and admittedly we wanted to believe—that he was a fraud, not a magician, and merely a man of science. In the process, he did us no harm and helped us to win several battles. Without using magic, or at least that we were aware of."

"This would be the fellow those Knights of the Holy Trinity

were seeking. They were convinced he was evil. They could be right," said Marco.

Turner nodded. "He said that he and you had a common enemy, but that you might wish to imprison him because had once worked for an enemy of Venice, a prince possessed by a demon called Chernobog."

"Grand Duke Jagiellon," said Marco.

"Then this man will be his assistant and chief researcher, Count Kazimierz Mindaug, later rumored to be working for Elizabeth Bartholdy and King Emeric of Hungary," said Petro Dorma.

"Evil associates for an evil man," said Marco.

"He may be that, Marco," said Francisco tiredly. "He definitely shared your opinion of Elizabeth Bartholdy. He said Lucia was like her. He's still the only person who seems to know what is going on. And I am sure of this, he might have fooled us about not being a magician, but I'll swear he is deathly afraid of Lucia. I was not, but I should have been."

"I think," said Petro Dorma, "that we should give him his wish. Put the mirror in a cell, but only if it can be bound against him making a similar escape. Can it, Marco?"

"It can. Or at least it can be made very difficult and damaging."

"Good. Then I think we should do that with this mirror—just in case that proves a real thing, too. I have an empty cell or two in the new prison. Now, Caviliero, I am sure Marco will do his best for...the man we shall refer to as...Signor Abello from Fruili, seeing as Captain Parolo is in the lazaretto. The question remains, Caviliero, what you will do now. You are a recognized and known man in Venice. I do not believe that any spies are yet aware that the trusted physician of Carlo Sforza is in Venice, but it will be merely a matter of time. Hours, not days—and then the story would disintegrate. You need to disappear or be hidden."

"Your Grace," said Francisco, "I've given my commander's care over to a man I trust. As little as I want to leave, I need to go back to Milan. I arranged to meet a troop at San Penti."

"Lord di Lesso will see you conducted there, in secret, this very morning. We will do our best for Sforza," Petro Dorma smiled briefly, "partly because I see this as a good investment, and partly because he sent me a physician and, as a prisoner, a poisoner."

Rimini

Count Andrea's spies, he had often felt, were overpaid and inadequate. This time, however, they had paid a handsome dividend. "Collapsed! Taken to Cantu Castle, with his personal physician, and the place shut up tighter than a siege! And the bastard get of Filippo Maria's saying that it is not too bad and all he needs is rest, and she'll be running the duchy to take the weight off his shoulders while he recovers! Ha. As if a woman could. Well, our allies were wavering and fading but this will put new heart in everyone. Without Sforza, they are lost."

He hastened to send out messages to the committed and to those who had been quietly withdrawing their support. To Florence, where Cosimo de' Medici still vacillated. That letter was a particular pleasure. Andrea despised the man, but he did have access to vast wealth, and they needed that.

Within two days, they would start to push into Milanese territory.

Chapter 40

Milan

Count Laglissio was a quivering jelly before Lucia's rage. "I thought you needed to know," he protested.

She paused seconds from ordering his death. She'd set her guards to the work of improving the attitude and morale around the palace. There'd been some show of fear and nervousness about that stupid pig being sick. Some beatings and a couple of summary executions had sorted that out. And then Laglissio had brought her this copy of Count Andrea's letter with every appearance of pride! The insulting reference to her had brought her to screaming rage. As if Milan's resistance to their armies would just fall over under her leadership! As if she were a figurehead and a sop! She'd show them. But...

He was... somewhat right. She did need to know.

"Let go of him," she said to the guards. "I do need to know what these fools think. You seemed pleased. That was your mistake."

"I was just pleased we had managed to get a copy of their document, Your Grace. It wasn't easy. The troops are already moving. Who should I notify...?"

Lucia stared at him, her eyes narrowed. The truth was she had no idea at all. Neither Sforza nor her father had ever let her into their confidences about the military and she'd had no real interest anyway. They were stupid games men played at, away from the real business of court politics. One told the condottieri and they dealt with it. Only... that was Sforza. She had not the faintest idea how the chain of command worked below him. She

302
Eric Flint & Dave Freer

thought that Sforza had his own network of spies for military matters. But now...these fools could threaten her with their stupid, clumsy military methods allowing no time for the mechanisms of politics, poison and suitably instilled fear and respect.

Sss, the great serpent has devoured many armies. He is hungry for them.

"Go to the central barracks. Have the senior officer there report to me," she said tersely to Laglissio. She turned to her senior bodyguard, one of those she'd had the asp hypnotize to utter loyalty. "I will need to increase the palace guards. Find more men."

Others might have questioned her, asked who or how many, but the asp had seen to that not happening. Later that afternoon, a lieutenant from the central barracks came to see her. After a suitable interval, she had him escorted in. He limped forward and made his bow. "Are you the senior officer here?" she asked incredulously.

"Yes, Your Grace. Almost all of the troops are on deployment."

She extracted the little the lieutenant knew, that there was a plan which Captain Turner and Di Nebbiolo seemed to be working to. He wasn't privy to the details, but yes, they knew that a counterattack was under way. He seemed quietly confident. She demanded to know why there were not more troops dedicated to the safety of Milan, and her person.

He blinked. "But then they'd know we were losing, Your Grace. You can be sure their spies report on our troop movements when they can. We're laying siege to two of their fortresses right now: Terdona and San Donnino. Better they worry about those than think of conquering Milan."

"And if those fall?" she asked.

"Well, I suppose they'd be scared about who would be next."

After the lieutenant left, the serpent stirred in her bosom. *They will, if you tell me to make it so. The rats like a siege.*

What rats had to do with it, she had no idea, but there was a sweetness in the concept of making their towns fall. It would be a kind of vengeance. "I think Terdona should die. I did promise the great serpent more."

Orkise will need to be told, by you. That is the bargain. But it does not know towns or limits easily.

"I command it and set the limits."

Oh, yes. Of course.

Then it would be done. But right now she needed dresses with looser waistbands. Filippo Maria's child was taking up too much space in her belly and was starting to take up space where her lungs needed it, making her short of breath. She would spend a day or two getting more clothes, making Milan know that she had no fear, and that, if anything, they had to fear her.

A few floggings and a few visits by the asp were called for, and she had a list of suitable courtiers for her work, which she must see to. Tomorrow she could go back to Arona and give the orders.

She needed more allies, too. It was time to call in the nobility and the Church. The Church could be useful. The Hypatians she'd heard were ascendant, and the Church wielded a lot of influence on the minds of the masses. She'd heard that the Hypatians wanted to expand at the expense of their Pauline rivals. She'd send letters to both, inviting them to send a delegation to Milan. She could play them against each other.

Francisco returned to Milan from Venice with alacrity. He realized that Venice spent a lot on spies who were considerably more efficient at it than Sforza's handful of agents had been. He was back with the escort waiting for him in San Penti within hours—in fact they'd barely gotten there. As it happened to be the easiest route to Pavia, he passed through the city of Milan.

There was a squad of soldiers in peacock blue and gold uniforms drilling. Well, ineptly trying to drill. "Has some sort of traveling fair come to town?" he asked one of his escort.

"They're Her Grace's new City Guard," explained the man, his tone carefully expressionless.

"I'm terrified we'll be out of a job," said Francisco wryly. They passed a few other signs of the duchess's new order, but there was a telling one at the city gates. There were quite a few carts with more-than-just-moving-cargo about them, clues such as a songbird in a cage, or a pet pug on a lead on the seat. A couple of those on the cart seats had skullcaps and long sidelocks.

"Not good. The Jews are leaving," said Francisco.

"Nobody cares if they do," said one of the other officers.

"The more the fool you, then, Voccia. They are always the people who get hammered first, when things go wrong. So they've gotten really good at reading the signs that something is about to erupt."

He dismounted and walked over to the nearest cart, motioning his guard back. He recognized the man as a jeweler, one he'd had occasional dealings with when turning campaign loot into cash. He smiled in what he hoped was a disarming manner. The man plainly recognized him as well, and did not regard him as a threat, judging by his posture and tone.

"And who will I sell to next time?" asked Francisco casually.

"Ah, Captain Turner...well, I am sure there will always be someone."

"Why are you leaving, David?"

The jeweler looked around cautiously. "It's a good time to do so, Captain. The new duchess..." Then he thought better of it "I just see opportunities elsewhere."

"Carlo Sforza would prefer you to see them here."

"So would I. But she's here and he isn't, if you take my meaning," said the man, now plainly nervous. "I never did you any wrong, Captain."

"True enough. Well, matters will settle soon. Carlo should sort things in weeks if not before, so I hope you'll be back."

"If they did, I would," said the man fervently. "I like Milan. Good place to do business."

"What is happening? I ask so that I can put a stop to it."

"Floggings, arrests. They were owed money and asked..."

"Sforza pays his debts."

"Oh, not the Lord Protector, or even the duchess. It was other people of influence. Favorites at the new court. I've said enough, Captain. I just want to get out that gate and down to Venice for a while. Go now, while I can, with my son and his new wife and no one getting hurt, before anything gets worse."

Three hours later, Francisco was in Pavia, at a council of war with the senior captains in Carlo's army, who had taken over a tavern for the purpose. The owner of the tavern didn't seem particularly aggrieved by the situation, which indicated that the officers were paying for whatever they consumed and the rooms they'd be using as billets. That was Sforza's normal policy, and Francisco was a bit relieved to see that discipline hadn't—so far, at any rate—slipped significantly.

The situation wasn't pretty though. The degree to which they relied on the reputation of the Wolf of the North was apparent in the worry on the faces, here, in private. The news that he was sick, or possibly, as rumor always grew, dead, had put new heart into their foes. They waited on Francisco's news like hungry dogs.

"The one thing I can tell you is that the physician he's with has halted the decline in the other patient who had been poisoned in the same way. She was slowly dying, but he's stopped that. He knows how to do that now, and Carlo had less time to survive before that corner got turned. My physician friend hasn't got a cure yet, but if anyone can develop it, he will. We just need to hold it all together until then."

Francisco said all that with every ounce of the calm conviction he had ever mustered to comfort a dying man. It sometimes worked there, and to a degree, it worked here. Soon they were busy discussing, planning, and working on ways to hold the principality and its territories. It was a big task, but they were tough men.

"And the sieges on Terdona and San Donnino?" he asked.

"We keep them up as long as we can. That shows that we're not retreating."

Florence

Archimandrite Klaus von Stebbens had wondered about the sense of the order to move to Florence. Apparently someone in Mainz had decided that the Venetian doge was entirely too sympathetic to the usurper, Carlo Sforza. And now they were dealing with Cosimo de' Medici, who made an eel seem like the shagreen on a sword hilt.

Finally, however, they had signs that Mindaug was coming out into the open with his magic use. "He summoned some ancient river monster, a killer of men," said Heinrich von Tarnitz.

"Back to his usual work, I see," said Von Stebbens grimly. "I am still getting nowhere with de' Medici, but I do have an interesting lead. Our host, the patriarch Adam, informs me that the Hypatians have had an invitation from Duchess Lucia to send a delegation to Milan to discuss the opening of a chapter there. God moves in mysterious ways. I have sent a request to Rome, begging that we could accompany such a mission, to protect them in the civil strife, and also to show that the old Pauline-Peterine rift is healing. We shall have to wait on their reply."

Arona, Duchy of Milan

Lucia made her return to Castello di Arona in fine style, accompanied by three hundred of her new civil guard. She liked the new uniforms. They were remarkably fashionable, which would draw recruits. The designer had been good at interpreting her wishes.

The castello looked even smaller and dowdier now. Imagine having been doomed to live out her life there! It was largely shut up, too, and as she had not sent word ahead, the caretaker and his family were badly prepared. His surviving family would pass the word around to prevent that from happening again.

Somehow, stepping over his dead body made going down into the cellars, alone, much easier. She'd told her guards not to allow anyone in there, and she had the castello to herself...

Herself and the serpent, Orkise.

Down in the inky blackness, it spoke before she did.

"You have come to turn me loose, at last. My appetite is whetted; I hunger. I must feed." Sibilant as ever, the serpent's voice seemed stronger, and more terrible now. It was followed by the echoing sound of many scurrying feet, and the occasional chitter.

"Rats..." She liked them possibly less than snakes.

"Yessss. My legions, and their legions on them, and their legions within them. Death to our foes and food to me."

"So long as they stay a long way from me. I want you to destroy a town. It holds out under siege."

"Most towns are alike to me. The names change. How would I know which one?"

She hadn't thought of that. "Terdona... you must know where Terdona is!" She would have to do something about that. What was the use of a weapon that could not find its target? Perhaps some stone from there...

"Ah, yessss. That I may. It was once called Derthona and stood to defend the crossroads between Genoa and Placentia on the right bank of the Scrivia. I ravaged it before, when I was in strength and new. The river was in flood and carried the corpses to the Po. Yessss. I remember it well. It will have the honor of being my first great sacrifice. Go, my legions, go. I will emerge and destroy."

And the distant rustle and chitter had become a mighty flood of rat sounds in the darkness.

Lucia fled the rats, her belly wobbling as she ran.

Venice

Marco had agonized over this course for some time. But as the Lion, he had little choice. He had gone to the new prison, to a cell where he had set wards and, to the best of his power, traps for anyone or thing that tried to escape.

The mirror had the spells written on it, in tiny script along the margin. They were enough of an "address" for the Lion of Etruria, looking into the mirror and calling on his will. A cool mist boiled from the mirror face, which cleared to reveal the face of a white-haired and heavily moustached man, looking very startled and extremely wary.

"My old master would have given anything for this opportunity," said the man. "It is very dangerous, Signor Valdosta. You need better warding, despite your strength."

Marco knew that. He also knew that there were few people who could teach him such magic. Eneko Lopez had set him on the path, and made him practice. He had, and had taken those skills as far as he could without further teaching. "You sent me Carlo Sforza, and some cryptic writings."

"Yes. There is more information, but it is scattered in many books, and distorted. I had hoped that that would be sufficient."

"Sufficient for me to recognize the enemy. Not sufficient for me to identify the cure."

"It's a kenning, an alternate meaning to the words. At that time, the reference would have been obvious. The thread is the thread of life, and the rose garden is what lies beyond, tended by a guardian of the dead. It is literally a place of souls, growing, tended. Possibly a place of passage, where the bloom of those who die before they have had a chance to flower in life can do so. A belief to shelter those whose beloved daughter, or brother, or parent was taken too soon, the promise they had unfulfilled, so it could not be weighed in the afterlife. Belief gives substance, as we know. The small rose garden exists—or did—but it is beyond my reach."

"Also possibly beyond mine. And yes, I can see that the lives Orkise cut off as the plague might be considered that, and bloom there."

"Orkise moves. I detected it today. I prepare to move myself and my retainers, and place ourselves at your mercy." The white-haired, sharp-faced man smiled—or at least that was what his eyes and cheeks suggested. "They are what you would term good people. I would ask that you deal fairly with them, and in exchange I will give you what help I can against Orkise."

"I cannot guarantee what the Doge will do."

"Then we will stay away as long as possible, until we are certain we either can do so no longer, or until you need us badly. Do you have any more questions for me? This is dangerous for both of us, especially me."

"No. Goodbye." Marco severed the magical connection.

The mirror was left to lie on the cell floor.

Chapter 41

The border of the Duchy of Milan

Francisco Turner turned his anxiety into hard riding and hard work. The days after his return had been a crisscrossing of Milanese territory. Summer had arrived, although the heat was still not intense, and the countryside was now green and lush. But Francisco barely noticed, he was so concentrated on the tasks at hand.

All those who saw him, bar a small handful of senior officers who knew otherwise, thought that he was the eyes and ears and, indeed, the mouth of the commander, and that he was carrying his instructions and carrying reports back to the master's sickbed in Cantu. Francisco wished that it were true. He always had to give reports of Carlo's progress and was frequently castigated for leaving his bedside. If only they knew how much he wanted news himself, and how little he'd wanted to leave!

Still, it was working. The inevitable reaction to the news, and the new heart it had put into the enemies of Milan, had not let them progress much. Pelta had beaten off an attempt on Peschiera del Garda, and instead crossed the river himself and held territory as far as Valeggio sul Mincio.

Of the two sieges, the one at Borgo San Donnino had been broken, but the enemy had not managed to advance from there, and they'd taken the fortress at Fogliani in lieu. Terdona, waiting on help from Genoa or the duke of Parma, had had the relief force resoundingly beaten off. Francisco rode there to investigate how things stood now.

Borghetti had been wounded in the attempted relief, but Francisco was relieved to see that the injury was not too serious. "I hope you're sending us more men," said the young lieutenant, his arm in a sling and his back perched against the wall of a still-intact farmhouse. From there, they had a good view of the besieged town. "Terdona is ready to fall. They're getting desperate in there. By the noises, people are dying. There's been a fair bit of wailing and crying going on. We've been able to hear it for four days now."

"Let's get a bit closer and have a look at the walls. Carlo likes a full report on the state of the defenses," said Francisco. "It's a bit early for them to be starving and desperate, surely?"

A soldier helped Borghetti come to his feet. "They might have had an outbreak of disease or something," said the lieutenant.

Francisco felt something in his stomach go cold. He didn't want to believe this. But not wanting something never stopped things from happening.

"Let's get a bit closer," was all he said.

There were entrenchments and earthworks, manned by Sforza's troops, in harquebus range. From these the ramparts of the city were clearly to be seen—battered but largely intact. Francisco knew why: Sforza had been using the town as bait, making its relief bleed the foes, for little gain. He'd planned to take Borgo San Donnino in their normal style, and that, too, had not worked out. Well, his strategy was in tatters, but they couldn't let the enemies know that, and perhaps they should smash into this little town instead.

Something arced over the battlements and landed on the open sward between the lines. It was a body, limbs and face puffy and swollen. The fall had burst the cotte open, and as it lay sprawled, the white chest was exposed to the besiegers.

"They're so desperate they're throwing their dead at us," said the lieutenant.

Francisco knew already, even before he stared intently at the corpse, what he would see there. And he did, just as it had been described in the text. He could see the purple bubo next to the armpit just down from the breast.

"Has anyone gone anywhere near those bodies?" he demanded, his voice harsh.

"Not yet. I was going to get some of the men to drag them

into a pit tonight under cover of the darkness. They don't shoot much in the dark."

"They won't shoot much at all at anyone now," said Francisco grimly. He looked around to make sure they were not overheard. "Nine out of ten are dead or will be soon. There's a deadly disease loose in that town, and we need to make sure that it stays there. They'll sue for surrender soon. We grant no quarter. We accept no surrender. Shoot any living thing that comes out of there, anything at all. And I want that sward and those bodies burned to a crisp ash. Now, to the disposition of your men. The people in there won't be able to fight much. I want your most injured, but those still able to shoot, for the inner cordon. They're to stay here for six weeks, and if they contain it... every one of them will be a rich man. But for that time, not a man is to leave. We will form a second perimeter to defend the town from relief and to shoot any man who tries to leave until that quarantine is lifted."

He looked at the horrified lieutenant. "We have to do it," he said quietly. "This must stop here. It must."

Lieutenant Borghetti nodded. "Those purple marks. It is the Plague of Justinian, isn't it?"

Still, a millennium later, they remembered the horror. Stories passed down, generation to generation. There was no point in lying now. No point in anything except stopping it. "Yes."

"Then I will take charge of the inner perimeter. I know the men to pick and who to put on the outer ring that will shoot us down if we try to leave."

Francisco looked at the young man, a younger son of minor gentry, a boy who had joined Sforza because there were few other options for younger sons, and because the Wolf had a reputation for derring-do and victory. Not the sort of young cub you expected to suddenly turn into a lion. "By the authority vested in me by our commander, you are now Captain Borghetti. If we get out of this alive, and contain the disease here, I'll see to it that Carlo honors that."

"If that happens, I might get around to being glad I am a captain," said Borghetti wryly.

Chapter 42

Venice

The lights on the mastheads had been sighted from the Lido lagoon barrier islands at dusk. The fleet was nearly home. Marco greeted the news with great relief. There were several reasons for that, not all to do with the joy of having his sister-in-law, of whom he was enormously fond and respected a great deal, in the house. His Katerina loved Maria dearly, and Alessia was a delight. But it had been a long time.

And then there was the still-present desire of a lot of Venice's people to go to war with Milan. Others might want the fleet home for that; Marco wanted it home to stop that. His brother Benito wielded a great deal of influence with the people.

Then there were the issues of the possible disease and dealing with it.

Finally, there was the fact that a day of research—after consulting as many experts as he could—had left Marco convinced that Mindaug had been correct. Laurin's rose garden was indeed some kind of kenning for a borderland of the dead, and one you could just see but never reach. The dawn light over the mountains of Tyrol was supposed to provide a glimpse of it. He wanted to ask Maria about Aidoneus and for help of some kind, but she had heard the news about the ships, too, and like most of the city, the excitement was not making her easy to talk to. And that one was a *turn and walk away from you* issue, it seemed. He'd explained about the rose garden, and had tried four times now to ask her if there was any way she could ask Aidoneus about it. But just mention of that name brought his sister-in-law's shutters down.

So he'd have to ask Benito to ask her—or hope she'd be easier to talk to in a day or two. He thought his patients had that day or two, for both had stabilized. There was some tissue necrosis around the bite on Sforza, but at least Marco knew how to deal with that effectively now.

And also, well, he just wanted his brother back. Benito had been all Marco had, back in tough times. That sort of bond endured.

He was not surprised that while the ships had yet to cross the shifting sandbars around the Lido islands into the shallower waters of the lagoon—a process which few captains would undertake in the dark—his brother showed up, just before midnight.

Benito tapped on his window, three stories up in the *Casa* Montescue, hanging like a bat from a beam, grinning from ear to ear.

Marco opened the window and Benito dropped in. "I wasn't too sure which was Maria's window. Besides, she'd probably shoot a window-tapper first and ask questions later."

"She's asleep. Alessia was very lively today."

"Well, I'll wake Maria in a minute or two, and I am glad to hear my daughter is keeping you all busy. I've only got a few hours and I'll need to get back to the fleet for the triumphal return. We nearly didn't have a fleet after that storm. Now my official excuse for getting a galetta to risk the bar in the dark is that I wanted to check things out and make sure all was well in Venice so at least if we sailed into a hornet's nest, Enrico and I were prepared. Anything I should know?"

"A lot—but most of it will take more than a few minutes. We have the possibility of war, and worse, the possibility of a terrible disease—the plague—in Milanese territory."

"Has Sforza gone mad? I thought he'd had enough of fighting Venice."

"Carlo Sforza is in my infirmary in the Doge's palace, in a coma caused by a magical snakebite."

Benito whistled softly. "Phew. No wonder we were wanted home. Will he recover?"

"I don't know. I've managed to stabilize him—both of them—but I've still got no cure. Maria might be the only person who can help, but right now the subject is off limits. Without the petals from the rose garden of Laurin, I doubt it."

"What?"

"Ask Maria. They're something that don't really exist in this world, as they are in some place on the border of death. I asked her if she could speak to Aidoneus about it and got the total stonewall. It is all that can save him, and possibly us, from disease and war."

Benito pulled a wry face. "I see life is as simple as ever. How is my daughter, besides lively?"

"Very well indeed. Noisy, permanently active, loving. A darling, but quite a handful, Benito. And you'll be an uncle soon, too, by the way."

Benito hugged his brother and slapped his back. "Now there is a job I feel right up to! I can't wait to tell your child about all the things you did as a child that you would like to pretend you never did. Now take me to my wife. I've got a boat to get back to well before dawn."

So Marco led him to the right doorway.

Maria had been having difficulty sleeping, despite the fact that Alessia had had her on the run all day. The ships were due in tomorrow. She longed for Benito.

She'd just slipped off into a sleep full of complicated dreams when Benito arrived...which was probably simpler than the awkwardness of meeting him at the quay surrounded by thousands of people. Then she might not have sat up and into his arms, and hugged him quite so desperately, which was the best way of telling him the really important thing she had to say: "Oh, Benito, I've missed you so badly."

"Now, love, you'll get over it soon. Be back to throwing plates at my head in no time," he said, stroking her shoulders. "And I'm sorry Marco and Kat have been so horrid to you."

"Of course they haven't. Your brother got all the good parts and you got all trouble-making and...oh, Benito. I love you."

"I love you, too, Maria. And very I'm pleased to be home."

"I don't think Venice is my home anymore," she sighed.

"Home is where you and my daughter are, dear. Anyway, my grandfather wants us to go to Ferrara."

"Ferrara? Why?"

"Why not? It's his city and he approves of my wife. Besides, he wants me to be his heir."

"I'm ... not your wife."

"Well, as you said, things have changed, so maybe you could become that now. What has happened there?"

"It wasn't working. I have arranged things differently. I told Aidoneus that it had to change. That he had to have a full-time wife. And that it couldn't be me."

He was silent for a while. Then he said in quite a different tone: "I am not sure I understand this. There was an agreement between the three of us."

She was about to say that it had nothing to do with him, when she realized that it did. "I have arranged for him to have a full-time bride. That is all. Someone from Venice who can worship him properly."

"And he was happy with this?" Benito asked.

"It is not his choice. I decided. He's a good man—well, male god—and deserves more."

Benito sighed. "I'm not following this at all. I didn't know it was about choosing. I thought it was a bargain that had to be honored."

Maria swallowed. "I thought you'd be pleased!"

"I am. But you're a canaler. So, by upbringing, am I. That's not how we make our bargains."

"It wasn't good for him!"

"Did he agree with you?"

"Ask him!" she said angrily. Damn Benito. He always did this to her. It had all seemed a good thing for everyone. Aidoneus had agreed! Well, if she found him another bride. Sort of agreed.

"Very well," said Benito. He turned his head. "Aidoneus, did you agree to this change in the bargain between the three of us?"

The god of the Halls of the Dead took misty form in the candlelight. Then gradually he became the man she'd spent four months as the bride of. He bowed slightly in greeting. "In my own way."

"Which, if I remember rightly, isn't straightforward," said Benito grimly. "What is the catch? I didn't agree to any changes and this is my bargain as much as Maria's."

"I would insist on your being party to the new bargain," said Aidoneus. "Maria offered to find a new bride, a bride who would remain with me all year around. Actually, she offered to find me many. Of course, that cannot be, but one, a suitable one, might be acceptable, although I was ... hurt, yes, a mortal feeling, but accurate. So I agreed that, if by the appointed time she had done so, we could make a new bargain. I did not tell her what my terms would be."

"You *testa di Cazzo!*" yelled Maria. "You . . . you . . ."

"She'll throw things any minute," said Benito, which immediately stopped her doing so.

"It makes no matter, Benito," said Aidoneus. "She has found me more worshippers . . . but not another bride to replace her."

Maria felt her mouth fall open. "What! There's that girl who is doing her best to clean herself up and live up to you. All she wants is a bit of comfort . . ."

"That may be what she wants. It is not what I need."

"Ah," said Benito. "So just what do you need? Or what don't you need?"

"Both fit together," said Aidoneus. "Until recently, I had only had what Maria seems to think I need again: women seeking escape. Women who fill my empty halls with endless 'I am not worthy' and averting their eyes, and telling me how they adore my mother, who is also a goddess they worship. She is my mother. I love her, I lend her my strength. But I know her, and they don't. I know I am a god. I know my need. I need their help to also be a man, bound to humanity."

"Oh," said Maria, thinking she'd encouraged the woman to worship.

Aidoneus nodded, understanding. "Yes. Not quite what I sought. Benito Valdosta, Maria was like a breath of fresh air for me. She did not worship me at all, she lost her temper often, she cared about all sorts of things that had nothing to do with the dead—and spent very little time in the rituals they've made up in the pursuit of fertility. You and I know what gets women pregnant, and it isn't just offerings and dances and prayers. The rituals help the mind, and that helps the body, but bodies have also gotten pregnant without it always, and will go on doing so. That's what women do, with the ones they desire, with the ones they love. What I got was the women who in your world become nuns. Very devout, and ready to give up the world. That's what Maria has 'arranged' for me to have more of."

"That was what I thought you needed—willing, eager devotees," said Maria, "instead of desperate sad women, who took the almond as a last resort. That's what I tried to do, to arrange for you."

"Willing, yes; eager, yes. Devotees? No," said Aidoneus. "You were very different from what I'd had for ... millennia, now. Can you imagine, an endless stream of devout women ready to leave the world and live alone as a bride with the Lord of the Dead?"

"Enough to make a fellow wish he were dead," said Benito with a wry smile. "I know what you mean. Women who say 'Oh, my husband would not like that.' They never ask him, or really know much about him. They play doormat, and put the fellow on a pedestal and treat him like some minor god. Some men like it. The weak and the insecure, particularly. The ones who are master of nothing, with no skill and no place, outside of their marriage. Such woman are good brides for weaklings. But not for me—and not for you."

Aidoneus didn't see the humor of it, he just nodded in agreement. "I thought they were all like that. Endless dripping wells who tried to worship me in between their crying. What the Halls of Dead need is life, striving, full of desires and laughter and determination, and not women training to be dead. Women who are people, not just a shadow of their husband. I have, since Maria, been studying them, among humans. There are many who add little but worship of their partners. I have no need of that from my wife. I have been looking into the threads of the lives of men. A man wants someone he can worship, too, and who can stand at his back and fight when things are desperate."

"That sounds like my ... our wife," said Benito.

"Yes," said Maria, still angry, partly with herself, partly with Benito, and partly with Aidoneus. "That's all very well, Benito, but Aidoneus needs a worshipper to do this. Going to live with the dead is not easy. They need some reason. They're afraid of the dead, and there's not much there for a woman. No company, no children, no shops ..."

Aidoneus looked thoughtful, as if these were things his kingdom lacked which had never occurred to him. "But yet many is the woman—or man—who forsook all those to be with someone, who went out into wild lands and built and dreamed and ... were alive. Yes, there is a kind of worship there. A kind of wishing to be worthy. But it's not that given to a god. I have seen that."

"It's called love, and you can't get it made for you," said Benito. "You want what I found."

"I suspect you are right. Unfortunately, that is what I would consider a better bargain. One I would be willing to unmake my old bargain for, without traps or conditions."

Benito scratched his head. "Look. I can help you. But I can't do it for you. And I'm an expert on this, which you aren't, because I'm human and you're not. You see, you'll have to go out and find it, Aidoneus. And I promise you, it's not always easy or smooth. It's worth it when you do find it, though."

There was a silence from the god. And then he said slowly: "Go ... and find a bride?"

"That's generally what men do," said Benito. "Unless it is an arranged marriage. And if you think about it, maybe that's what has been wrong for you all these years. Why don't you try it?"

There was a longer silence. And then the god of the Halls of the Dead nodded. "I accept your help, Benito Valdosta. And your advice. If I can find a bride ..."

"Then you can invite us to the wedding," said Maria. "And I'll try to introduce you to some candidates ..."

"But they must not know I am a god, or what power I wield, who my mother is, or what a terrible task I must do."

"If they love you and accept you and all of that, you'll have found someone worth having. It's not impossible. Maria accepts me, and I'm not all joy."

"You can say that again," grumbled Maria, but deep inside she felt like getting up and dancing. She hadn't realized that this had been what was troubling her, or why or how. "But I love him anyway, Aidoneus."

Benito decided it was time to change the subject, now that a resolution seemed to have been reached. "I gather my father is here and sitting at death's door. I don't know whether to be upset or pleased. He isn't quite what I thought he was."

"What did you think he was?" asked Aidoneus.

"When I was a little kid, a god. And after Mama and he fought, a monster out to kill us all. And now I find out that he was just a man."

"Marco wanted me ask you, Aidoneus, about the rose garden of Laurin," said Maria, glad now to escape the conflict of emotions and, she had to admit to herself, a little guilt.

"The dwarf. In a way, Laurin is a vassal. It is a matter of appearances really. He is his own master, and the master of any man—as long as he has his belt of strength on."

"Well, apparently the petals from this rose garden are supposed to be a cure."

"They could be. Do you know what the rose petals are? They are the virtues of the too-soon dead. The dead need their full bloom to go beyond. And yet some would gladly give that bloom to the living."

"Probably to the living that they loved," she said.

"Yes. Considering the matter makes me think you are right, Maria. But Laurin does not allow that choice to happen easily. I will speak with him, but I think it unlikely he will agree."

The next morning brought the triumphal return of the fleet. And if anyone thought the hero Benito Valdosta looked half asleep, no one mentioned it. Well, no one bar the Doge and that in a private interview, later. Benito smiled and blamed it on anticipation of seeing Venice and his darlings.

Chapter 43

The Duchy of Milan

Francisco Turner was a very worried man, riding away from the dying city of Terdona. Nothing could be done to save it, he knew—which was just rendered all the more horrible by the fact that, once you got a short distance away, the countryside of the Po Valley was as verdant as it always was in late spring and early summer. Farmlands alternated with mixed stands of oak and hornbeam, with elderberries scattered here and there.

Combining the facts in his head with what he knew of Carlo's poisoner, and what the man he knew as Kazimierz had said, he knew they faced desperate times, which called for desperate measures. He rode with his escort first to Val di Castellazzo. There he was greeted by the ever grateful Emma, and taken to see Kazimierz, who was at his desk surrounded by books.

Francisco did not beat about the bush. "There has been an outbreak of plague in the town of Terdona, a town we had under siege. I've burned the sward around it, and put a guard on it that should see nothing leaves it alive."

Kazimierz closed his eyes and sighed. Then, he put his hands to his head. "I knew it had happened. And her power and that of Orkise have grown as a result. The agony of death feeds them both, because she is being devoured by Orkise."

"You said she was the only person who could control this monster. We need to capture her and force her to make it go away. I can bring all of Sforza's troops to bear on this, if need be. We outnumber her little guards, and we're real soldiers. I think we will need your help, though. You're the only one who seems to know what we're dealing with."

Kazimierz pulled his hands down from his temples and steepled his fingers. "The Lion of Etruria—your friend Valdosta— knows. His strength within his demesne may suffice; yours—or mine—would not. What do you think I have been working at here? Traps. Ways to constrain, without us dying. I don't think you understand, and possibly she does not either, but Orkise will soon be out of his lair. The serpent will stalk the countryside, driving its legions, who, if the text is correct, bear their legions, and those legions each carry legions. I don't know quite what that means, but it suggests that Orkise will command enough force to overbear all of Sforza's men. What I do know is that some form of compulsion is being laid on her minions. They will fight to the death for her, and cannot be reasoned with."

"Then we need a clever trap, one that can separate her from her men. She's just a woman—"

"I have heard slightly stupider statements, but not many," interrupted Kazimierz crossly. "Elizabeth Bartholdy was also 'just a woman' and she could have killed fifty men on her own, before she called on the power at her command. This woman is, if anything, slightly worse in that she is already partly dead and cannot be saved. The poison of Orkise is in her veins. Not even black lotos could do much more to her mind. If she is hurt by a knife or an arrow or bullet, her body will be weakened and she could die. And if she dies, Orkise will be loose, without any leash. She is also not without the ability to kill or infect. Lucia carries in her bosom a snake. I know, because I have seen it. It must be a part of Orkise. It would be lightning fast to strike, and I believe it can call the serpent to her rescue."

It was Francisco's turn to sigh. "So then, what do you think we should do? We have to do something."

"Burn Terdona. Burn it as hot as you can. Orkise, it seems, does not like fire. In the meanwhile, I am working on magical traps. There are many but there is little information as to what the power of Orkise can merely override."

"There will still be some live people in Terdona. Possibly women or children. The plague doesn't kill quite everyone."

"I know. But wars kill women and children, and grandmothers, and people like me, who just happen to be passing through this one, without intent. The plague is worse. It does not even try to target soldiers, but kills indiscriminately."

"I'll call a council with Sforza's senior officers...and send a message to Venice."

"Do that. But give me a token of yourself. Something you have worn close to your skin. If I find an answer or a way to entrap her, I will summon you."

"You are actually a very powerful magician, aren't you? What are you doing here?"

Kazimierz grimaced. "Believe it or not, I came here looking for a place to grow old peacefully. I have been avoiding using magic so as not to call attention to myself. If it had been any-thing else—a new Elizabeth Bartholdy, even a new Jagiellon—I would just have moved on to some other place. But the plague will destroy too much. When there is no fuel, people burn books. When there is no food, they die or eat each other. There is no trade, and precious little your gold will buy. It affects everyone, everywhere. There really is no 'other place' when this disease ravages."

Florence

Archimandrite von Stebbens received the message and the mes-sengers from Rome two days after the thaumaturgic watch had been effectively destroyed. The glass orb they'd been using had melted abruptly, and gobbets of melted glass had hit the blessed water and exploded into daggerlike shards. The Knights doing the ritual would have been killed, but for the armor Von Stebbens had insisted they wear.

What they had seen—the vast bruise-purple serpent—had told them that Mindaug had succeeded in his purpose.

The riders from Rome were nearly exhausted. It was a very long way in a short time for clerics. But they, too, knew that something—something that had been killing eagerly—was on the loose in northern Italy. Now was not the time for bickering between factions in the Church...or anyone else.

"I am Father Thomas Lüber of Baden," said the tired man, accepting an arm to help him stand, as he almost fell after dis-mounting. "I have with me a letter of authority from the Grand

Metropolitan in Rome, responding to Duchess Lucia Sforza's invitation. And in response to your request, you are to be my escort."

"It will show unity in the Church, where she sought to sow discord—and will get us into striking distance of Count Mindaug."

"That is the Grand Metropolitan's intent, but I beg of you... well, have you anything for saddle sores?" asked the priest plaintively.

"That is an area in which we Knights tend to have more experience than most," said the archimandrite, foregoing a smile. "Contrary to rumor, we are not born in the saddle, but the order does require long training in it. And we will be unable to leave for Milan until early tomorrow morning. Food and rest you must have, Father Thomas."

The next day they set out for Milan.

The seal of the Duchess Lucia did indeed allow them to pass, escorted, into Milanese territory, and into the city itself.

Chapter 44

It was the evening after the fleet had returned, when feasts and celebrations were still the order of the day, and the worries and business of the next few days were yet to come, that the household at the *Casa* Montescue had an unusual visitor. They had all just returned from a sumptuous dinner at the Palazzo Ducale, and the various members of the family were going to bed, when Benito noticed there was someone else in the salon. Just standing there, watching them. Katerina and Lodovico had already left, and Marco was in the act of bidding them a good night.

Not part of the family or a retainer. A man who was dressed in clothes that were, in spy parlance, so ordinary that most people would not have noticed them—certainly in contrast to the men of the *Case Vecchie* dressed for the court of the Doge. A man so ordinary of feature it would be hard to describe him ... except for his eyes.

Maria recognized him first, seconds before Benito. But then, she had seen much more of him. "Aidoneus?"

He bowed slightly. "My lady."

"Why, um ..."

"The appearance? I have certain powers."

"Why are you here in the flesh?" asked Marco, in a voice that said there was more than Marco present. He was not entirely pleased.

Aidoneus bowed, far more deeply. "I ready myself to go courting. To search for a bride who will take me as a man. I

324

would begin that quest here, in your demesne. A gesture, one hopes, of trust."

"That is a great ambition. I grant you permission for your search."

"I gather it is not easy," said Aidoneus.

"No, but the rewards are great," said Benito, a little amused by the appearance of the man.

"You are a lot more handsome than you've made yourself look," said Maria critically, "and it's rather late at night for me to introduce you to anyone."

"I came, rather, to deal with another matter you asked me about, that of the petals from the rose garden of Laurin. I have spoken with the dwarf, and he will permit a mortal to wrestle with him."

"To wrestle?"

"That is his traditional challenge to any who want to gather the petals that the roses let fall. It must be in Tyrol, in his mountain home, before this dawn, in the garden itself. I can guide you thence, through the paths not taken by mortal feet. There are terms, of course."

"There always are," said Benito. "Let's hear about all the tricks and traps, Aidoneus."

"The fight takes place in the rose garden itself. Damaging or breaking flowers, as Witege did, has a proportional cost. In limbs. Eyes. Ears... whatever Laurin can take off and yet leave you alive. And the garden itself is surrounded by a single thread. That thread is your life-thread. If you break it, you will die."

"Well, I don't see what else I can do," said Marco. "Any last-minute tips on wrestling, brother?"

"He will not allow you to go to his garden, Lion. My consort, he cannot refuse, or my consort's partner, because Laurin is some kind of vassal of mine."

"But I can't ask that of you. Either of you," said Marco.

Benito shrugged. "Carlo Sforza is my father, Marco, not yours. Better me than Maria. I think I'm a better wrestler than she would be." Wrestling was something he'd done a little of with Erik Hakkonsen—enough to know that he wasn't all that good at it. "I suppose this Laurin is a champion wrestler, too?"

"I do not believe he is very skilled, actually," said Aidoneus. "With his advantages, he doesn't need to be."

"And what are those advantages?" asked Benito.

"He has a belt of strength that lets him toss people around, and a cloak of invisibility that lets him close with them without them seeing him. And he rides a deer-sized horse, faster and more agile than any mortal steed, but he will dismount to fight a man on foot."

"I think the chances of me fighting on horseback are about the same as the chances of my staying on one. Hmm. Invisibility and a belt..."

"You mustn't do this, Benito. I want you alive, with all your limbs," said Maria firmly.

"There is a reason why he must, Maria," said Aidoneus quietly. "I can tell no man of his passing, but there are points in the weave... Let me say this bluntly. I cannot tell you what will happen, but I value you... and I have met your daughter..."

"He's trying to tell us that the disease will kill Maria and Alessia," said Marco, "and somehow that ties to curing Sforza and Violetta de' Medici."

"You see too much, too well, Lion of Etruria."

"I have advantages that most men do not," said the voice that wasn't quite Marco.

"I would also guess that's why Aidoneus arranged this whole thing," said Benito suspiciously. "He wasn't particularly encouraging yesterday, and now it is suddenly all arranged?"

Slowly, Aidoneus nodded. "I stand in a difficult position. If I could do it myself, I would. But I cannot cross the thread because I have no thread to break. There are no over-too-soon lives blooming on the other side for me or for the mother. It is for mortals, and I am not that. I will lend you aid to get there. But we must go soon, Benito Valdosta."

"If he is going, so am I," said Maria tersely.

"You can't do that, Maria!" protested Marco.

"Why not? If Benito fails, I'm dead and our daughter is dead. What have I got to lose, bar a few limbs? If there are two of us, Benito can keep him busy while I pick flowers. That is very ladylike."

It was difficult to argue with her, and Benito had the intelligence to not even try. "I can think of no greater honor," he said. And then rather spoiled it by saying: "Besides, I can't wait to see you picking flowers like a lady born."

Aidoneus saved him from a thick ear, before the fighting even started, by saying: "Under no circumstances can you pick the flowers! You must take a basket and only gather any petals they let fall."

"And I suppose sticking a knife between this Laurin's ribs is right out, too?" said Maria, crossly.

"He wears koboldwerk, and it is cunningly wrought. He is armed as if he is the greatest of knights, with a magical sword that is always faster than any other, and armor that is proof against any blade. It is magical in its construction, as is his sword. Your only chance is to wrestle with him. He is a small fellow and enjoys flinging men around. He lost against Theoderic, who was clever enough to steal his belt and cloak."

"Koboldwerk." Benito grimaced. "Then I will take a bucket of canal water with me. The only time I've seen Erik in any remote danger of being defeated was when he was upset about getting salt water on his armor. He was so busy thinking about how hard that would be to clean that he wasn't thinking about fighting. And it sounds like I might as well have a bucket with me as anything else."

"Water from my lagoon has my virtue about it, as well as quite a lot of other things," said his brother, who right then was more than his brother. "A joke sometimes has an element of truth in it, and this time I feel it does. You must take that water."

"Get your bucket and your basket—but we must away," Aidoneus said. "We have many miles to cross to be in the high Alps before the dawn, which is the only time that the rose garden touches this world."

Hand in hand, they walked through a grayness that was certainly no part of Venice. It was not fog-shrouded mud, but like it in appearance—and just as depressing and hard to walk though, Benito thought, even if you weren't carrying a bucket of canal water. Personally, he felt that winged horses had more going for them than the ways of the dead, even if it involved being on horseback.

It grew steadily colder and, oddly, even darker...and then there were stars. Staring intently, Benito could just work out where the starry sky ended, and the darker, jagged skyline met it. Underfoot now something crunched...and Benito realized it was the first sound he'd heard for some time.

"I must leave you here," said Aidoneus. "Reach your hand

forward, slowly and carefully, and you will feel the thread. Do not break it, or the only way out will be through Laurin's kingdom. And that is unlikely, so just don't. Step over it and you will find yourselves in the rose garden. Laurin will come to challenge you. You only have until the sun is up."

Benito realized that the light was improving by the second. There was almost a hint of purple above the darker spikes of the skyline. He knew from many nocturnal expeditions that it wasn't actually darkest before the dawn, and that first light was not far off. There was no point in waiting. Besides, it was too cold to stand still.

He let go of Maria's hand with a last squeeze and felt cautiously for the thread. It was a thin strand, quite taut and not hard to step over.

Inside the garden, it was much lighter. Not from the dawn yet, but from the blossoms. They seemed to glow slightly, and there were a vast number of them in a small space. They were growing where no ordinary rose could, into the bare rock and through the drifts of snow. Fighting here without breaking the plants would be very difficult. Benito picked out a monolith of rock, about fifteen feet high, with a little open ground in front of it. "Let's go there, love. It's about the best spot I've seen here to try and fight."

"If you hit him from behind, while I—" started Maria as they walked to it—when she was interrupted.

"Hit who? You can't even find me, hee hee hee!" There was a flick and the cloak's hood was pushed back, revealing a dark-eyed face with a big bulbous nose and a bushy white beard. There was another brushing movement, and the cloak must have been pushed back and there was Laurin, dressed from head to foot in fine chainmail, except for his steel cap. Around his waist was clasped a broad, ornate belt of large golden plates. He carried a two-handed sword . . . casually, in one hand. Laurin himself stood only about four foot high, but the sword was easily half again his height.

Laurin edged his dainty pony forward from behind the roses. "What do you want in my garden?" he demanded as he dismounted gracefully, which Benito could only envy. His own dismounting usually added up to more or less controlled falling off. And unlike Laurin's pony, most of the horses he had anything to do with usually didn't just stand quietly.

"It's a beautiful garden," said Benito, judging his distances and taking in details in the growing dawn light.

"I tend it carefully, and protect it. Have you come to talk or fight?" asked the dwarf.

"To wrestle, if you put down the sword."

"Ho. I thought you had come to water the plants," the dwarf sniggered, as he set the sword down.

In answer, Benito slung the bucket and its contents at the dwarf. He didn't miss with it, either. The dwarf staggered back... and vanished.

"Gather petals," shouted Benito, "while I argue with Shorty." And he jumped sideways and ducked and rolled.

He had some small advantage in that the bare rock showed very clearly where his opponent was, in wet footprints. It was still no way to fight. So he took to what he knew best—the heights. A small ledge, a heave or two, a long reach and he was on the top of the little pinnacle.

"Come down and fight!" yelled a furious voice from the space above the dripping puddle.

"Did you have a nice watering?" said Benito, sticking his tongue out and blowing a raspberry. "Maybe you'll grow now. Come up, if you can reach." He was working on being as annoying as possible, but Maria, instead of gathering petals, had ruined his plan of jumping down behind the dwarf, because she was sneaking up behind Laurin herself, a knife in hand. Benito blew another loud raspberry.

"I'll use you like a scythe! I'll have every limb off you and... *arwh!*"

At this point, Benito jumped down anyway, his intention to hit Laurin as hard as possible, as the dwarf had obviously grabbed Maria. He could tell by the way she was being pulled down. But it was a bit too late for Laurin, as she had cut his belt. Benito's feet hit the invisible dwarf and knocked him down. Maria stumbled free, backward, nearly falling into a rosebush, only just saving herself at the last moment. The cut belt lay on the ground. Now Benito was grappling and rolling on the ground with an invisible, wet, steel-clad foe. A strong one, but not that strong.

"Collect petals!" he yelled. "I can handle this—*ouch! You little bastard!*"

He found an arm and twisted it. Laurin managed to rip away from him and Benito faced a foe he couldn't see—but could certainly feel when Laurin punched him in the stomach. Gasping, he felt a hand grab his cotte, trying to pull him forward. So he sat down, and was lucky enough to sit on the foot Laurin had been trying to sweep him over. The dwarf had no choice but to fall with him. This time Benito's hands found cloth, and he wrenched really hard. The cloak tore off, and Benito could at least see his opponent. Now that he could do that, it was a lot less difficult. Laurin wanted to get up, somehow, to try to throw his opponent around. But Benito stayed down. Even when Laurin broke free and swung a furious kick at his head, Benito managed to duck forward, catch the foot and make the dwarf fall. And then he grabbed hold of him, while Laurin tried to roll the two of them to the flowers. Benito felt the scratch of thorns, which gave him enough strength to roll the other way and pull Laurin under him, and end up sitting astride the dwarf's chest, holding his arms down, while Laurin humped and strained futilely.

It was Benito's first chance to look around. The sky was pink with dawn. Maria was hurriedly scurrying between the rows of rosebushes and sprawling climbers.

"Let me go and I'll take you to my palace beneath the mountain. It is full of treasure," said the dwarf. "You've been lucky so far, but you can't hold me forever."

"I don't want to go beneath your mountain, Laurin. No one comes out of there. And as for treasure, I have mine collecting rose petals. When she's got her basketful, I'll let her get out and then let go of you. Fair?"

The dwarf struggled some more as the red fingers of the dawn transformed the garden. And then, as the first gold of the sun finally sent its rays across the mountains to the garden, Benito found himself sitting down with a wet thump. The garden of roses amid the snow and rocks . . . now had just snow and rocks. And Maria, with a basket of petals, was running to him.

They were in the high Alps, far above Italy, far from Venice. Fortunately, as Benito was fairly wet and it was briskly cold up here, Aidoneus was there. He gave them his hand and led them back into a place that is no place but everywhere.

He brought them out again to the room in *Casa* Montescue, where Marco had plainly spent a very stressful night, waiting.

"We have your petals for you," said Maria, handing him the basket.

Marco looked at the orange-pink petals in the small basket.

"I could only pick up the fallen ones," said Maria. "That was the agreement. There isn't a lot." The scent rising from them was heady, even so.

"The scent of heaven," said Marco.

"In a manner of speaking, perhaps," said Aidoneus. "Heaven obviously means different things to different people. But Diderich's men did use it against Orkise's poison. And now, I must leave you. There is a new day out there, and I must go to meet people." And with that, he faded away like smoke in the new day's sunlight that was streaming through the window.

Benito yawned. "Is Alessia up yet?"

"She'd be here if she was," said Marco, looking up from the basket. "Do you have all your limbs?"

"Amazingly, yes. But don't ask for more petals!" said Maria.

Marco looked critically at the basket of petals. "I think it is too little to make a distillation, really. But perhaps just the smell of them may help. They certainly have a beautiful scent."

"If the smell will help, then you'd better make a little tent over their heads, like Mama used to do with the wintergreen when we were sick. It always made my eyes water and my nose run," said Benito.

"That's a brilliant idea! I'll put their heads together, and put this bowl between them over some hot water. I'd better get it to them at once." Marco took the basket and strode off towards the front door, still talking to himself.

Maria and Benito were left holding hands. Benito moved, and winced. "Are you all right?" asked Maria.

"Yes, I think that little fellow half wrenched my shoulder off."

"Serves you right," she said, kissing it, "for the things you said about me throwing things at Aidoneus."

"I missed you, you know," he said, putting his arm around her. "And you can always wrestle with me and attempt to pull my arms off. I'd enjoy that."

"You probably would!" Maria snorted. "But now let's go upstairs, before we're joined by Alessia. I love my daughter more than breath itself, but she does put a crimp on some things."

Chapter 45

Venice

Carlo Sforza knew he was somewhere very close to the gates of death. Earlier, he had seen a poison-spewing dragon without legs. Then a lion, roaring somewhere in the darkness. It was all very confusing. His last coherent memory was holding that bitch by both shoulders...and the snake lunging at him out of the space between her breasts, going for his face. He'd gotten his arm up in time to save his eyes.

That obviously hadn't saved him, because he was lying here under a scented shroud. At least it did not smell of Lucia's damned scent, and the shroud was slightly raised off his face. But he could see the fine weave of the muslin. He closed his eyes again, and just lay there, breathing. Even that was hard work. He felt as weak as a half-drowned kitten.

After what must have been quite a long time, he tried to move. His muscles seemed to have turned to jelly. Disobedient jelly, at that. Eventually he got his head to turn slightly. Not a handbreadth away, sharing his shroud, was a young woman. At least a young woman's head. He wondered if she were also dead, or nearing it, but by staring intently, he could see that there was just the slightest movement from her nostrils as she breathed...so quietly.

Her eyes were closed and long-lashed, her skin as white as alabaster, her nose aquiline. Those slightly moving nostrils looked almost as if they'd been carved. She had too big a mouth for classical beauty, set above a firm chin. It must be her scent he could smell. He could breathe that forever.

He lay there for a long time trying to focus his mind, trying to work out what was going on. With effort, he worked his mouth...and swallowed. He tried to speak.

The shroud moved aside. Carlo Sforza found himself looking up into a face he hadn't seen for the better part of ten years, but recognized instantly.

"...arco?" was all he managed. The effort was enough to make the world waver and set a roaring in his ears, as darkness closed in again. The roaring seemed to tell him to rest, and that he was safe. He'd known that when he'd seen Marco's face anyway. A good boy, if a little soft.

There was something about his face that had not seemed soft now, though.

Violetta heard the roaring of the Lion as it dueled with the terrible serpent. And there was just the faintest light, somewhere ahead, along with the scent of roses. The strange thing was that it was drawing her away from the rose garden. She struggled towards the light. The weakness was almost too much, but she would not give in. There was a crack of light there...ahead. Just a little more...

It took a while to realize that it was that her own eyelids that needed to open. She opened them to see a handsome, delicate-featured young man looking down at her through a raised veil of fine muslin. He smiled. "Signorina de' Medici, I am glad to see you awake at last. Don't try to move yet. Please be calm and rest. You are safe and getting better."

He put his hand on her shoulder, and then withdrew, pulling the sheet over the reed frame that kept it above her head.

She wondered, briefly, how those long slim hands could be so like vast velveted paws, but she needed that rest still. But it was not darkness and snake-full now, just sleep.

When she awoke again, she was a little more in control of her mind and able to think more coherently. She lay there trying to work out just what was going on. She remembered the snake, her mother being bitten and screaming in agony, and rushing to try to help, before it lunged at her. The pain. The terrible pain and fear. Vague brief images that included her Uncle Cosimo, and a stranger. Not the man who had leaned over her and told her she was safe...but somehow, similar.

Something gave a slight sigh next to her ear. Terror that it might be the snake gave her enough strength to turn her head and open her eyes. It wasn't. It was a man, his head at 180 degrees to hers. He was older than she was, by perhaps two decades. His curly hair was grizzled and he had a solid, chunky, determined face. His skin showed signs of exposure to the sun and wind. He had been shaved, but not today.

She didn't quite manage a scream, but came close. She made enough noise to call someone anyway. The young man lifted the cloth veil again. "Man," she said weakly. "Next to me."

"Ah. Do not worry. That is Signor . . . Carlo. He was also bitten. We have so little of the scent we are using to treat you that both of you have to share it. This is the only little bit that's been available for the last nine hundred years, so I doubt we'll get more. He is on a separate divan, and there are servitors here all the time, my lady. You are perfectly safe. Would you like to try drinking something?"

It hadn't been her virtue that had worried her. More the shock. But she would like to drink something. "Yes. Please."

He helped her to sit up a little. She could not have done it herself. She sipped the watered wine, aware that those watching were smiling and, in the case of the portly little man in the corner, hastily scribbling on a pad, and both beaming and crying. She thought she recognized him. One of Uncle Cosimo's men, perhaps?

"Where am I?" she asked as they let her sink back on the daybed, feeling exhausted, giddy and . . . alive.

"Venice, Signora. In the Doge's palace. I am Marco Valdosta. You were consigned to my care by your uncle and my physician friend, Francisco Turner, who saved your life. I don't know if you remember, but you were bitten by an extremely venomous snake. You are lucky to be alive." He took her pulse. "You need to remain under the tent and continue to breathe in the scent of the roses of Laurin. We don't know how much is needed, and how long it will take for you to recover, and in this case, I believe more is better. Be patient. You have been unconscious for many days."

Carlo Sforza had actually been lying there, awake for some time now, trying to muster the strength for his next move, and also trying to work out just how he thought he had seen Marco Valdosta. Now, listening to that interchange, that at least was clear. It was also clear that Marco was not advertising who he was to Violetta de' Medici. She was actually a pretty girl, not that it mattered now.

Sforza was not too sure how he'd gotten here, or how long he'd been here, but at least he knew where he was. That might not be all that safe in the long run, but was certainly better than being at the tender mercies of his dear wife. He'd bet Francisco had had some hand in getting him here. He must get back to Milan to keep things together there. There were a lot of men relying on him, and that was always something a good commander took very seriously. He relied on them, they relied on him. He did not fail them, and most of the time, they wouldn't fail him either.

His thoughts were interrupted by the tiniest little ladylike snore from his fellow snake victim. He had to smile at that. He'd been told he could snore a house down, so when her turn came she'd have a lot more to listen to.

He tried calling out. "Marco." It came out as a feeble croak, but the man heard him.

"I will speak to M'lord alone," Carlo heard Marco say. "I think you might alarm him."

It was neatly done. The boy had learned Venice's ways.

Marco pulled the tent covering away. "I think that, if you are understanding me clearly, you should keep your identity secret."

"Yes. Drink?"

Marco helped him more upright, pulled a pillow under his head, and held a goblet for him. "A little only."

That was fine. He didn't feel up to quaffing much. The taste of it was very intense... and, perhaps for the first time in his life, his nose wasn't at least partly blocked. Snakebite, as a way to cure catarrh, was never going to be popular though.

"Thank you."

"A pleasure," said Marco, putting it down.

"Not for the drink. For saving my life."

The young man smiled, looking very much as he had when he was ten or so. "Thank Francisco. He brought you to me."

"Where is he?"

"He went back. He said that you had given him the responsibility of seeing you had a principality to return to. I'll send him a message about you, but you must rest now. Breathe as much of the scent as you can. It is very precious."

"I heard. And I will. And . . . thank you again, Marco. I never loved you as much as I should have."

The young man nodded. "But I shouldn't have believed you wanted to kill us, either. Now rest. There will be time to talk later."

He pulled the cushion out, pulled down the tenting fabric, and Carlo Sforza was left to his thoughts and the smell of roses. He thought quite a lot about the past, and about the future. Nearly dying did that to a man. It would make him into a priest yet, he thought wryly. Then, because it was what he would do whenever he had to wait, which was often as a soldier, even as a commander, he began reconstructing campaigns in his head, working out the possibilities, and in doing so fell asleep.

When he awoke again, it was much brighter outside the fabric, and he was feeling a great deal stronger and far more alert than he'd swear he'd felt for months. He was aware of movement outside the little tent. The movers opened it, and it was Marco and two other men.

"Good morning. How are you feeling?" Marco took Carlo's wrist and felt the pulse.

"Better. I could try to get up."

Marco shook his head. "These gentlemen will take you, wash you, shave you, and change your clothes. You will try to do as little as possible for yourself. As I remember, you gave a lot of orders." He smiled slightly. "It is my turn now, and you will please cooperate. Seriously, overdoing it now could set you back—or worse. Your pulse is still fast and not as strong as I would like it."

Carlo nodded. Even that was still an effort. Marco was probably right, drat him. And by the time he returned to the tent, he was glad to simply slip off into sleep.

The young woman was not there when he went to sleep, and was when he woke later. She was being fed some gruel—and being firmly told by Marco: no, she could not feed herself, and that her stomach would have to grow used to solid food first. There was more officer material in the boy than he'd realized. He was given a small meal of steamed fish, which he'd never liked, but found himself hungry for, and told to drink a moderately vile tisane to help clear the poisons out of his system.

Later that day he found himself awake, alert, while still feeling weak lying in the tent. He set about the battle of Bella di Torra and found that, as usual, he could not remember the name of the company of pikemen on the south ridge. He muttered something to himself.

"What?" said the young woman, to whom he had yet to be formally introduced.

"Oh, nothing. I was trying to remember something about Bella di Torra."

"One of Duke Enrico Dell'este's masterpieces," she said.

He was almost as surprised as when the snake had lunged out of Lucia's bosom. "Well, well. I don't suppose you would know the name of the company of pikemen on the south ridge?"

"They were under the command of a Frankish fellow, von Mandelbohm. Four hundred men, mostly Swiss, and a bit green. In my opinion, the battle turned on their inexperience."

If he hadn't been lying down and feeling as if a feather was too much weight to bear, you could have knocked Carlo Sforza down with one. "Yes, I have always suspected Dell'este must have known that."

"He did. They had tried to contract to him that spring," she said.

They covered the campaign in some detail, and then moved on to others. To his secret amusement, Sforza found his own tactics as a junior officer in Balco's company, when he'd been about this girl's age, dissected by her. "Sforza was just lucky and had the confidence of his men. It was strategically stupid. If he'd taken the high ground instead . . ."

Carlo knew he'd been enormously lucky and had had a good sergeant who had dissuaded him from going any further. He'd had a plan. It had been, with twenty years hindsight, a terrible plan, but as a wet-behind-the-ears officer, it had seemed good. He avoided saying too much about it though, and the talk moved on. And then, abruptly, she fell asleep midsentence. Carlo realized he, too, was exhausted, and fell asleep as well.

When he awoke later, he found himself drawn into an argument about armor. She had strong points of view and was not in the least afraid to express them, or to change them—or not—depending on the skill of his argument. She was strong-willed, but not stupidly pigheaded. Both of those were traits Carlo approved of, since he was much the same way himself.

"You are better at this debate than I am. Do you spend all your time sparring the gentlemen of your acquaintance into submission? I detest koboldwerk, but I might even wear it after this."

She paused. "I do not often have the chance. It's not a subject ladies are supposed to know anything about. So I used to argue with Cosimo, and with my father. But Signor Valdosta told me something I don't wish to think about. So I was talking about battles I have never seen. It . . . is easier. My mother is dead, and I don't know how to deal with that. We were very different, and now I regret that I didn't try harder for her. I cried for a month when my father was killed. Now I just feel sad for my mother. And that makes me feel guilty."

"You were very nearly dead yourself. And that drains you. I am glad to talk, if that helps. As long as it is not about fashions. I have always had to confess to ignorance about them. The ladies informed me that I had no taste, which absolutely devastated me."

That got a small snort of laughter from her. "I am sure your knowledge of court gossip redeemed you no end."

"Another of my weak points, alas."

"And no doubt many of them thought you were boring as a result of these confessions. I wonder how many of them realized you were being sarcastic at their expense?"

"Oh, some of them did, but not many, I admit. Come, let us talk more of battles."

Florence

"Get an escort ready for me," commanded Cosimo de' Medici, after he finished reading the letter from the man he'd sent to watch over Violetta's treatment. "I'm departing for Venice immediately."

Chapter 46

The Duchy of Milan

Lucia admitted to herself that she was worried about the military might her spies reported were massing against Milan. She'd known that there were enemies, but had had no idea of the numbers, and of the different forces attacking Milan. What had Sforza done to let it get to this? She thought he'd beaten them back before she'd fed him the poison!

They're dying in Terdona. The city cannot hold. The asp's tone was triumphant. *Dying, dying, dying. Orkise devours!*

There was a terrible, irresistible urge to go there, to see her victory. She called Lord Laglissio. "I plan to go to inspect the war. Arrange an escort. I believe we are about to capture the city of Terdona.

He blinked. "I had heard the siege still held, Your Grace."

They're dying, dying. The few live people try to fight, or hide. They cannot flee.

"I also have sources of information. Do not question me. I will need a suitable escort. Perhaps a thousand men."

"Er. We only have eight hundred in uniform so far," answered Laglissio nervously.

"I should imagine eight hundred will be adequate. Sforza... my husband's mercenaries are still in control and beating back our foes."

"Yes, Your Grace. When do you wish to leave?"

"Tomorrow morning will be acceptable."

The escort was ready shortly after sunup the next day. There were a few matters that Lucia had forgotten that had been planned for that day, however, so in fact it was only the following afternoon that they set out, eight hundred men, escorting her traveling carriage, and those of her ladies-in-waiting. And their luggage.

The countryside bored her, but she did sleep, and had one of the ladies read to her, until the woman threw up. Lucia's brief rage was quieted by the asp reminding her that this "trusted confidante" was under the snake's spell, and could scarcely have planned to vomit down the side of the gilded carriage. And she was feeling slightly queasy herself from the swaying and bumping. So they had stopped at the next town, where suitable lodging was acquired. She so liked the villa in which they stayed that it restored her humor. And the former owners quite deserved what they'd gotten.

Before crossing the Po, her view from the windows had showed little signs of war. She'd begun to suspect that the tales of war had been greatly exaggerated for effect. That changed on this side of the river. There were soldiers, checkpoints, and some signs of war damage. There were some minor delays when Sforza's mercenaries foolishly held up their progress, disputing with her officers. But she was the duchess. She was allowed to pass, all the way to within half a league of the small city of Terdona.

There, the guards on the road were tense, actually firing a shot in the air when one of her captains attempted to ignore the order to halt. He fell off his steed. Several of her men had their weapons readied rapidly, and Lucia's bodyguard massed around the carriage. At first, it looked ugly—the guards might be outnumbered but they had given a warning call, and had retreated into their little fort. But when the captain got up, unhurt, and an officer of Sforza's men came riding up hastily, the situation was defused.

The officer was brought to her carriage to speak to her in person. He at least knew who she was and treated her with suitable respect.

"I'm sorry, Your Grace. There is a disease loose in the city. I cannot, for your safety, allow you to proceed any closer."

The kiss will not affect you. You are Orkise's chosen, said the asp.

"In Sforza's illness, I must act for him," she said, aware of the sinuous slither emerging from her cortege. None of her guard would react, but the mercenary officer's eyes bulged briefly ... before the asp brought him to her will.

She was escorted through the lines, a mile through uninhabited countryside. To the inner perimeter, to the burned ground around the city—and its far less able guards. Less able perhaps, but far less biddable as well. Captain Borghetti and his men were not what she thought of as proper soldiers.

A gust of wind brought the stench of rotting corpses wafting from the shattered walls. Up on the count's tower, his flag still fluttered in a last weak defiance. That was the only sign of movement from Terdona. That, and the crows.

"Well, sir?" demanded Lucia. "Why do you still wait like useless cowards? Why does that flag still fly?"

There was something oddly alluring about that smell. Yes, it was decay and death. But it was also victory. Thus would die all her foes.

The scruffy captain and his battle-worn men stood stock-still, staring at her, not moving toward the fallen city, across the burned sward of land that surrounded it.

She had become accustomed to instant obedience to her slightest wish, in the Palazzo Ducale and with the guard there. They'd seen to it, rapidly, that the citizens of Milan understood appropriate respect as well.

Not so among these mercenaries. They were ragged, bandaged, some on crutches, some not even trying to stand.

"Well?" Lucia repeated herself. "Answer me, Captain Borghetti, or I'll have you flogged here, in front of your men." She had her personal guard with her, quite capable of seeing the threat carried out.

The captain did not seem to care. "I have my orders. Nothing leaves there alive. Not a dog, nor a cat, nor a rat. Not even the crows if we can shoot them. You can send one or all of your pretty boys in"—he sneeringly gestured at her escort—"but if they try to cross the sward to come out again, we'll kill them. The plague is loose in there. You shouldn't even be in this layer of the cordon. Your Grace." The last part was an obvious afterthought.

Lucia neither knew nor cared what they thought had killed the people of Terdona. She knew perfectly well what it had been and that it was hers to command.

"Plague," she sneered. "They dared to withstand us and that is the fate of all who resist. Yours, too, Captain. Understand this. I give the orders in the Duchy of Milan while my husband is indisposed. When he recovers, those who balked will pay the price."

She knew that was not going to happen, but they did not, and among the mercenaries, Sforza's name probably still carried a greater weight than the principality of Milan.

The captain shrugged. "They tried to throw their dead at us. That's why Francisco ordered the sward burned. It looked enough like what I had heard of plague to me, and to Turner. He's no fool. The buboes, the swelling . . . I want no part of it. I make war for a living, but not like this. You can guard your own cordon, and take your own town, Duchess."

Instinctively Lucia knew, despite her fury at his insolence, that she had gone too far. If the rumor spread that Milan—or rather, she herself—had caused the plague to get loose, soldiers would desert, and not just mercenaries like this one.

But you will not need them, whispered the asp concealed in her bosom. *They will do your will, or die. Or just die. The dead cannot defy you.*

"You have misinterpreted me, Captain," said Lucia, keeping her voice calm and silky. "I mean they have brought this on themselves, and if there is an outbreak of some infectious disease, what better thing could we have done but to besiege them, to isolate them? Good work!"

The captain, for the first time, looked a little uncertain. He would still die for his insolence and temerity, when the time came.

Later, said the asp.

Lucia returned to Milan directly, but by the time she got there, she found that rumor had ridden on faster steeds. There was a jam of carts and wagons at the gates of Milan. Her men had to use their whips to clear a way through.

"What is going on here?" she demanded.

"A panic, Your Grace. Seems someone has started a tale that the soldiers are using the plague to conquer towns. They're blaming Sforza, saying he is sick with the plague, too. It could get ugly, Your Grace. We'd best ride on."

She nodded, and the carriage was driven out of there, entirely too fast, making her feel very sick. It was worrying. She said so to the asp. It seemed to misunderstand her.

They always try to run. That spreads the kiss of Orkise wider and wider. Some try to hide away.

"But I said I just wanted that town destroyed. I told him that!"

And your orders are obeyed... by Orkise. But humans carry the kiss wider. And then the kiss of Orkise must be used to deal with them. Never fear, mistress. They cannot stand against you.

"I won't allow that. We need more soldiers to control the behavior here. We want the plague in their cities, not ours. Is that clear?"

Orkise will do as you order, and he will control his legions. But once the kiss goes to humans, they flee in terror and they pass it on between each other, and then Orkise cannot control them.

"Then I will."

Later she called Lord Laglissio to her chambers. "We need to quash this plague rumor. We need more troops on the gates. Get a list from the central barracks of all the troops of Sforza's mercenaries, too. Any stationed here can be taken for duty. I shall sign the necessary orders."

A little later he was back. "There are very few of his mercenary company's men within the city, Your Grace. Here is the list. Here are the orders I have had the scribes draw up."

She signed them all, including one for the troops on the Val di Castellazzo. The name brought back an errant memory. Ah, yes. Her source of the poison, that Sforza had somehow detected. He'd still be useful later.

"And I want the man who issued those ridiculous orders about Terdona brought to me: Francisco Turner. Unless I am much mistaken, he is the fellow who disrespected me before. I'll have his head."

"I will order that he is brought to Your Grace in chains," said Laglissio.

Chapter 47

The Duchy of Milan

The news of a warrant for his arrest for the quarantine of Terdona was something of a surprise to Francisco Turner. It shouldn't have been, but it was.

"Treason. On the orders of Her Grace, Lucia, Duchess of Milan, for preventing the capture of Terdona by the forces of the Protector," said the officer who had loftily informed Francisco he was here to arrest him.

Francisco was tired. He'd always wondered just how his commander had come by the energy and the mental acumen that a war required. Now he found that even harder to fathom. Perhaps one got used to it or something. Right now this party—you couldn't really call it a troop—of the duchess's peacock soldiers outnumbered his escort by three to one. They were still obviously wary about actually seizing the man they carried a warrant for. That wasn't all that surprising since Francisco's men were battle-hardened veterans. Neither the officer attempting to arrest him nor his troops had been in more than a barfight, most likely.

There was no sense in making it easy for them. "You wish to arrest me for obeying Protector Sforza's direct orders?" he said incredulously. "There is disease in Terdona; it is under quarantine. If that quarantine is broken you'll have the disease in Milan. Do you want that?"

At least that would possibly stop that quarantine being broken, as the story would get around.

"No, but I have a warrant for your arrest signed by the duchess. I cannot go against that. I . . . I am sure that once the matter is clarified, then all will be resolved, Captain," said the man stiffly.

"I am sure my corpse will be very interested in that. No, gentlemen. A warrant bears the signature and seal of the Lord Protector of Milan. What is your name?" asked Francisco, reaching calmly into his saddlebag. He took out an oilskin document pouch.

"I am Captain Count di Neiro of Her Grace's guard," the officer announced.

Francisco took one of the documents from the pouch. The pouch was set up for writing while traveling, with a small ink bottle and quill.

"A letter won't do. You will accompany us voluntarily or I will order my men to take you by force," said Di Neiro.

"One moment," said Francisco. "Di Neiro has an e before the i—correct?"

"You can't bribe me!"

"Bribe you?" Francisco snorted, holding up the document. "Do you recognize this signature and this seal, Di Neiro?"

"Uh. The usurp— ah, Protector," said the man. "But even if you have orders to quarantine that town, I cannot carry them to Her Grace for you, and the order specifically states you are to come before her in chains."

"This is an order for your immediate execution," said Francisco, loudly and clearly. "I'd be very sure that everyone who witnessed this and does not act dies, or Sforza will want their heads, too. The Wolf is recovering well. Do you think his personal physician would be running around the country otherwise?"

"Excuse me, Captain," said Francisco's sergeant. "Might do to tell these play soldiers that we've got four less men than we had, because I sent two forward to tell Lieutenant Balchi and two to the barracks in Brescia."

If the knot of Francisco's men were four less, the melt of Di Neiro's troop was considerably larger . . . and he plainly realized this, by his sudden desperate lunge for his horse. If he'd been fitter and less of the epitome of fashion—not designed for fast movement—he might have made it, too.

As it was, he just ended up dead.

It was a good short-term solution, but Francisco knew his time in Milanese territory was likely to cause more problems than it solved. He just wasn't sure quite what to do now, except to inform the other captains.

Venice

So far as she could ever recall afterward, there was never a specific moment at which Violetta realized that the man she shared the rose-scented healing tent with was Carlo Sforza. The knowledge simply dawned on her over time, very much like the sunrise itself.

A number of things led her to that understanding. First, the simple fact that he knew too much. The man knew details concerning the battles they discussed and sometimes argued about that only a man who'd actually been there could have known— and, at least in some instances, could only have known if he'd been in command. Second, although she sometimes disagreed with his tactical assessments and more often had doubts about his strategic opinions, she soon realized that she was completely outclassed when it came to practical issues.

Violetta had met the commander she most admired, Enrico Dell'este, on several occasions. Once, she'd even been able to discuss a couple of his victorious battles with the old soldier. The thing that had struck her the most about that conversation was the very different way Dell'este looked upon those events than the way she did.

As he'd put it to her at one point: "Your grasp of tactics is superb, Signorina de' Medici—amazingly so, for someone who has never even seen a battle. That would be true of a man, much less a young woman like yourself. But you tend to overlook the issue that is always the central concern of an experienced soldier."

"Which is?" she'd asked, just a bit miffed. She'd only been nineteen years old at the time.

"Supplies. What we sometimes call 'logistics.' More battles have been lost, throughout history, because a commander failed to properly match his resources to his tactics than because of a flaw in the tactics themselves."

Time and again, as their discussions under the healing tent continued, Violetta was reminded of that conversation with Dell'este. The man she shared the tent with had that same hard-headed and practical view of a soldier's work.

He knew so much she'd never even thought about. For instance, Violetta considered herself quite a good equestrienne, but her knowledge and understanding of horses was pitiful compared to what the man knew.

At what point in a heavy rain do cavalry mounts became unreliable? That point at which dirt became mud, it turned out. Like most big animals, horses grew anxious when their footing was unreliable.

How thickly massed did pikemen have to be in order to repel cavalry? Horses were dumb, even by animal standards, and could be forced to charge directly into pikes and fortifications. But only to a point—and knowing that point could be critical in a battle.

How early in the spring could a given-sized cavalry force or artillery force—any unit that required livestock—depend on there being enough grass to keep a campaign from being stalled? That varied from place to place, of course, but the man in the tent could tell you what the answer was for every region of Italy and parts of Europe beyond.

At first, she'd simply taken him for a very experienced soldier. A mercenary, in all likelihood. But as their discussions went on, she began realizing that he always viewed military affairs from the top down, as it were. The man had all the understanding of the practical realities of military affairs that you'd expect from a grizzled middle-aged sergeant, but he never looked at those affairs the way a sergeant would.

Looking back, she should have reached her conclusion earlier. But there were also things about the man that she had never associated with Carlo Sforza, which had veiled the truth from her for a while.

He was good-humored, for one thing. Who would think that of the man they called the "Wolf of the North"?

Even more surprising—astonishing, actually—was that he never patronized her. Indeed, he seemed genuinely interested in her opinions. Few men, in her experience, would have reacted that way to a woman expressing her views on military matters. True, they would be polite, given her status and position. But within a short time it would become obvious to Violetta that they were paying no attention at all to what she said.

The man in the tent did. Close attention, in fact.

❀   ❀   ❀

Once she comprehended the truth, she tried to figure out what to do about it.

Demand that Sforza be removed from her presence?

That seemed...churlish. Not to mention unreasonable, presuming that what Marco Valdosta had told them was true, that he had only a very limited supply of the precious rose petals.

But, most of all, what dissuaded her from that course of action was that, if she did succeed, she'd just wind up being bored. Imagine doing nothing with your mind except enjoying the scent of roses!

Which were not her favorite flowers anyway.

As it was, she woke each time with the cheerful thought that the period of consciousness which followed would be filled with intelligent conversation with an older man whose views she found both interesting and stimulating. There weren't many men like that, in her experience. Uncle Cosimo, of course, and...

Well. Carlo Sforza.

Chapter 48

Val di Castellazzo, Duchy of Milan

"If anyone sees Knights of the Holy Trinity scouting, word will almost certainly come to Count Mindaug," Father Thomas Lüber said calmly. "A solitary priest, however, attracts no such comment. And it appears Duchess Lucia plans to keep us kicking our heels here. So I shall take my mule out to this Val di Castellazzo, and see what can be seen."

He had returned some hours later. "The villagers told me the guard had been marched away last night. I walked to within sight of the house itself."

Archimandrite von Stebbens took a deep breath. "God moves in mysterious ways. We will proceed there as soon as we can. Father Thomas, we bid you thanks and farewell."

"I shall come with you. If indeed this is the source of the plague, I may find out more."

"Father, it is quite possible that we will all be killed. I do not know that we will be able to overcome Mindaug and, even if we do, if we can then escape from the wrath of the Milanese."

"And if I stay here, once your actions are known, I will be executed," said Father Thomas calmly. "I am known to be with you, so I may as well actually be with you."

That was an impossible argument to counter, so the tall spare priest rode with them when later that afternoon they set out through the gates of Milan, unchallenged.

"The key will be to give him as little time as possible to

respond," said Von Stebbens. "Speed is of the essence. Father Thomas, I must ask you to stay back and out of the way."

So Father Thomas Lüber walked in behind the armored phalanx that charged up to and smashed its way into the apparently undefended house, and rushed forward, seeking their quarry in the book-lined hall, and broke into the first salon.

The floor under Von Maelenberg suddenly gave way and, in a cloud of debris and dust, the man disappeared. The rest of the Knights halted their rush.

Standing on the far side of the hole, Count Mindaug looked at them, his face almost expressionless.

The archimandrite looked at the hole between him and their quarry. It could be an illusion—or it could be the maw of hell. Knowing Count Kazimierz Mindaug, it was likely to be the latter.

"We will get you, you foul fiend!" he screamed at the monster, the sorcerer who had raised the plague demon.

Count Mindaug had made the trap for the serpent Orkise. He couldn't have been more surprised by what it had caught, had a troupe of traveling players fallen into it.

"My apologies," he said. "I had intended the trap for our foe. You should have knocked, like anyone else. I did not know who had broken down my door, and I took appropriate steps. I am afraid your companion has fallen a long way. Actually, he's still falling."

Archimandrite von Stebbens could deal with defeat. He could deal with death. This, however, sent him to the edge of fury. "Let that which cannot abide the name of Christ, be gone!"

There was no sign that that did any good, or had any effect. He raised his sword, about to—

A voice behind them said: "Put your weapons down. Now!"

He turned to see what this new possible threat was. He swallowed, looking. She was not a very large woman and was certainly very pregnant, wearing an apron over the bulge. She also held a large hand-cannon with two hands, rock steady.

"Armor won't protect you well enough," she said. "Klaus has loaded the hand-cannon with steel fragments for me. Some of them will go through your visors and blind you."

"And," said Count Mindaug, "I do not know what brings you to my house, but we share a common enemy. I have already

spoken with the Lion of Etruria, and I wanted to send a message to Emperor Charles Fredrik, the Church, and particularly
to the Knights of the Holy Trinity. A thing—call it a god or a
demon—has been awakened by..."

"Do not try to deceive us!"

"Do not interrupt the master," said the girl with the gun.

There was only one of her, and fifteen—now fourteen—of
them. But...she was a young, pregnant, and plainly peasant
woman. Even from here he could see the cross hanging between
her breasts. This must, by the accent, be one of the peasant servants who had gone to the church.

"Daughter, you have been misled," said Von Stebbens, knowing
full well that, if necessary, he would have to kill her. "Please put
the gun down. We do God's work, and you have been deceived."

She snorted. "If breaking into Master Kazimierz's house is
your idea of God's work, then your god must have horns and
a tail. He's the best and kindest of men. If we didn't look after
him, he'd be robbed blind."

"I am not a particularly good man, actually," said Kazimierz,
"but I am not your enemy. I could kill all of you a great deal
more easily than Emma could, but I actually need to talk to
your masters."

"We know who and what you are, Mindaug," grated the archimandrite, weighing the possibilities, "and where you came from."

That got a derisive snort. "Come now. I am absolutely certain
the Church did not scry within Jagiellon's defenses. Or Bartholdy's,
for that matter. And I nearly destroyed the former, and caused
the downfall of the latter."

"Do not pretend you fought for good. We know—"

"Oh, no. I did it for my own survival. But now, well, I have
learned some interest in the survival of others. I like it here in
the West, more than I could have dreamed. In fact, I had begun
to think I loved it, until you burst in here."

Like Satan, he was the prince of lies, thought Von Stebbens.
And then the side door burst open, with a shout of "Master, are
you all right?"

Hartz reacted to the entry and slashed at the man who had
just rushed in. He was a knight with a broadsword. The man
was an unarmed peasant carrying a box.

❈   ❈   ❈

The asp in Lucia's bosom suddenly twisted and thrashed and burst out of her décolletage. *Magic! Powerful magic!*

"Am I being attacked?" demanded Lucia.

No. But it is a danger to you, to Orkise. And so close! The serpent will go. You must send soldiers, too, the ones my eyes have bent to your will.

"But they're my special guard." She knew precisely which troops the asp meant. Like her mother, they'd looked at the swaying serpent. The asp said such loyalty was best for those close to her, and she'd agreed with him.

Orkise is your source of power, mistress. I am part of Orkise, too. So close is danger!

"But he is safe under Arona's castle."

Oh, no, mistress. The kiss is loosed, his power rises with each death. And you are the one who made the sacrifice. He is close to you, readying his kine, and their legions. He goes as fast as he can to the place you took me to. Val di Castellazzo.

Count Mindaug saw Tamas come rushing in, just too late. He had the spell ready, waiting only for the activation, and they were all within the trap. It had been planned for the troops Duchess Lucia might turn loose against him, but would be just as effective against the Knights of the Holy Trinity. They were proofed against direct magical assault...but everything needed air. Within the sphere they stood in, the air wanted to leave and leave now. And while they might wish to leave with it, the floor would not make it easy. It did not truly become liquid, but more like the jelly that formed around cold pork, trickling slowly into the pit trap he had made for Orkise.

The wind rush shattered windows and slammed open doors. It was slower than a sword stoke or the floor spell. The floor suddenly liquefying did have some effect, but it did not stop the terrible scream from Tamas or the boom of Emma's hand-cannon.

Von Stebbens's yell of "Hold" came too late. Hartz cut at the peasant boy and the girl shot him. And before the archimandrite could do more than take a step, the floor began to swallow him; he gasped for breath as he sank down into it. There could be no chanting, no charge, no effective magic or physical attack in this. Desperately, he flung his sword at the evil count, who had run to the very edge of the pit and was balancing his way along the thin fringe of surviving boards on the edge of the room.

The count simply ducked and the sword bounced off the wall and into the pit. Mindaug leapt across the remaining chasm to kneel next to the girl who was already cradling the boy in her arms. Blood was pumping out from the upper thigh, spurting in a way that Von Stebbens knew most likely meant death. Then, without the rites of protection or any further ado, the magician stood up and performed a summoning...not of some vile demon, but a very surprised-looking man—who took one look and hastily knelt next to the wounded man.

But the archimandrite's personal problem was that he could not breathe.

One moment Francisco Turner had been leaving the meeting of Sforza's officers, en route with his escort to Venice, or at least the Venetian border, and the next...

He found himself in the ruins of the front salon of the villa at Val di Castellazzo, where Kazimierz had once entertained Carlo. He might not have recognized it had not been for Kazimierz, blood on his cotte, and the pregnant Emma, cradling the wounded Tamas.

One of the young man's hands had been cut, badly enough that he would probably never have the full use of it again. He'd probably thrown it forward in an attempt to block a sword strike, but Francisco spent no more than a moment on that. Tamas had a far worse injury.

One look at the blood pulsing from the femoral artery was all Francisco needed to rip his waist sash free and lift the leg and put it around, just above the wound; then, using his sheathed main gauche as a lever, he twisted it to stem the blood loss.

"Hold this," he ordered, using his knife to cut another strip of cloth, which promptly blew away. "Blasted wind!" he growled, starting to cut another. The wind stopped, but Francisco was too busy trying to contrive a bandage for Tamas's ruined hand to wonder why. When that was tied off, he went back to the savage cut in the leg.

Now he could absorb that the man holding that tourniquet was the former bombardier, Klaus. Emma clung to her man, and Kazimierz knelt next to her. Francisco noted the magician's face was wet with tears.

"Can you keep him alive for a few minutes?" asked Kazimierz, his voice gravelly. "I see there is a priest among these."

"How long ago did this happen?" asked Francisco.

"Perhaps thirty heartbeats. I called you as quickly as I could," said Kazimierz. Kneeling next to his servants, he reached out and squeezed their shoulders. "Tamas, my boy. Emma. I am sorry."

"Am I dying, master?" gasped the boy between clenched teeth, "Look after...Emma. Baby. Please. Thought..." he gasped weakly, "I'd...be good father, husband." He slumped back.

"Please, a priest, master," sobbed Emma. "At least then his soul..."

"I will see to it," said Kazimierz. He looked around, and stood up. "I must take certain actions."

He took a thin-bladed stiletto from his sleeve and carved symbols on the wooden board. He was muttering words at great speed as he did this, and then he walked across the strange quagmire that embedded the knights. They looked like Knights of the Holy Trinity, from the quick glance Francisco had spared them, before attending to his patient. The girl was now praying and holding her man, who was moaning weakly, plainly in shock.

"What happened, Klaus?" Francisco asked.

"Dunno, Captain. Young Tamas and I were fetching some of those flying stars and some small rockets for the master, and we come in the back, and Tamas hears a noise and runs to help. I'm not so fast. I come in to this mess."

"What happened to the guards?"

"They got ordered to Milan. The duchess signed the orders."

Kazimierz returned with a man in Hypatian robes.

The boy looked up. "I've only got...one thing. On my conscience."

"Confess and I will ask God to grant you absolution."

"I...not married. Asked long ago... Got absolution, last Sunday."

"But the priest wanted us to stay and have the banns read! We couldn't!" said Emma. "It's not Tamas's fault. And the good master gave permission," she sobbed. "He gave me my trousseau. It has just...not yet happened. It was to be this Sunday."

"If that is your only great sin, my son, God forgives easily," said the priest.

The boy nodded. "Will you marry us, Father?" he croaked.

The priest, to give him credit, simply said, "Yes."

"Kazimierz," said Francisco, as the priest knelt next to the two and held their hands together. "I need some instruments. A small clamp of some kind, some small knives and cloth, and the finest needle and silk thread. And the strongest grappa you can find and a bowl. And something for him to bite on. This is going to hurt, and he's in a lot of pain already."

The count blinked. "He hasn't long to live, Francisco. They bleed out in a few minutes if cut there. I have some strong poppy juice that will at least make it painless."

"I've all but stopped the bleeding, and with some sewing, luck, and no infection, we might save his leg. His hand, no. I'm sure the tendons are all severed. But it is his left hand, and there are many men who live with the use of only one."

"Oh." The expression on the older man's face told plainly that he had expected the boy to die. The relief was open and honest. "Well, yes, I have all manner of tools. Klaus, a small clamp? Which do you think would be best?"

"I will go to the workshop and fetch some, master. If you could hold this?" said the bombardier of the tourniquet twist which he was still holding.

"I'll tie it off," said Francisco, taking control of it, as the scarred bombardier got to his feet. "What about that lot behind us?" he asked, directing an elbow at the chest-deep Knights. He'd just heard one of them say something.

"Them?" said Kazimierz irritably. "They destroyed my trap for Orkise and wrecked my house and injured my good loyal servant nearly to death and cost him his hand. I have slowed and hardened the flow, so that I could haul the priest out, but it will slowly take them down into the hole and set around them. They deserve it."

"Can one of you be spared to witness their oath?" asked the priest. "And please, I would like to beg for the lives of the Knights. They are men of God, doing their duty."

"No quarter!" said one of the Knights.

"I order you to be quiet," said another, their officer by the ornate extra row of gilded spikes. "It is still a Christian marriage. We may die but we will do so with honor, dignity and prayer. We are all witnesses to their vow."

"For that, I will let you live," said Kazimierz.

❊   ❊   ❊

Archimandrite Klaus von Stebbens, having very nearly died from a lack of air, and having lost his sword, had not lost his wits. He was a skilled magic worker himself, though he now realized he was completely outclassed by Count Mindaug. The Empire had severely underestimated the man. It took very little time to realize that the trap they were caught in had been carefully engineered to reduce the possibility of using any form of magic to escape it. There was a weave of counterspells about them.

Von Stebbens finally admitted to himself that perhaps he and the other Knights, and indeed the Emperor, had not quite gauged this man aright. The Aemiline hesychast Dimitrios had continued to insist that the Knights of the Holy Trinity were misreading the situation.

Von Stebbens tended to be distrustful of the monk's assessment, mostly because he was an Aemiline. They were a very pacific order, which was why they inclined toward the Peterines rather than the Paulines. And while that attitude might speak well of their souls, it did not necessarily speak well of their good sense. Being pacific toward someone like Count Mindaug was likely to lead to disaster.

Still, by now Von Stebbens accepted that Dimitrios had been able to keep a closer watch on Mindaug than anyone else. And there was one feature of the Lithuanian count's behavior that the archimandrite himself had always found difficult to explain.

Von Stebbens had grown up in a noble family in the Marches. If these two young servants of Mindaug's were anything but mere Hungarian peasantry, he'd be amazed. The girl had been praying steadfastly and aloud . . .

And Mindaug, whom they had assumed to be without feeling and utterly cold-blooded, a murderer of his own family, had shown more emotion than most noblemen over the injury of a loyal servant—a young man who seemed to consider his worst sin not yet having married this girl. Von Stebbens knew that on the order of things that both Bartholdy and Jagiellon had done, that did not even register as a peccadillo.

Could the young people have been that ignorant? Could Mindaug have kept evil blood magic that secret from his own servants? In the confines of the wagon in which they'd spent most of their time together?

Or, as Brother Dimitrios had suggested, had the count turned his back on those practices? But there was still the great magical flux that had happened a bare fortnight ago. And the traffic with the water-demon...

And then, just after the vows, just after the maimed man who was plainly a soldier returned with things he'd been asked for, there was the distant sound of things breaking, coming ever closer.

It was a sound reminiscent of someone snapping kindling, but vastly magnified.

"Dear God!" said Father Thomas, pointing out the blown-in window. Across the parkland, an enormous serpent was advancing toward the house. It forced its way between the trees, uprooting or breaking whatever resisted the lateral pressure of the sinuous slither. That was what they'd heard.

"Orkise," said the count grimly. "The dying in Terdona has fed him, given him strength, raising him from his lair as I feared it would. He is aware of my little magics and has now come to destroy any possible threat. We must flee."

"How?" asked the surgeon, lifting his head from the bandaging.

That was a good question, thought Von Stebbens. The creature would outrun a horse, by the looks of it.

"Tamas is in no shape to get on a horse, Kazimierz. Have you a coach?" asked the surgeon.

Mindaug shook his head. "We will have to depart by magical means. I am sure Orkise's mistress will have her soldiers hunting the countryside anyway, even if some could escape the serpent. I have it all prepared. Do you remember that mirror you took to Venice for me? We will need to carry Tamas to the next room. Klaus, call as many of my people as possible. I must save what I can. I have set traps that will delay Orkise slightly."

He pointed to the men trapped still, chest deep in the floor. "I wasn't expecting these Knights, though. I just hope we have enough time."

"Mindaug," said the archimandrite. "Free us and we will buy you that time." At that moment, he was not sure if this was guile, but one thing was certain, remaining there would mean certain death.

The magician's forehead wrinkled briefly. He looked around. Then he nodded.

❖   ❖   ❖

Mindaug had been shocked at his own rage and despair at the boy meeting his end as he had. He hadn't realized just how much he had come to care about Tamas and Emma. A part of his mind still said, *but they are merely serfs.* Another less logical but more dominant part of his mind said, *look at the promise, the loyalty . . .*

Mindaug dismissed the thoughts. However it had happened— whenever it had happened—he had come to care deeply about both of them. Caring was something he was unpracticed at, that he'd always distanced himself from. It had only been the knowledge that they faced a very slow unpleasant death that had saved the Knights. He'd always shied from actually using too much of his power or skill. If he did, he could be perceived as a threat and not as a source of support.

And then Francisco had turned his despair for the boy into relief and hope. His mind, always quick, recovered some of its tone, and he saw the Knights as the tools they could be. He was not merciful or kind, but he was not given to mindless cruelty either.

"It would be a pointless death," he said, as he began the spell to release the Knights. "Orkise is the enemy of all that lives."

Chapter 49

"The only effective weapon against Orkise is fire," said Mindaug. "I do not think the serpent itself can actually be killed, for it is not truly alive. I had hoped to trap it, to encase it in stone, which would have delayed it considerably. Its breath is poisonous, and its bite deadly. But it fears fire." The count nodded toward the one-eyed bombardier. "Klaus will show you how to operate the star rockets. He always has slow matches with him. Light them. Charge towards it. Fire the rockets and then retreat back here. With luck, we'll still be here and you can escape with us. Otherwise—flee. As fast and far as you can. Duchess Lucia's troops will probably hunt you, too." Mindaug was as cool as if he had not nearly killed them all and, it appeared, been quite willing to watch them die.

Von Stebbens had no time, right now, to work this all out. He was close enough, perhaps, to kill the man. But, firstly, Mindaug had proved trickier in defense than they had guessed, and secondly, that vast serpent out there was real. His men—bruised, half-suffocated and having been chest-deep in the magical trap—showed why they were the Empire's finest fighting men because, despite this, they were ready and able to go to battle...barring Hartz, who had died with a fragment of steel in his brain from the young woman's shot. It had, indeed, gone straight through his visor.

This could be a deceit, still. But what was out there was a vast snake, and what Mindaug and his retainers were doing was preparing to flee, not to consort with it.

"God willing, we will hold it off," said one of the Knights.

Mindaug visibly took a deep breath. "I will help magically as much as I can. And I will beg the Lion of Etruria to lend us his strength. I will attempt to build a big enough portal to take all—or at least as many of you as survive—to safety in Venice. We'll sound the call when it is ready. Cry truce until then."

"Truce," said Von Stebbens. "Now let us out and mount, men."

Venice

The next time Violetta awoke, Sforza wanted to discuss something other than military affairs.

"I'm curious," he said. "I presume you know a great deal about the current situation with Milan? Ruled, as it now is, by the usurper Carlo Sforza."

Wondering where he was headed, she replied cautiously: "Well, yes, I do—at least, up to the point when I was poisoned. But a lot of time has gone by since then. In the sort of predicament the Wolf of the North found himself when I last knew anything about it, every day can mark a turning point or a crisis. A week is like a month, a month is like a year, and a year might as well be eternity."

"Truly said," he agreed. "I was poisoned quite a bit later than you were, however. Allow me, if you would, to fill you in on the main features of the more recent events."

What followed was a terse but excellent summary of the course of the conflict—which had now reached the scale of an outright war—since Violetta had been poisoned.

Once he was finished, Violetta pondered the matter for a bit. She had to shift her viewpoint, first. Her own keen interest in military affairs tended to overshadow other considerations, she'd found. Well...more precisely, she hadn't "found that out" herself so much as Uncle Cosimo had pointed it out to her.

Um. Several times, in fact. Her second cousin was a master-ful strategist on a level that even Duke Enrico of Ferrara rarely attained. War, for Cosimo de' Medici, was first and foremost a grotesque waste. A waste of people; a waste of resources; a waste of money—most of all, it was wasteful of the future. So, as the ruling duke of Tuscany, he approached all strategic issues with the aim of avoiding war if at all possible.

Usually, he managed to do so. Many of northern Italy's small mob of princes sneered at Cosimo de' Medici for what they perceived as his pusillanimity. But what they overlooked was that Tuscany's reluctance to engage in warfare also meant that Tuscany had become—by far—the richest region of Italy. Not even the much larger territories controlled in one way or another by the Church were as prosperous and wealthy.

And wealth meant power. Usually, so long as Cosimo was in charge, power held in check rather than power used. What Violetta had once heard one of the scientists who clustered around the court in Florence—yes, there was that, too; Tuscany was rich in scholars as well as merchants—call potential energy or stored energy. He'd distinguished between that sort of stored energy and what he called "kinetic energy," which was energy actually manifesting itself.

"Think of the immense power of the water held in check by a dam," he'd used as an example. "The water just sits there, to all outward appearances a completely placid phenomenon. But now imagine that whoever owns and controls the dam decides to open the sluices—perhaps because an enemy army is marching up the valley toward his realm. That army will soon vanish, won't it? As if it never existed at all!"

Such was the nature of Tuscany under the rule of Cosimo de' Medici. His duchy had the strongest and best-designed fortifications, probably in all of Europe, not just Italy. Tuscany could also afford the best condottieri, and Cosimo paid his mercenaries well enough that there was no significant risk that they might turn on him.

So, other rulers of the area came and sneered—privately, not to the duke's face. But they also saw the great fortresses and the fine guns—the *many* fine guns—and the well-trained and ready soldiery. And...

Decided there was probably easier prey to be had elsewhere.

"Sforza's big mistake was the converse of his great strength," she said. "There's no denying the man is a brilliant battlefield tactician, even better in that regard than Dell'este"—that was the first time she'd made that admission in their conversations—"but he relies on it too much. He has a tendency, I think, to neglect strategy in favor of tactics and, what's probably worse, tends to think of strategy almost entirely in military terms, which is too narrow."

The man whose head lay right next to hers grunted. "You may well be right," he said. "But I—ah, can you give me an example of what you mean by that last remark? The one about too narrow a focus on military strategy, I mean."

Her own thoughts had been moving ahead along those lines, so her answer came immediately.

"The critical problem Sforza faces is twofold: first, he's a usurper; and, second and probably worse, he has no lineage that any Italian nobleman will respect. Well, not most of them, anyway. So what he needed to do first and foremost was devote all his energy and intelligence to solving *that* problem. As best it could be solved, at least."

"And therefore he should have...?"

"Chosen his bride more carefully," she said. "Instead, he made his choice based on hurried considerations. His decision was completely slapdash. The way he *never* would have handled a military problem."

She discovered, to her surprise, that she was feeling quite cross. "How could the man possibly have thought Lucia Maria del Maino would make a suitable wife for him under *any* circumstances, much less the ones he was working within? If he'd done the slightest bit of careful reconnaissance, he would have soon realized that the Del Maino creature combines a treacherous and selfish heart with a dull mind. It's not as if anyone who's ever spent any time with the woman couldn't have told his spies! She would have been no help to him at any point, and was bound to stab him in the back sooner or later—probably sooner."

She stopped, and tried to breathe more slowly. *Why was she so agitated on this subject?*

Sforza chuckled, although it was hard to tell that from a grunt. There was no humor in the sound at all.

"Except she used a snake instead of a blade," he said. "All right, I accept your criticism of Sforza's decision to marry Lucia. But what other option did he have? There were only three possibilities after all: Lucia, Eleni Faranese, and Violetta de' Medici. Eleni was murdered almost at once—obviously, now, that was Lucia's doing—and the de' Medici girl made it quite clear that she had no interest in marrying him."

"Oh, that's ridiculous," she said, then, waving her hand, continued, "I don't doubt the girl was initially unwilling. Lots of young women don't react positively to the first indication that someone wishes to wed them. Why? There are a host of reasons, which men hardly ever think about. Do you want me to list them? I warn you, it will take quite a while."

Again, there was a chuckle, but this one came with humor in the sound. "No, no. I don't doubt you at all on that matter. So what should Sforza have done instead?"

"Exactly the same thing he should have done with the Del Maino witch. Pressed a careful but rigorous reconnaissance. Tried to discover exactly what the de' Medici woman's objections were—and, at the same time, what factors might work in his favor should she become aware of them. Instead, after that initial rebuff, he simply dropped the matter and rushed out to marry a two-legged viper."

She took another slow breath. "Of course, he might simply have been uninterested. By all accounts I've heard, Violetta de' Medici was a corpulent girl. They called her 'Butterball,' you know. That sort of obesity usually indicates a slothful nature. Often a dull-witted mind, too."

"Not necessarily," Sforza countered. "There's another possible explanation for her being so fat."

"Which is?"

"You touched on it yourself, just a moment ago. The host of reasons a young woman might be wary of marriage. Let us suppose, for the sake of argument, that we are dealing with a young woman whose family position makes her quite a prize as a bride. As a result, she's deeply distrustful of all suitors. She's a very bright girl whose guardian—that would be Cosimo de' Medici, the ruling duke of Tuscany—indulges her, which means in turn that she's not at all unhappy with her unmarried state."

He waved his own hand. The gesture, as had been true of hers, was languid. They were both still very weak.

"To make things worse, she's a pretty girl. So—I suspect this was not a conscious decision, so much as an instinctive one—she chose to turn herself into a—what was the term you used?—'butterball,' I believe. You might think of it as a tactical maneuver to fend off as many suitors as possible."

Violetta was so surprised by that answer that she was speechless for some time. Long enough for sleep to draw her down again.

Chapter 50

Count Mindaug had dared terrible dangers—but cautiously, as was his nature. Never had he opened himself up to attack by taking chances. Now he did so. The way he chose to contact the Lion of Etruria, the magical being who was a part of Marco Valdosta, left him wide open. The creature would know that, and could possibly decide that Kazimierz Mindaug was worth more dead, or enslaved, than alive. But it was fast and effective, and Kazimierz Mindaug had crossed his Rubicon and burned the bridges behind him. He would do what had to be done. He would unlearn the habits of a lifetime, if need be.

Trust! came the roaring in his mind. *A rare coin from one such as you!*

Mindaug realized he had opened a great deal of himself, and not just his defenses, to the ancient denizen of the marshes of Etruria. The Lion read his motives, his instincts, and his past—not in detail, but in a broad brushstroke. "Yes. And I have need of help."

That, too, is new to you. Help not for yourself, but for others.

"I could save myself. But not them."

And thus you have risked all to trust one who can. Very well done. I will give trust for trust. But the serpent lies outside my demesne, and even I can only stand in its way, not kill it. I will lend my strength to you and the Knights. I will defend their minds. I will multiply the strength of your spells.

"The mirror portal will take time to accumulate the energy and power to make it large enough. I will have to leave my books."

Power I will lend. Time you must win.

Mindaug nodded and rushed to it. There were symbols that had to be changed. Different invocations made. There was a moment of regret that even the crates of the most precious books would have to be left. Once he would never have considered that.

Von Stebbens and his men were mounted and riding across an open field towards the serpent, which was the height of a house. It had just broken through a grove of Aleppo pines, leaving several of the trees half destroyed and scattering branches, needles and pine cones everywhere. Right now, it was raised up and struggling with what looked like nets, which sparkled with spellwork—undoubtedly the work of Mindaug. The vast creature would tear them up soon, he was sure.

It cast its gaze on them . . . and the Knight felt a vast compulsion, too strong to be held off, almost so strong that it felt like his own idea, to go and cut loose the great Orkise. He was like a leaf in the wind, trying to resist, while galloping towards it.

And then, just before it would have been too late, there was a roaring in his ears, as if from a great lion. He—and by their behavior, the other Knights—regained control of their faculties, and turned away.

"It uses magic to compel. Sing the battle hymn!" The battle hymn of the Knights was a prayer as well as a hymn—a spell of power and protection in itself.

Even the finest of warhorses, bonded and trained to their Knights' will, do not face a giant serpent easily or well. Several of the Knights had an almost impossible task with their horses. And then the snake turned and opened its purple mouth on the left phalanx.

Horses and men reeled and then fell before the foul breath. Only a handful of Knights managed to flee. Von Stebbens, leading the right flank attack, ordered his men to fire as the great head swayed towards them. Those who had retained the devices and slow matches responded.

The shriek and sparks of gunpowder devices caused even more panic among the horses, so much so that Von Stebbens had no chance to see what happened when they struck the serpent. But a few moments later he was able to look again. They were burning on the ground around and before it, with a fierce light and spitting sparks. The creature did pull its head away from the burning stars. Away . . . but not into retreat.

And then, one by one, the burning devices went out.

The snake began to advance again. It had been a temporary stop and now they had no more of the devices. If only they had not fired them all at once . . .

"Do we press on?" asked one of the Knights.

Von Stebbens touched the crosses embossed on his shield with the sword in his hand. "What else can we do? Let us sing our battle hymn and die."

Von Stebbens wished for a lance, but that he did not have.

The serpent began to turn its head toward them.

He put his spurs to his reluctant horse.

Something struck the head of the snake with an exploding gout of fire, and once again he had to struggle to control his horse. And now he could see hundreds of riders behind the snake, spurring their horses to the charge. His twenty-odd men were doomed, whatever happened.

Count Mindaug finished readying the new, expanded circle, deliberately ignoring any sounds from outside. The task of conveying a group of people was a far larger, more magically demanding and exhausting process than merely taking himself would have been. He left it to the Knights to hold off Orkise for a few minutes. Only when he was ready to transport them did he look out. The serpent had plainly destroyed some of the Knights, and the others did not have long to survive.

Then Klaus, from outside the villa, fired one of the rockets. It was too much to hope it would kill the beast, but it would hold it for a few moments. But the gathering of the circle's energies would take more time. So Mindaug left the relative safety of his circle—safe until they entered the netherworlds, at least—and went out to stand beside Klaus, who was readying a second rocket. Mindaug placed his hands on the device, ignoring the bombardier's yell, and called up a well of strength that he knew would cost him dearly. He had used it before, on two occasions. This time was different. He had the strength of a lion, and not just any lion, but a vast immortal one who drew his power from all that lived and breathed in the ancient marshes of Etruria. And somehow Marco Valdosta was there, too. As he flung the rocket at Orkise, Marco was telling Klaus to light the next, and the next.

The Lion of Etruria lent not only superhuman strength and accuracy to his arms but, it seemed, force to the explosions. The serpent lashed backwards, pulling its head away, and the charge of those who were ensorcelled to follow the snake found themselves showered in shrapnel. Klaus and Tamas's rockets could not kill Orkise, but they had no problems doing that to its followers.

"I think we have won the time you needed," said the tall fine-featured Venetian.

So he cast his voice at the Knights. A voice of power, a voice that carried echoes of a roar of defiance. *"Come back, we are ready to go!"*

The Knights did not need much urging. Soon they were all scrambling inside the house, inside the circle.

Within the circle, Mindaug ordered them all to take hands. He crossed the final line on the spell script with a pointed toe and it whisked them hence.

Count Mindaug feared what he might find waiting in the netherworlds. But now they would take neither him, nor his burdens, from him. And the roaring he heard echoing was merely a warning to anyone that this time, he had allies. And this time he had finally begun to find his own strength.

It occurred to him, a few moments later, that he should have asked the Venetians to put the mirror in a bigger cell.

Chapter 51

Venice

Standing before the Doge, the white-haired man with the huge mustache whom Marco knew was Count Kazimierz Mindaug, magician and once the henchman of not one but three of the great evils of the world, shrugged. "There was a small chance that the traps I had prepared might hold it, Your Grace. You realize such creatures do not live entirely on our physical plane, and thus physical entrapment is only a partial restraint. And I was trying to hide the fact of my existence from other practitioners of the magical arts, to say nothing of beings on the other planes."

"Why were you hiding?" asked the Doge.

"Because it was widely assumed that I had died. I have enemies"—he raised an eyebrow at the battered Knight of the Holy Trinity—"even ones I was not aware of."

"We know you have continued your magical work, Count," said that man. "You've trafficked with man-devouring water monsters."

Mindaug blinked. And then laughed. It was an odd sound. "I still have not entirely mastered this laughing," he said, reading their expressions. "It has come to me very late in life. Can you place a date on this 'traffic'?"

"About two weeks ago. I can work out the precise date," said Von Stebbens stiffly.

Mindaug nodded. "Ah, yes. I think that you refer to my calling up the nyx that transported the snake-bitten...man, to Venice. I do think he was not devoured by the nyx, but rather that it saved his life, albeit temporarily."

"To call the nyx a monster is to call a lion a monster because it will eat men. It is their nature," said Marco. "And yes. I can definitely confirm that a nyx brought... well, you know whom, Doge Dorma, to us. Francisco said it was done with Kazimierz's help. And now, I must return to assist him in his surgery on that poor boy. All should be ready by now."

"Not a bit of use," said Petro Dorma, slightly peevishly to Benito. "Tell your brother that I, and the affairs and defense of Venice, ought to command more respect than helping Francisco with an injured man."

"No," said Benito. "That's pointless. Medicine will always come first with him."

He looked at the slight white-haired man with the enormous mustache who was supposed to be a powerful and evil magician, and did such a poor job of looking it. Perhaps that was part of the skill of the man. The others—the archimandrite Knight of the Holy Trinity; the priest, one Father Thomas Lüber of Baden, who was apparently a powerful Hypatian scholar; and the Doge—all looked more dangerous. Mindaug looked to be not much of a threat to anything tougher than cheese.

"I was told that Duke Enrico has just come from Ferrara," said Benito, "and he is good at unraveling complicated matters. Why don't we call him in here, too, Doge? He is as good at keeping secrets as those of the Council of Ten who watch and listen to us right now. And he is very much our ally."

"A most sensible suggestion," said Dorma, nodding. "It will be done. And during the explanations maybe it can all become clear to me, and to you, because in the end, I think it may come down to military matters, or at least strategy and tactics."

So, a few minutes later, Benito had his grandfather there, who, as usual, cut through at least some of the confusion. "This Orkise. Where did it suddenly come from?" He looked at Count Mindaug. "I've been to Milan, and even the merchants there are not quite snakes."

"He woke it," said the archimandrite. "Maybe Mindaug regrets that now. Maybe he can help us to destroy it. But I have thought about it, and the count knows too much. Why else would it suddenly appear in Milan?"

Mindaug shook his head. "It has been there—or at least in

Visconti holdings—for centuries. It shows plainly on their coat of arms. I am not stupid, Knight. I have always held back from that which could devour me. No power is worth that price. I conclude that the plague god was awakened by Lucia Maria del Maino, the woman who now rules the Duchy of Milan. She is certainly stupid enough—very vain, too. She has much in common with Elizabeth Bartholdy. She is also the only way we can control the plague."

"But . . ." said the archimandrite.

"Hush, let me plumb this," said Enrico calmly, authoritatively. "So is Sforza behind this?"

The "No" came from the most surprising of people: Petro Dorma. "I would guess that the woman merely used Sforza to get onto the ducal throne. The fact is that the better candidates for Sforza to marry to legitimize his rule, were murdered—or at least someone tried to kill them both. We know not how the one was killed, but Violetta de' Medici was attacked by a small snake that looks very like the Visconti charge. She killed it but was still bitten. Marco is treating her, with some success, I gather."

"I knew her father," said Enrico. "But I would not put it past Sforza to discover all of this and then use it."

"I have reason to know otherwise," said Petro, in such a way that it indicated that the debate was over.

That didn't work on Enrico Dell'este. "I hear he's very sick," he said with some satisfaction.

"Yes," said Petro. "A snakebite. Now, let us stop talking of blame, unless it helps us to deal with this, and talk of strategy. You call this a plague god . . ."

"Yes, it has devoured one town, and it will spread and grow stronger," said Mindaug.

"So how do we counter it?" asked Enrico. "Kill this Lucia woman?"

"That would be the worst thing we could do," said Count Mindaug forcefully. "Orkise is bound to her. If she dies, the wyrm is released. We have to find some way to snare them both—for a very long time."

He shrugged. "If I can retrieve my library, I will look for a way to do that. Otherwise, Orkise will ravage until it runs out of prey."

"Prey?" asked Benito.

"Us," replied Count Mindaug. "Humans. Any and all regardless of age, religion, goodness or otherwise. Needs must that we stand together, or we will all die separately."

The Doge of Venice sighed. "Very well. I need to consult with some people before I can made any decisions." He made a vague gesture at one of the walls. Benito knew that the "some people" referred to by Dorma meant the Council of Ten. At least one of the men on the council would have been listening to this discussion.

"Meet again tomorrow, then?" he asked.

The Doge nodded. He looked very weary in that moment.

When she awoke, Violetta turned her head to see if Sforza was awake also. He was—in fact, he seemed to be studying her intently.

"Yes," she said.

"Yes, what?"

"If you ask me again to marry you, Carlo Sforza, the answer is 'yes.'" She frowned a little. "Of course, you'd have to figure out a way to have your current marriage annulled."

The grunt that came this time sounded exactly like a wolf's. "That's not much of a problem. Becoming a widower is a fine way to have a marriage annulled, I'm thinking."

The man could be scary sometimes. But...

...Always interesting. That was what she'd been looking for, when it came to a husband, she realized. And had now found, after what could fairly be described as a true heroic quest.

Chapter 52

Venice

"There's nothing more I can do for the lad at the moment," Francisco said to Emma and Klaus. The girl and the bombardier were hovering over the now heavily bandaged figure of Tamas, who was lying asleep in a bed in one of the rooms in the Doge's palace. Turner was amused to see that despite Emma's anxiety over the medical state of her new husband, she was almost equally anxious over the damage that might happen to the bedding. He was quite sure she'd never seen such a magnificent bed in her life—and the sheets! Silk, they were.

"What should we do?" asked Klaus. "In case . . . I don't know . . . something happens."

Francisco shook his head. "The boy is in generally good health, leaving aside his wounds of the moment." *Terrible wounds,* he could have said, but there was no point in spreading pointless alarm. "I've stopped the loss of blood from his leg, which was the great danger to his life. As for the hand . . ."

He shrugged. "There's really nothing to be done for that. We'll just have to hope the damage isn't too bad. At least it's his left hand."

"But what if something bad *does* happen?" asked Emma insistently.

"Marco Valdosta will be coming by to examine Tamas sometime later this morning. In the unlikely event that anything happens before Marco arrives, send for me. I won't be far away since the council I've been summoned to is right here in the palace."

Emma didn't look very reassured. By her architectural standards, the Doge's palace was enormous, not to mention labyrinthine.

"Just ask someone for directions," Francisco said, trying not to sound impatient—which he was. There really was nothing further he could do for the injured boy for the moment, and he needed to deal with other pressing matters, such as a patron still on the edge of death, a dukedom in the balance... oh, there were many things he had to deal with. *Now.*

He turned and strode out of the chamber. Behind him, he heard Klaus's comforting voice saying to Emma "Everything will be fine."

Which was most likely not true at all, of course.

Francisco himself got lost twice, trying to find his way through the palace. The main problem, in his case, was that he didn't really know where to go in the first place.

So, he asked one of the guards standing at the intersection of two corridors. The man was wearing an elaborate red and white uniform and was armed with the most absurdly designed halberd Francisco had ever seen. He was pretty sure that if anyone tried to kill a mouse with the weapon he'd do nothing more than wrench his own back.

The guard leaned forward slightly, placing his weight on the halberd—so it was good for something after all—and pointed down the corridor to his left. "Sala del Maggior Consiglio," he said.

A minute or so thereafter, Francisco entered a huge chamber whose walls were covered by portraits of men whom Turner presumed to be the former doges of the city. The painting that hung on one wall, overlooking a great dais, was the largest Francisco had ever seen and seemed to depict Paradise—or, at least, someone's conception of Paradise.

Not Turner's, however. There was not a glass of beer to be seen.

Other than that, and two guards standing beside a far entrance, the enormous room was completely empty.

More enquiries produced directions from the two guards which Francisco followed meticulously that wound up bringing him to another chamber, considerably smaller than the Sala del Maggior Consiglio but even more elaborately decorated—and also completely empty.

Fortunately, there was another guard in that chamber and the directions he provided Francisco took him to a chamber on the floor above where he found the people he was looking for. And a squad of guards—six of them, very alert and armed with lethal-looking weapons—who were a lot less willing to take Turner's *bona fides* for granted. He wasn't allowed to pass through into the chamber beyond until one of the Doge's advisors came out and vouched for him.

Finally, though, he found himself where he needed to be.

The Doge was there, of course, reclining half erect on a chaise lounge, well-upholstered and colored a rich burgundy. Sitting to Petro Dorma's right was a very big man Francisco had never met. He matched the description he'd gotten of Prince Manfred, the younger of Emperor Charles Fredrik's two nephews—which placed him second in line to the Imperial throne, since the Emperor had no children of his own.

Simple deduction would then make the tall but much slimmer man standing next to the prince his Icelandic friend and body-guard, Erik Hakkonsen. But that hardly required any deduction at all, since the young woman standing next to him had to be the Mongolian princess Bortai; by now that story was well known in Venice. Probably in half of Italy, in fact.

Francisco didn't know the two Mongolian men standing just behind Erik and Bortai, but he assumed they were officers in the princess's entourage.

He paid them little mind, however, because the two men standing in the center of the chamber were the focus of atten-tion for everyone there.

By his distinctive uniform, the large man on the left had to be a Knight of the Holy Trinity. This would be the leader of the group of Knights who had come into Italy in search of Count Mindaug. If Francisco remembered correctly, his name was Klaus von Stebbens and he held the rank of archimandrite in the militant order.

Obviously, the Knights had found Mindaug, for the small, somewhat elderly sorcerer was standing right next to Von Steb-bens... and speaking.

"...very worst thing you could do, as I said yesterday," Min-daug was saying. "The Lucia woman is the only thing restraining Orkise at all."

Petro Dorma was frowning. "She hardly seems powerful enough to do that."

Mindaug shook his head. "Her control—call it her power, rather; no, a better word would be 'influence'—over the great snake is because she is the one who summoned him."

"But how would she have done that?" demanded Von Stebbens. "Is she a sorceress herself?"

"No, I doubt that very much. She would have roused Orkise..." Mindaug's eyes narrowed a bit. "Some sort of great blood sacrifice. From the researches I had time to do before—"

Here he gave the archimandrite a none-too-admiring glance. "Before I was interrupted."

Von Stebbens's lips seemed to tighten. But he said nothing beyond: "Please go on."

"Lucia apparently had a younger sister who died some years ago of a mysterious disease. If my supposition is correct, Lucia would have fed her to Orkise. Perhaps unwittingly, but it hardly matters. Once the serpent was roused, it would have begun controlling her as well as being controlled by her. By now, the two of them are inseparably linked. If you kill Lucia, whatever restraint she has over the monster dies with her."

The big broad-shouldered prince shifted a little in his seat, and issued a skeptical sort of grunting noise. "Does she restrain the thing at all?"

Mindaug nodded. "Oh, yes. I'm sure she does. Orkise is motivated by nothing beyond his lust for killing. But Lucia, for all that she is something of a monster herself, has broader and more subtle ambitions. She wants to rule Milan—perhaps more than Milan eventually. Killing almost everyone in Italy would hardly serve that purpose."

"So where do you think Orkise is now?" Dorma nodded toward the armored figure of Von Stebbens. "Given what the archimandrite has told us of the battle between the Knights and the great serpent at Val di Castellazzo, the monster was wounded but certainly not killed."

From the movement of Mindaug's huge mustache, Francisco thought he must be grimacing. "No, no, they didn't kill it. They *couldn't* have, no matter how badly they injured the thing."

Von Stebbens seemed to bridle a bit. Mindaug gave him a glance that was half-apologetic and half-amused. "Please don't take that as a criticism, Archimandrite. I doubt if anyone—or anything at all, short of direct divine intervention—could kill

Orkise. The creature is something in the way of a divinity himself. A snake god who embodies the plague—probably all forms of death brought by disease. How can anyone kill disease? It's one of the Four Horsemen of the Apocalypse. Could you kill any of the other three—war, famine and death itself?"

The little sorcerer shook his head. "No, Orkise can't be slain. What we have to do is figure out a way to trap him. And do so in a trap that will hold the monster for centuries."

"Is that possible?" asked the Doge.

Mindaug made a little gesture that could be taken as a shrug. Just a twitch of the shoulders.

"I . . . think so." He reached up and tugged at his mustache, but only briefly. Francisco had the impression that Mindaug grew suddenly worried that his mustache tugging might be somehow inappropriate. Or was there something about his teeth that he was disguising?

"I can think of at least two possible ways it might be done," said the Lithuanian sorcerer. "But I would need to study the matter carefully, and for that, I need my library."

Archimandrite von Stebbens's face twisted into a grimace of skepticism. "There wouldn't be anything left of it by now. Books are valuable. The duchess's soldiers would have plundered the library. Or, if they were so ignorant they didn't realize what the tomes were worth, they would have simply destroyed it."

Mindaug's mustache wiggled in that manner that Francisco had come to recognize as a smile. "Oh, I doubt that, Archimandrite. Unless they had a very capable magician with them—*very* capable—they couldn't have gotten past the seals and wards. And even if somehow they did manage that, they . . . ah . . ."

For a moment, Francisco thought the elderly count looked downright shifty-eyed.

Prince Manfred chuckled. "They'd be dead."

Yes, he *did* look shifty-eyed.

"Not exactly," said Mindaug. "They would no longer be in this world. And in the one they found themselves, well . . . let's just say they would wish they were dead." Now, the sorcerer from Lithuania looked downright malevolent. "I really dislike it when people meddle with my library."

Manfred chuckled again. "So it would seem." His eyes moved to Von Stebbens. "Can he be trusted, Klaus?"

The archimandrite's expression became quite sour. "Well..."

Before he could go any further, Mindaug shook his head and said: "Trust is not something I am very familiar with, Prince. There's precious little of it—none at all, actually—in the circles in Lithuania I grew up in. That was true even before Jagiellon became possessed by Chernobog."

He puffed out his extravagant mustache with an exhalation. "What I *can* assure you is that you can rely on me. Well, probably. It depends on what you want. But if you can't rely on me, I won't lie about it. Why would I?"

Here, he shrugged. "I have by now burned every bridge behind me in the lands to the east of your uncle's empire. My only chance of survival is to reach an accommodation with someone of power here in Italy." He glanced at Francisco. "My preference would be Milan, so long as Sforza is in control. But wherever it might be, I would hardly make myself welcome if I developed a reputation for being unreliable."

Manfred's gaze had been on Mindaug throughout that little speech. Without shifting it, he said: "Klaus?"

The archimandrite grunted. "I...will vouch for that much, Your Highness. My experience with Mindaug is that he keeps his word."

"Good enough." Manfred now looked up at Erik. "Do you have any need for the Knights who came with us to Venice?"

Erik shook his head. "I can't see why I would. If anything comes up that requires military assistance"—he nodded toward Bortai and the other two Mongols—"I can call on them."

Manfred planted his hands on the armrests of his chair and pushed himself up to stand erect. The movement was quick, easy, even graceful. Despite his bulk, the big prince was obviously athletic.

"Very well," he said. "Klaus, your men still need to rest and recover. But the Knights we brought with us are well rested and they should be enough. Count Mindaug, let us be about the task of recovering your library."

He grinned down at the sorcerer. "Mind you, I'm only offering to deal with whatever troops Duchess Lucia still has at your villa. The wards, the seals—those I'm not getting anywhere near. I like this world just fine."

Mindaug started to say something, but he was interrupted by

a commotion at the door. Apparently, on the other side of the closed portal, the men standing guard were taking exception to something.

Or someone.

Francisco heard a male voice saying: "You can't—"

That was as far as he got. A rather piercing and very imperious female voice rode over him. "Just open the door, blast you! What? Do you think I'm going to assault the Doge in my condition, you ninny?"

"Ah," said Francisco, moving quickly toward the door. Over his shoulder he said: "That will be Violetta de' Medici. I'd recommend letting her in, Doge. She's clearly recovering and, ah, quite strong-willed."

After Francisco opened the door, the first person to come through was Violetta de' Medici, sitting in a wheelchair being pushed by Marco Valdosta. The next person to come into the chamber was Carlo Sforza, also in a wheelchair. His attendant was one of Marco's assistants. Francisco couldn't remember his name.

Francisco gave Marco a quick, worried glance. *Are they up for this?* his eyes said.

Marco understood the silent query. After bringing Violetta's chair to a halt not far from the Doge, he turned to Francisco and shrugged. "They insisted—and to be honest, while they're still both weak, I think some activity would be good for them."

Francisco himself had long held to the heretical opinion that physical activity was good for ill or injured people, within reason, so he could hardly object now. Besides, while he still looked weak, Carlo was obviously alert. Indeed, he seemed quite cheerful, judging from the expression on his face.

"Some introductions are in order," said Petro Dorma. He used a forefinger to point at people as he named them.

"Prince Manfred, this is Carlo Sforza, the current ruler of Milan. The young lady next to him is Violetta de' Medici, whose uncle is Duke Cosimo." He didn't bother to add "the ruler of Tuscany" since Manfred would know that already.

Presuming on a personal acquaintance that didn't exist—but neatly sidestepped the awkward issue of Sforza's title—Petro now pointed at the prince and said, "Carlo, Violetta, this is Prince Manfred. His uncle is—"

"Emperor Charles Fredrik, and Manfred is second in line to the throne," Sforza finished for him. "Yes, I know." He then added with a sly little smile: "You're looking well, Petro"—presuming a personal acquaintance that didn't exist. "I hear you were poisoned also."

"So I was." Dorma's finger pointed to Erik and Bortai. "This is Erik Hakkonsen and his wife Bortai. She is the sister of Kildai, Great Khan of the Golden Horde." He hesitated for a moment. "I just realized that I don't know what title Erik holds at the moment."

The tall blond shrugged. "For the moment, I'm still just Manfred's bodyguard and...ah..."—he gave the prince a sly little smile of his own—"mentor, I guess you could say."

"And closest friend," said Manfred, a bit gruffly.

Sforza nodded politely at both people, but immediately turned his attention to Francisco. "What news?"

"Duke Umberto seems to have recovered from his setback at Fidenza—or thinks he has, at any rate. He's launched a new attack, approaching from the east."

"By way of Cremona. I thought he'd do that." Grimly, Sforza added: "It's time the duke of Parma learned his proper place in the world. I'll have his head—one of his hands, too, the bastard—on a pike."

Dorma looked a bit startled. The fury in the voice of Milan's new duke was unmistakable, for all that his tone was level and even.

Seeing the expression on the Doge's face, Francisco explained: "We sent an envoy to Duke Umberto. He had the poor man maimed—his hand cut off."

Throughout the discussion, as had been true the day before, Princess Bortai had been following the discussion intently—but also with obvious difficulty. She seemed to have enough familiarity with Italian to make broad sense of what was being said, but missed many of the specific details.

Now, she rattled off a burst of words in what Francisco assumed to be her native tongue. That would be the Mongolian dialect used by the Golden Horde.

Erik said something in reply, in the same language. As soon as he finished, Bortai and both of the Mongolians standing behind her got expressions on their faces that...

Boded very, very ill for somebody.

The duke of Parma, Francisco was pretty sure. He wasn't very familiar with the Golden Horde and its customs, but he assumed they shared the typical Mongol attitude on the subject of envoys. However ruthless Mongols might be in other respects, envoys—any sort of ambassador or emissary—were considered sacrosanct. They were never harmed, or even threatened with harm.

Bortai rattled off something else. Grinning coldly, Erik looked down at Sforza and said: "If your troops can open a path for us whenever you meet this Umberto fellow in the field, we'll be glad to reap his parts for you."

Startled, Petro Dorma looked at Manfred. "Ah, Your Highness..."

The prince shrugged. "I'm not going to tell Erik and Bortai what to do with their own troops. Besides, I think"—he glanced from Dorma to Sforza to Violetta—"we can discuss the political implications later."

While that exchange took place, Sforza had been studying Erik; then, gave the two Mongol soldiers a quick study; then, looked back at Erik. "How many men do you have? And are they really that good?"

Before Erik could answer, Carlo held up his hand. "Hear me out, please. I'm sure I can defeat that bastard Umberto in any battle"—here his expression became somber—"but I doubt if I can rout him. Not with the number of men I'll have. The problem is that we're being invaded by others besides Parma, so I have no choice but to divide my forces."

He looked now to Francisco. "Who else will we be facing? In the next fortnight, I'm talking about."

Turner tugged at his beard, thinking. "Malatesta, for sure. I don't know about Lippi Pagano and his Imolans. The viscount is being his usual cagey self. But what I'm more concerned about at the moment is this silly notion that *you* will be leading anybody in the field. For the love of all that's holy, Carlo, you're still a very sick man."

The duke of Milan shook his head impatiently. "I'm not proposing to lead any charges—in fact, I won't even be on horseback. I've gotten used to riding in a carriage. Maybe it's my advanced age. And it's no harder—well, not much, anyway—to sit in a carriage than it is to lie on a couch."

"Sitting in a carriage, no," said Manfred, "but what you're

proposing is that you'll be directing a battle from that carriage." The big prince made a face. "I've commanded soldiers in a battle. No matter what position you do it from—standing; on horseback; sitting in a carriage; lying flat on your back, for that matter—it's...ah, what the word?"

"Stressful," Francisco supplied forcefully. "Carlo, this is unwise. Let me deal with Duke Umberto. You have other officers who can handle Malatesta."

"No." Sforza's response was just as forceful. "Yes, I've got other men who can deal with Malatesta. But we're fighting on three fronts, not two. You seem to have forgotten that Milan itself is now in the hands of my treacherous wife. I want it back—and you're by far the best man I have for that purpose."

Francisco started to argue but fell silent. Carlo's assessment was...

Probably accurate. The Wolf of the North was such a dominant figure that, while he had plenty of capable military subordinates, he really didn't have very many good political advisors and assistants. He didn't usually need them.

A slight commotion behind him drew his attention. Another person was being ushered into the chamber, whom Francisco had met before.

The duke of Florence had joined them. Cosimo must have just arrived in Venice.

Violetta didn't notice, however. Her attention was concentrated entirely on Sforza. Now she spoke up, for the first time since her entrance. "Are you sure of this, Carlo?" She sounded genuinely concerned. "If anything goes wrong..."

"Nothing's going to go wrong. At least, nothing that would pose a threat to me personally." Sforza glanced again at Erik and the Mongols. "Whether they can do their part...we'll see."

Bortai frowned. The other two Mongols had no reaction to the Milanese ruler's somewhat skeptical remark—probably because they hadn't understood him. Their command of Italian was obviously rudimentary.

Erik Hakkonsen, on the other hand, just looked amused. "I've got the best light cavalry in the world, Duke. And anyone stupid enough to have an envoy mutilated isn't likely to be any more astute on a battlefield, I'm thinking."

Sforza studied him for a moment, then grunted. "You've got

the right of that. Parma's an ass and a drunkard—and those are his best qualities."

He swiveled in his wheelchair to look at the woman in the wheelchair next to him, and gave her a big smile. "You can probably manage a carriage ride yourself. Would you like to see a battle, instead of just reading about them?"

Violetta brightened immediately, as if Carlo had offered her some fine jewelry rather than a view of carnage. "Oh, yes, Carlo! That would be splendid."

While that exchange was taking place, Duke Cosimo had advanced to the center of the chamber and come to stand just behind his niece. "What would be splendid, Violetta?"

Startled, she looked back at him. "Uncle Cosimo! I didn't know you were here." She pointed at Sforza. "Carlo's offered to let me watch one of his battles. Isn't that exciting?"

It was Cosimo de' Medici's turn to be startled. Not at the notion of his niece going to a battlefield, but at Sforza's new status with her.

"Carlo," was it now? And he hadn't missed the undertone of affection.

Well, this was interesting.

Chapter 53

Val di Castellazzo, Duchy of Milan

As it turned out, Prince Manfred and his Knights of the Holy Trinity had no role to play at Val di Castellazzo—beyond that of simple laborers. When they got to the villa, they discovered that the whole compound was now in ruins. And it was completely deserted. Having done their wreckage and plundering, Duchess Lucia's troops had apparently returned to Milan.

As he and Manfred surveyed the scene from horseback, Count Mindaug started tugging at his mustache. The gesture somehow managed to combine anger and thoughtfulness.

"Doesn't look like there's much left," commented Manfred. He waved at the ruins with a large, gauntleted hand. "If it hadn't rained yesterday, everything here would probably still be smoldering."

"With respect to the edifice, you're right. But my library—the books, at least—will still be intact. We'll need to dig them out from under the rubble, of course."

Seeing the surprised expression on the prince's face, Mindaug left off his mustache tugging and smiled. Or so, at least, Manfred presumed from the little heave in the enormous mustache. You couldn't actually see any part of the Lithuanian magician's mouth.

"I assure you the fire those miserable arsonists started won't have damaged the books, Prince. The reason I know that is because one of the wards I set upon my library protects them by incinerating any would-be reivers. That would hardly do me any good if my library got incinerated at the same time."

He began climbing down from his horse. "Let's go see what needs to be done."

Venice

Marco looked over the five Knights of the Holy Trinity resting on their cots in the same room in the Doge's palace where he'd healed Carlo Sforza and Violetta de' Medici. These were the Knights who'd survived Orkise's breath, which the monster had spewed upon them in the battle at Val di Castellazzo.

Survived—but only for the moment. The plague god's venomous breath had poisoned them badly. Unless Marco could neutralize its effects, they would all die soon.

He'd decided to try the same treatment he'd used to good effect with Sforza and Violetta. He didn't know if he had enough left of the rose petal attar, but there was only one way to find out. So, he'd had the knights' cots arranged like a five-pointed star, with their heads clustered together. That way, he could have the same sort of tent covering them, within which they'd be able to breathe as much of the attar as possible.

"Will it work?" asked Patriarch Michael. He and Father Thomas Lüber were standing next to Marco. Just behind them stood the Aemiline hesychast, Brother Dimitrios, who'd arrived in Venice the day before at the patriarch's summons.

Marco spread his hands in a gesture of uncertainty. "I don't know, because I don't know how much of the essence of those rose petals hasn't been steamed out of them already. You can tell just from the smell that the attar has become weaker. We'll just have to see. They won't heal quickly, no matter what."

He turned away from the tented cots and gestured toward the door. "Let us continue our discussion in the chamber beyond. These men don't need to be disturbed; they need to rest."

The chamber next door was one of the many moderate-sized salons that could be found throughout the Doge's palace. The building served as the seat of the Venetian government, not simply the Doge's residence, and had been designed accordingly. At any given time, many of La Serenissima's multitude of councils and committees would be holding meetings within the palace, both formal and informal.

The walls and ceiling of this chamber had the usual murals and paintings that decorated most of the rooms in the palace—not including the cells holding suspects, of course. The palace also served Venice as a prison.

After the four men had taken seats, Patriarch Michael looked from Marco to Brother Dimitrios, and then back again. "I suspect the two of you have a better understanding of this Count Mindaug than anyone else in Italy—or in the Holy Roman Empire, for that matter. What do you think of him?"

Marco glanced at the Aemiline hesychast. Brother Dimitrios's expression was pensive; that of a man who would take some time to deliberate on his answer.

Left to his own inclinations, Marco would probably have done the same, but the ancient power whose spirit he shared was not given to hesitation. So, almost as if he were hearing someone else speak, Marco heard his own voice filled the room. It was not a loud voice, just . . . powerful.

"I would not call him a good man, certainly. But he has made his choice and he is neither indecisive nor someone who second-guesses himself. And, in his own fatalistic way, he is courageous. You can rely on him to fight on your side and not betray you."

Patriarch Michael frowned. "You are sure of this?"

"Yes." So might granite sound, if stone could speak.

Brother Dimitrios ran fingers through his hair, which was now a bit thin on top but still dark. "I concur. I spent many hours observing the man. I don't doubt he is capable of great—even extreme—ruthlessness. But I never detected any cruelty. Indeed, he was often kind to the little mice who shared his wagon, sharing bits of food with them and taking care not to frighten them. I think he rather enjoyed their company."

"But they posed no threat to him, either," pointed out Father Lüber. "What you describe as kindness might simply have been forbearance."

The Aemiline smiled. "You can say so, if you wish. But I have spent a great deal of time in Lithuania, Father. In Chernobog's realm, forbearance is no more common than kindness."

After a moment, Patriarch Michael nodded. "No, I suppose

not—and I think we have little choice, in any event, between Orkise and Mindaug?"

Father Lüber issued a soft little grunt, that even had some humor in it. "Put that way, we have no choice at all," he said.

Milan

"I leave you in charge of the city, Lord Laglissio." Impatiently, Lucia headed for the entrance to the ducal palace. Behind her, she heard the count say: "But, Your Grace, what would you have me—"

"Just do it! I have pressing business to attend to in Arona."

Pressing, indeed. As she climbed into the carriage, she heard the asp's hissing voice. It sounded louder than usual, but that was probably an illusion brought on by her own anxiety. The snake's speech was not really a voice, just thoughts in her mind.

Orkise is hurt. And enraged, of course.

The carriage set off with a lurch. Lucia, unprepared, was slammed back into the seat. Normally, that would have resulted in punishment leveled on the coachman, but she was so preoccupied she barely noticed. She hadn't actually been hurt, after all.

"Will he survive?" she asked, now frightened. Without Orkise...

The answer had a derisive tone. *Orkise can't be killed. How could he, since he is death himself? But he will sulk for a time. He is not accustomed to being thwarted.*

Lucia wondered what "sulk for a time" would translate into, if measured. Hours? Days? Even weeks? *Months?*

Hours were not a problem. Days...she could manage, especially if they were just a few. But weeks—certainly months—could be disastrous.

"And you say Sforza still lives?" That came out almost as a whisper.

Yes. I do not understand it.

Disastrous.

Count Laglissio's thoughts were similarly dark-hued, but the time frame was reversed. He was hoping for as much time as possible, before someone from the duke of Milan's entourage— perhaps even Sforza himself, God forbid—showed up in Milan. The new military units that Duchess Lucia had assembled in the capital were still large in number, but they were poorly trained and probably had a morale to match their training.

His fears proved well founded. In midafternoon, a sizeable cavalry force showed up at the city's southern gate. The officer in command demanded entry and the fools manning the gate were browbeaten into compliance.

The first act of the cavalry commander was to replace the existing guards with men from his own force. His second act was to lead the remainder of the force—still upward of four hundred strong—to the ducal palace.

There—this was incomprehensible!—the commander succeeded in browbeating the guards into allowing his cavalrymen entry. The ducal palace of Milan was a *fortress*, which could have successfully resisted a much larger army.

Perhaps they would have, except that the guards couldn't find Lord Laglissio when they sent couriers to fetch him and get his instructions. They looked everywhere they could think of—

—but, sadly, did not think to look in the treasury vault. Had they done so, they would have found the count hurriedly stuffing a sack with specie, before he headed to the stables and rode his horse out of the city via one of the smaller gates on the northeast wall.

Let Lucia do what she would. Laglissio didn't think she would be alive much longer anyway. Nor would he, if he didn't get out of the duchy fast enough. The officer who'd led the cavalry force into Milan was that Turner fellow that Sforza seemed to dote on.

Frightful man, for all that he claimed to be a simple healer. Turner was the same brute who'd had poor Captain Count di Neiro summarily executed. Cut down right in the street! As if he were a common criminal!

It was well for Laglissio that he made his escape from Milan. Francisco Turner did indeed have a warrant for the count's arrest, signed by Sforza himself—and a not-thin batch of other documents, also signed by the duke, that authorized Turner to execute anyone he chose.

He used four of them to execute the top officers of Lucia's so-called "City Guard." Or, at least, the four top officers who still remained in Milan. Lord Laglissio and two other leading figures in Her Grace's City Guard appeared to have fled the city.

"Should we set out in pursuit, Captain?" asked one of Francisco's lieutenants.

Turner shook his head. "It's not worth the effort, and it's certainly not worth diverting the needed men." He gestured toward the four captured officers. "Just hang that lot—nothing fancy; we don't need to erect a gallows for the likes of them—and see to it that there aren't any organized units of Lucia's 'City Guard' still at large."

He thought for a moment. "Put up a proclamation announcing that anyone still wearing that ridiculous blue-and-gold uniform by tomorrow morning will be executed on the spot. That should do it, I think."

Val di Castellazzo, Duchy of Milan

The next morning, Manfred and Mindaug and the prince's retinue of Knights left the ruins of the villa. They escorted two wagons loaded with the count's library, one of them driven by Mindaug himself and the other by Klaus the bombardier.

Manfred rode alongside Mindaug's wagon. He was sucking his left thumb.

"Still hurts," he complained.

Mindaug grimaced with sympathy; so, at least, the prince interpreted the motion of his mustache. "That volume has always had a nasty disposition."

"Who ever heard of a book that bites?" grumbled Manfred.

"Um." Count Mindaug puffed air through his mustache. "At least that one doesn't have a digestive tract. So you were never in much danger of losing your thumb."

The prince stared down at him. Mindaug's view of the world was . . .

Odd. Sometimes, quite disconcerting.

Chapter 54

Left bank of the Adda River
A few miles northwest of Cremona

Violetta fell asleep as they neared the site where Carlo predicted the battle would be fought. Her fatigue was not surprising, though. It had been a long and arduous journey, at least for someone still as weak from poisoning as she was. The carriage holding herself, Cosimo and Sforza, guarded by the soldiers her uncle had brought as an escort from Florence along with a sizeable force of Venetian cavalry, had left Milan several days earlier. They'd passed through Padua and Verona before striking west toward Cremona where most of Milan's army had been awaiting Sforza's arrival.

Once he had an army back under his command, Sforza had marched them south through the Val Seriana, the valley formed by the small Serio River. They'd moved quickly, as Sforza's armies always did, until they reached the Adda River, which they then followed toward its confluence with the Po due west of Cremona.

Throughout, to Violetta's surprise—and some unease—Carlo had stayed on the east bank of the two rivers. She would have expected him to follow the opposite bank, which would allow him to easily interdict an enemy force marching northwest toward Milan.

When she'd asked him the reason, his explanation had been terse—and, she realized, opened a window into the man's soul. Or at least, the military facet of that soul.

"I trust my army more than Umberto or any of his officers will trust Parma's. Don't forget that if I'm not on the west bank to block a Parmese army marching on Milan, they'll not be on this bank to block me from marching on Parma. My army will move at least half again—maybe twice as fast as the drunkard's forces will. I'll reach Parma long before he gets to Milan—which has better defenses to begin with, and by now will be under Francisco's control. I can trust Turner to hold my capital long enough for me to take Parma, and once that stinking Umberto loses Parma he'll lose his army, too. Most of it, anyway."

Violetta had glanced at her uncle to see if Cosimo shared that confidence, but the duke of Tuscany's expression had revealed nothing. In all likelihood, she decided, Cosimo was simply declining to second-guess a man who was widely recognized as one of Europe's most capable generals. Her uncle had many skills and talents—a great many; more than most rulers—but military tactics were not among them.

Once they reached the confluence of the Serio and the Adda, Cosimo left the carriage in order to ride one of his horses. Despite her own fatigue, which was still too great to risk trying to stay in a saddle, Violetta soon came to envy him. The road that ran alongside the River Adda was crude—more of an ox cart path than anything that could properly be called a road. The rocks and tree trunks had been removed but no one had bothered to do the same for the many large roots that came to the surface. The carriage was jolted back and forth unpredictably, to make everything worse.

After one particularly rough battering, Sforza had patted the seat next to him. Violetta had been sitting across from him the whole way since they left Venice.

"Stop being proud, girl," he said. "Put your head on my lap and brace your feet against the side of the carriage. That'll cushion you a lot better—and I can keep you from being thrown onto the floor."

She considered the proposal for a moment—but not a long one. True, it was immodest, even perhaps improper. Despite their private discussions, she and Sforza were not formally betrothed. But Violetta had never cared that much for proper public opinion; better her reputation pick up a bruise or two than her whole body wind up black and blue.

Her new posture was surprisingly relaxing, as well as more comfortable and safer. Within a few minutes, she was sound asleep.

❁   ❁   ❁

She was awakened by the sound of cannon fire.

"We're here, girl. Welcome to your first battlefield," said Carlo. There was a hint of humor in his voice. "Just hope it's not your last."

Violetta sat up abruptly. "Oh, surely not!" she said. "This is so exciting!"

Her first impression was nothing much more than chaos and confusion in the distance. The carriage had come to rest atop a small knoll that gave a fairly good view of the confluence of the Adda and Po rivers, perhaps four hundred yards away. But while Violetta could see what was happening well enough, she had trouble making any sense of it.

Fortunately, she had one of the world's best *let's-make-sense-of-a-battlefield* experts at her side.

"My officers have done extremely well," Carlo said with great satisfaction. "Just what I told them to do." He pointed to the nearby river, which, here, was the Adda. "See how our troops have been forcing the Parmese down the bank? They're using the spring and early summer muck along the river to tangle up the bastards. It's hard to fight in those conditions. Instead of forming a solid bulwark behind you where you can make a stand, the river keeps betraying you."

As if to illustrate his point, Violetta saw a squad of Parmese soldiers slip into a pile by the riverbank, with several of them being forced into the water itself. They scrambled back onto land soon enough, but Violetta could just imagine how disheartening the experience must be—especially given that the rate of Milanese cannon fire being brought to bear on the soldiers half-trapped along the bank was almost astonishing. Violetta had known that Sforza was famous—notorious, among his enemies—for the superlative quality of his field artillery, but that knowledge had been abstract. This...

Was anything but. Even at the distance she could see how terribly the cannonballs were careening through the Parmese ranks. A man was literally *cut in half* by one of those projectiles. She watched as the upper part of his body was sent pinwheeling through the sky, trailing and spewing about...

Best not to dwell on that. Whether intentionally or not, Carlo distracted her at that moment, to her relief.

"It's just spring-summer muck," he said, "mostly concentrated right by the river. So we're still getting good grazing shots as long as the artillerymen do their job properly."

She saw that he was right. A "grazing shot" was a ball that struck the ground five to ten yards short of the enemy ranks. So long as the ground was solid, the ball would bounce rather than dig into the soil—and thus come smashing into the soldiers at roughly waist height. It was almost impossible to dodge from such shots, and a single ball could kill as many as a dozen soldiers.

Again, abstract knowledge she'd had in her possession. What she hadn't considered was, first, the sheer volume of noise produced by such cannon fire. It was hard to keep her mind concentrated instead of taking flight like a startled bird.

And, second...she realized now that she'd never considered just how much blood was contained in a single human body, and what would be the effect on a battlefield of dozens—hundreds—of ruptured bodies. There seemed to be bright red paint everywhere she looked.

Men screaming, too. Those sounds rose even above the cannon fire.

"Are you all right?" Sforza asked. Turning her head, she saw that he was studying her intently. "A battlefield is difficult enough for even veterans to handle. You..."

"I'm fine," she said firmly. "A bit shaken, but...I can handle it. And if I'm to be the duchess of Milan, I had better be able to. No?"

"Ah...Well, yes, that would be handy." He gave her a quick, quite wolfish grin. Then he pointed further down the rivers—to the banks of the Po this time.

"See that cluster of men?" he asked. "That'll be Duke Umberto and what passes for his command cluster. Looking pretty ragged, aren't they? By now, the bastards won't be in much better shape than their sorry troops. A perfect target..."

His gaze ranged across the landscape. "Don't see them yet, though."

Sforza couldn't see Hakkonsen and his cavalrymen because Mongols—Icelanders, even more so, given the barren landscape of their island—were masters at using terrain to disguise their movements. The Po Valley was generally flat, but very few "flat" areas of the Earth really had no undulations at all. Erik and Bortai and their men had found a sunken road that was low enough, given its surrounding vegetation, to allow them to approach within two hundred yards of the Parmese forces without being spotted.

Now, nestled out of sight in a small grove, Erik studied the enemy that was being hammered down the riverbank.

"It won't be long," he said softly.

Bortai's expression was more skeptical. "The duke of Parma might be trying to rally his men—in which case he won't show up until his troops have already overrun this position and we'll have had to move."

Erik's smile was a very shallow thing. "We could make a bet on it, if you'd like. I'll place three of my best horses down in a wild gamble that Duke Umberto is leading his men to the rear rather than rallying his rear guard. What say?"

Bortai didn't bother to dignify that proposal with a response.

Arona, Duchy of Milan

For once, the sight of Castello di Arona coming into view didn't fill Lucia with disdain. Indeed, she was relieved to see it. If there was anywhere in the world she could restore her self-confidence and resolve, it was here. The buildings might be rundown, but what lurked in the cellars below was anything but that.

Once she got out of the carriage and went inside—unusually, to her staff, making no criticism of any kind—she headed toward the entrance to the cellars, a gaggle of servants following in her wake.

"I do not wish to be disturbed," she said, making a dismissive motion with her hand. "Under no circumstances, is that understood?"

Hastily bobbing heads indicated the staff's full and complete comprehension of their mistress's desire. Within seconds, none of the servants was still in sight.

Lucia took down the heavy key to the cellars from its hiding place. In truth, it wasn't much of a secret compartment. She'd never bothered to hide the key more thoroughly because the staff was frightened of those cellars and would hardly be likely to steal the key in order to explore them.

And if they did, so what? A snake god would enjoy a little snack.

As ever, despite the many times she'd made this same journey, the descent into the cellars filled her with dread and unease. All the more so when she reached her destination and was terrified to see the huge face of the serpent looming out of the darkness. Even with the dim lighting produced by the lamp in her hand, the fury in that flat-headed visage was obvious.

"They *hurt* me," hissed the monster. Its jaws gaped wide, the fangs looking like so many swords. "It *hurt.*"

If the creature blamed Lucia for that...

More petrified than she'd ever been in her life, Lucia held completely still. She said nothing. What was there to say?

To her relief, after perhaps half a minute Orkise pulled back its head. The jaws closed. "What do you want?"

"To help you get your revenge," Lucia said, thinking quickly. "It was outrageous, what they did!"

A faint look of something like humor came to the serpent's face. Something in the eyes, perhaps—the lips were hardly suited to expressions.

"And what do you care about that?" it demanded derisively. The monster curled away and slid further into the cellars. "There's nothing to do but wait," Orkise said. "It's still not warm enough out there."

"Wait?" She didn't like the sound of that. Every day's delay gave her enemies time to gather their strength. "How long?"

"A week. Perhaps two. However long it takes. If I hadn't been so cold, those cursed Knights never would have escaped. Not one of them."

Left bank of the Po River
A few miles northwest of Cremona

"Now," said Erik.

An instant later, the Mongol cavalrymen began swarming out of the grove of trees and the sunken road in which they'd been hiding. The terrain they now found themselves on was quite level—and, best of all, hadn't been rained on for a couple of days. The ground was solid, firm, unobstructed by anything more substantial than grass and a few scattered shrubs—just the sort of footing that the Mongol horses preferred.

They were small horses, though not ponies: a typical Mongolian horse weighed around six hundred pounds. They were not especially fast horses, either. Over a short distance, they could be outrun by many European mounts. But what the Mongolian horses lacked in size and speed, they made up for with extraordinary endurance. Horse racing was second only to wrestling as a Mongol sport, but the length of the races was far longer than Europeans were accustomed to—anywhere up to twenty miles. A Mongol horse could manage that distance without losing its wind, long after a European horse was too exhausted to continue.

Relative speed mattered little at the moment, though. Erik hadn't ordered the charge until Duke Umberto and his immediate cluster of officers and bodyguards were no more than one hundred and fifty yards away. It would take them about twenty seconds to get there—and once they'd gotten within fifty yards, they could start firing their bows.

Twenty seconds is a long time for well-trained and alert soldiers to take good defensive positions against a cavalry attack. But Erik would have been willing to bet ten of his best horses that the group of men they were charging toward were neither alert to external threats—they'd be completely preoccupied with the quarrels and debates they were obviously embroiled in—nor well trained. "Well trained," at least, in the sense of infantrymen who were accustomed to such maneuvers. Abstractly, the Parmese officers would know how to defend against a cavalry attack. But not more than a handful of them would have actually had to do so personally in years.

In the event, Erik and Bortai and their Mongols had crossed half the distance before Umberto and his entourage began anything one could call a coordinated response. They only had ten seconds left—and only three or four before the arrows came slicing through their ranks.

Not enough time. Not nearly enough time.

"Ha!" shouted Sforza, his fist clenched and raised above his head. "Ha! That drunken swine is a dead man!"

Violetta had never seen any sort of cavalry charge in person, much less the exotic Mongolian version of the tactic. But even at the distance—this was all happening a good third of a mile away from their knoll—she could see that Carlo was probably right.

Soldiers accustomed to harquebuses and muskets tended to be derisive of bows and arrows. "Antique weapons." But the truth was that at short range, bows in the hands of men who knew how to use them were deadly—and they had a much greater rate of fire than even the most skilled gun handler could manage. The real advantage of a gun over a bow on a battlefield was that it took years for a man to become truly proficient with a bow, where he could be trained to shoot a gun in only a few weeks.

But these Mongols *had* been training for years; for their entire adult lifetime, in fact, since Mongol boys started learning mounted archery from a very young age.

By the time Erik and Bortai reached Umberto, half of the duke's bodyguards and officers were either dead or badly wounded, and half of those who'd survived were galloping away in full retreat. The group that remained—perhaps a dozen men—were too confused and agitated to put up a coordinated defense. They were just milling around, waving their swords and shouting incoherently.

Erik and Bortai ignored everyone but Umberto—who still hadn't spotted them coming at him.

Bortai drove her lance into the neck of the duke's mount. The warhorse screamed, stumbled, and fell to the ground. It was Umberto's turn to scream then. The duke favored a boot holster whose pistol grip rose just above his knee, which had been trapped between the falling horse and the weapon. The knee was broken so badly he would never have been able to walk well again.

Not that it mattered. Erik was already on the ground, kneeling next to the duke. A quick smash with the head of his hatchet stunned Umberto. It took no more than a handful of seconds to sever the head. Then—

Sforza hadn't specified which hand he wanted. Probably he'd have preferred the right, but that had been trapped under the horse as well.

The left would do. Erik was not sentimental about such things and he'd be surprised if a condottiere of Sforza's stature and experience would be either.

Standing up with a trophy in each hand, Erik saw that Bortai was already holding a sack open for them. As he dropped them in, glancing around, he saw that the little cavalry battle—skirmish, really—was already over. What few Parmese had survived were now also racing off.

A nice day's work, if he said so himself.

Which he saw no reason not to. "A nice day's work."

"Stop bragging," said Bortai.

It took a bit of effort for Violetta and Duke Cosimo to persuade Sforza to forego a pursuit of the now hastily retreating Parmese army. The Milanese condottiere was like a tiger smelling blood. That retreat—it had hardly any leadership at all!—could be easily turned into a rout. And the slaughter that could be inflicted on a routed enemy was something no professional soldier wanted to relinquish, unless he knew for a certainty that he'd never have to face that enemy again.

But Orkise was still lurking somewhere. With Umberto dead, there was no chance Parma wouldn't sue for peace. Without Parma still in the war, the Imolan Viscount Lippi Pagano would also seek a settlement—just something face-saving—and not even Malatesta would be foolish enough to continue the conflict under those circumstances. "Lord of Rimini, Forli, Cesena, Pesaro, Marquis of Ravenna, and Protector of Romagna" was a splendid-sounding list of titles, but on his own, Malatesta would be no match for Sforza's Milan, and even that arrogant bastard understood as much.

"I'll still take Cremona!" Sforza insisted. "I need a good estate for my maimed officer, and there'll be several for him to choose from in Cremona."

Duke Cosimo made a little placating gesture with his hand. "Yes, of course. Cremona's but a few miles away and the garrison won't put up any resistance. By all means incorporate the city and its hinterland into the Duchy of Milan. Who's going to resist? Umberto's ghost?"

Violetta said nothing. She was still preoccupied with digesting everything she'd seen that day. Many lessons had been there to learn.

Perhaps the greatest lesson, she thought, was that an army was made up of men, not toy soldiers or stick figures seen at a

distance. A great deal of the reason Sforza was such a formi-
dable adversary was the way he trained his men and chose his
officers. It wasn't simply that the man was a superb tactician on
a battlefield. He also, except possibly when he faced Ferrara, had
the *best army* on the field. Officers and men he could count on
to implement his brutal, ruthless tactics . . . and, most of all, *press
on, press on, press on*. Carlo and his troops had never relented
that day. Not once, that she'd been able to see.

It had been a little frightening to watch. She could only
imagine the terror that must have seeped into the souls of the
Parmese who'd been battered by Sforza and his methods, and by
the men he had to do the battering.

She was very tired now. She laid down on the seat of the
carriage, her head nestled in Sforza's lap.

"Are you all right?" he asked. She didn't miss the genuine
concern in his voice.

There was that about the man, too. "Oh, yes," she said.

Chapter 55

Venice

"Yes, I can do it," said Mindaug. "More precisely, I can *try* to do it." He waggled a hand back and forth, indicating uncertainty. "Whether I will succeed or not..."

"What are the parameters involved?" asked Archimandrite von Stebbens. "What I mean is, what factors—"

"Work in our favor, and which against?" Mindaug paused for a moment, thinking, then said: "In our favor, the fact that I am generally very knowledgeable about such matters and the fact that the grimoire's instructions are, in this case, unusually clear and precise."

He puffed out his mustache. "*Unusually* clear, for this sort of magic. As a rule, the guidelines for affecting anything in the infernal regions are distressingly vague. You're as likely to summon a specter as an eidolon—or a simple slab of beef. Or the Prince of Lies himself, in which case your continued existence will be brief in duration though near endless if measured by pain."

Von Stebbens made a face. "And working against us?"

"Is the ambition of the project itself," said Mindaug. He looked around the chamber, at each of the occupants therein. Besides the archimandrite, those consisted of Petro Dorma, Patriarch Michael, Father Thomas Lüber and Marco Valdosta. All of them were standing in a semicircle around the Doge, who was resting in a chair.

"Understand—understand *clearly*—what it is I propose to do. If the enchantment works—well, it's more like a conjuration—Lucia will find herself in a portion of the netherworld that has been separated from all others. I will, in effect, have changed the very topography of damnation. She will be trapped in an endless loop from which there is no escape—nor any means of rescuing her."

He glanced around the room. Spotting a small writing desk against a side wall, he asked: "Is there any paper in that drawer?" Without bothering to wait for an answer from the Doge—which he wouldn't have gotten anyway, since Dorma had no idea what was in the drawer—he went over and pulled it open.

"Ah! Perfect." He came back to the center of the room, tearing a sheet of paper down its length as he did so. Once he arrived back in the center, he folded the paper half over so that one side rested atop the opposite side at the end of the strip.

"You see?" he said. "Imagine yourself walking down this strip of paper. Eventually you would loop around to the other side, yes. But since that side has now become the same side you started on, you will continue to walk endlessly."

"Will Orkise be trapped as well?"

"Not...exactly. The wyrm will, at no time, be in the same place as Lucia. Its body will remain behind, wherever it is—probably in the cellars of the Castello di Arona, if my guess is right. But, as I've told you, the two are now inseparably connected. So long as Lucia wanders in that netherplace, Orkise will be in a stupor. A trance, you might say. Only when she finally dies will the monster's mind be free again."

Von Stebbens issued a little grunt. "An ingenious trap—and I see what you meant by 'changing the topography of damnation.' What will snare the evil woman are not chains which might be broken, but the very nature of her new surroundings."

"Precisely." Mindaug grimaced again. "What makes the whole business so dangerous is not the peril of the enchantment itself. It's that there is no way to make such a profound transformation in Satan's realm—even a small part of that realm—without alerting him. Leaving aside his generally unpleasant temperament, the Prince of Darkness is particularly inflamed by anything which trespasses upon what he views as his dominion."

Von Stebbens nodded. "Which Hell would certainly qualify as."

Father Lüber raised an admonishing finger. "Technically, that's not true. The underworld—all parts of it—were created by God along with everything else. The Devil is really no more than a tenant."

The archimandrite gave him a level, flat gaze. Father Lüber smiled. "I grant you, Satan would dispute the matter."

"And while he would lose the argument with God," said Mindaug, "he would probably not lose it with me." He puffed out his mustache again. "Not unless I had some aid."

The patriarch frowned. "What sort of aid?" Uncertainly, he looked at Father Lüber and then at Von Stebbens. "I'm not sure..."

"They would be of almost no help at all," said Mindaug, shaking his head. He said nothing further, simply stared at the floor.

Marco chuckled—very drily. "What he needs is the Lion. Am I correct, Count, in thinking that Satan would send an emissary to chastise you? What I mean is, he would not intervene personally."

Mindaug shook his head. "Satan could not do so without triggering the same sort of—ah, what to call it?—territorial jealousy on the part of the Lord, let's say. Which not even he would dare to do. So, yes, he will send an emissary—more like an executioner really."

"And what are the spatial parameters of this enchantment... conjuration, whatever? How close to the Devil's realm do you need to be in order to cast it?"

Mindaug looked momentarily confused, as if Marco had asked him a question so basic the sorcerer had forgotten the answer. Then, after a terse little headshake, he said: "That question has no meaning."

Patriarch Michael interrupted. "You'll have to forgive my young friend for his ignorance, Count Mindaug," he said, with a smile: "His studies have been concentrated on the healing arts, not the darker ones that you, and I as well—no high churchman can be oblivious to these things—have spent so much of our lives examining."

He turned to Marco. "The 'location,' as you call it, of Satan's demesne is everywhere and nowhere at the same time. The distance it lies from us—any of us—is measured by the soul, not by a yardstick of any kind." Now, pointing a finger at Mindaug, he added: "I daresay he can get very close to it."

"More than close enough," Mindaug said. "Certainly closer than I'd like. Still, it would help if I could cast the enchantment from some place already attuned to perdition. Some place whose past has left a blot upon it. A desecrated monastery, perhaps, or—"

"I know of several such places in my lagoon," said Marco. "Do you want one as isolated as possible?"

If you want to limit the side damage, yes."

The young physician nodded. "There's a small island in the northern reaches of the lagoon that would be suited for the purpose. It was blighted a long time ago when it was used for human sacrifices."

"By whom?" asked Father Lüber. "I know of no such—"

Marco made an impatient gesture. "*Long* ago, I said." There was a slight undertone to his voice. A growl, maybe, like that of an ancient creature annoyed a little by the chattering of infants. "Trust me, the place is there and will suit our purpose."

He turned back to Mindaug. "You will have to do the magic, Count. I would have no idea where to begin. But I will be there with you, and if this emissary . . . executioner—call it Satan's own sacrifice—dares to appear in *my* lagoon, I will deal with it."

Marco was a slender man. But for just a moment, there was a sense of a huge form filling the space where he stood. Huge— and monstrous.

Mindaug held his breath for a second or two. Then, he exhaled. "That would . . . ah . . . be quite nice."

Petro Dorma was frowning up at the young physician. "Marco, are you quite sure of this course of action? It will be most dangerous."

"*My* lagoon," Marco repeated. The sense of a monstrous presence in the chamber was now thick, almost palpable.

"Ah . . . yes, of course."

Once outside and standing in the Piazza San Marco, Archimandrite von Stebbens said, "I will come with you as well." He tapped the front of his shield, where the cross favored by the Knights of the Holy Trinity was prominently displayed. "I believe this will help against what we will face."

Count Mindaug gave him a look he hoped was inscrutable. Had it been scruted—was there such a word?—the meaning would have been quite obvious. *Splendid. With that ridiculously ornate armor, the Knight is bound to draw the attention of Satan's creature, allowing wiser fellows to make their escape if the affair goes badly.*

He didn't say it aloud, though. In Lithuania, the matter would have been obvious to a child. Here in the Western Lands . . . not so much.

Instead, he turned to practical issues. "How will we get there? By boat, I assume."

Now it was Marco's turn to look inscrutable. "Let me handle that. Just be ready shortly before dawn tomorrow. We will meet here again."

Milan

As soon as Sforza's army began passing through the Ticino gate, not far from the Basilica de San Lorenzo, Sforza gave orders to his staff to see to it that Duke Cosimo and his niece Violetta were provided with quarters suited to their station.

"Somewhere in the ducal palace," he specified, waving his hand in a vague gesture. "Wherever they like."

And off he went, with no further ado. *Where was Turner? What was the balance of power in the city?*

"He's a brusque man at times," said Cosimo.

Violetta smiled. "I can deal with brusqueness. It's boredom that terrifies me."

Cosimo gave her a sidelong gaze. "Are you sure of this, Violetta?"

"I thought it was what you wanted."

He shrugged. "From a political standpoint, yes, I do. Very much so, in fact. An alliance between Tuscany and Milan would go a long way toward quieting the Italian political factions, which would be a blessing for everyone—especially with the risk of plague hanging over our heads. Still, I would not wish you unhappy."

"I will be fine, Uncle." She shifted in her seat. "Especially once I can get out of this blasted carriage and into a proper bed. I'm still easily fatigued."

Sforza found Turner reclining at his ease in a chaise in one of the many chambers in the palace. He had a book in one hand and a glass of beer in the other.

"I thought you'd come to greet me at the gate," the duke said, a bit crossly.

"Pressing matters of security kept me at my post," Turner said stoutly. He declined to elaborate; Sforza declined to enquire. Some matters were best left unstated. Subordinates who could hand over a stable capital city in the middle of a semi-civil war did not grow on trees.

"Where is my beloved wife?" was the question he asked instead.

If a wolf could smile, that would have been the expression on the predator's face.

"She's back in her estate in Arona."

"You're sure."

"Oh, yes. One nice thing about the woman's foul habits and casual cruelties—she leaves a wake wherever she goes."

Sforza grunted, then lowered himself into a chair close to Turner's. That done, he handed over the leather sack in his hand. "Have this taken care of."

Turner set down his beer and book, took the sack in both hands, and opened it up.

"Well, Umberto's looking a bit worse than usual," he said. "Where would you like him displayed?"

Sforza waved over a nearby servant. "Some wine," he said. To Turner: "Use your imagination. I don't care, as long as the swine is widely visible."

Venice

"Are you sure about this, Marco?" Kat asked worriedly. Standing close to her in the salon in *Casa* Montescue, Benito and Maria looked just as worried. The only one present who didn't seem concerned was 'Lessi.

"Uncle Marco," the child gurgled happily, beaming up at him. "Give me a ride."

Marco smiled down at her. "Not right now, 'Lessi. I have to do something first."

When he looked back up at the adults, his expression was as savage as Marco's could ever get. "*My* lagoon," he said.

Chapter 56

Venice

The three men who would be making the journey to the island assembled in the Piazza San Marco shortly before sunrise. Benito was with them also, having accompanied his half-brother from *Casa* Montescue.

"How do you do this?" he asked Marco.

"Do what?"

Benito made vague gestures with his hands. "You know... transform into the Lion. Or whatever you do. I was told that there was a big ceremony involved."

Marco smiled. "That was the first time I took up the Mantle and the Crown. It's much more straightforward now." He looked to Von Stebbens and Count Mindaug. The first was encased in full armor, holding a two-handed great sword. The other was wearing a simple hassock and holding a slender volume. There was something odd about the book's spine—it actually looked like a spine from a reptile of some sort.

"Are you ready?" he asked. Von Stebbens nodded. Mindaug shrugged.

An instant later, all three men vanished into some...

Thing. Benito couldn't tell if it was a cloud or a phantom; perhaps a cross between the two. All he could make out clearly was a huge pair of wings that swiftly bore the *thing* out of sight.

"That's the Lion, I guess," he muttered to himself.

❀   ❀   ❀

From Mindaug's point of view, the situation was even less clear. He could tell that he was being swiftly borne somewhere— through the air, he supposed, although he could see nothing around him but a gray mist. Next to him—near to him, rather; the exact distance was unclear—he could detect although not see the archimandrite.

He had no sense of time passing. The journey might have taken seconds, minutes—possibly hours. Not days, though. He was sure of that for some reason.

Then he felt a thump under his feet, as if he'd hopped off a short ledge. Within seconds, the mist that had surrounded him cleared away.

And now, he could see the Winged Lion of St. Mark, the ancient guardian beast of the lagoon and the marshes, who predated even the Etrurians.

He almost wished he couldn't. The creature—he struggled mightily not to think of him as a monster—was squatting on his haunches almost right next to him. Mindaug had to look up... and up... and up to see the Lion's eyes.

Which were looking right back down at him.

"Well?" rumbled the Lion. "Hadn't you best get started?"

The sun was just beginning to come up over the horizon. The Winged Lion had timed their arrival perfectly, for this was the moment when the diurnal balance of power shifted against the forces of darkness.

The count moved toward the center of the island, which wasn't hard to determine, since the island was quite small and mostly barren of any vegetation. That in itself was unusual since most uninhabited places in the Venetian Lagoon were marshland. Normally, even a small island would be dense with cattails, sedges and sawgrass. But on this island there was very little beyond an occasional low shrub or patch of glasswort. Most of the island was as empty as a desert, although a haze that would never be found in a desert shrouded everything more than thirty yards offshore.

The island was eerily silent. Normally, in any of the marshlands of the lagoon, birds were plentiful—and noisy. Ducks of all kinds, herons, seagulls; they all lent their distinctive voices to the landscape.

But on this island... nothing. Mindaug could hear the faint sounds produced by birds on neighboring islands, but here the sound also seemed to be obscured by the haze. The ancient evil that had produced this unusual environment was palpable to him. The wickedness was much too old to have any direct effect on the magic he'd be using, thankfully. Still, it was unpleasant.

And about to become a lot more unpleasant.

Once he reached the place he estimated to be the island's center, he crouched and opened up the book he'd been carrying. Off to the side, he could see Von Stebbens frowning fiercely. No doubt the upright archimandrite was wondering why Mindaug was using none of the wards that Christian and Jewish sorcerers—the Strega as well, although the specifics could be quite different—employed as a matter of routine.

Of course, such more-or-less saintly magicians were not generally trying to *raise up* the forces of darkness. Under the current circumstances, wards would have been worse than useless—a downright nuisance to Mindaug's purpose.

He began reciting from the appropriate page in the text. The language was an ugly one—spiky, as it were. And he could only hope that he was approximating the pronunciation closely enough. That was hard to say, since no one—no man nor any creature—had used the tongue in centuries. Hopefully, Satan's minions had no more familiarity than he did with the fine points of diction, inflection and elocution.

Halfway through the passage, he was able to descry the form taken by the geographic manipulation he was producing. Visually, it was confusing—to be expected, of course. But the main aspect of the twisting infernal topography was what could only be described as a discarnate stench.

He spotted Lucia only once, and that dimly and at a great distance. But the glimpse was enough for him to be sure that she was being properly snared in the trap. So, by the time he finished reciting the entire passage, he had a sense of fulfillment.

A fairly mild sense, though, compared to the horror that he could also sense approaching.

He tucked the volume into his hassock. Looking around, he saw that the Lion and the archimandrite were both scanning the skies, alert for the nearing enemy—they, too, could sense its coming.

As if even a devil would launch an attack through the air into a place guarded by the Winged Lion of St. Mark!

Granted, devils and demons usually sported wings of some kind. That didn't mean they were obliged to use them.

"I'd keep an eye on the ground, myself," the count said loudly.

As if that were a cue, a low hillock toward one side of the island suddenly erupted. Water and steam spewed up as if it were a geyser, but what actually emerged from the soil was a horrid behemoth.

Very large—even larger than the Lion, though not by much. A round head with only a short snout, but a snout that sported a pair of tusks that would have been the envy of any boar. They made the razor-sharp teeth that filled the rest of the demon's maw seem puny.

There was a red, glaring eye under a looming brow. Incongruously, the other eye was covered by an eye patch. Bat wings were now uncurling. Two raptorlike limbs ended in huge talons; scaled like a reptile's, not feathered like a bird. Much smaller forelimbs—still massive—were similarly shaped.

"It's a malebranche," Von Stebbens said grimly. He gripped his huge sword with both hands and raised it high. Apparently he'd decided his shield would be of little assistance here—a judgment Mindaug concurred in.

The Lion bellowed his fury. It was as if the island was being shaken by an earthquake.

Bellowed—and pounced. The seconds which followed made clear to Mindaug that the ancient Etrurian guardian had not much use for the fine points of combat. Bite—claw—strike—rend: that was pretty much the Lion's repertoire.

The malebranche was given to no greater tactical subtlety. Bite—gouge—rend—tear.

Von Stebbens issued a great shout, charged the devil and struck it a mighty blow with his sword. Had that strike landed on a human, even an armored one, he'd have been hewed down; possibly even cut in half.

Here, against the malebranche's scaled hide, the sword did no worse than leave a shallow gash. It did succeed in infuriating the devil, though, which resulted in a blow from a clawed forelimb that sent the knight reeling backward. He didn't fall, but he did slip down to one knee—which may have saved his life, since the malebranche's backswing passed just over his head instead of striking full on his neck and taking the head off altogether. As if was, the helmet was knocked askew.

Von Stebbens was effectively blind now. He dropped his sword and wrestled frantically with the helmet, trying to bring the visor back into position so he could see again.

He wouldn't have made it in time to avoid another blow, except that Mindaug uttered a prepared spell that briefly shrouded the archimandrite in a coruscating ball of light. Now striking blindly, the malebranche's blow went amiss—hammering Von Stebbens on the shoulder and knocking him down, but not killing him or even badly wounding him. The design of the armor favored by the Knights of the Holy Trinity featured especially robust pauldrons.

The red glare was now turned on Mindaug. The malebranche surged toward him. The count turned and raced off, running as fast as his short legs could manage.

Which was nowhere nearly fast enough, of course. A man, even one far more athletic than Mindaug, had no more chance of outrunning a malebranche over a short distance than he did a bear.

But Mindaug understood the true calculations. He didn't have to outrun the malebranche, he just had to stay ahead of it long enough for—

An incredible bellow announced the arrival of the Lion, followed almost instantly by the meaty sound of its claws tearing into the flesh of the malebranche—using the term "flesh" liberally. The substance was actually more akin to xylem or phloem than to meat.

Mindaug flung himself to the ground, then twisted to see what was happening.

Then, he hurriedly scrambled to his knees and flung himself closer to the shore. The Lion and the malebranche were now tangled into a knot of snarling fury that was rolling toward him. He had to fling himself to the side twice more in order to avoid being crushed by them.

The count was getting worried. As immensely powerful as the Lion was, here in his own demesne, it was becoming clear than he was probably outmatched by a devil as mighty as a malebranche—an old one, too, to make things worse. There was no danger of the Lion being defeated quickly...but over time...he'd already suffered a bad gash on his flank from one of the devil's tusks.

Then, the break happened. As the two giants spun around, still grappling each other with their claws and talons, the malebranche threw out one of its wings and pressed it to the ground, in order to maintain its balance.

Seeing his opportunity, Von Stebbens shouted something incoherent—to Mindaug anyway; the cry might have meant something to another Knight of the Holy Trinity—and leapt toward the malebranche.

He actually *leapt*—in full armor. Mindaug was astonished. As he flew through the air, the archimandrite raised the sword in both hands, the blade pointing down. As he landed, he used his own weight as well as his strength to drive the sword blade right through the bat wing, pinning it to the ground. Whether by design or luck, the blade passed between the wing's carpus and its immensely long phalanges. It was as if a human had been crucified in one of his wrists.

The malebranche screeched as its own furious attempt to pull free caused still greater damage to the wing. It was immobilized... just partially, but enough—long enough—to give the Lion the opening he'd been looking for. The favored killing maneuver of the great cats—in this, the ancient Etrurian guardian was no different—was to clamp its jaws over the throat of its opponent, thereby suffocating it.

The huge leonine maw closed over the malebranche's neck and the Lion applied a bite pressure that Mindaug could only estimate. It must have made even a crocodile's bite seem like a nibble. The jaws of the malebranche gaped wide—as did its one flaming eye—but no sound emerged. Not even a wheeze.

The monster struggled furiously, even shredding its own wing in its desperate attempt to pull free from the death grip of the Lion. But it now had no more chance than a deer to escape.

Suddenly, with a great poof of air and a swirling black cloud, the malebranche vanished. Vanished as if it had never existed. In the corner of his eye, Mindaug could see the ruptured soil from whence the devil had emerged folding itself back into its previous state.

The Lion spit, partly from fury and partly from—

"Tastes *horrible!*" he roared.

Mindaug nodded. "Well, yes, it would. It's a devil, after all."

The Lion bellowed his fury again. Then, glaring about, he snarled: "It *cheated!*"

Mindaug nodded. "Well, yes, it would. It's a devil, after all."

Von Stebbens came up, carrying his sword. "What happened?" he asked. "Is it coming back?"

Mindaug shook his head. "No, it won't be back." He pointed to the patch of now apparently undisturbed soil. "Once it was clear the malebranche was doomed, his master recalled his beast to the pit."

Von Stebbens grunted. "I suppose even Satan watches over his underlings."

Mindaug made no reply. In point of fact, the Prince of Darkness would have summoned back the malebranche to punish it for its failure. The creature was in for a very long period of what human criminals would have called "hard time."

But the count saw no reason to dispel the archimandrite's tender illusions.

Chapter 57

Venice

The delegation from Milan arrived two weeks later. It consisted of Duke Carlo Sforza and a small Milanese bodyguard, along with Duke Cosimo and his niece Violetta. The Tuscan ruler's bodyguard was considerably more numerous than Sforza's. This did not reflect distrust on the part of the Tuscans, since the bodyguard was no larger than one would expect. The contrast with the Milanese escort was entirely due to Sforza's discretion. The Milanese duke's escort was purely a token formality since, if violence did erupt, there was no way they could have fended off the forces the Doge of Venice could bring down upon them in his own city.

But no one feared violence—or, indeed, any sort of unpleasantness. From the standpoint of four of the five major parties attending the convocation called by Patriarch Michael, the outcome of their deliberations seemed well-nigh certain to be positive.

Those four parties being Venice, Tuscany, Milan and the Church. The oddball, the outlier, the one party who was exceedingly and vocally skeptical of the outcome of the deliberations, was Ferrara.

More precisely, the Duke of Ferrara, Enrico Dell'este. Had most inhabitants of Ferrara been asked their opinion, they would have been quite positive in their responses.

But Enrico was a sullen man, a sour man, a disgruntled man... and, as had been true his entire life, was not at all hesitant in expressing his opinion.

"You're all a bunch of damn fools," he said again. "Sforza

will stab you in the back within a year—most likely before the summer is out."

By the time the delegations from Milan and Florence arrived, however, the duke of Ferrara had outlived his welcome. Long since outlived it, to be honest. Under the best of circumstances, even people a lot more saintly than the ones already assembled in Venice would have tired of the old man's constant warnings and predictions of disaster. Given that no one had ever suspected Petro Dorma of being a saint—such status was pretty much ruled out from the beginning for a Venetian doge—and Patriarch Michael was too rigidly orthodox in his theological views to make much of a diplomat, tempers had gotten rather badly frayed.

All the more so since the one person in that august group who *did* have a disposition that bordered on saintliness—that would be the great doctor Marco Valdosta—was in a, for him, unusual mood. He was quite grouchy, this sentiment being occasioned by the slowly healing wound in his side.

The Winged Lion could shrug off most injuries. Indeed, by the time he returned his human aspect to his normal state, most injuries had already been healed. But a deep gash caused by the tusk of a malebranche is hardly what one would call a "normal wound," and it was taking its own sweet time to heal.

At the best of times, it itched fiercely. Usually it hurt—and it always stank a little. As one might expect from a serious wound inflicted by one of the great powers of damnation, it was prone to infection.

No, not simply infection. It was also prone to rot, decay, pustulence—it was quite the horrid business.

So, unusually for him, Marco Valdosta was in a foul mood. Every bit as foul a mood as that of Duke Enrico—and, unlike the duke of Ferrara, when he chose to be, Marco was also the embodiment of a huge, unbelievably powerful and ferocious, ancient guardian spirit.

"WILL YOU JUST SHUT UP ABOUT SFORZA!"

When the windows stopped rattling, Marco continued in a more normal tone of voice: "Just shut up about it! Nobody agrees with you, old man! I'm sick of hearing your carping and whining!"

The footman who'd entered the chamber half a minute before decided he had an opening. "Duke Cosimo and Duke Carlo have arrived, Your Grace," he announced in a most sprightly manner.

Then, hurriedly and without waiting for the Doge's instructions, he opened the door wide to allow the newcomers to enter.

Violetta was the first to speak the moment she took a seat. The chairs had been arranged in a circle, thereby avoiding the awkwardness of making any one person present the overseer of the meeting.

"The duke of Milan has asked me to marry him and I have agreed," she said. Then, moving at once to the ungainly aspect of the business, she looked at Patriarch Michael.

"The Church will have to annul his marriage to Lucia Maria del Maino, of course. Unless you choose the option of declaring her to be dead—which, for all practical purposes, she is."

The patriarch made a face. Michael was generally inclined to be cautious when it came to theological issues; very attentive to the rules.

"Ah . . ." he said. Then, clearing his throat, he looked to Father Thomas Lüber, whom he had come to rely upon for doctrinal advice. "Would you agree that the Del Maino woman is deceased?"

Lüber shook his head. "Oh, no, she's certainly not dead. Dying, yes, according to Count Mindaug. But it will be quite some time before she is no longer alive."

He looked at the Lithuanian sorcerer. "Is that not correct?"

Mindaug puffed out his mustache. "Yes—allowing for some gray area as time passes. She'll not die for several centuries, but toward the end she'll barely be what you'd call 'living.' And, in any event, the time passing will seem much shorter to her than it will to us."

The patriarch looked startled. "Do you mean to tell us that you can actually *see* her in that"—he made a vague, uncertain gesture—"whatever you call that place you sent her."

"I think the term 'scry' is more accurate than 'see,'" replied Mindaug. "But, yes, I can observe her. So long as I'm still alive, at any rate." He made a gesture that was not quite as vague and uncertain. "But by then, I'm confident I can train others to maintain the observation."

Michael tugged at his beard. "So, clearly the duke of Milan cannot be declared a widower. As for the possibility of annulling the marriage . . ."

He eyed Sforza cautiously. "Is there any chance the marriage was not consummated?"

Carlo grimaced. "Sadly, no."

"Um."

Perhaps unwisely, Benito chose that moment to intervene. "As long as we're on the subject," he said, "I think it's long past time the Church agreed to marry Maria and me. The...ah... situation that you found questionable no longer exists, so there shouldn't be any problem."

Stoutly, he added: "Let bygones be bygones, I say."

"I agree," chimed in Maria, very firmly.

Benito gave Enrico Dell'este a look that bordered on an outright glare. "Tell him," he commanded.

The duke of Ferrara scowled, but spoke without any hesitation. "As I already told you, Patriarch, I plan to declare Benito to be my heir."

Hearing that, Carlo Sforza got a very intent expression on his face. You could practically see the condottiere making the political calculations. Fortunately, Dell'este was not looking his way at the time.

Instead, he had now transferred the glare to Patriarch Michael. "So if you refuse to marry Benito and Maria—this whole thing was never more than damn foolishness on the part of the Church to begin with—then after my death, Ferrara will no longer have a legally clear line of succession. Is that really something you want to deal with, Patriarch? As if Italy hasn't had enough succession crises over the centuries! That's got to be the cause of half our wars, you know."

"Um." Michael cleared his throat. "Well, it's all very complicated and it will take quite a bit of deliberation—"

The whole palace seem to shake. The Lion had manifested himself and roared his fury.

Then, roared again.

"JUST DO IT, YOU WRETCHED LAWYER! JUST DO IT!"

The debate got much more focused after that—and certainly briefer. Father Lüber's hurriedly proffered doctrinal advice proved most helpful in the matter.

"I knew the Church would see its way clear," said the Doge, quite cheerfully.

That evening, Benito did his best to settle accounts with Enrico Dell'este.

"Just get over it, Grandfather," he said. "I don't care if you want to keep hating the man—and I'm quite sure he cares even less. The fact is that Carlo Sforza was not responsible for killing your daughter and"—he glanced at Marco—"our mother. He simply didn't do it, that's all. We know who murdered her, and that man is dead."

"He's right, Grandfather," chimed in Marco.

"So just get over it," Benito repeated. "The feud with Sforza is over. Whatever wrongs he committed in the past to our mother"— he nodded toward Marco—"or him, or me, Sforza made up for, by rescuing my daughter."

"He certainly did," said Marco.

Dell'este's expression was still sullen. But he said nothing. Benito knew his grandfather very well by now. That silence meant . . . not agreement, certainly. But it did signify acquiescence.

Good enough. He turned in his chair and bestowed a huge smile on Maria, who had 'Lessi perched on her lap. "So. Have you given any thought yet to the wedding?"

Maria frowned. "Something modest. Money doesn't grow on trees, you know."

"Be serious," said Benito, and Marco, and Enrico Dell'este.

Elsewhere in the ducal palace, a more cold-blooded political discussion was taking place. The participants here were Petro Dorma, Duke Cosimo of Tuscany and Violetta, Carlo Sforza—and Prince Manfred, who was perhaps the most critical person present.

"Nothing less," Violetta was saying. "An outright alliance—a military alliance, mind you, with duties and obligations precisely spelled out, not some vague and namby-pamby political mishmash." Her expression grew fierce. "The sort of treaty that has no more room for sleazy lawyers and diplomats than the stones in a flour mill. Crush them into a bloody paste if they try to squiggle."

Sforza grinned coldly. "Nicely put."

Cosimo tried to visualize a diplomat being fed into a flour mill. The huge, heavy stones slowly turning, driven by a great waterwheel . . . the shrieks of the fellow as his flesh was drawn into . . .

The image was horrendous. He suspected his niece would make a poor diplomat herself.

Until you needed something resolved, anyway.

"A four-part alliance," mused the Doge of Venice. "Do you

really think you can get Enrico Dell'este to agree?" Petro glanced at Sforza. "You know how strongly the duke of Ferrara feels about... ah..."

"Me," said Carlo, still grinning coldly.

Manfred waved the thought away. "I also know how strongly Benito feels on the matter. He'll bring his grandfather into line, I'm quite sure of it."

The prince of Brittany sat up straighter, to give emphasis to his next words. "And I can tell you something else. My uncle—that would be the Emperor of the Holy Roman Empire—is going to be just as adamantly in favor of such an alliance."

Sforza and Petro Dorma gave him somewhat skeptical looks. "Why so?" asked Sforza. "I'd think..."

Manfred waved his hand again. "That silly ultramontane business? The decrepit ghosts of the Ghibellines? The last thing any sensible emperor wants is to have to rule over disputatious Italians. What we *do* need is a stable Italy, especially in the north, instead of the constant squabbling we have now."

Violetta looked fierce again. "He's right! The way it is, northern Italy's almost always in a state of warfare. One petty principality trying to aggrandize itself at the expense of its neighbors. The Scaligeri are the worst, but they have plenty of company. Who else but an Italian dynasty would have the symbol of the plague as part of its coat of arms? It's time to end it!"

Sforza grunted. "Which a quadripartite military alliance between Venice, Tuscany, Milan and Ferrara would certainly do. Even if it's just a defensive alliance, those four powers would overwhelm any possible opposition."

"With the two richest Italian provinces included," mused the Doge, "and the two with Italy's most respected—and feared, by their enemies—military leaders? Yes, I'd say so." With a smile that bordered on sly, he added: "We could probably lay claim to having the best navy as well."

Manfred nodded. "Yes, all that. And not any too soon, either. While you damn Italians have been preoccupied with your own petty quarrels, things in the North and the East have been getting steadily more dangerous. Never forget that the real enemy—of ours, of yours, of all civilized nations—is the demon who rules Lithuania."

He looked around the room, his brow lowered and his gaze as fierce as Violetta's. "Chernobog, they call him. The Black Brain."

Epilogue

Somewhere

Lucia was livid. *Someone was going to suffer for this!*

What made her particularly furious was that she had no idea who the culprit was. "Someone" was a most unsatisfactory target for an outraged duchess.

She came around another bend in the...what to call it? Corridor? Except it was too wide for a hallway, but too long and narrow to be called a room.

It was all quite infuriating. She hated being lost.

Where *was* she anyway? For a time, she'd assumed she was in a portion of the cellars that she'd never encountered before. But she'd walked much too far for that to be true. This floor was quite unlike the cobblestones of the cellars. Much drier, too. The one thing to be thankful for.

At least she wasn't hungry—good thing, for there was nothing to eat.

Someone was going to suffer for this!

Venice

After Mindaug finished his tale, he leaned back in his chair and looked at the three people facing him in chairs of their own. Tamas, his hand still bandaged, but able to walk with a crutch, at least; next to him, a now very pregnant Emma; on his other side, Klaus the bombardier.

The faces of Tamas and Emma were very pale; their expressions, frightened.

Klaus, on the other hand, simply looked pensive. "Explains a lot," he said. "I always knew you had to be a sorcerer—and a much more powerful one than you'd let on to be."

Kazimierz turned his head and looked at the two men standing to the side. Those were Archimandrite von Stebbens and Father Thomas Lüber, who'd led the group into this small salon in the Doge's palace and waited while Mindaug finally told his servants who he really was.

In considerable detail, some of that detail being quite ghastly.

"It's all true, what he says?" Klaus asked.

Father Lüber nodded. "Yes, it is. Count Mindaug is a very notorious figure, to those knowledgeable about these matters. At one time or another, he was a top advisor to three of the most evil creatures in the world—Grand Duke Jagiellon of Lithuania, Countess Elizabeth Bartholdy and King Emeric of Hungary."

Then Father Lüber shrugged. "As for his claims that he had few choices when it came to his past, I am inclined to agree with him. Growing up as a high nobleman in the realm ruled by Jagiellon—it's true, by the way, that he's a demon under the surface—is . . ." He shook his head. "Horrible to contemplate."

Von Stebbens cleared his throat. "And it's also true that when Mindaug came into the West, he began making different choices. Sometimes quite different."

The archimandrite gave the three servants a considering gaze, especially Tamas and Emma. "That was what puzzled us the most as we spied on him. How had he managed to hide his true nature from such as you? We had thought that to be impossible. For a time—quite some time, being truthful—that led us to be suspicious of you as well."

Tamas and Emma looked at each other. "Us?" asked Emma, practically squeaking. "What did we do?"

"Nothing," replied Von Stebbens. "That was the puzzle."

Klaus spoke up again. "So what do you think?" he asked, looking up at the archimandrite and the priest. "What do you think we should do?"

Von Stebbens and Lüber glanced at each other. The archimandrite opened his mouth, closed it. A moment later, the priest did the same.

The bombardier chuckled. "Let me rephrase the question: what do you *want* us to do?"

Von Stebbens looked distinctly relieved. "We'd like you to accept the count's offer. Resume your positions with him."

"Back at the villa in Val di Castellazzo," Lüber added. "We're going to rebuild it completely."

"Why?" asked the bombardier.

Again, Von Stebbens and Lüber exchanged a glance. "Because we think you're a good influence on him," said the priest.

Von Stebbens spoke next, his tone very solemn. "Listen, Klaus. And you two as well, Emma and Tamas—especially you two. We've come to the conclusion that despite his past, Count Mindaug is not actually an evil man. He's not a good man, either—but he clearly has a personal attachment to you. We're facing some terrible times ahead, and we'd rather have Mindaug on our side if it's possible."

"And you'll be a help in that," said Lüber. He glanced at Mindaug, whose head was lowered. "I think he'd agree on this— you're good for him."

"Yes," said Mindaug, murmuring the word. "And I would miss you greatly."

Hearing that, Emma took a deep breath and sat up straight. "All right, then."

"Yes," said Tamas. "All right, then."

Petro Dorma made a face. "I have to admit, I'm glad Mindaug will be living in Milanese territory. I'd really be quite uncomfortable having him close to Venice."

Manfred grinned. "You have such a pessimistic way of looking at things."

The Doge frowned. "Please explain how there could be an optimistic way of contemplating Count Mindaug as an ally."

"Isn't it obvious? I think having someone so close to the line of succession in Lithuania—Hungary, too, you know—might prove to be very handy in the time to come."

Arona

After Von Stebbens and the contingent of knights he'd brought with him set up their watch inside the castle near Arona, the

Aemiline monk Brother Dimitrios arrived. He had been asked to come by the archimandrite, to see if he could assist them.

"Are you quite sure you understand the situation?" asked Von Stebbens sternly.

In contrast to the archimandrite's dour view of the situation, Dimitrios seemed quite cheerful. "Oh, yes," he said. "I'm quite confident I can maintain a watch on Orkise without having to go down into the cellar where the great serpent dwells—and without the monster even being aware of my presence. That's obviously not something you and the knights could do."

Later that afternoon, the monk set up his mat and wards, lay down and closed his eyes.

"What 'little friends' do you expect to find down there?" Von Stebbens asks.

"Oh, there are bound to be lots of rats."

"*Rats?* You must be joking!"

"Oh, no. Rats are a much-maligned lot, I'm afraid. They're certainly not harmless, but they're really quite innocent little souls."

Eventually, Dimitrios came out of his trance, and his eyes opened.

"Well?" demanded Von Stebbens.

The Aemiline monk smiled serenely. "I'd say that is one very unhappy wyrm. The rats are getting quite annoyed with its surly and cranky behavior. Nothing they can do about the situation, of course." He sat up, shaking his head. "Have you ever considered what a rat's life is like, Archimandrite?"

"No." Von Stebbens held up a firm hand. "And I don't want to know. This time I'll just take your word for it."

Venice

When she awoke, Violetta saw that Carlo was propped up on an elbow in the bed, looking down on her. His gaze combined satiety and a great deal of affection.

They were both naked.

"I'm surprised," Sforza said, smiling. "I would have thought you'd insist on waiting until after the wedding."

Violetta shook her head. "I'm very curious by nature. I wanted to find out finally what it's like, not being a maiden any longer. And I saw no reason to wait. It's not as if there's any chance you were planning to seduce and abandon me."

Sforza chuckled. "Well, that's certainly true."

She smiled back at him. "It was very nice, Carlo. And here I thought conversation would be our only source of entertainment! Who but a virgin would be that uninformed?"

She rolled toward him, sliding a bare leg over his abdomen. "Francisco assured me that you're still quite vigorous, despite your advanced years. It'd be nice if you could prove him right. Again."

After a while—a very short while—she added: "Now, O great condottiere."

Cast of Characters

Aidoneus: God of the dead.

Borghetti: Milanese captain; in command of the siege of Terdona.

Bortai: Mongol princess.

Chernobog: A demon; the "Black Brain."

Da Corregio, Umberto: Duke of Parma.

De' Medici, Cosimo: Duke of Tuscany.

De' Medici, Violetta: Niece of Duke Cosimo.

Dell'este, Enrico: Duke of Ferrara: "The Old Fox," Grandfather to Benito and Marco Valdosta.

Del Maino, Lucia Maria: Illegitimate daughter of Filippo Maria Visconti, the duke of Milan overthrown by Carlo Sforza; later, married to Sforza.

Dimitrios: Hesychast of the Aemiline monastic order.

Dorma, Petro: Doge of Venice.

Emma: Servant of Count Mindaug.

Hakkonsen, Erik: Icelander; bodyguard to Prince Manfred.

Hohenstauffen, Charles Fredrik: Holy Roman Emperor.

Jagiellon: Grand Duke of Lithuania; possessed by the demon Chernobog.

Klaus: Bombardier; assistant to Count Mindaug.

Laglissio: Milanese count; courtier in service to Duchess Lucia.

Laurin: Dwarf, master of a magical rose garden.

Lüber, Father Thomas: Priest, advisor to Patriarch Michael.

Malatesta, Andrea: Count of Sogliano al Rubicone, Lord of Rimini, Forli, Cesena, Pesaro, Marquis of Ravenna, and Protector of Romagna.

Manfred, Prince: Earl of Carnac, Marquis of Rennes, Baron of Ravensburg; nephew of the Holy Roman Emperor Charles Fredrik.

Michael: Patriarch of Venice.

Mindaug, Kazimierz: Lithuanian count, former advisor to Jagiellon.

Montescue, Lodovico: Head of House Montescue.

Pagano, Lippi: Viscount of Imola.

Rhene: Nyx, courier for Francisco Turner and Marco Valdosta.

Sforza, Carlo: Condottiere, usurper of ducal power in Milan. "The Wolf of the North." Benito's father.

Tamas: Servant of Count Mindaug.

Turner, Francisco: Doctor; soldier; chief advisor to Carlo Sforza; friend of Marco Valdosta.

Valdosta, Benito: Grandson of the Duke of Ferrara; illegitimate son of Carlo Sforza.

Valdosta, Katerina: Wife of Marco Valdosta.

Valdosta, Marco: Grandson of the Duke of Ferrara; Benito's half-brother; the embodiment of the Winged Lion of St. Mark.

Verrier, Maria: Former canaler, married to Benito Valdosta.

Verrier, Alessia: Daughter of Maria and Benito.

Visconti, Filippo Maria: Former Duke of Milan; overthrown and killed by Carlo Sforza. Father of Lucia Maria del Maino.

Von Stebbens, Klaus: Archimandrite of the Knights of the Holy Trinity.